BARACK OBAMA

BARACK OBAMA

AMERICAN HISTORIAN

Steven Sarson

BLOOMSBURY ACADEMIC
LONDON · NEW YORK · OXFORD · NEW DELHI · SYDNEY

BLOOMSBURY ACADEMIC
Bloomsbury Publishing Plc
50 Bedford Square, London, WC1B 3DP, UK
1385 Broadway, New York, NY 10018, USA

BLOOMSBURY, BLOOMSBURY ACADEMIC and the Diana logo are trademarks
of Bloomsbury Publishing Plc

First published in Great Britain 2018

Cover design by Adriana Brioso
Cover image © Dennis Brack-Pool/Getty Images.
President Barack Obama in the Oval Office, 4 August 2015.

A catalogue record for this book is available from the British Library.

A catalog record for this book is available from the Library of Congress.

ISBN: HB: 978-1-3500-3234-7
PB: 978-1-3500-3233-0
ePDF: 978-1-3500-3236-1
eBook: 978-1-3500-3235-4

Typeset by Newgen KnowledgeWorks Pvt. Ltd., Chennai, India
Printed and bound in Great Britain

To find out more about our authors and books visit www.bloomsbury.com
and sign up for our newsletters.

To my students

CONTENTS

Contents

Contents

Contents

ACKNOWLEDGMENTS

Barack Obama believes that making a more perfect union is a collective endeavor. So, on a rather smaller scale, is writing a book. I thus owe many and major thanks, first to everyone at Bloomsbury who helped to make this happen, especially to Academic History Editor Emma Goode, who was not only immensely helpful at every turn, but also provided that perfect balance of patience and perseverance that authors often need. Thanks also to Bloomsbury's academic readers for their excellent advice and kind encouragement—two of them remain anonymous, but it's a great pleasure to be able to thank Frank Cogliano by name. Others who offered valuable advice at my behest at various points are Elaine Chalus, Sam Chambers, Jean-Daniel Collomb, Heather Dubnick, Jacqueline Fear-Segal, Alan Finlayson, Jean Kempf, Nathalie Morello, Pierre-Antoine Pellerin, Marie Plassart, Allan Potofsky, Marie-Jeanne Rossignol, Bertrand van Ruymbeke, and Anne Verjus.

An extra thanks goes to many of those named above for helping me move to France, where a new birth of academic freedom has allowed me to write this slightly offbeat book. Thanks too to all my colleagues at Jean Moulin University in Lyon (again including some of those named above) for hiring me and helping provide such a collegiate environment to research and teach in. Very special thanks to Nathalie Morello, without whose skills and sacrifices the move could never have happened.

In fact this book has been one of those happy occasions when research and teaching come closely together. When I arrived here, in the fall of 2014, I was asked if I'd teach a master's course in education, and I was delighted to oblige. Then, when asking myself what I might give that's of practical use to trainee teachers and their students, how I might combine my specialty in early American history with something more obviously appealing to younger people, I remembered reading Barack Obama's speeches and writings and how impressed I was by how informed they were by historical knowledge and perception, and so I thought I'd do a course on that. And as this book arises from that course, it seems fitting furthermore to dedicate it to my students. To all of them, all those I've taught and in fact learned from over the course of many years now. Many necessarily remain nameless, but shout-outs must nevertheless be made to those who have most directly influenced me or this book or both. Special thanks, then, to Marine Abinal, Julien Agostini, Diego Alvez, Louise Beaver-West, Guillaume Braquet, Raphael Costarella, Lucas Daly, Sacha Debard, Domitile Dubois-Athenor, Selsebil El Blidi, Marie Ferandji, Claire-Anne Ferrière, Etienne Gimenez, Steven Gray, Charline Grimaldi, Richard Hall, Adrien Halliez, Elizabeth Hargrett, Loic Henry, Narimene Ibrahim, Melissa Kemel, Caroline Laplace, Sarah Loustalet-Turon, Marwa Maghrabi, Charlotte Maillet, Adeline Mary, Khaled Naimi, Lauralie Possenti, Lucie Ratail, Stella Rofi, Edwin Rose, Camille Seidlitz, Divine Servant, Carissa Sims, Camille Tardy, Mervé Taspinar, Cassandre Thibert, Ciara Thompson, Esther Wright, and Luye Zhang.

INTRODUCTION
THE LANDSCAPE OF OUR
COLLECTIVE DREAMS

A more perfect union

Barack Obama announced his arrival on the American national political scene at the Democratic Convention in Boston, Massachusetts, on July 27, 2004. He commenced his keynote address that evening by saluting his audience on "behalf of the great state of Illinois, crossroads of a nation, land of Lincoln"—instantly connecting the history of the nation with that of his adopted state. The substantive section of the soon-famous speech started with personal stories that similarly coalesced with the country's history. Of how his father "got a scholarship to study in a magical place, America, that's shone as a beacon of freedom and opportunity to so many who had come before him." Of how his mother's father signed up to "Patton's Army" the "day after Pearl Harbor," and how his grandmother "raised their baby and went to work on a bomber assembly line." Of how the two subsequently "studied on the GI Bill, bought a house through FHA, and later moved west, all the way to Hawaii, in search of opportunity."[1]

Then the longer-term and larger picture: "our pride," Obama said, "is based on a very simple premise, summed up in a declaration made over two hundred years ago: 'We hold these truths to be self-evident, that all men are created equal. That they are endowed by their Creator with certain inalienable rights. That among these are life, liberty and the pursuit of happiness.'" And he spoke as he so often does of hope, again grounding living individuals' biographies in a national history of collective experience. Of John Kerry, the presidential candidate in 2004: "the hope of a young naval lieutenant bravely patrolling the Mekong Delta." Of John Edwards, Kerry's running mate: "the hope of a millworker's son who dares to defy the odds." And of his own: "the hope of a skinny kid with a funny name who believes that America has a place for him, too." And all these he said were the same as hopes that rang through the ages: "the hope of slaves sitting around a fire singing freedom songs; the hope of immigrants setting out for distant shores."[2]

Barack Obama has been equally historical in outlook on other oratorical occasions. "Hope," he said on the night of his victory in the Iowa Caucus that gave his presidential campaign the momentum that eventually carried him to the White House, "is what led a band of colonists to rise up against an empire; what led the greatest of generations to free a continent and heal a nation; what led young women and young men to sit at lunch counters and brave fire hoses and march through Selma and Montgomery for freedom's cause." And, once again seeing his own story in the context of his nation's history, he continued: "Hope—hope—is what led me here today—with a father from Kenya, a mother from Kansas, and a story that could only happen in the United States of America."[3]

When first announcing his initially unlikely run for the presidency on February 10, 2007, he did so in Springfield, Illinois, and he made sure he drew attention to the historical resonances of the location: "in the shadow of the Old State Capitol," he said, "where Lincoln once called on a divided house to stand together." He found inspiration indeed in Abraham Lincoln, who, "through his will and his words ... moved a nation and helped free a people." Obama even implicitly identified himself in the physical, professional, and philosophical images of Lincoln: "a tall, gangly, self-made Springfield lawyer" who "tells us that a different future is possible." Obama quoted the sixteenth president: "As Lincoln organized the forces arrayed against slavery, he was heard to say: 'Of strange, discordant, and even hostile elements, we gathered from the four winds, and formed and fought to battle through.'" And in his concluding words he paraphrased the Gettysburg Address, adopting Lincoln's eloquence as his own: "let us finish the work that needs to be done, and usher in a new birth of freedom on this Earth."[4]

And not only Abraham Lincoln. Barack Obama tied the campaign he was commencing to a tradition of triumph over tribulation dating back to the American Revolution: "The genius of our founders," he said,

> is that they designed a system of government that can be changed. And we should take heart, because we've changed this country before. In the face of tyranny, a band of patriots brought an Empire to its knees. In the face of secession, we unified a nation and set the captives free. In the face of Depression, we put people back to work and lifted millions out of poverty. We welcomed immigrants to our shores, we opened railroads to the west, we landed a man on the moon, and we heard a King's call to let justice roll down like water, and righteousness like a mighty stream.[5]

And so he told his supporters that he and they were continuing the mission first begun by the country's Founders, as "one people, reaching for what's possible, building that more perfect union."[6]

These are themes that Barack Obama returned to when his bid for the Oval Office was in danger a year later. The media had uncovered sermons in which his pastor, Reverend Jeremiah Wright, was a lot less positive about America's past than Obama was, and the candidate responded with a speech entitled "A More Perfect Union," delivered in Philadelphia's Constitution Center on March 18, 2008. Obama began with some of those same words from the US Constitution: "WE THE PEOPLE, in order to form a more perfect union." And then he delivered the most historically informed oration he had ever given, possibly the most historically literate one ever given by any US president or candidate for that position. "Two hundred and twenty one years ago," he said, "in a hall that still stands across the street, a group of men gathered and, with these simple words, launched America's improbable experiment in democracy. Farmers and scholars; statesmen and patriots, who had traveled across an ocean to escape tyranny and persecution, finally made real their declaration of independence at a Philadelphia convention that lasted through the spring of 1787."[7]

He spoke next of how the Founders' work "was stained by this nation's original sin of slavery." Though also of how "the answer to the slavery question was already embedded within our Constitution." Of his own African and American heritage and of Michelle Obama's and others' enslaved ancestors. Of Reverend Wright's and others' bitter recollections of segregation and disfranchisement, and of further burdens that African Americans have not been allowed to lay down yet. And of the hardships others too have suffered. But he spoke above all of how, "through protests and struggle, on the streets and in the courts, through a civil war and civil disobedience and always at great risk," generations of Americans had endeavored to "narrow that gap between the promise of our ideals and the reality of their time." Of how "America can change." Of how, in spite of everything, it has still somehow become "a more perfect union."[8]

And when Obama bade a presidential farewell to the American people in January 2017, he did so in his adopted hometown of Chicago, Illinois. "This is where I learned that change only happens when ordinary people get involved and they get engaged, and they come together to demand it," he said. And then he turned once again to the past as a way of understanding the present and the future. "After eight years as your President," he said,

I still believe that. And it's not just my belief. It's the beating heart of our American idea—our bold experiment in self-government. It's the conviction that we are all created equal, endowed by our Creator with certain unalienable rights, among them life, liberty, and the pursuit of happiness. It's the insistence that these rights, while self-evident, have never been self-executing; that We, the People, through the instrument of our democracy, can form a more perfect union.

For 240 years, our nation's call to citizenship has given work and purpose to each new generation. It's what led patriots to choose republic over tyranny, pioneers to trek west, slaves to brave that makeshift railroad to freedom. It's what pulled immigrants and refugees across oceans and the Rio Grande. It's what pushed women to reach for the ballot. It's what powered workers to organize. It's why GIs gave their lives at Omaha Beach and Iwo Jima, Iraq and Afghanistan. And why men and women from Selma to Stonewall were prepared to give theirs, as well.[9]

And he concluded this passage with a reference that quietly placed more recent happenings in historical context. "Yes, our progress has been uneven," he noted. "The work of democracy has always been hard. It's always been contentious. Sometimes it's been bloody. For every two steps forward, it often feels we take one step back." But he remained optimistic all the same: "the long sweep of America has been defined by forward motion," he said, "a constant widening of our founding creed to embrace all and not just some."[10]

The landscape of our collective dreams

We can find these same themes in Barack Obama's books as well, but in his writings more than in his speeches he takes the opportunity to make longer and more philosophical reflections on the meanings of American history. At the very end of *The Audacity of Hope*, for example, the then US senator from Illinois reflected on the highs and lows of elected office. He explained that when the lows came he liked to take a run along the Mall in the nation's capital, the site of so many American monuments, memorials, and museums. He often stopped, he said, at the Washington Monument, but other times he carried on—to the National World War II Memorial, the Vietnam Veterans' Memorial, and finally the Lincoln Memorial.

Describing the mood the latter inspired in him, Obama wrote: "At night, the great shrine is lit but often empty. Standing between marble columns, I read the Gettysburg Address and the second inaugural address. I look out over the Reflecting Pool, imagining the crowd stilled by Dr. King's mighty cadence, and then beyond that, to the floodlit obelisk and shining Capitol dome. And in that place," he continued, "I think about America and those who built it." About the "nation's founders, who somehow rose above petty ambitions and narrow calculations to imagine a nation unfurling across a continent." About Abraham Lincoln and Martin Luther King, "who ultimately laid down their lives in the service of perfecting an imperfect union." And also about the not-so-famous: "all the faceless, nameless men and women, slaves and soldiers and tailors and butchers, constructing lives for themselves and their children and grandchildren, brick by brick, rail by rail, calloused hand by calloused hand, to fill in the landscape of our collective dreams."[11]

For Barack Obama, then, the past isn't something simply to mine for a few crowd-pleasing sound bites. It's something that informs and inspires him. Americans' hope is still to this day for him "the hope of slaves sitting around a fire singing freedom songs. The hope of immigrants setting out for distant shores." Americans are still today, as they were in 1787, "one people, reaching for what's possible, building that more perfect union." And each generation connects to the next in a continuing mission "to narrow that gap between the promise of our ideals and the reality of their time."[12]

For Obama therefore the past is not apart from the present but a part of the present. In the speech in Philadelphia and in his autobiography as well he quoted William Faulkner's famous words to that effect: "The past isn't dead and buried. In fact, it isn't even past." And for Obama the Founders, the great figures since, and also the "faceless men and women" who built America did so not only "for themselves," but also for "their children and grandchildren." We therefore live in their posterity, in a world that they created. They are therefore in a sense still with us, part of a single historical continuum, as we live still as they did in that "landscape of our collective dreams."[13]

Barack Obama: American historian

We can see from the above that Barack Obama uses the tools that historians use. He exploits history's raw materials, primary sources such as the founding documents and the words of Abraham Lincoln. He employs analytic concepts such as continuity and change. And he deploys interpretative themes such as tyranny and liberty, audacity and hope, struggle and progress, and the making of a more perfect union. This book is about how Barack Obama as a historian applies these materials, concepts, and themes to the American past, although I hope the book also contributes to our understanding of Obama as a person, a politician, and a president as well.[14]

Obama has never written a whole book about or given a speech about the whole of American history. Common as his comments on the subject are, they are scattered throughout and threaded through his writings and speeches. Yet it's possible to gather his comments together and reconstitute them into a narrative or a set of related narratives that comprise Barack Obama's American history.

After this general Introduction, then, this book continues with a Prologue that traces the origins and explores the nature of Obama's general theory of American history. Of course many before me have traced Obama's ideas to such intellectual inheritances as Judeo-Christian religiosity, Classical Greek and Roman philosophy, the Renaissance, the Enlightenment, and utopianism. Others have attributed them to more specifically American traditions such as puritanism, transcendentalism, African American religion, and philosophical pragmatism. Others still have connected them to people, institutions, and events in Obama's own life. Many see in Obama a mixture of a number of these influences, and I do too. But these other analyses have focused most on Obama's political thought. While that political thought is closely related to his historical thought, my aim has been to focus more specifically on Obama's ideas about history, most especially American history. As we'll see, his political ideas about consensus, conflict, and progress manifest themselves in a Whig theory of American history. Or, more precisely, in a Radical Whig theory of American history as a continuing endeavor and an often difficult struggle to implement the ideals that in his view inhere in the Declaration of Independence and the Constitution.

The Prologue focuses on Obama's historiography, then, but the rest of the book focuses on his history. Chapter 1 is about British colonial America. In *The Audacity of Hope*, Obama called the Declaration of Independence "our starting point as Americans," which emphasizes the importance of the American Revolution, and seems by the same token to dismiss the rich history and formative influences of the previous colonial period. Yet in this and other writings and speeches, he finds various American starting points in this earlier era. His colonial America seems to have had little equality or liberty, but he does seem to find in it some precocious pursuits of happiness. Migrants who "traveled across an ocean to escape tyranny and persecution" were, for example early exemplars of Obamian audacity and hope. In the New World, according to Obama, these people and their descendants created communities, practiced "homespun virtues," and experimented with "local democracy." Yet, as we'll also see, Obama cleverly conflates the founding of the colonies and the founding of the country, folding exemplary aspects of British American colonial history into the history of the United States.[15]

Barack Obama's history of colonial America is actually therefore rather teleological, comprising tidbits and tropes that illustrate fledgling aspects of national character that existed before Independence and which he selects from a postindependence perspective. In other words, it's more a prehistory of the United States than a history of the British American colonies in their own right. Yet that tendency, with its elisions of colonial history and inclusions of aspects of it in the later national history, helps Obama establish what he sees as the radically revolutionary nature of American Independence. It also helps us see more clearly the greater completeness, coherence, and complexity of Obama's postindependence American history.

Chapter 2 explores Obama's American Revolution, in particular how the abstract ideas of seventeenth- and eighteenth-century philosophers were transformed into what Obama calls "the substance of our common creed" when they were written into the Declaration of Independence, the nation's founding charter.

The principles in the Declaration were also for Obama "the foundation of our government," and Chapter 3 explores how for him the Constitution completed the creation of a nation and established the conditions for its perpetual renewal. That conception of the Constitution contains what may be Obama's single most powerful historical message: that the Founders' "original intent" was not to set the values of the eighteenth century in stone but to create what Obama and others have called a "deliberative democracy" in which later generations could discuss how to make the Founders' "more perfect union" even more perfect in their present and for the future—what we might call the founders' evolutionary intent. Obama thus rejects both the determinism of originalist readings of the Constitution and the indeterminism of relativist readings. He prefers instead a historicist reading that conceives the Constitution as containing core principles that subsequent generations have adapted or extended in line with the values and needs of their own times. In other words, Obama doesn't so much reject originalism as redefine what originalism is. The Founders' original intent was, he believes, evolutionary—they intended that we adapt their words to our world. The Constitution has thereby been and should remain a bridge to the future and a pathway to progress, not a chain to the past and a barrier to change. Obama knows he is not the first to say these things, but he is better placed than anyone to make these points heard.

This book is thus somewhat weighted toward the revolutionary era, in particular to the Declaration of Independence and the Constitution. This is because, for Barack Obama, the American Revolution was truly revolutionary and determinative. It not only turned colonies into an independent nation, but also transformed the character of the American people and the nature of their polity. The Declaration's creed motivates Americans to deepen and expand the reaches of its ideals of equality and liberty. "WE THE PEOPLE" then do the work of transforming these ideals into day-to-day realities, either consensually, or via compromise through the operations of the Constitution, or in a more contested fashion through protest, or through some combination of the three. For Obama these documents are not only foundational, but also formative. The "creed written into the founding documents," he said, "declared the destiny of the nation." Not only the existence of the nation, then, but also its "destiny." And on another occasion Obama quoted the Constitution as follows: " 'We the People ... in order to form a more perfect union' " and the Declaration of Independence: " 'We hold these truths to be self-evident, that all men are created equal." And he then proceeded to say: "These are not just words. They're a living thing, a call to action, a roadmap for citizenship and an insistence in the capacity of free men and women to shape our own destiny." And so the rest of this book is about how Obama sees America's "destiny" as defined by these documents as working itself out over the course of time.[16]

Although the Founders formed a "more perfect union," they knew their Union wasn't perfect. As Obama amply acknowledges, the stain of slavery remained until what his hero Abraham Lincoln called "a new birth of freedom" emerged from mortal conflict. As Obama admits, the histories of slavery and Civil War, explored in Chapter 4, are exceptions to the rule that America's "deliberative democracy" has promoted progress either by consensus or by compromise or by peaceful protest. And while abolition made America more perfect, it didn't erase racism, as enslavement eventually gave way to segregation and disfranchisement. Chapter 5 therefore explores Reconstruction, Jim Crow, and the Civil Rights Movement that finally made the "more perfect union" even more perfect with its determination that "We Shall Overcome." Though that lyric came from a gospel song made famous in the fight against racism, for Obama it also applies more widely to struggles for equality for and by poor whites, immigrants, women, LGBT people, disabled people, and others.

The above chapters provide a narrative of some of the political and social histories of the United States as Barack Obama sees them. But there are also other and overlapping narratives, one of them social-economic, though still political in many ways, and the other one concerning foreign policy. Chapter 6 goes back to the founding eras to explore the history of American economy and society, and in particular the relationships of property and liberty. "The chief business of the American people" may be business, but Obama uses this phrase in a different way than did its coiner Calvin Coolidge. For Obama, Coolidge's entrepreneurs are not only private businessmen, but also public officials and workers too. Hence Obama's historical interest in government as an enabler of employers since Alexander Hamilton's time as secretary of the Treasury. Hence also however his un-Hamiltonian interest in government as a protector of employees and of the poor or vulnerable more generally from the time of Franklin Roosevelt's New Deal. For Obama, then, the American economy has promoted wealth and opportunity for many, but with a little nudging from people power and government it might one day provide greater wealth and opportunity for many more and maybe even all—in the spirit of the American creed of equality, life, liberty, and the pursuit of happiness.

Yet the absence of an Obamian colonial American history obscures the origins of the American economy in the slave trade, slavery, and other extreme forms of exploitation, and perhaps therefore obscures the difficulty of eradicating historical inequality. Furthermore, and perhaps more fundamentally, the absence of an Obamian "critical theory" of capitalism obscures the extent to which economic imperatives on the one hand and political ideas about "property" and "liberty" exist in tension with each other both in the past and in the present.

Chapter 7, "Beyond Our Borders," goes back to the beginning once again, exploring first the Founders' imperfect avoidance of entangling alliances and then onwards to the also often imperfect entanglements of more recent times. But because Barack Obama's definition of "America" depends to a great extent on adherence to ideas in the Declaration of Independence and on citizenship under the Constitution, his American history necessarily categorizes Native-American nations (though not all Native-American people) as at least partly non-American. It's to accommodate this aspect of Obamian historiography that his Native-American history appears in the same chapter here as his history of foreign policy (as indeed happens in Chapter 8 of Obama's own *The Audacity of Hope*, itself entitled "The World Beyond Our Borders"). Like many Americans, Obama is deeply troubled by the imperialist aspects of America's westward expansion, yet it's hard for him as it is for many to imagine American history without some sort of manifest destiny.

On relations with America's first peoples and the world's other peoples, then, Obama admits that "our record is mixed," but he still believes there has been progress. And that assessment is consistent with his internal history of the United States. The Union has always become "more perfect" and yet remained less perfect than it could be. Progress has always been made, but almost always slowly and hard-won. But when progress has been won, those victories for Obama have always depended on the many working together in common cause: in the Union in the form of the American nation under its Constitution and in union in the form of American people acting in concert with each other to promote their creed.

That's a theme that recurs in Obama's American history and therefore throughout this book. But it's also the assumption underlying Obama's recounting of the stories of individual people. Obama invariably situates the history of individuals in the context of communities and their histories, as we saw in previous pages, sometimes in specific communities but always in a national community. He thus renders biography as American allegory: hence the Epilogue, "Out of many, one." And he renders autobiography the same way: hence "American history's Barack Obama."

The order of this book's chapters as well as their contents reflect the narrative of Barack Obama's American history, at least as I understand it. To reinforce this effect—of this book as a reconstruction of as well as a running commentary on Obama's American history—the chapter titles and all the subheadings consist of Obama's own words or words by historical figures who he quotes (with a few exceptions, the reasons for which will be clear when you see them). There is some repetition of these titles and subtitles, but that reflects how certain refrains regularly reappear in Obama's oeuvre. There is also throughout this book some repetition of longer quotes, some repeated recounting of moments in Obama's life, and some re-rendered explanations of historical events. Some of these reprises are required because the material mentioned needs to be reexamined in the different contexts in which it respectively arises. But some is necessary simply because I'd like each chapter to stand on its own for readers who are interested in one or more of them but not in all of them.

There are comments, where relevant, describing the nature of the sources used and the problems involved in using them. Not the least of these, for example, is the issue of when and to what extent Obama is writing or speaking to please himself for personal reasons or when and to what extent he's writing and speaking to please others for political reasons. Those are the kinds of issues I address as I come to them in particular instances throughout the course of the book. But I should say a few general words about these kinds of issues here to be clear from the off about a couple of things—things not to do with sources as such, but to do with the perhaps more fundamental matter of how an academic historian like me should approach the work of a different kind of historian like Obama.

Barack Obama is neither a professor of history nor otherwise a professional historian. He's first and foremost a politician, of course, and as such he represents and seeks to speak to all citizens, some of whom like history and know a lot about it, some of whom don't. So while Obama expounds extensively on aspects of American history in his books, especially *The Audacity of Hope*, and occasionally in certain speeches made in certain contexts, such as "A More Perfect Union," much of his historical commentary is brief and sometimes even somewhat opaque. Yet there is substance in the brevity and significance in the opacity.

Some of Barack Obama's historical references, for example, are rendered as imagery. Yet these images are meaningful. For instance, a city upon a hill, a revolutionary struggle against tyranny, a nation unfurling across a continent. Sometimes the images come in human form—a tall, gangly self-made Springfield lawyer, a preacher from Georgia, a voter in Atlanta. Other times they are or at least seem more abstract—that all men are created equal, the audacity of hope, a more perfect union. Some commentators see such images as simplistic soundbites. In fact, each of them is a symbol and therefore suffused with meanings, unspoken significations that audiences understand. This book explores these symbols and their significances.

There are omissions in Barack Obama's American history. Yet these omissions are meaningful. For instance, Obama says relatively little about the history of Native Americans, except when mentioning their partly forced and partly chosen exclusion from the political nation as defined (for Obama) by the Declaration of Independence and the Constitution. But it's precisely that fact that makes Native Americans less a part of Obama's US history and more a subject of the country's foreign policy (hence their appearance in this book's Chapter 7). This fact reminds us that Barack Obama's "American" history is defined and bounded by a political union, not by geographical location, the history of a people rather than the history of a place. He can therefore recognize wrongs done to outsiders such as Native Americans without (in his opinion) contradicting his convictions about the United States as, in and of itself, an ever "more perfect union." This book thus examines not only what Obama says but also the significances of his silences.

There are elisions in Barack Obama's American history. Yet these elisions are meaningful. For instance, Obama confounded the founders and the foundings of the colonies and the country when he claimed in "A More Perfect Union" that "farmers and scholars; statesmen and patriots, who had traveled across an ocean to escape tyranny and persecution, finally made real their declaration of independence at a Philadelphia convention that lasted through the spring of 1787." Yet Obama obviously knows that the men who founded the original colonies were not the same men who drafted the Constitution 180 years later, so this elision is probably no error. It is more likely a conflation created by a rhetorical sleight-of-hand, one that establishes continuities across different generations of Americans—of the audacity and hope and the clamoring for liberty that links the spirit of the colonial founders to that of the country's Founders. So, once again, this book aims to explore the meanings of these elisions.

There are errors in Barack Obama's American history. Or possibly "errors." Yet these errors are meaningful. For instance, as above, Obama speaks of "a Philadelphia convention that lasted through the spring of 1787." The Convention sat in fact from May to September, through the summer of 1787, not the spring. There may have been a momentary lapse of memory, but the magna cum laude Harvard Law School graduate, onetime president of the *Harvard Law Review*, and former professor who taught constitutional law at the University of Chicago for over a decade surely once knew the Convention dates. And anyone can easily check them. So why would he make this mistake, or why would he make this "mistake"? First, it's not a significant error in that it doesn't undermine the analysis that follows of race in American history. So some license is surely allowed for a trivial change of detail if there's some reason for it. And the reason for it may be that for Obama the Founders sowed the seeds of nationhood in a springtime that followed a cold winter of colonialism, as he's implied in other rhetorical contexts. Strict factual accuracy thus surrenders to what Obama offers as a deeper metaphorical truth. This book also thus examines the significances of such rhetorical errors.

I cannot stress enough, though, that this book is not about debunking much less deriding or in any way demeaning Barack Obama's American history or his different way of doing history. A necessarily different way of doing history. Obama is after all or was a politician first and foremost, and his principal goal in that role was and still is to persuade people to think and to act. Elaborate explanations of the historical premises of his politics and policies, especially in speeches, are more likely to send people to sleep than onto the streets. The brevity afforded by rhetorical shortcuts such as symbols, omissions, elisions, metaphors, and even meaningful errors is therefore nothing more or less than we demand of politicians. And rhetorical techniques and even tricks need not equate with twisting history for political purposes, and in Obama's case they don't. Obama's political ideas represent the continuation of what he sees as American historical traditions, so there's a natural continuity between the past and the present as he sees them, and a logical consistency in his history and his politics.[17]

If the principal purpose of the politician-historian is to persuade, that of the professional historian is to explore and explain. But to do so effectively requires us to try to see the world as the subject sees it and to do so with respect. And Barack Obama deserves tremendous respect as a historian. He has enormous historical knowledge, especially considering that his education was largely in literature, politics, and law, and that his various day jobs have always been busy ones, even before he became the most powerful person on the planet. And he processes that prodigious knowledge into coherent historical narratives and interpretation. And he tells history well—exceptionally well. One of his greatest gifts as a historian, for example, is an uncanny knack, perhaps a political skill, certainly a rhetorical art, for weaving smaller scenes into a bigger picture. He has a genuine genius for historical synthesis.

But my main point here is that the point of this book is not to identify "good things" and "bad things" but to try to understand things. When I identify symbols, omissions, elisions, metaphors, errors, and so forth, it's to try to explore and explain the deeper meanings of Barack Obama's American history in the ways outlined previously and explained in more detail in the pages that follow. And when I dispute his interpretations, it's to try to see them more clearly in the light of a different perspective. But whether I agree with him or not is irrelevant. What interests me is what interests him. What matters is Barack Obama's American history. And it matters because his history has shaped his politics, and so in turn it should shape our understanding of his presidency and his legacy. Because Barack Obama built his White House on that "landscape of our collective dreams."[18]

PROLOGUE
A MORE PERFECT UNION: BARACK OBAMA'S AMERICAN HISTORY

Let's begin to understand what Barack Obama's American history is by looking first at what it isn't.

God damn America

In the fading days of 2001, Reverend Jeremiah Wright gave a sermon called "The Day of Jerusalem's Fall." The name evokes the tone of the Puritan Jeremiads of seventeenth-century Massachusetts, sermons in which ministers warned of God's avenging anger at New Englanders' numerous apostasies. And this modern-day Jeremiah reported that recent events represented divine retribution for America's sins overseas. The attacks of September 11 showed, he said, that "America's chickens are coming home to roost."[1]

In another sermon, in April 2003 and this time entitled "Confusing God and Government" and therefore equally evocative of Puritan Jeremiads' critical political and social commentary, Jeremiah Wright made more wide-ranging criticisms of the United States' historical mistreatment of African Americans and other nonwhite people both at home and overseas. The Founders had "lied," he said, "about their belief that all men were created equal ... The government lied in its founding documents and the government is still lying today." And he added that the government "wants us to sing 'God Bless America.' No, no, no, not God Bless America. God damn America—that's in the Bible—for killing innocent people. God damn America, for treating our citizens as less than human. God damn America, as long as she tries to act like she is God, and she is supreme."[2]

ABC News first reported the sermons on March 13, 2008, and not just to mock the minister's apparent attribution of "God damn America" to the Bible. Those words—"God damn America"—all the more resounding as anaphora, were serious. Or at least they were taken seriously. Or at least they were taken seriously several years later, because the actual spectacular aspect of this story was that Reverend Wright was the pastor at Trinity United Church of Christ in Chicago, the place of worship of a leading contender for the Democratic Party nomination for president of the United States.

Barack Obama may have seen something like this coming, as he'd already established a degree of distance from Jeremiah Wright with a last-minute un-invitation to give the invocation at the announcement of his presidential candidacy back in February 2007.

That had followed an article in *Rolling Stone* about other possibly inflammatory sermons by the sometimes fiery preacher. But the men remained close nevertheless. After all, Reverend Wright had introduced Obama to his Christian faith and had officiated at his wedding to Michelle Robinson and at the baptisms of their daughters, Malia and Sasha, as well as being Barack Obama's long-time pastor. At the beginning of the media storm of March 2008, Obama defended Dr. Wright on ABC by saying that "it's as if we took the five dumbest things that I've ever said or you've ever said in our lives and compressed them and put them out there," although Wright was rapidly relieved of his responsibilities on the Obama-supporting African American Religious Leadership Committee. Then, as Wright continued to defend his words in the following weeks, Obama finally rid himself of his troublesome priest. At the end of May, the Obama family withdrew their membership of Trinity United Church of Christ, stating that "the divisive statements of Reverend Wright ... sharply conflict with our own views."[3]

America can change

Although the controversy thus staggered on for some time, Barack Obama had already ended the immediate crisis with a speech he'd delivered on March 18, 2008, one that's widely credited with turning his campaign away from the political wilderness that it seemed to be heading to and back on track to the White House. "A More Perfect Union" is the most analyzed of all of Obama's oratorical oeuvre, and there's even a book-length collection of scholarly essays about *Race and Barack Obama's "A More Perfect Union,"* the main title of which is simply *The Speech*. Sections of this speech, sometimes long ones, will duly appear and reappear in this book. But my main point for now is that in this moment of crisis, when Barack Obama needed to clarify what he was fundamentally about, he used this oratorical opportunity to show how deeply steeped he is in American tradition. In doing so, he condensed a great deal of what he thinks about the course of his country's history.[4]

As Obama made clear on that occasion, Reverend Wright was not completely wrong. In part, the preacher was channeling African American anger at over three centuries of historical injustices and their deeply divisive persisting legacies. We need, Obama said, "to remind ourselves that so many of the disparities that exist in the African-American community today can be directly traced to inequalities passed on from an earlier generation that suffered under the brutal legacy of slavery and Jim Crow." After detailing many of those inequalities and their lingering effects, Obama noted: "For the men and women of Reverend Wright's generation, the memories of humiliation and doubt and fear have not gone away; nor has the anger and the bitterness of those years."[5]

Yet, for all this realism, Obama distanced himself from his pastor's historical pessimism. "The profound mistake of Reverend Wright's sermons," Obama said, "is not that he spoke about racism in our society. It's that he spoke as if our society was static; as if no progress has been made; as if this country ... is still irrevocably bound to a tragic past. But," he said, "America can change. That is the true genius of this nation. What we have already achieved gives us hope—the audacity to hope—for what we can and must achieve tomorrow."[6]

In that last sentence—in a phrase highlighted by hyphenation in the transcription given to the press and in the Obama campaign's later publication of the speech— Barack Obama boomeranged Jeremiah Wright with the latter's own words. The term "the audacity to hope" obviously echoes *The Audacity of Hope*, the title of Obama's book-length *Thoughts on Reclaiming the American Dream*. And as well of course "The Audacity of Hope," the title of Obama's national-name-making speech at the Democratic Convention of 2004. The audacity *of* hope is Obama's slightly misremembered or altered borrowing of "the audacity to hope," the phrase he used in Philadelphia, from a sermon he heard by Reverend Wright and one regularly repeated by him.[7]

But Barack Obama didn't only want to say that America can change and that there is hope. He also wanted to explain—to explain *how* America can change and *why* there is hope. To do so, he began at the beginning. Obama started the speech of March 18 with some of the opening words of the United States Constitution: "WE THE PEOPLE, in order to form a more perfect union." And then: "Two hundred and twenty one years ago, in a hall that still stands across the street, a group of men gathered and, with these simple words, launched America's improbable experiment in democracy. Farmers and scholars; statesmen and patriots, who had traveled across an ocean to escape tyranny and persecution, finally made real their declaration of independence at a Philadelphia convention that lasted through the spring of 1787."[8]

Starting that speech with these words was a clear and clever way for Obama to identify himself immediately with the nation's Founders, with their Declaration of Independence, and with their Constitution. As of course was delivering the speech in the National Constitution Center in Philadelphia, "across the street" indeed from Independence Hall, where the Founders adopted the Declaration of Independence in 1776 and drafted the Constitution eleven years later. As was doing so in front of a gallery of flags, a visual framework of stars and stripes. All these signals were implicit but unmistakable ways for Obama to identify himself with the "group of men" he referred to and thereby to signal his allegiance to America's Founders rather than with their fiercest critics, which was the main political objective of the day. Yet opening the speech this way was no empty gesture aimed only at refuting Reverend Wright, mollifying the media, and reassuring public opinion. The words he used form the foundation of his understanding of American history.

The Declaration of Independence that Barack Obama mentioned contains what he called in *The Audacity of Hope* America's "common creed": "WE HOLD THESE truths to be self-evident, that all men are Created equal, that they are endowed by their Creator with certain unalienable Rights, that among these are Life, Liberty, and the pursuit of Happiness." This "common creed" was "our starting point as Americans," Obama also wrote in the same place, and it formed "the foundation of our government" because at least implicitly the Founders made it "real" in the Constitution of 1787. The Constitution didn't create a perfect union, as the histories of slavery and segregation amply attest and as Obama abundantly affirmed then and on other occasions. But it did create a "more perfect" one in which such enormities as slavery and segregation could in the future be cast into the past. And so people with the audacity to hope have had the means to make their "more perfect union" more perfect still.[9]

At its best, this historical process is a consensual one in which progress emerges from civil conversation and compromise. Often, though, it's a contentious one in which progress is only achieved through widespread protest and in one instance through civil war. And the process is never-ending. To this day there is more to do. Nevertheless, Obama claimed, "America can change."[10]

The substance of our common creed

The rest of this book builds on the very brief summary above of Barack Obama's American history. Before we go there, though, what are the underlying principles of history that shape Obama's understanding of the American past? What is Barack Obama's historiography?

For Barack Obama, American history is driven by the ways in which ideas, institutions, and actions interact. How that happens in Obama's historical scheme of things is in brief as follows. The abstract ideas of European philosophical writings about equality and liberty gained "substance" in the form of the moral imperatives of the "common creed" advanced in the Declaration of Independence. That common creed and "foundation of our government" were then "made real" by being institutionalized in the Constitution. The Constitution created a "deliberative democracy" in which, ideally, the creed could be transmitted into day-to-day reality via legislation, eventually even making its way into everyday custom.[11]

Or, if that process doesn't work by itself, the Constitution at least guarantees the right of the people to take actions to improve their own and others' lives and thereby bring America more into accord with its founding creed. The process is often fraught with struggle, not least in the Civil War, and can take time, and there is always more to do. As Obama put it in "A More Perfect Union":

> words on a parchment would not be enough to deliver slaves from bondage, or provide men and women of every color and creed their full rights and obligations as citizens of the United States. What would be needed were Americans in successive generations who were willing to do their part—through protests and struggle, on the streets and in the courts, through a civil war and civil disobedience and always at great risk—to narrow that gap between the promise of our ideals and the reality of their time.[12]

It's worth observing here the pronouns that Obama applies respectively to "ideals" and "time" at the end of this passage, and the plural and singular attached to each. When he says "the reality of their time" he signals the era of particular generations. When he says "our ideals" he signals the common aspirations of "successive generations" of Americans from the nation's founding onwards. The "reality" is thus historical, belonging to a particular time. The "ideals," however, are timeless. Making the two match more and more, and thereby making that more perfect union, is what Barack Obama's American history is basically about.

Barack Obama's American history is therefore only rarely concerned with the specific and multiple causes of individual events. He barely mentions, for example, the British parliamentary taxes and other measures that provoked colonial rebellions and the American Revolution, simply subsuming them under the generalizing description of "tyranny" as a natural outcome of imperial rule. He also passes over the structural transformations of American economy and society that gave rise to the more militant and widespread abolitionism that arose from the 1830s and that perhaps paved the way to Civil War and Emancipation. Nor does he mention much of the suffering of slaves, saying far more instead about slaves' struggles for freedom and eventual emancipation. And he says little about the interplay of factors that gave rise to the renewal of the fight against Jim Crow during and after World War II. Again, he prefers to focus on the fight itself and the extended equality and expanded liberty that resulted. For Obama, then, what ultimately matters, and what ties all these events from the American Revolution to Emancipation to the defeat of segregation together and to each other, is that each one is a logical if eventual outcome of America's ongoing revolutionary mission to extend equality and liberty in accord with the creed of the Declaration of Independence. It is this long-term and continuous progress of extending equality and liberty that matters more to Obama than the passing histories of injustice and oppression.

There are, of course, multiple, complex, and interrelated reasons for Barack Obama's choosing of his historical priorities. As a politician, he naturally needs to avoid unnecessarily alienating people, and not dwelling on taxation and other oppressive measures obviates offending a former mother country and imperial nation that is now an American ally. And not dwelling on the details of slavery and segregation avoids aggravating Americans who are not so willing or not yet able to confront the fullness of these realities of American history. Obama has done more than any other president to move African American history to the forefront of popular consciousness, but he is in this, as he is in other matters, a gradualist. Certainly, Obama's preference for the art of persuasion over big sticks and bully pulpits encourages him to focus at least in public less on the negatives and more on the positives of the past, less on oppression and more on inspiration.[13]

For Barack Obama then the meta matters more than the miniature, the macro more than the micro, and he thus gives precedence always to what he sees as the bigger picture. And for that reason, as a historian rather than as a politician, he privileges the long-term-narrative over narrower approaches to the past that focus on individual events, institutions, groups, or individuals. Hence he's generally more interested in the outcomes of historical processes than he is in the details of those processes themselves, and thus more interested in the abolition of oppressive institutions than in the details of the onetime existence of those institutions. Of course causation is crucial to narrative history, unavoidably so indeed, but long-term narratives naturally tend to privilege sweeping interpretations explaining the whole course of things rather than the particular causes of individual events. And as a historian, Obama believes that the fundamental cause of change is the "creed" defined by the Declaration and its progressive implementation through Constitutional means or through other means that the Constitution guarantees as the natural and civil rights of American citizens.

The audacity of hope

This positivity is so prevalent in Barack Obama's spoken and written words that cultural and political historian Mark S. Ferrara styles Obama's discourse as "the rhetoric of hope" and his ideas as "utopian." Utopian not so much because Obama's aspirations are located in a "no place," as in the original meaning of the word in Greek, but because of Obama's ability "to imagine a better place" than the world as it is and because of his preoccupation with the "dialectical tension between the status quo and the ideal world." It is certainly true, as noted and quoted above, that Obama adamantly argues that the United States should live up to its ideals. And indeed therein for him lies the idea that "America can change." But, as informative, insightful, and interesting as Ferrara's ideas are, it seems to me that utopianism doesn't quite capture the full nature of Barack Obama's American history. As a historian, Obama is too sensitive to the messy complexities of the past—to the contingent nature of ideas, to the continuities of things, to the limits of the possible at any given moment, and to the unpredictability of the future—to propose the kind of before-and-after scenarios that any definition of utopianism inherently implies.[14]

Even the expert Ferrara's sophisticated definition of "utopian" seems to me to be too binary in two ways to contain the complexities of Barack Obama's American history. First, for Obama there are no "two poles of the ideal and the actual," as Ferrara posits, no simple dichotomy of ideal and real, for all that Obama sometimes uses such terms as a kind of shorthand. To begin with, ideas are not merely abstract concepts in Obama's mind. They are also for him, at least in America, active forces that can change and have changed economic, social, and political conditions. As aforementioned, the essence of Obama's American history is that the abstract ideas of the Enlightenment were given tangibility when turned into a "creed" in the Declaration and then yet more so when "made real" in the law of the land by the Constitution. And then even more so still through subsequent constitutional amendments, legislation, and the evolution of everyday custom. Ideas therefore operate on many levels, from the entirely abstract to the totally "real" and at all points in-between.[15]

Consider Obama's own words. The "self-evident truths" of the Declaration of Independence that "all men are created equal" and are "endowed by their creator with unalienable rights to life, liberty, and the pursuit of happiness" are not only "our common creed" but "the substance of our common creed." It's difficult to know exactly what Obama means here by "substance," but in the context of other things he says he seems to me to mean two closely related things. First, that even though the Declaration has no legal standing, its words are nonetheless literally the founding words of the nation and therefore the moral standard the nation should and often does hold itself to. And, following from that, it's the power of those founding words to motivate people to act, the moral imperative embedded in them, that gives ideas their agency. As Obama said when citing them in a speech on the semi-centenary of Bloody Sunday in Selma, Alabama: "These are not just words. They're a living thing, a call to action, a roadmap for citizenship and an insistence in the capacity of free men and women to shape our own destiny."[16]

As Obama also said in the next sentence in the same speech, "For founders like Franklin and Jefferson, for leaders like Lincoln and FDR, the success of our experiment in self-government rested on engaging all of our citizens in this work." Thus the words from the Declaration are also, for Obama, "the foundation of our government." These particular words do not appear in the letter of Constitution, but in Obama's opinion they are in its spirit—in the idea of popular sovereignty embedded in the words "We the people," in the political mechanisms designed, Obama believes, to create an ever "more perfect union," and in the legal and political protections proffered by the Bill of Rights and other constitutional provisions. Consider something else Obama says in "A More Perfect Union": that in the Constitution, the Founders "finally made real their declaration of independence." Made real. Obama's world, past and present, is thus not just about utopian idealization. It is a world of creeds that are starting points rather than perfect endings, and a world of ideas that have "substance," form "foundations," and are "made real."[17]

And let's consider too a certain other concept that also implicitly undermines ideal-real binaries: the "more perfect union" that Obama often mentions and that provided the title of the speech in Philadelphia. Like the language of the Founders themselves, Obama's vocabulary is sufficiently supple to accommodate such modified absolutes as "more perfect." The Union the Founders formed was not perfect or imperfect, but "more perfect," more perfect than the Articles of Confederation that it replaced. The Union Obama describes has similarly never since the time of the Founders been perfect or imperfect, but has become "more perfect." And if Obama's grammar has no perfect or imperfect past or present, it also has no perfect future. As Obama said in Philadelphia, "This union may never be perfect, but generation after generation has shown that it can always be perfected."[18]

Indeed, while Obama often writes and speaks of a more perfect future, he has never detailed a perfect one. And indeed in a moment of historically minded political introspection he explicitly disclaimed the confidence required even to foresee such a thing. Discussing the absolutism of abolitionists, Obama noted that "it has sometimes been the cranks, the zealots, the prophets, the agitators, and the unreasonable—in other words, the absolutists—that have fought for a new social order." And he said he therefore "can't summarily dismiss those possessed of a similar certainty today—the antiabortion activist who pickets my town hall meeting, or the animal rights activist who raids a laboratory—no matter how deeply I disagree with their views." Even when the absolutists turn out to be right in hindsight, only these few prophetic zealots had the foresight to see that in advance. And in any case more often than not they turn out to be wrong. Hence Obama does not count himself as one of them, even when expressing admiration for some of them. Obama is therefore at most a half-way utopian: idealistic, but without imposing prescriptive ideas; visionary, but free of blinding visions.[19]

In his uncertainty about the future, Barack Obama is once again one with America's Founders. Or at least with what he sees as their sense of their own epistemological limitations. Obama argues that the Founders eschewed prescriptive visions of the future precisely because they knew they could not know what the future would be like. But they were sufficiently visionary to provide a constitutional means through which succeeding generations could find their futures for themselves. As Obama tells it, "the Founding Fathers and original ratifiers have told us *how* to think but are no longer around to tell us *what* to think. We are on our own, and have only our own reason and our judgment to rely on." Obama thus sees the Founders as the historian and political scientist James T. Kloppenberg sees Obama: as "philosophical pragmatists." That is, as idealistic but also practical, grounded in ideals but grounded by reality. One of those realities is that different people have different ideals, including differing ideal futures. Obama thus accepts that pursuing one's individual ideals potentially betrays the more important ideals of democracy itself—the accommodation of different points of view. He thus accepts in turn the necessity and in fact the virtuousness of compromise as embedded in America's polity. While Barack Obama is indeed idealistic, then, he's also ecumenical. He therefore prefers to aim for the greatest happiness for the greatest number, rather than the perfect future for a few. And so he's ultimately too utilitarian to be utopian.[20]

WE HOLD THESE truths

If Barack Obama is not a utopian historian, then what kind of historian is he? His central historical themes—the power of ideas, the struggle for equality and liberty against the forces of injustice and tyranny, and above all the theme of progress, all of which feature in the making of that "more perfect union"—suggest to me that he's a Whig.[21]

But let me qualify that. The term "Whig" is often deployed as a weapon in historian-on-historian verbal violence. To say someone is a "Whig historian" is usually to accuse them of exaggerating the existence of equality, liberty, and consensus, of understating the existence of inequality, oppression, and conflict, of naively believing in historical progress, and of antiquated attachment to the Great Man Theory of History. But I don't think or mean to say any of these things about Barack Obama. While Obama most certainly believes in the historical existence of the ideals of equality and liberty, and in their very real material progress, these things are for him much contested and therefore have to be fought for. And so for Obama progress is not linear, it can be painfully slow, there can be setbacks, and it's often the people as well as or even rather than their leaders who do the fighting for it.

It's often forgotten furthermore that Whig historiography originally emerged from the polarized ideological conflicts and deadly revolutionary struggles that transformed England, Britain, Europe, and North America in the seventeenth and eighteenth centuries. And it's also often forgotten that there were and are different kinds of Whigs, and also that Whiggism has changed over time. Barack Obama's historiography is deeply influenced by the eighteenth-century Radical Whigs. Most deeply by America's "Founding Fathers," men who called themselves Whigs.[22]

The term "Whig" actually originated in English politics as an insult derived from "whiggamors," referring to western Scottish cattle drovers. It first appeared in political discourse during the 1678–81 Exclusion Crisis as a term of abuse aimed at those aiming to prevent James, Duke of York from inheriting the English throne on account of his preferences for Catholicism and absolute monarchy. James's supporters, believers in the divine right of kings and in nonresistance to authority, were nicknamed Tories, from the Irish word *tóraí*, meaning outlaw. The Tories ensured that James ascended to the throne in 1685, despite Whig efforts to exclude him, but Whigs and Tories briefly combined with each other and with William, Prince of Orange to overthrow James II in 1688, after he proved indeed to be too "papist" and absolutist. After this Glorious Revolution, however, Whigs and Tories turned on each other once more and remained the principal protagonists in British politics until the rise of the Liberal Party in the mid-nineteenth century and the Labour Party in the early-twentieth. The Tories are still with us, endlessly ensuring that progress toward equality and liberty is a long and often painful process.[23]

While the Whigs had in common with each other a commitment to constitutional and limited monarchy, they were never a homogenous lot. At one end of the spectrum were moderate Whigs who believed that political authority derived from an Ancient Constitution under which parliaments ruled alongside and occasionally overruled kings, and which thereby guaranteed the "rights of freeborn Englishmen." At the other end were radical Whigs who believed that political authority derived from natural or God-given rights. Men (usually meaning men exclusively but sometimes more inclusively meaning "mankind" or humankind and thereby encompassing women as well) were born equal and had natural and unalienable rights to life, liberty, and property. People originally lived in a "state of nature," but by way of a "social contract" they voluntarily consented to be governed, the better to secure their lives, liberties, and property. But if government was destructive of these ends, the people had the right to alter or abolish it, and to institute new government in such form as they believed would best secure their future safety and happiness.

The chief English exponents of radical Whiggism in the late seventeenth and eighteenth centuries were John Locke, author of *Two Treatises of Government* (1690), and a little later "commonwealthmen" such as John Trenchard and Thomas Gordon, the initially pseudonymous authors of *Cato's Letters*. *Cato's Letters* were first published as newspaper articles between 1720 and 1723 and then in collected form as *Essays on Liberty, Civil and Religious, and Other Important Subjects* in 1724, and in successive editions in subsequent decades. Moderate Whiggism dominated English and British politics for a century and a half after the Glorious Revolution, but the radical Whiggism of Locke and of Trenchard and Gordon was the most widely read version in eighteenth-century America. As the paraphrasing in the previous paragraph indeed unsubtly suggests, the American Declaration of Independence was written in the language of the Radical Whigs.[24]

We can see the American Radical Whig in Barack Obama in the frequency with which he notes or quotes that Declaration of Independence. And we can perhaps see his depth of commitment to its principles in the manner in which he sometimes does so. In *The Audacity of Hope*, for example, Obama began a section of a chapter on "Values" by quoting the Declaration with the following typography: "WE HOLD THESE truths to be self-evident, that all men are Created equal, that they are endowed by their Creator with certain unalienable Rights, that among these are Life, Liberty, and the pursuit of Happiness." Some sections of *The Audacity of Hope* begin with capitals, others don't, so that alone may not mean much. But the other capitalizations here are not copied from any original or early version of the document that I know of, and appear therefore to be either Obama's own or his editors' presumably author-vetted inventions. The typographical style nevertheless resembles that of the eighteenth century, and the effect is therefore one of transcription even if it is not exactly copied. And the intended effect may even relate to the biblical origins of the term transcription. Indeed we've already seen Obama call these words a "creed," the same term used by the Swedish sociologist Gunnar Myrdal to describe the ideals of equality and liberty embedded in the Declaration, even as he pointed out how America failed to live up to its ideals in regard to race. And it's the same term used by Martin Luther King to describe the Declaration in his "I Have a Dream" speech of 1963. As the great historian Pauline Maier showed, the Declaration became a kind of "American Scripture," a part of what philosopher and social scientist Robert Bellah called America's "civil religion."[25]

Barack Obama's near-religious reverence for the Declaration of Independence might indicate an affinity with a particular brand of American Whig historiography: Providentialism. The Providentialist Whigs saw the Revolution and other American advancements as not only struggles for equality and liberty against iniquity and tyranny but as cosmic battles between good and evil, with God on the side of American freedom. Some have perceived an Obamian Providentialism and ascribed it to Puritanism, others to Transcendentalism. These ideas are intriguing but for me ultimately unconvincing. First, notwithstanding the likes of Jeremiah Wright, the influence of New England Puritanism on later American thinking is generally exaggerated, as we'll see in Chapter 1. And while Obama evokes the inspirational influence of the Puritans' sense of mission, he's intolerant of their intolerance.

The Transcendentalist thesis on the other hand may have more to recommend it. In the speech in Selma, Alabama, for example, marking the semi-centenary of the famous voting rights march from there to Montgomery, Obama summed up the collective vision and mission of Americans as follows: "We are the people Emerson wrote of, 'who for truth and honor's sake stand fast and suffer long;' who are 'never tired, so long as we can see far enough.'"[26]

And yet Barack Obama's historiography is ultimately decidedly sublunary. We saw above how his "philosophical pragmatism" grounds his idealism in practical realism. We can also see a decisive rejection of the admitted temptations of unearthly theories in one of his discussions of the Constitution and the Bill of Rights, which, he writes, "seem so incredibly right that it's easy to believe that they are the result of natural law if not divine inspiration." He therefore "understands" the view that "our democracy should be treated as fixed and unwavering; the fundamentalist faith that if the original understanding of the Constitution is followed without question or deviation, and if we remain true to rules that the Founders set forth, as they intended, then we will be rewarded and all good will flow." All this though leads to his very practical point that the Constitution "is not a static but rather a living document, and must be read in the context of an ever-changing world."[27]

That reference to "fundamentalist faith" and the other gentler but still satirical imitations of religious idioms reflect a rejection of providential perception. Indeed, as we'll see in some detail later, Obama's religious rhetoric, genuine though it is, resembles the Enlightenment secularists of the eighteenth century, rather than the Evangelical sophists of today. It resembles, for sure, the abolitionist and anti-segregationist preacher-activists of the nineteenth and twentieth centuries, and to that extent it's very righteous indeed. But that's just another way of saying that it's grounded in the good of humanity rather than aerated by the glory of the Almighty.

What makes us exceptional — what makes us American

Barack Obama therefore has more in common with the non-providentialist Whigs of the American revolutionary era and with the neo-Whigs of more recent times than he does with nineteenth-century historians who saw God (as distinct from belief in God) as an actual agent in human and especially American history. But Obama does share with many American Whig historians of all eras a belief in "American exceptionalism"—up to a point. As Obama noted in his second inaugural address:

Each time we gather to inaugurate a President, we bear witness to the enduring strength of our Constitution. We affirm the promise of our democracy. We recall that what binds this nation together is not the colors of our skin or the tenets of our faith or the origins of our names. What makes us exceptional—what makes us American—is our allegiance to an idea articulated in a declaration made more than two centuries ago: "We hold these truths to be self-evident, that all men are created equal; that they are endowed by their Creator with certain unalienable rights; that among these are life, liberty, and the pursuit of happiness."[28]

American exceptionalism is sometimes seen as problematically parochial, as ascribing as "American" things that may have originated elsewhere or that may be widely shared or both. But the man who sees the part of his childhood that he spent in Indonesia as a formative experience, and who has carefully nurtured his African family ties, is hardly likely to be so narrow-minded. Indeed Obama appreciates that many ideas embraced by Americans actually originated elsewhere, and he duly namechecks Englishmen Thomas Hobbes, John Locke, and quotes though doesn't name Thomas Paine as examples of writers who have informed the American mind. What is "exceptional" for Obama, as we've seen and will see further, is that the United States has transformed these ideas into realities by declaratory creed and constitutional means.

But the idea that adherence to the Declaration of Independence, the Constitution, and American democracy "binds the nation together" raises again the question of whether Whig history in general and Obama's Whiggism in particular puts too much emphasis on historical equality, liberty, and consensus, and too little emphasis on iniquity, oppression, and conflict. In the late nineteenth-century Gilded Age through the Great Depression of the 1930s, "Progressive" historians were in the ascendance, understandably stressing the enormous inequality and conflict between rich and poor in the past that they saw reflected in their present. The end of that Depression, and America's role in the victories over German Nazism and Japanese Imperialism, plus the new threat of totalitarian Communism, saw the neo-Whig emphasis on a unified struggle for liberty against tyranny rise once again to historiographical eminence. The Civil Rights Movement and the Vietnam War, however, drew attention back again to injustices at home and overseas, and encouraged neo-progressive historians to stress historical iniquities to which neo-Whigs were allegedly complacently oblivious. Indeed Obama's "A More Perfect Union" and other speeches have been criticized for overemphasizing historical harmony and underemphasizing racial and other kinds of conflict in the past and in the present.[29]

There are certainly tendencies in Barack Obama's American history that may make his interpretation of the past appear as excessively focused on equality, liberty, and consensus and as inattentive to their opposites as some of his critics claim. Obama pays little attention, for example, to internal conflicts in the American Revolution, abolitionism, and the Civil Rights Movement. When writing and talking specifically about these movements, he's generally more interested in their successful outcomes than he is in the internal disagreements that were often a part of what made them dynamic.

But when writing and speaking more broadly about American history, Obama actually does acknowledge American revolutionaries' dilemmas about such sometimes deeply divisive matters as liberty and license, liberty and equality, and—above all—liberty and slavery. For Obama, moreover, conflict of one kind or another is part of the dynamic that drives American history generally. And it's often only through bitter struggle and bloody conflict that the American Union was made more perfect, especially in the fight against slavery and the struggles for Civil Rights. Indeed a tellingly notable feature of Barack Obama's American history in this respect is the importance of African American history. For Obama, as we'll see, the struggle for African American liberty and equality is not a subplot in the American story; it's a principal driving force of the central narrative.

In sum, Barack Obama's American history may seem on the face of it to emphasize consensus over conflict, equality over inequality, and liberty over oppression. Yet his consensus is not unanimous, but presupposes the existence of conflict. His equality is not ubiquitous, but presupposes the existence of inequality. And his freedom is not universal, but presupposes the existence of oppression. In other words, history is truly complicated, and Obama's analysis of it is duly sophisticated.

The arc of the moral universe

Barack Obama's American history may also seem on the face of it to overemphasize progress, a concept that professional historians rightly tend to be skeptical about. And indeed Obama knows and was reminded by the election of 2016 that sometimes darker demons defeat the better angels of our nature. As he said in his farewell address of January 10, 2017, in regard to American history generally but also in more pointed reference to recent events: "Yes, our progress has been uneven. The work of democracy has always been hard. It's always been contentious. Sometimes it's been bloody. For every two steps forward, it often feels we take one step back."[30]

Indeed the winners-versus-losers attitude of the Tea Party and of Barack Obama's successor in the Oval Office is the very antithesis of the inclusive ends of Obamian politics. But the differences between forty-four and forty-five are not only about ends but also about means, and in the area of means America may have taken more than one step back in 2016. Obama's successor's mode of politics as war by means of weaponized lies represents an existential threat to American constitutionalism, subverting the democratic deliberating and constructive consensus-building that for Obama are the political analogues of the philosophical concepts of truth and reason. So it's all the more remarkable that Obama retains his faith in the resilience of the American system and above all in a creed he believes is adhered to by the majority of Americans if not their current leader. As he said in the next words of his farewell address: "But the long sweep of America has been defined by forward motion, a constant widening of our founding creed to embrace all and not just some."[31]

But all of this is no more or less than Barack Obama believed a decade before when he spoke of progress but noted in *The Audacity of Hope* that "nowhere is it ordained that history moves in a straight line." His historical narrative as related in this book duly includes the breakdowns and backtracking that happen on the road to progress. And as Obama has observed on more than one occasion, quoting Reverend Martin Luther King quoting the nineteenth-century abolitionist Reverend Theodore Parker: "the arc of moral universe is long, but it bends towards justice."[32]

But Obama often adds his own coda when citing this dictum. At the sixty-fifth birthday celebrations in 2005 of the great Civil Rights leader and later Congressman John Lewis, Obama spoke of the attacks on voting rights marchers, including Lewis himself, in Selma, Alabama, in 1965. Obama said that "two weeks after Bloody Sunday, when the march finally reached Montgomery, Martin Luther King Jr. spoke to the crowd of thousands and said 'The arc of the moral universe is long, but it bends towards justice.' He's right," Obama added, "but you know what? It doesn't bend on its own. It bends because we help it bend that way. Because people like John Lewis and Hosea Williams and Martin Luther King and Coretta Scott King and Rosa Parks and thousands of ordinary Americans with extraordinary courage have helped bend it that way." On other occasions Obama credits King himself with this addendum. A few months earlier, when Barack Obama won the race for the US Senate in November 2004, he said that "Dr. King said, 'the arc of moral universe is long, but it bends towards justice as long as we help it bend that way.' "[33]

Either way, Obama's point is that progress presupposes the existence of opposition and therefore conflict. Progress is not natural, easy, or linear, and achieving it is often a struggle, and one that can only be won by "We the people." Which brings us to a final general point about Barack Obama's American history that needs to be mentioned before we move on to explore its particulars in the subsequent chapters.

Where the perfection begins

Barack Obama believes that historical progress or its opposite doesn't depend only on who happens to inhabit the White House or other positions of power at any given time. For Obama, American democracy and its history is also about "all the faceless, nameless men and women, slaves and soldiers and tailors and butchers" that he wrote of at the end of *The Audacity of Hope*. And, furthermore, Obama's "more perfect union" is not only built at dramatic moments but also on a more gradual basis, "brick by brick, rail by rail, calloused hand by calloused hand." His is not just political history therefore but also social history, or at least the social history of politics.[34]

Which brings us back to Philadelphia in 2008, and by extension back to that same city in 1787. Barack Obama began his oration on "A More Perfect Union" with the Founders, as we already saw, but he ended it with a story of those he sees as their modern-day successors. The tale tells of how for Obama the phenomenon of people working together to make their lives better, to make real the creed of the Declaration of Independence, belongs in a tradition dating from the constitutional convention. Obama's telling of it also illustrates the gift he has for linking long-term progress to collective action, and more generally for describing the synergies he sees between historical processes and everyday lives-as-lived. "There is one story in particular that I'd like to leave you with today," he said:

> —a story I told when I had the great honor of speaking on Dr. King's birthday at his home church, Ebenezer Baptist, in Atlanta.
>
> There is a young, twenty-three year old white woman named Ashley Baia who organized for our campaign in Florence, South Carolina. She had been working to organize a mostly African-American community since the beginning of this campaign, and one day she was at a roundtable discussion where everyone went around telling their story and why they were there.

And Ashley said that when she was nine years old, her mother got cancer. And because she had to miss days of work, she was let go and lost her health care. They had to file for bankruptcy, and that's when Ashley decided that she had to do something to help her mom.

She knew that food was one of their most expensive costs, and so Ashley convinced her mother that what she really liked and really wanted to eat more than anything else was mustard and relish sandwiches. Because that was the cheapest way to eat.

She did this for a year until her mom got better, and she told everyone at the roundtable that the reason she joined our campaign was so that she could help the millions of other children in the country who want and need to help their parents, too.

Now Ashley might have made a different choice. Perhaps somebody told her along the way that the source of her mother's problems were blacks who were on welfare and too lazy to work, or Hispanics who were coming into the country illegally. But she didn't. She sought out allies in her fight against injustice.

Anyway, Ashley finishes her story and then goes around the room and asks everyone else why they're supporting the campaign. They all have different stories and reasons. Many bring up a specific issue. And finally they come to this elderly black man who's been sitting there quietly the entire time. And Ashley asks him why he's there. And he does not bring up a specific issue. He does not say health care or the economy. He does not say education or the war. He does not say that he was there because of Barack Obama. He simply says to everyone in the room, "I am here because of Ashley."

"I am here because of Ashley." By itself, that single moment of recognition between that young white girl and that old black man is not enough. It is not enough to give health care to the sick, or jobs to the jobless, or education to our children.

But it is where we start. It is where our union grows stronger. And as so many generations have come to realize over the course of the two-hundred and twenty one years since a band of patriots signed that document in Philadelphia, that is where the perfection begins.[35]

CHAPTER 1
OUR STARTING POINT AS AMERICANS:
THE AMERICAN COLONIES

Our starting point as Americans

"WE HOLD THESE truths to be self-evident, that all men are Created equal, that they are endowed by their Creator with certain unalienable Rights, that among these are Life, Liberty, and the pursuit of Happiness." Barack Obama describes these words from the Declaration of Independence as "our starting point as Americans." In some respects this claim is true. As a political action rather than just a random announcement of abstract principles, the Declaration helped bring the United States into being, which certainly seems like a starting point of some sort.[1]

And yet. Obama acknowledges that there was in fact an earlier America. That earlier America is alluded to in the earlier words of the Declaration of Independence. The more famous ones above form the opening of the Declaration's second paragraph. The Declaration actually begins as follows:

> When in the course of human events, it becomes necessary for one people to dissolve the political bands which have connected them with another, and to assume among the powers of the earth, the separate and equal station to which the laws of nature and of nature's God entitle them, a decent respect to the opinions of mankind requires that they should declare the causes which impel them to the separation.[2]

While the Declaration of Independence was certainly the starting point for the United States, then, these words remind us that it was also the ending point of something else. That is, that the newly self-created citizens of the United States were abandoning their long-held status as colonial subjects of Great Britain.

On the eve of independence, the American colonies that would form the United States comprised thirteen among twenty-five diverse British colonies scattered from the farms and fisheries of icy Canada to the sugar plantations of the broiling Caribbean. These colonies and their peoples were connected politically to each other and to the "mother country" by common allegiance to the British crown. They were also connected together through trade networks governed by Navigation laws that confined colonial commerce within a British mercantilist trade system. British trade networks tied Britain and its American colonies closely to Africa too. Victims of the slave trade and their descendants, along with people from all over the British Isles, parts of continental Europe, and some other parts of the world were all thus members of a rich if often deeply riven "British-Atlantic World."[3]

The more fortunate among the people of British America were united by a sense of inheritance of "the rights of freeborn Englishmen," by a broadly common culture, and by ties of family and friendship. Historians of this British Atlantic World have shown how deep and extensive these common connections, inheritances, and allegiances were, despite the many differences between the colonies and despite the many divergences of religion, race, gender, class, and status within them. Even the most unfortunate people of British America, early members of the African diaspora, established new roots in this New World. They did so initially involuntarily and merely as a matter of survival, but in so surviving they founded African Caribbean and African American cultures that enrich our world immeasurably today. The continent's original inhabitants also enriched the lives of the newcomers in a variety of ways that we'll explore in more detail in Chapter 7. In short, at least from the defeat of the French in the Seven Years' War of 1756–63 and possibly before that, the British Empire comprised the most powerful extended political and economic entity and the richest and most diverse cultural region the world had ever known.

Barack Obama does not explore the richness or dynamism of this world, however. Rather, for Obama, the American colonies were simply arenas of tyranny from which eventually a new people broke free. As Obama put it in his weekly radio address on Independence Day in 2013, for example: "On July 4th, 1776, a small band of patriots declared that we were a people created equal—free to think and worship and live as we please. It was a declaration heard around the world—that we were no longer colonists, we were Americans, and our destiny would not be determined for us; it would be determined by us." On the South Lawn of the White House earlier the same day, Obama said the same thing, but then expanded on the theme. "At that time in human history," he added, "it was kings and princes and emperors who made decisions. But those patriots knew there was a better way of doing things, that freedom was possible, and that to achieve their freedom they'd be willing to lay down their lives, their fortunes and their honor. And so they fought a revolution."[4]

Barack Obama had iterated this idea of empire before, and had also previously even more clearly connected national self-determination with individual liberty. Obama urged the 2006 graduating class of the University of Massachusetts at Boston, for instance, to "pursue the happiness you hope for," but reminded them not to take for granted their historically privileged position. "Today," he said, "this dream sounds common—perhaps even clichéd—yet for most of human history it's been anything but. As a servant of Rome, a peasant in China," he said, "or a subject of King George, there were very few unlikely futures. No matter how hard you worked or struggled for something better, you knew you'd spend your life forced to build somebody else's empire; to sacrifice for someone else's cause."[5]

These views may well have been shaped more by Barack Obama's family memory than by a deep familiarity with British American history. Obama provided a brief insight into his perspective on the impositions of imperialism in "The Audacity of Hope," his address to the Democratic National Convention of 2004. "My father was a foreign student, born and raised in a small village in Kenya," Obama said. "He grew up herding goats," he continued "went to school in a tin-roof shack. His father—my grandfather—was a cook, a domestic servant to the British." This was a tale he told in many of his earlier speeches when it was still necessary for him to introduce himself to audiences.[6]

On occasion Obama has connected British imperialism in Africa with slavery and Jim Crow in America, perhaps more as a way to establish his own ancestral credentials as a black American, despite not being descended from African American slaves. In an early primary campaign speech in 2007 in Selma, Alabama, the site of the "Bloody Sunday" violence against voting rights marchers by state troopers, Obama told the crowd, "My grandfather was a cook to the British in Kenya. Grew up in a small village and all his life, that's all he was—a cook and a houseboy. And that's what they called him, even when he was 60 years old. They called him a houseboy. They wouldn't call him by his last name. Call him by his first name. Sound familiar?" Obama's autobiographical *Dreams from my Father* further illustrates the individual stories of lives limited and human potential wasted as well as the better-known murderous atrocities committed to sustain British colonialism in Kenya. Although David Remnick's biography, *The Bridge*, has shown that Obama's forebears enjoyed certain opportunities under British rule, there is no doubt they would have enjoyed more had they had the individual liberties that are more likely to exist with national self-determination.[7]

There were many oppressions and atrocities committed by the British Empire in America as well as in Africa. But it was nevertheless a different kind of imperialism than the one Obama describes. The military, monetary, and other resources available to the English state in the early seventeenth century were less abundant than those available to the British state in the nineteenth and twentieth centuries. In the later empire the British were able to occupy and administer "colonies of exploitation" centrally from London with relatively few civil and military personnel on the ground. Generally, in this "second" British Empire, indigenous peoples were exploited so their resources could be expropriated.

By contrast, in the "first" British Empire, indigenous peoples were expropriated so their resources could be exploited. The earlier and less well-resourced English state had to colonize in collaboration with private enterprise. The standard method was for the crown or parliament to grant charters to private companies or proprietors who would then occupy and administer "colonies of settlement." To attract migrants and settlers to repeople America required allowing relatively extensive economic opportunity and the ability to enjoy it. Colonial promotional literature thus promised migrants such enticements as religious and political freedom, low taxes, and, above all, cheap land.

Of course, that land had previously belonged to Native Americans and a great deal of it was worked by Africans and their enslaved descendants, so there was in many ways even worse violence and suffering in the early British Empire than there was in the later one. And promotional literature understated the hardships and dangers involved in oceanic travel and American settlement, and overstated the extent of opportunity available to individuals. Nevertheless, significant numbers of free Europeans were able to build something for themselves as well as "to build somebody else's empire." And many certainly enjoyed better prospects in colonial America than they would have done if they had stayed at home.

Otherwise, Barack Obama mentions certain aspects of life in the colonies that we explore below, but mostly isolated ones that don't provide a complete or coherent picture of colonial British America. Indeed, in some respects Obama's colonial America was not what it was but what it wasn't. As we saw in the prologue and as we see in greater detail in later chapters, Barack Obama's American history is driven by the "common creed" of the Declaration of Independence that infused the law of the land in the form of a Constitution that created a "deliberative democracy" so that Americans with the audacity of hope could and can keep on building an ever "more perfect union." What makes his history of the United States complete and coherent is therefore precisely what in its absence makes his history of colonial America incomplete (though not incoherent). Colonial America did not even have this common creed and starting point.

But there are elements in Barack Obama's colonial America that would later coalesce in a coterie of phenomena that in his view helped shape the United States. Namely, religious migration, communitarianism, "homespun virtues," the "local democracy" of town meetings, late-colonial British tyranny, and America's "original sin" of slavery. These are things that are relevant to Obama's sense of what America became after Independence, and he thus sees them from a postindependence perspective. They comprise therefore less a history of colonial America than a prehistory of the United States. Historians consider such teleological approaches to history to be bad practice, but on the other hand Obama never pretends to do anything more than mine the colonies for the origins of things that cohere into a more consistent form as a consequence of Independence. It does mean, though, that he sees Americans as having a number of starting points deep in the pre-Declaration past.

With the exceptions of imperial rule and enslavement, the isolated features of colonial American life that Barack Obama identifies are ones he finds positively inspiring for later Americans. The migratory escape from seventeenth-century religious tyranny and persecution, the building of new communities, those homespun virtues, experiments in democracy, and the revolutionary escape from eighteenth-century political tyranny and persecution all feature in his scattered comments on colonial American history, all appearing as early examples of Obamian audacity and hope. There was little equality and liberty in Barack Obama's early America, but there were these pursuits of happiness.

Sometimes Obama draws a direct line between precocious pursuits of happiness in the colonial era and those that arose after the revolution. So we can begin again with the founding of the country and work our way back in time from there to the founding of the colonies.

In a hall that still stands across the street

In common with his comments on the Declaration of Independence, Barack Obama's remarks on the Constitution can tell us much about what he thinks about colonial America. In the introduction to "A More Perfect Union," the career-saving speech of

March 18, 2008, Obama focused first on the Founding Fathers and their formation of a new nation. He started the speech and set the scene for his theme by quoting some of the opening words of the Constitution: "WE THE PEOPLE, in order to form a more perfect union." And then he explained the provenance of this phrase as follows:

> Two hundred and twenty one years ago, in a hall that still stands across the street, a group of men gathered and, with these simple words, launched America's improbable experiment in democracy. Farmers and scholars; statesmen and patriots, who had traveled across an ocean to escape tyranny and persecution, finally made real their declaration of independence at a Philadelphia convention that lasted through the spring of 1787.[8]

What the bulk of this passage refers to is the fact that while the Founders declared Independence in 1776, they did not immediately create a lasting political settlement for the new United States. From 1776 to 1781, the United States was overseen by the same Continental Congress that issued the Declaration of Independence. Or, more accurately, the United States *were* overseen by the Continental Congress, as they remained a confederation of states and were not yet a federal nation. After a subsequent period of what many saw as still insufficiently substantive governance under the Articles of Confederation from 1781, the Founders at the 1787 Convention, calling themselves "We the people of the United States," finally drafted the Constitution "in order to form a more perfect union." Most of the states ratified the document in 1788, and the new Constitution began its operations on March 4, 1789. The creation of the Constitution was finally completed with the adoption of the Bill of Rights, the first ten amendments, in December 1791.

We return to this process of nation formation in greater detail in subsequent chapters, and to Barack Obama's contestable claim that the Constitution was an "experiment in democracy." For now, though, I want to attend to certain aspects of Obama's abbreviation of these events in this speech, including some elisions and even errors that reveal a great deal about what Obama thinks about colonial America. Most especially, how he elides the era in order to emphasize the rupture that for Obama the American Revolution represents.

First, there is that peculiarly American sense of time embedded in Obama's words, manifest in the apparent notability that a building should still be standing after 221 years. This emphasis on the age of Independence Hall actually draws attention to America's youth rather than its age, as no one would find it literally remarkable that a building should still be standing after more than two centuries in, say, Europe. And indeed Obama's comment here implicitly takes thirty-four years off the age of the building. Independence Hall was in fact built in 1753 to be the Pennsylvania State House, so it had actually been standing for 254 years at the time Obama was speaking. Maybe that's a trivial observation, and in any case Obama's rhetorical reference point was 1787 and not the earlier date. But, on the other hand, there is a difference between the just over two centuries that Obama spoke about and the more than a quarter of a millennium that he might otherwise have mentioned.

In any case, this emphasis on America's youth is silently strengthened by dating its age to the creation of the United States in 1776, and most especially by dating it to the drafting of the Constitution in 1787. Again, this seems reasonable considering that Obama's subject at that moment was indeed the creation of the United States. But, like his comment about the Declaration of Independence as "our starting point as Americans," there is an elision of colonial America in operation here. One might equally date "our starting point as Americans," for example, to the founding of the first permanent English colony at Jamestown in 1607, four centuries and a year prior to the time Obama was speaking. But that would not have the effect of emphasizing America's youth, or, more importantly, its revolutionary rupture. Obama does occasionally date the origins of Americans to the colonial era, at least to the Pilgrims and the Puritans of the 1620s and 1630s, but only so as to incorporate that aspect of colonial history into the history of the United States, as we shall see shortly.

The spring of 1787

Next though there is an error in the above passage from "A More Perfect Union," or perhaps an "error." And it too but in a different way serves to emphasize the youthful and revolutionary nature of America as Barack Obama sees it. The Constitutional Convention to which Obama referred actually assembled on May 14, became quorate on May 25, and sat until the last of the delegates finally dispersed on September 17. The Convention thus lasted through the summer of 1787, and not "through the spring" as Obama incorrectly recollects. This may have been an error made due to the words being written in a rush and delivered only once. The speech was crafted after all in the political crisis of mid-March 2008, created by the media uncovering some old sermons in which Obama's then pastor, Reverend Jeremiah Wright, had suggested that the attacks of September 11 represented America's "chickens coming home to roost," and in which he responded to racism in America's historic and recent domestic and foreign policy with the words "God damn America." The subsequent emergency speechwriting did not go through the usual process of penmanship and proofing. Rather than speechwriter Jon Favreau drafting and then Obama editing his words, the two men reversed their by then usual roles. Obama drafted the deeply personal speech and then Favreau edited, with the two working day and deep into the night on both the campaign and on the oration before the March 18 day of reckoning. Maybe some mistakes were made due to these departures from normal procedures. And as the speech was a response to a passing crisis, it was a one-off rather than a staple of the stump in subsequent months. It would not therefore be repeated and in the process perfected in the course of the campaign.[9]

Or maybe the spring thing was not exactly an error. Barack Obama graduated *magna cum laude* from Harvard Law School, was president of the *Harvard Law Review*, and later taught constitutional law at the University of Chicago for twelve years. He knew at least then when the Constitutional Convention sat, and in case of a memory lapse he could have googled it. Or Jon Favreau might have mentioned it, or checked it himself.

So the relocating of the season of convening was more likely the result of a rhetorical decision to forget the facts and evoke instead the symbolism of springtime. Or else it may have been the result of that symbolism having already seduced the speechwriters, unconsciously perhaps, but all the more revealingly if so. Whatever the case, spring evokes positive images of warmth, growth, and new life. Rhetorically, metaphorically, it implies awakening or reawakening, renewal, fresh possibilities. The same kind of dawning that Ronald Reagan was evoking in his 1984 reelection campaign when he made the otherwise bizarre claim that "it's morning again in America." Favreau is a fan of the rhetoric of Reagan.

And of course spring follows winter. If spring represents the birth of a new nation, then winter perhaps presents the British Empire as old, cold, and dying if not dead. Barack Obama has on other oratorical occasions associated British rule with wintertime, and not in a Christmas-cardy kind of way. The following passage from his first inaugural address is more factually accurate than the lines in "A More Perfect Union" in the sense that the events described actually took place in the season ascribed to them, but as imagery the words are similarly evocative:

> In the year of America's birth, in the coldest of months, a small band of patriots huddled by dying campfires on the shores of an icy river. The capital was abandoned. The enemy was advancing. The snow was stained with blood. At a moment when the outcome of our revolution was most in doubt, the father of our nation ordered these words be read to the people: 'Let it be told to the future world ... that in the depth of winter, when nothing but hope and virtue could survive ... that the city and the country, alarmed at one common danger, came forth to meet [it].'[10]

When you put it like that, calendrical literality doesn't really matter. Obama presents us instead with America's birth as a metaphorical transformation from winter into spring, from death into life, from darkness into light.

Farmers and scholars; statesmen and patriots

Positing an American starting point in the late eighteenth century and nudging the Constitutional Convention from the summer back into the spring of 1787 are not the only ways in which Barack Obama rhetorically frees the United States from its British colonial past. Obama also spoke in Philadelphia of "Farmers and scholars; statesmen and patriots, who had traveled across an ocean to escape tyranny and persecution." These farmers and scholars and statesmen and patriots are obviously Obama's revolutionaries. They are the "group of men" who "gathered" and "launched America's improbable experiment in democracy" and who "made real their declaration of independence at a Philadelphia convention." But who precisely were these people, these farmers and scholars and statesmen and patriots? Who did Obama want us to think of when he said these words? And why?[11]

The most obvious early American candidate for the description of "farmers and scholars" is John Dickinson. Dickinson adopted the nom de plume "A Farmer" when authoring his *Letters from a Farmer in Pennsylvania*, initially published as a series of newspaper articles, the first one on November 5, 1767, and then published again in pamphlet form the following year. He opened the first of his twelve epistles as follows: "I am a *Farmer*, settled, after a variety of fortunes, near the banks of the river *Delaware*, in the province of *Pennsylvania*. I received a liberal education, and have been engaged in the busy scenes of life; but am now convinced, that a man may be as happy without bustle, as with it. My farm is small; my servants are few, and good; I have a little money at interest; I wish for no more; my employment in my own affairs is easy; and with a contented grateful mind, undisturbed by worldly hopes or fears." Dickinson was in fact a highly educated lawyer, and a practicing politician as well as a political writer. He was, in other words, a scholar, and the self-styled Pennsylvania farmer is remembered to this day as "The Penman of the American Revolution."[12]

The letters objected to British parliamentary "taxation without representation" imposed by the Sugar Act (1764), Stamp Act (1765), and Townshend Duties (1767). Also to the Quartering Act (1765) that billeted soldiers in the provinces at colonists' expense; an added offence to the stationing of troops on American soil without the consent of the colonial legislatures after the end of the Seven Years' War in 1763. Dickinson objected, furthermore, to the Declaratory Act of 1766 that asserted parliamentary authority over the colonies "in all cases whatsoever." Dickinson was a member of the Continental Congresses that sat from 1774 in objection to further British measures, though he didn't sign the Declaration of Independence as he persisted in pushing for reconciliation rather than opting for a separation that was in his opinion premature. He later compensated for this recalcitrance by leading a Delaware militia unit in the War of Independence and later still serving as a delegate at the Constitutional Convention.

And so, as well as a self-styled farmer and genuine scholar, Dickinson was also a statesman and a patriot. He and his fellow members of Congress and the later Convention were by definition statesmen: they fought a revolution and founded a nation. And by self-definition they were patriots: that's what they called themselves (as well as Whigs) in opposition to the loyalists (aka Tories) who supported British measures. We return in Chapter 2 to the egalitarian and democratic implications of Obama's characterization of American revolutionaries as "farmers and scholars; statesmen and patriots," and to their possible personification in John Dickinson. But, for now, had these farmers and scholars and statesmen and patriots really "traveled across an ocean to escape tyranny and persecution," as Obama also says?[13]

Who had traveled across an ocean to escape tyranny and persecution

In a word, no. Although more migrants than ever before were crossing the Atlantic Ocean to British America in the years immediately preceding Independence, only eight of the fifty-six men who signed the Declaration had done so. And none of them because of tyranny and persecution. All eight had in fact traveled across the ocean to gain from the opportunities offered by the relative fluidity of British American colonial society. Of the other forty-eight, many had traveled across the ocean variously for educational, political, business, and legal reasons, but all of them were born in the colonies, including John Dickinson.

John Dickinson's great-grandfather Walter had migrated from England to Virginia in 1654. A Quaker, the original American Dickinson knew tyranny and persecution, but by 1659 he had established a tobacco plantation named Croisadore in Talbot County, Maryland, where John was born on November 8, 1732. John Dickinson spent most of his childhood at the family's other property, Poplar Hall in Kent County, Delaware, and he divided most of his adult life, as a lawyer, politician, and penman, between there and Philadelphia, Pennsylvania. He had traveled across the ocean in 1753, in an easterly direction the first time, to study law at Middle Temple in London, traveling back west again three years later. He was getting himself a very fine education; he was not escaping tyranny and persecution.

In any case, the words "traveled across an ocean to escape tyranny and persecution" ritualistically evoke early migrants to the colonies, most especially the Pilgrims who travelled across the Atlantic aboard the *Mayflower* to found Plymouth Colony in 1620, and the Puritans who travelled across the ocean aboard the *Arbella* and other vessels to found Massachusetts in 1630. But of course Obama knows about these people and when they lived. He wrote in *The Audacity of Hope* that "Pilgrims came to our shores to escape religious persecution and practice without impediment to their brand of strict Calvinism." And in a commencement address at the University of Massachusetts in Boston in 2006 he said that "the earliest settlers arrived on the shores of Boston and Salem and Plymouth, they dreamed of building a city upon a hill." Obama may consider the Founding Fathers as America's secular patriarchs, but he knows perfectly well that they didn't live as long as their scriptural counterparts.[14]

Besides Plymouth and Massachusetts, the former of which was absorbed into the latter in 1691, the other New England colonies were founded as follows: New Hampshire in 1629, although it was also later absorbed into Massachusetts and only became a permanently separate entity in 1691, and Connecticut and Rhode Island in 1636, respectively chartered by the crown in 1662 and 1663. Nor were these the first to be established. The first permanent English colony in America was in fact Jamestown, Virginia, settled thirteen years before Plymouth and almost 500 miles to the south. The other one founded in North America in the early seventeenth century was Maryland, adjoining Virginia, which was chartered in 1632 and settled by Englishmen two years later.

The civil wars of the British Isles in the 1640s and the subsequent interregnum interrupted imperial progress, except for Oliver Cromwell's "Western Design," which resulted in the English capture of Jamaica from the Spanish in 1655. But a new wave of North American colonization followed the Restoration of the monarchy in 1660. The Dutch New Netherland was conquered by England and became New York in 1664, and what had previously been part of New Sweden and then part of New Netherland became

New Jersey in the same year in the same process. The Quaker William Penn founded Pennsylvania in 1681, and four counties in its southern quarters, which had previously been variously Dutch, Swedish, and had been part of Maryland as well as Pennsylvania, finally became the colony of Delaware in 1701. Further down the Atlantic coast, Carolana was first chartered in 1629, though not settled by the English until rechartered in 1663, and it split into North and South Carolina in 1712. Finally, Georgia was chartered in 1732 and settled the following year, the last of the thirteen colonies that would form the United States via the Declaration of Independence and the Constitution—in 1776 and 1787, several generations after the founding of Jamestown.

Given the precarious state of Barack Obama's presidential candidature and political career in March 2008, he certainly had more pressing things to do in "A More Perfect Union" than list the founding dates of all the thirteen American colonies. But, with Obama's literary skills, not to mention those of his chief speechwriter Jon Favreau, he or they could certainly have found a way to avoid confusing the founders of the colonies and the founders of the country. Yet they seem to have used their literary skills to the opposite effect, for the grammar of the phrase reinforces the temporal elision, perhaps confirming that what we have here is deliberate conflation rather than an accidental confusion of the two groups of founders.

;

A semicolon, as in "Farmers and scholars; statesmen and patriots," of course isn't designed to signal a new direction or a switch to different subject matter, but to go in the same direction and elaborate on the same subject. What the semicolon in the speech therefore does is affirm that the "farmers and scholars" were one and the same as the "statesmen and patriots" of the revolution, and yet had indeed travelled across an ocean to escape tyranny and persecution. If we take out the semicolon and break the sentence down, then what we have is this: There were some farmers and scholars. These farmers and scholars were also statesmen and patriots. The farmers and scholars and statesmen and patriots had also traveled across an ocean to escape tyranny and persecution. And they also made real their declaration of independence at a Philadelphia Convention in 1787.[15]

One cannot of course hear a semicolon in the spoken word, but TV and YouTube show no sonic or visual indication of any resolution to these temporal anomalies. And in any case that semicolon was in the script handed to the press on the day and it's also in *Change We Can Believe In*, the Obama campaign's official publication of the speeches from the 2008 election. And besides the semicolon, we have a perfectly audible pluperfect tense in the phrase that also assists in the rhetorical effort required to compress historical time and thereby further confirm the conflation. In both spoken and written versions of the speech, Obama's farmers and scholars and statesmen and patriots were men "*who had* travelled across an ocean to escape tyranny and persecution." And of course they "*finally* made real their declaration of independence at a Philadelphia convention."

Barack Obama famously admires the quality of audacity, and this temporal elision is fantastically audacious. It drags events in English history across one and a half centuries of time and folds them into the history of the United States. But why would he do such a thing? It seems perhaps that for Obama some colonial Americans possessed the same kind of "audacity" and "hope" that he sees in revolutionary and later Americans. The Pilgrims' escape from tyranny and persecution is perhaps analogous to the patriots' Declaration of Independence, and the Puritans' city upon a hill is perhaps analogous to the statesmen's Constitution. So analogous indeed that Obama merges them rhetorically. And in doing so he establishes a kind of continuity between the monumental men of each founding and the momentous deeds of both. And that continuity in turn implies a powerful sense of historical destiny: a long, sweeping history in which America was always about escaping tyranny and persecution, that America was founded on freedom, whenever the founding might have happened.

And that's not the end of the cleverness of this piece of rhetoric, as there's a touch of historiographical genius to it too. Because, although extending the history of the country's founders back to the deeds of the colonial founders creates an impression of a sweeping history of American freedom, the extending of the history of the colonies' founders forward to the deeds of the country's founders leaves intact the sense of revolutionary rupture that Obama is otherwise keen to create. To put that in the terms of the great French historian Fernand Braudel, Obama rhetorically constructs a *longue durée* and a dramatic *événement*—and they happen *at the same time*.[16]

For Barack Obama perhaps, the colonies' founders were in their audacity and hope the first practitioners of the pursuit of happiness, while the country's founders articulated the idea and added equality, life, and liberty to America's creed. But Barack Obama's positive assessment of New England's colonial founders is somewhat qualified. If these colonies' founders were proto-American in the audacity of their escape from tyranny and persecution and in the hope inherent in their adventure, they were distinctly pre-American in the tyrannous tendencies and persecutory proclivities of their religion, at least according to Obama's liberal and inclusive sense of what "American" is, as we'll see a little later.

Also, though, Obama's picture of migration to and the settling of the colonies is highly selective, though silently so. Contrary to popular mythology, the Pilgrims and Puritans were neither the only, nor the first, nor the most typical of early American settlers. First, the Pilgrims predominated in Plymouth and the Puritans in Massachusetts and in most of the other New England colonies. But few ventured far beyond this northeastern corner of colonial America. Most migrants to the colonies as a whole were not Puritans at all, certainly not the earlier arrivals in Jamestown, nor the founders of the other colonies either.

And far from escaping "tyranny and persecution," most migrants to America went there either seeking a living or seeking a better one. Or some, like the Quaker and tobacco-planter Walter Dickinson, were doing both. Others still were convicts who were transported rather than hanged for their crimes and thus travelled to America for their lives rather than their livelihoods. And most European migrants arrived in America as indentured servants rather than as free people. And all of them of course were invaders of or settlers on what had hitherto been or still were other people's lands. And there were yet other migrants too, who, far from escaping "tyranny and persecution," were being involuntarily taken to it, violently kidnapped in Africa and forcibly transported to America in chains.

Obama does not ignore these other people—these other free and enslaved migrants or Native Americans—but, as we see later in this chapter and later in the book, he writes and speaks of them in other and different historical contexts. He writes and speaks most extensively, for example, of slaves, but almost always in the context of slavery as a social institution and most especially as a political issue, rarely writing or speaking of slaves as forced migrants to American shores. The phenomenon of migration is thus reserved for Pilgrims and Puritans escaping tyranny and persecution. Pilgrims and Puritans can thus be represented as archetypal early settlers, even though they were far from typical. And migration can thus be ascribed exclusively to the heroic history of American freedom rather than the tragic history of American slavery or other forms of ill-fortune. This kind of selectivity means that it can remain for Obama as it does for many others an article of faith—an American origins myth—that early colonial migrants and settlers were religious refugees.

We'll look now a little more at Obama on the Pilgrims and Puritans of New England before returning to other colonists and other colonies a little later in the chapter.

A city upon a hill

As Barack Obama says in an interestingly ambiguous sentence in *The Audacity of Hope*, "The Pilgrims came to our shores to escape religious persecution and practice without impediment to their brand of strict Calvinism." These are of course the same people brought to mind by Obama's reference in "A More Perfect Union" to those "who had traveled across an ocean to escape tyranny and persecution." We'll come back to the strictness of the Calvinism later. For now, let's focus on the escaping of the tyranny and persecution.[17]

English religious and political authorities had opted for a moderate form of Protestantism in the reign of Elizabeth I, but pejoratively so-called puritans increasingly objected to the tie between the Anglican Church and the English state, the retention of the episcopal hierarchy of Bishops and Archbishops, the wearing of vestments by the clergy, and other such vestiges of "papist" idolatry. Some preferred Presbyterianism, Calvinistic theologically but with church government by elected elders, as became the basis of the Church of Scotland. Others favored Congregationalism, also Calvinistic theologically but with church government by members of independent congregations.

Most English Puritans preferred to push for reform of the Church of England from within. But in 1581 Robert Browne withdrew his Bury St. Edmunds congregation from the Anglican Communion, accelerating the growth of Separatism. The 1559 Act of Uniformity had made church attendance compulsory, and this and other laws imposed fines and imprisonment for nonattendance at the Anglican parish church and for conducting separate services. A Religion Act and a Popish Recusants Act in 1593 made matters even more dismal by directing that separatists reconcile with the Anglican Church within three months or else forfeit their property and leave the kingdom on pain of death. The acts targeted Catholics primarily, but Puritans feared for themselves as well, especially after the execution that same year of Henry Barrowe and John Greenwood for supporting separation.

Many Separatists sought sanctuary in the Netherlands. Even there they weren't safe, though, as demonstrated by the attempted arrest in Leyden in 1618 of William Brewster for publishing attacks on the English Church. Combined with their being country people in a city, and unhappily seeing their children acculturate to their host culture, some began to consider a more distant America as a possible refuge from English tyranny and persecution, and also from Dutch toleration. After patenting land from the Council of New England—the state thereby aiding and abetting their escape—thirty-five dissenters left Leyden in July 1620, joined up with others in England (including some non-dissenting laborers known as "Strangers"), and embarked for America aboard the *Mayflower* in September. In December, 102 people led by William Bradford founded Plymouth Colony on Cape Cod. Half the settlers perished in the harsh winter that followed, but the colony survived, initially thanks to food buried by local Native Americans who had subsequently died of European diseases, and then by cultivating crops under the tutelage of the Wampanoag people. A celebratory feast in the autumn of 1621 has since become known as the First Thanksgiving.

The Plymouth Pilgrims were not the only Puritans to settle in America. Plymouth colony was absorbed by Massachusetts in 1691, which had been founded by non-separatist Puritans in 1630. Though not persecuted as the Pilgrims were, conforming Puritans became increasingly distressed at the direction the Anglican Church was taking under Charles I and his church leader William Laud. After his investiture as Archbishop of Canterbury in 1633, Laud began appointing Arminian bishops, followers of the Leyden University theologian Arminius, who theorized that people could choose whether or not to accept God's grace—an unacceptable offence to Calvinist believers in predestination. Laud's insistence on moving communion tables from the middle to the east end of churches seemed to confirm dark suspicions of papist predilections.

Puritans had already found themselves ejected from public posts, including John Winthrop, a one-time Justice of the Peace and attorney to the Court of Wards and Liveries in Groton, Suffolk. In August 1629 he and eleven other Puritan elders convened in Cambridge and resolved to move to Massachusetts. The most significant phase of the Great Migration began the next March, as the first of about 20,000 people made their way to New England before Civil War erupted in the old one.

It's from these Puritans that Barack Obama borrows the trope of America as "a city upon a hill," a refrain repeatedly misrepresented by presidents and would-be presidents for many years. Its most eloquent expositors before Obama were John F. Kennedy as president-elect when addressing the General Court of Massachusetts in January 1961, and Ronald Reagan on the campaign trail in 1980 and in his farewell address in 1989.

Obama used it in his commencement address at the University of Massachusetts in Boston on June 2, 2006, observing that it "was right here, in the waters around us, where the American experiment began. As the earliest settlers arrived on the shores of Boston and Salem and Plymouth, they dreamed of building a city upon a hill. And the world watched, waiting to see if this improbable idea called America would succeed."[18]

Though biblical in origin, deriving from the parable of salt and light in Jesus's Sermon on the Mount, the image first acquired American iteration in a sermon by John Winthrop entitled "A Model of Christian Charity," purportedly preached aboard the *Arbella* on arrival at Massachusetts in 1630. In the first part of the following extract, Winthrop expresses exactly Obama's own kind of can-do communitarianism (and also the latter's love of anaphora and generally rhythmical prose):

> We must be knit together, in this work, as one man. We must entertain each other in brotherly affection. We must be willing to abridge ourselves of our superfluities, for the supply of others' necessities. We must uphold a familiar commerce together in all meekness, gentleness, patience and liberality. We must delight in each other; make others' conditions our own; rejoice together, mourn together, labor and suffer together, always having before our eyes our commission and community in the work, as members of the same body.[19]

Winthrop's sermon subsequently became more scriptural than Barack Obama's speeches ever do, but I quote the next section to put the simile of the "city upon a hill" in its proper place in Winthrop's world:

> So shall we keep the unity of the spirit in the bond of peace. The Lord will be our God, and delight to dwell among us, as His own people, and will command a blessing upon us in all our ways, so that we shall see much more of His wisdom, power, goodness and truth, than formerly we have been acquainted with. We shall find that the God of Israel is among us, when ten of us shall be able to resist a thousand of our enemies; when He shall make us a praise and glory that men shall say of succeeding plantations, "may the Lord make it like that of New England."[20]

Immediately after the above arrive the famous words so frequently recollected: "For we must consider that we shall be as a city upon a hill." These words, though, are less a happy summary of the meaning of the Massachusetts mission than a transition to fearful forebodings of failure. Right after "we shall be as a city upon a hill" comes the following:

> The eyes of all people are upon us. So that if we shall deal falsely with our God in this work we have undertaken, and so cause Him to withdraw His present help from us, we shall be made a story and a by-word through the world. We shall open the mouths of enemies to speak ill of the ways of God, and all professors for God's sake. We shall shame the faces of many of God's worthy servants, and cause their

prayers to be turned into curses upon us till we be consumed out of the good land whither we are going.[21]

Perhaps it's not surprising, then, that many Puritans spent most of the rest of the seventeenth century haranguing and sometimes hanging each other for every form of God-angering unworthiness they could imagine each other guilty of.

For Barack Obama, though, the "city upon a hill" is something other than a socially and culturally homogenous colony under the rules of a particular notion of a one-true-religion. Obama's "city on a hill" (as rendered later in the Boston commencement speech) is a metaphor for a tolerant inclusiveness that's the antithesis of Winthrop's "city upon a hill" simile of intolerant exclusivity. As Obama put it to Boston's UMass graduating class: "In the most diverse university in all of New England, I look out at a sea of faces that are African American and Hispanic American and Asian American and Arab American. I see students that have come here from over 100 different countries, believing like those first settlers that they too could find a home in this city on a hill—that they too could find success in this unlikeliest of places." That was not Winthrop's plan.[22]

You would have thought I was Cotton Mather

Although Barack Obama is inspired by the Puritans' escape from tyranny and persecution, he has no tolerance for the intolerance that was part of the Puritan mission as they themselves defined it. On occasion Obama has himself been accused of moral censoriousness, but his amused recollection of one such instance reveals how far removed he actually is from seventeenth-century Massachusetts. Recounting a speech he gave to the Kaiser Family Foundation regarding their finding that "the amount of sex on television has doubled in recent years," Obama recalled that he too "wasn't too happy with ads for erectile-dysfunction drugs popping up [lol] every fifteen minutes whenever I watched a football game with my daughters in the room." Nor with "a popular show targeted at teens, in which young people with no visible means of support spend several months getting drunk and jumping naked in hot tubs with strangers." He argued therefore that television companies "should adopt better standards and technology to help parents control what [is] streamed into their homes." He did not argue that the government should regulate, much less censor, broadcasting. Yet, judging by reactions to the speech, he recalled, "You would have thought I was Cotton Mather."[23]

Cotton Mather (1663–1728) followed his own family footsteps into the Puritan ministry and prolific theological quill-pushing. His grandfathers, John Cotton and Richard Mather, were among the earliest Massachusetts migrants, whose piety the younger Mather praised in his *Magnalia Christi Americana* (1702). His father was Increase Mather, famous as one of the "Jeremiahs" whose sermons attacked the alleged apostasies of New England's second generation.

Increase and his increase are also infamous for supporting the Salem witch trials of 1692. Cotton Mather's *Memorable Providences*, an account of the bewitchment of a number of the Goodwin family children in Boston, published in 1689, has been (dis) credited with stirring passions that boiled over in Salem three years later. He also supported the appointment of hawkish witch-finder William Stoughton as Lieutenant Governor of the colony and as head of the Salem tribunal. And he promoted the use of spectral evidence in the trials, even while cautioning that the Devil could plant false evidence by concocting visions of the spirits of the innocent in the minds of credulous accusers. His father, Increase Mather, also warned against use of this evidence for this reason, and in January 1693 Governor William Phips ruled it out of court, a move that resulted in a rapid decline in the number of prosecutions and indeed in the end of the outbreak of accusations. Before that happened, however, nineteen people were hanged, four died in custody, and another was pressed to death between stones in a vain attempt to extract a plea from him.

Cotton Mather wasn't all about the witch hunting. He trialed the hybridization of corn, for example, and his scientific interests extended to experimentation with smallpox inoculation. The latter effort was inspired by Onesimus, a slave of Mather's who had been immunized against the disease as a child in Africa. Mather's support for inoculation even got him into trouble with other ministers, who thought it interfered with the disease-creating works of God.

Unlike others, however, neither of the Mathers nor William Stoughton recanted for their roles in the witchcraft trials of 1692–93, and so their reputations remain haunted to this day by the ghosts of the Salem dead. This is the kind of thing that Barack Obama may have meant when he made reference to "their brand of strict Calvinism." Strictly speaking, Obama was referring to the Pilgrims who had separated from the Church of England, as opposed to the Puritans who hadn't. But that was a political choice by the different groups of dissenters; theologically, both groups adhered to the same brand of strict Calvinism. And for Obama, as for many others, Cotton Mather is therefore a symbol of something un-American, or perhaps pre-American. Barack Obama's Cotton Mather was an oracle of bigotry and intolerance upon which little of the Enlightenment ever cast its glow. The Puritan preacher may have lived in the city upon a hill, but he was no beacon to the world.[24]

Barack Obama is not fond of certain modern forms of piety either. Though a Christian himself, it gives him no satisfaction that "substantially more people believe in angels than believe in evolution." Nor is he impressed when "football players point to the heavens after every touchdown, as if God were calling plays from the celestial sidelines." And "organized religion," Obama reminds us, "doesn't have a monopoly on virtue, and one need not be religious to make moral claims or appeal to a common good." Indeed the normally preternaturally implacable Obama gets as close as he gets to palpably angry when he denounces modern political and persecutory pieties. He takes pains to respect those who are religious but respectful of others (as he is himself), including a doctor who successfully challenged him to change the wording on his website about "right-wing ideologues who want to take away a woman's right to choose." He nevertheless notes that he has "no sympathy" for anti-abortion activists "who bullied and intimidated and occasionally resorted to violence."[25]

In sum, then, while understanding "the impulse to restore a sense of order to a culture that's constantly in flux," and while "certainly" appreciating "the desire of parents to shield their children from values they consider unwholesome," Obama has "little sympathy for those who would enlist the government in the task of enforcing sexual morality. Like most Americans, I consider decisions about sex, marriage, divorce, and childbearing to be highly personal—at the very core of our system of individual liberty." Barack Obama is no Pilgrim, no Puritan, and nor indeed are most Americans.[26]

We are no longer just a Christian nation

There were other early American religious refugees most likely more to Barack Obama's liking. Among them perhaps are Puritans against puritanism. One of these was Roger Williams, an early Plymouth migrant and one-time minister at Salem (long before the witch trials) who first got into trouble for attacking Massachusetts leaders for continuing commitment to the Church of England. After apologizing to the General Court for this effrontery, he found further disfavor by arguing for the radical doctrine of freedom of conscience, after which (albeit with John Winthrop's connivance) he fled to Narragansett Bay and founded Rhode Island as a refuge from a religious refuge. Among those who also went there was Anne Hutchinson, excommunicated in 1638 for making the Antinomian claim that divine grace was a direct revelation—one only known between God and the individual—thereby threatening the Puritan ministry's claim to authority in proclaiming who was saved and who was not. And, as a woman, implicitly threatening the patriarchal social order also.

The un-Puritan religious diversity of English America is also manifest in the fact that it was even sometimes a haven for those at the other end of the Christian spectrum. George Calvert was a courtier of James I, but had to withdraw from public life in 1625 as his Catholicism rendered him unable to take the newly required Oath of Supremacy. Granted the Irish title Baron Baltimore by a regretful but grateful king, Calvert began casting about for a colonial venture. But it was shortly after his death that his son Cecilius received a patent for Maryland in 1632, first settled by Catholics and Protestants alike in 1634. Maryland offered a degree of religious toleration, although Catholics practiced their religion privately so as not to cause offence. After many years of religious and political conflict, however, the proprietary was overthrown and replaced with definitively Protestant royal rule under William III and Mary II in the wake of the Glorious Revolution of 1688–89. The Calverts finally received their colony back in 1714, but only after the fourth Lord Baltimore, Benedict Leonard Calvert, converted to Anglicanism.

The early seventeenth century was not a golden age of peace, love, and understanding between different Christian denominations. So a more successful experiment in toleration had to await the chartering of Pennsylvania in 1681 and its settlement the following year. From their emergence in the 1650s, English Quakers (including the aforementioned Walter Dickinson) were persecuted for withdrawal from the state church (a Puritan one during the interregnum from 1649, but once again Episcopalian after the Restoration of the Monarchy in 1660), for their opposition to oath-taking and to displays of deference, and also for their adherence to freedom of conscience and to pacifism. These ideas and experiences, as well as Quaker belief in an Inner Light—God's voice in every individual—led logically enough to William Penn's "Holy Experiment" in religious freedom.

Non-Christians were not especially welcome there, but it's perhaps in the spirit of Pennsylvania more than anywhere else in early America that Barack Obama is able to say: "Whatever we once were, we are no longer just a Christian nation; we are also a Jewish nation, a Muslim nation, a Buddhist nation, a Hindu nation, and a nation of nonbelievers." For Obama, then, America today is a "city upon a hill" not because it adheres to one true religion, as per the Puritan ideal, but because of later and opposite traditions of religious freedom and ethnic pluralism.[27]

Community, democracy, and homespun virtues

While rejecting Puritan-style religiosity, Barack Obama nevertheless valorizes Puritan communitarianism (as well as the Pilgrims' and Puritans' audacious escape from tyranny and persecution and their hopeful sense of mission). That communitarianism is very evident in the Mayflower Compact of 1620 that bound one and all to "covenant, and combine ourselves together into a civil Body Politick, for our better Ordering, and Preservation." New England towns were typically founded on similar covenants that required residents to live together in harmony.[28]

We've already seen the communitarianism at the heart of John Winthrop's "Model of Christian Charity." Obama's communitarianism is famously central to his political ideals too, and sometimes his words closely echo those of Winthrop. For example, in a 1988 article entitled "Why Organize? Problems and Promise in the Inner City," in the journal *Illinois Issues*, Community Organizer Obama expressed frustration at the fractious nature and behavior of different groups trying (or, more aptly, vying) to help people in Chicago's poorer neighborhoods. He wrote that "we must find a way to knit together the diverse interests," thus using the same metaphor for mutuality that Winthrop did when the latter said that "we must be knit together, in this work, as one man." Obama's "Why Organize?" was written in a very different context and his concept of organization was much more inclusive, but the sentiments and their intended effects are very similar.[29]

Barack Obama has even proven willing to qualify the much vaunted quality of American individualism in favor of a modernized echo of Winthropian communitarianism. When introducing himself to the nation at the Democratic Convention of 2004, Obama made clear that "alongside our famous individualism, there's another ingredient in the American saga. A belief that we're all connected as one people." As he explained (even using a biblical reference, suitably re-gendered for our era, to reinforce his point):

If there is a child on the south side of Chicago who can't read, that matters to me, even if it's not my child. If there's a senior citizen somewhere who can't pay for their prescription drugs, and has to choose between medicine and the rent, that makes my life poorer, even if it's not my grandparent. If there's an Arab American family being rounded up without benefit of an attorney or due process, that threatens my civil liberties.

It is that fundamental belief—I am my brother's keeper, I am my sister's keeper—that makes this country work. It's what allows us to pursue our individual dreams and yet still come together as one American family.[30]

As those inclusive words attest, though, Obama's beliefs are based on values in general rather than any religious doctrine in particular. As Obama also says, "We value community, the neighborliness that expresses itself through raising the barn or," letting his imagery travel through time to the present, "coaching the soccer team." When discussing the political models that the Founders considered as possibilities for the new United States, Obama references "the direct democracy of the New England town meeting." He also noted in *The Audacity of Hope* that "of my favorite tasks of being a senator is hosting town hall meetings."[31]

Historians have long debated the nature of community in colonial New England, including the issue of how "democratic" the New England town really was. New England town covenants invariably required the maintenance of harmony among inhabitants, which was often achievable among like-minded people who had traveled across the ocean for similar reasons. Many had even crossed the Atlantic with their neighbors from Olde England and recreated their former neighborhoods together in the New one.

As time passed, however, more and more tensions arose. New generations needed new lands further and further away from their original settlements, especially as the first generation enjoyed remarkable longevity, many making it to more than seventy. New covenants for new towns could renew senses of community to some degree, though sometimes reinforced by the "warning out" of the antsy and otherwise awkward, but these were often not as binding in practice as covenants agreed among members of the first generation. So it was that preachers denounced in thunderous "jeremiads" the second and third generations' "declension" from the supposedly superior piety of the first. And the aforementioned outbreak of witchcraft accusations and executions in 1692 is partly explained by traditionalists of Salem Village accusing those residing near the more commercial port of Salem Town of doing deals with the Devil.

In the early years especially, New England town meetings frequently peacefully resolved individual conflicts, decided on local affairs, appointed local officials, and elected representatives to the General Court—the colonial legislature in Boston. These representatives often acted as delegates, expressing the opinion of their townspeople even if they differed from their own. Anyone could speak at such meetings. However, while all "freemen" could vote, only men, and only men with property, could be "freemen." Also, at least in the early years, town meetings were often more about creating consensus and concealing conflict than they were about encouraging the expression of divergent points of view. It was perhaps only during the conflict with the British over taxes and other measures after the Sugar Act of 1764 that town meetings became "democratic" in any kind of modern sense; gatherings at which dissent could be acceptably articulated.[32]

It's also the enabling aspects of community that Barack Obama values, and sometimes indeed carefully contrasts with inhibiting ones. In *The Audacity of Hope*, for example, Obama echoes Isaiah Berlin's *Two Concepts of Liberty* (1958). Obama writes of "negative" liberty, the "right to be left alone," whether by the excessively conformist demands of a community or oppression by law and government. Hence the aforementioned assertion that such matters as "sex, marriage, divorce, and childbearing" are "highly personal" and "at the very core of our system of individual liberty." On the other hand, Obama further notes that "we understand our liberty in a more positive sense as well, in the idea of opportunity and the subsidiary values that help us realize opportunity—all those homespun virtues that Benjamin Franklin first popularized in *Poor Richard's Almanack*."[33]

Benjamin Franklin published his almanac every year from 1732 to 1758, with regular print runs of 10,000. Though considered an American phenomenon, the publication had many very British origins. Franklin printed it pseudonymously as Richard Saunders, after the seventeenth-century English physician and astrologer who founded the London almanac *Rider's British Merlin*, published under the name of Cardanus Rider well into the eighteenth century. As Franklin worked in a London printer's shop he was readily familiar with this work. Franklin, furthermore, based his "Poor Richard" figure in part on Isaac Bickerstaff, pseudonymous writer of the "Bickerstaff Papers," Jonathan Swift's three satirical letters of 1708–09. Like Bickerstaff, Richard called himself a "Philomath" and an astrologer, and made a habit of mockingly predicting and falsely reporting the deaths of other astrologers. And some of Poor Richard's aphorisms originated with the Restoration writer and politician George Savile, the first Marquis of Halifax.

Over the years, though, the almanac became more and more a mirror of its author. As well as astrology, aphorisms, and proverbs, Poor Richard was famous for poems, word plays, and mathematical games, as well as information on such matters as astronomy, the calendar, and the weather. Franklin is of course famous also for practical inventions, above all bifocals, the lightening rod, and the eponymous stove.

He lived usefully

Barack Obama mentions Benjamin Franklin more than once in *The Audacity of Hope*. The second time was when reflecting on how he himself had initially imagined his own career. Obama recollected thinking about Franklin explaining to his mother his devotion to public service: " 'I would rather have it said, He lived usefully, than, He died rich.' " Franklin was certainly one of the most noted colonial and revolutionary Americans, and in many ways a great model for Obama. He may indeed have been one of the scholars, statesmen, and patriots Obama had in mind in mid-March 2008, although farmer was not among Franklin's numerous vocations. Perhaps that's why, in one of his July 4 addresses to the American people, President Obama reformulated his characterization of the Founders as "farmers and businessmen, doctors and lawyers, ministers and a kite-flying scientist."[34]

Benjamin Franklin was born on January 17, 1706, in Boston, Massachusetts. He moved to Philadelphia aged seventeen and by 1729 was publishing *The Pennsylvania Gazette*. It was *Poor Richard's Alamanack* though that gave him the fame and fortune that he parlayed into his highly distinguished public career. Not all of Franklin's public service was political. His private passion for learning manifested itself publicly when he became a founder and the first secretary of the American Philosophical Society in 1743, and he was also its first president when he helped relaunch the society in 1769. Franklin was, furthermore, a founder and the first president from 1751 of The Academy and College of Philadelphia, later the University of Pennsylvania. His business interest as a printer led him to his role as Philadelphia postmaster and in turn deputy postmaster general for the British colonies in 1753. He was later the first United States Postmaster General.

Franklin's postmaster's interest in communication between the colonies as well as within each one helped lead him into politics. In 1754 he attended the Albany Congress, an intercolonial conference to discuss how to deal with French northwestern imperial expansion and the threat it represented to the interests and security of the British American colonies. Franklin was responsible for the famous "Join, or Die" cartoon of a divided snake, aimed at encouraging the intercolonial cooperation that eventually helped win the French and Indian War of 1754 to 1760 and in turn the global Seven Years' War of 1756 to 1763. Although his Albany Plan of Union proposing an intercolonial government came to nothing at this stage, as with a plan for union presented shortly before the declaring of independence, these ideas later influenced the creation of the United States—as opposed to thirteen non-united and potentially dis-united states. That in turn made the 1787 Constitution possible, drafted by a convention in which Franklin was a by-then revered elder statesman. Franklin is thus a key figure in the early evolution of America's more perfect union.

In 1757, the Pennsylvania Assembly appointed Franklin as its representative in London, and other colonies subsequently adopted him for the same purpose. Franklin thus became a kind of unofficial American ambassador in England, relaying provincial interests and protests to the British king, ministers, parliament, and people. He later became the first American Minister to France, after Paris recognized United States independence and formed a political, military, and economic alliance with the new nation in 1778. Franklin fulfilled this role until 1785, although he had already been instrumental in securing secret military and civil supplies from the French as soon as Britain and the colonies went to war ten years before.

War had indeed broken out in April 1775, after British soldiers fired on Massachusetts militiamen at Lexington Green and then got fired on themselves in Concord, although the conflict did not become officially a War of Independence until over a year later. Franklin was one of those who urged caution about independence until there was sufficient support to ensure its success. As he darkly but wittily warned the Continental Congress, "We must all hang together, or, most assuredly, we shall all hang separately." But he was decidedly for separation as soon as it was practicable, and on June 11, 1776, he was appointed along with John Adams of Massachusetts, Thomas Jefferson of Virginia, Roger Sherman of Connecticut, and Robert Livingston of New York to the Committee of Five charged with drafting a declaration of independence. Jefferson got the job of writing a first draft, but Franklin played a major part in suggesting revisions and guiding a finished product through the Continental Congress. And as aforementioned Franklin was also among those who "finally made real their declaration of independence at a Philadelphia convention" that lasted through the summer of 1787.[35]

There was at least one respect in which the British colonial Benjamin Franklin wasn't very American by Barack Obama's standards. Franklin wrote of his concern about the migration of Germans to Pennsylvania in his *Observations Concerning the Increase of Mankind*, published in 1751. "Those who come hither," he complained, "are generally of the most ignorant Stupid Sort of their own Nation." And indeed "why should the Palatine Boors be suffered to swarm into our Settlements, and by herding together establish their Language and Manners to the Exclusion of Ours? Why should Pennsylvania, founded by the *English*, become a Colony of Aliens, who will shortly be so numerous as to Germanize us instead of our Anglifying them, and will never adopt our Language or Customs, any more than they can acquire our Complexion," he asked.

That comment on "Complexion" may seem strange to us today, but Franklin explains from the eighteenth century:

> the Number of purely white People in the World is proportionably very small. All *Africa* is black or tawny. *Asia* chiefly tawny. *America* (exclusive of the new Comers) wholly so. And in *Europe*, the *Spaniards*, Italians, *French, Russians* and *Swedes*, are generally of what we call a swarthy Complexion; as are the *Germans* also, the *Saxons* only excepted, who with the *English*, make the principal Body of White People on the Face of the Earth. I could wish their Numbers were increased. And while we are, as I may call it, *Scouring* our Planet, by clearing *America* of Woods, and so making this Side of our Globe reflect a brighter Light to the Eyes of Inhabitants in Mars or *Venus*, why should we in the Sight of Superior Beings, darken its People? why increase the Sons of *Africa*, by Planting them in *America*, where we have so fair an Opportunity, by excluding all Blacks and Tawneys, of increasing the lovely White and Red?[36]

Barack Obama never mentions this side of Benjamin Franklin. Yet Franklin's evolution proves perfectly the significance in Obamian terms of the American Revolution and the nation's Independence. For, like America, Franklin changed. Which brings us to a final aspect of Franklin's life that reflects what Obama thinks Americans moved away from and moved toward in their transition from British subjects to American citizens.

Early in his life, Benjamin Franklin owned slaves, and as a printer he published advertisements for slave sales and for owners aiming to recapture runaways. His *Pennsylvania Gazette* also published antislavery articles, however, and gradually Franklin turned against slavery as he turned against Britain. By 1770 he had freed himself of human property, although it wasn't until after independence that he openly criticized the institution. In 1787, while governor of Pennsylvania (actually "President of the Supreme Executive Council" under the pre-1790 state Constitution), he became president of the Pennsylvania Society for Promoting the Abolition of Slavery. He subsequently wrote several essays against enslavement, and in early 1790 the Pennsylvania abolition society sent a petition to the First Congress of the United States. Its concluding words were these:

> From a persuasion that equal liberty was originally the Portion, It is still the Birthright of all men, & influenced by the strong ties of Humanity & the Principles of their Institution, your Memorialists conceive themselves bound to use all justifiable endeavours to loosen the bounds of Slavery and promote a general Enjoyment of the blessings of Freedom. Under these Impressions they earnestly entreat your serious attention to the Subject of Slavery, that you will be pleased to countenance the Restoration of liberty to those unhappy Men, who alone, in this land of Freedom, are degraded into perpetual Bondage, and who, amidst the general Joy of surrounding Freemen, are groaning in Servile Subjection, that you will devise means for removing this Inconsistency from the Character of the American People, that you will promote mercy and Justice towards this distressed Race, & that you will Step to the very verge of the Powers vested in you for discouraging every Species of Traffick in the Persons of our fellow men.

> Philadelphia, Febry 3ᵈ: 1790   B. Franklin
>   Presidt of the Society[37]

This was the last public act of "a long and useful life" that finally ended, after eighty-four years, on the evening of April 17, 1790. And it brings us to the subject of what Barack Obama and others have called America's "original sin." Before addressing that directly, though, we should return to the issue of exactly where America's Garden of Eden was in which this original sin was committed.[38]

The first settlers

As we saw earlier, it's commonly assumed that the first and most typical English settlers in North America were the Pilgrims of 1620 and the Puritans of 1630, even though they were neither. In his University of Massachusetts commencement speech in Boston in 2006, Barack Obama referred to the "first settlers," by which he might have meant the founders of New England specifically rather than English America generally. Except that he also referred to "the earliest settlers" who "arrived on the shores of Boston and Salem and Plymouth," suggesting these as the first places of settlement and therefore the arrivals there as the first settlers in all of English North America.[39]

About 20,000 migrants traveled to New England during the Great Migration of the 1630s, most of them Puritans, but that's a small fraction of the total of 800,000 migrants who traveled to English and British North America during the whole of the colonial period (and an even smaller proportion of the 2.6 million who went to all British colonies, including those in the Caribbean). And, as also mentioned earlier, the first permanent colonial settlement there was founded at Jamestown, Virginia, in 1607, some thirteen years before the arrival of the Pilgrims and twenty-three years before that of the Puritans.

The 105 first settlers at Jamestown were not Calvinists, Separatist or otherwise, and nor were they escaping tyranny and persecution or founding any kind of city on a hill. They were officials, employees, and servants of the Virginia Company, and their initial mission was to enrich the company's owners by finding gold and other treasures in the manner of Spanish Conquistadors. Hence over half of the first settlers were soldiers, another forty were gentlemen, and the remainder comprised a doctor, a preacher, and a few artisans and laborers, and they founded a fort and not a covenanted town. They were not a population capable of forming a community—there were no farmers, no families, no women, no children.

Settling near swamps and tidal waters, the early settlers suffered malaria, saline poisoning, and dysentery contracted from unknowingly drinking their own and each other's effluence as it washed unwashed back and forth in the tide. Half the earliest settlers expired within six months of arriving in this American Eden, and people continued to die in similar proportions of "seasoning" until the 1650s when residents finally realized that an autumnal rather than a spring arrival would give newcomers better odds of survival. In the autumn of 1609 a supply fleet heading for Jamestown was partly sunk and partly scattered by a storm—events that inspired William Shakespeare's *The Tempest*—and therefore failed to reach Chesapeake Bay. Half the Jamestown settlers died during the subsequent winter "Starving Time." Between 1607 and its bankruptcy and collapse by 1624, the Virginia Company sent some 7,500 settlers to Jamestown, but due to disease, hunger, and warfare with Native Americans the population was only 1,200 when Virginia became a royal colony in 1625.

Even so, and even though the colony stayed insecure for some time still, the seeds of Virginian prosperity had already been sown. Native tobacco was too bitter for English tastes, but when temporarily stranded on Bermuda by the storm of 1609 John Rolfe had discovered a sweeter kind of sot weed. After some experimentation, in 1614 Rolfe sent off a first commercial crop. Virginia was never a monoculture in the manner of the Caribbean sugar colonies, but the tobacco staple became the basis of Virginia's and then Maryland's economy and society.

Tobacco is a highly labor-intensive crop, and in early 1620 John Rolfe noted in a letter to Virginia Company Treasurer Edwin Sandys the beginnings of what would eventually be the solution to the Chesapeake labor-supply problem. "About the latter end of August" 1619, he recounted, "a Dutch man of Warr ... arrived at Point-Comfort, the Comandors name Capt Jope, his Pilott for the West Indies one Mr Marmaduke ... He brought not any thing but 20. and odd Negroes, which the Governor and Cape Marchant bought for victuals." These "20. and odd Negroes" were the first recorded of about 300,000 Africans or African Caribbeans to arrive in colonial British North America—fifteen times the number of Puritans who made the Great Migration of the 1630s. And these first twenty and odd black people arrived over a year before William Bradford and more than a decade before John Winthrop.[40]

It took time for slavery to become the dominant labor system in the Chesapeake region, though. Planters initially relied most heavily on indentured servants, who were cheaper to import than slaves because of the expensive brutalities required in kidnapping and forcibly transporting people across the ocean. Most though by no means all indentured servants were young and male (in contrast to the more common family migration to New England). Most in the seventeenth century came from England and Wales, but more and more came from Scotland, Ireland, and other parts of Europe in the eighteenth. They generally came from backgrounds where acquiring property was unlikely if they stayed where they were, either because their parents had none or had too little of it to leave substantial enough inheritances for all their offspring to enjoy economic independence. Some moved within England to find new livings, many gravitating to the rapidly growing capital of London. Some went either from there or straight from home to seek their fortunes overseas, many to Ireland, some to other parts of Europe, some to the Caribbean, but many also to North America. Some were enticed by colonial promotional literature that often overplayed the opportunities available and underplayed the dangers and hardships involved in migration and settlement. Large numbers of convicts also migrated after the 1718 Transportation Act, causing considerable consternation among colonists already in America.

Servants sold themselves to merchants or to ships' captains in England in return for their passage overseas, and once in America their indentures were sold on to colonists needing laborers, most commonly in agriculture. Length of service varied but was usually between five and seven years, and servants would live either in the house of or in accommodation provided by their masters. Masters were also responsible for feeding and clothing servants, and they or the colonial governments were obliged to provide freedom dues at the end of servants' terms. At a minimum such dues comprised a suit of clothes, work implements, and seeds; enough material to start the former servant off in their free life. Sometimes freedom dues included land, though more often people had to work for wages or rent farms or workshops in the hope of one day affording the means to make their own livings. Sometimes servitude really was a route to economic independence. In some places up to three-quarters of those who survived their period of servitude eventually owned their own farms, although such success stories grew scarcer over time as land filled up and became more expensive to rent and buy.

In some ways, though, the colonial indenture system was similar to forms of servitude long-known in England, and early planters preferred to rely principally on these more familiar kinds of laborers. By 1660, then, there were still fewer than 2,000 Africans or African Americans in Virginia and Maryland, outnumbered by around twenty to one by nearly 34,000 whites. And not all those black people were enslaved, as slavery remained relatively undeveloped in such demographic circumstances and in the absence of English laws or customs that defined slavery as systematically as would later be the case. There is evidence of early racial discrimination, not least the white-European sense of entitlement to enslave Africans in a way they would not do to each other. But there's also evidence that slavery was by no means as solidified as it would become later on. In some cases slaves were even freed after a number of years in the same manner as servants, and a few of those so freed went on to be owners of farms and even of slaves.[41]

America's original sin

In the second half of the seventeenth century, however, things began to change. The English economy improved and the number of alternative destinations available to English and other migrants increased with the capture of Jamaica from the Spanish in 1655, of New York and New Jersey from the Dutch in 1664, and with the settling of Carolina from 1663 and Pennsylvania from 1681. At the same time, though, Chesapeake planters had more land, and more capital to invest in their consequently increasing need for laborers. In addition, the Company of Royal Adventurers Trading into Africa, chartered in 1663 and revamped as the Royal African Company in 1672, started cultivating Chesapeake planters as alternative customers to their Caribbean consumers, increasing the supply and decreasing the price of their human imports to the North American market. Thus it was that between 1660 and 1710 the black population of the Chesapeake rose from under 2,000 to over 30,000, and from one-in-twenty of the whole population to one-in-three. By the 1760s, the black population of the Chesapeake reached 200,000, or 40 percent of a total population that by then reached half a million.

In the late-seventeenth and early-eighteenth centuries, the legislatures of Virginia and Maryland passed laws that defined slaves as property, established enslavement as a condition for life, and subjected its victims to distinct forms of discipline and cruel and unusual punishment. As slavery was simultaneously defined as inheritable through African ancestry (as opposed to contingent on religion or as a merciful commutation of death for prisoners of war), the invention or at least evolution of enslavement in British America was accompanied by the invention or evolution of the concept of "race." As is clear although implicit in Barack Obama's American history, "race" is not something that somehow inheres in us. For all the appalling practical consequences of acting on the concept, it is really nothing more than an ideological or cultural construct.

Slavery was by no means confined to the Chesapeake colonies of Maryland and Virginia. It first appeared in English America as a highly articulated economic and social system with the Caribbean sugar boom of the 1640s, although of course plantation slavery was long known in Spanish and Portuguese America. From Barbados in particular it migrated to the Carolinas in the 1660s. Once again it was a relatively loose system there initially but became a more articulated one with the establishment of rice as a staple product from the mid-1680s. South Carolina had a black-majority population by the early eighteenth century, and in 1760 its black population was over 57,000, almost two-thirds of a total population of 94,000. Generally less wealthy and with tobacco planting predominating above Cape Fear, North Carolina's black population was 33,000 of 110,000 at that time.

Slavery was initially forbidden when Georgia was chartered in 1732. The new colony was meant to be a buffer zone between South Carolina and Spanish Florida, its population to act as a counterweight to South Carolina's dangerous enslaved majority. And it was also supposed to serve as an idealized province of modest, independent white farmers. But under political and economic pressure the Georgia proprietors relinquished the ban in 1749, and eleven years later 3,500 slaves formed about a third of the colony's population of 9,500.

Nor was slavery confined to the southern plantation colonies. In 1760 there were nearly 13,000 black people in a total population of a little under half a million in the New England colonies of Massachusetts, New Hampshire, Connecticut, and Rhode Island— another reason to caution against the Puritan myth of early America. And there were nearly 30,000 black people in a total population of just under 430,000 in the Middle Colonies of New York, New Jersey, Pennsylvania, and Delaware. While most of these people were enslaved and some worked on farms and even on large plantations, especially in northern New York, they were more commonly city-dwelling domestic servants, artisans, general laborers, often dock workers and sometimes sailors. That meant high concentrations of slaves in some northern places. The one-third of the population that was enslaved made New York the most unfree city in eighteenth-century British North America after Charleston, South Carolina.[42]

Barack Obama has more than once referred to slavery as America's "original sin," and many others have used that metaphor too. It might actually be more right to reserve that phrase for what settlers did to America's original inhabitants. The first records of enslavement in North America date to 1619, as related earlier, which of course is some time after the first permanent English incursions on Native American land in 1607 and the first Anglo-Indian War of 1610 to 1614. It is also even longer after the first attempted English settlements at Roanoke and outrages committed against Native Americans there in the 1580s. We examine these issues further in Chapter 7, but all the above should show the indisputable significance of enslavement in colonial America. Subsequent chapters show the centrality of slavery in the story of the early United States, as rightly reflected in Barack Obama's history of the same.[43]

A question that divided the colonies

In "A More Perfect Union," Barack Obama described slavery as "a question that divided colonies." That's either right or wrong, depending on exactly what he means. If he means that it divided American colonists along racial lines, then he's certainly right. We've seen above the invention or at least evolution of "race" as a system of human categorization in the Anglo-Atlantic World (although it already was one in the Spanish and Portuguese Atlantic Worlds), and we've seen how that concept was employed to entrench the enslavement of Africans and their African American descendants.[44]

But we also know that enslavement existed in every single colony. There was thus substantial unity among white people about this institution, or at least a generally shared presumption that enslavement—of others—wasn't a problem. Furthermore, in the plantation societies from Maryland south, slavery and race helped unify white society across class lines. Even poorer, non-slaveholding whites, whether they liked it or not, were co-opted into the slave system by laws requiring them to participate in patrols that policed the countryside and the slave quarters, and in posses that pursued black people lurking unlawfully off their farms and plantations. Other whites worked as overseers and many non-slaveholders hired slaves if they didn't own them. Some poor whites who might otherwise have resented being of a lower class were thus compensated by the sense of being in a higher caste.

There was precious little white protest against enslavement in colonial America. Some Germantown Quakers asked as early as 1688 whether slavery was compatible with the Golden Rule to treat others as you would have others treat you. They thought it wasn't, but the issue was kicked into the Pennsylvania long grass until the 1750s when John Woolman finally convinced many in the Society of Friends to exclude slaveholders from their Meetings. The Massachusetts minister and repentant Salem witch hunter Samuel Sewall questioned the Godliness of the slave trade in a pamphlet entitled *The Selling of Joseph* published in 1700, but few fellow white people paid any heed. Until the era of the American Revolution, that is. As we see in the following chapter, the outcry about the metaphorical "slavery" imposed by British imperial policies from 1764 inspired considerable introspection among many whites about the very real slavery they themselves imposed on Africans and African Americans.[45]

Our starting point as Americans

The tendency to see the Pilgrims and the Puritans as the first and most typical or at least archetypal colonial Americans can unintentionally obscure the variety of peoples who migrated to and settled the colonies, and can deceive us into believing that the slave trade and slavery were incidental rather than fundamental parts of the American past. This was in a way the very purpose of the Pilgrim-Puritan paradigm when it was first elaborated as a then new American origins myth in the early to mid-nineteenth century. At the height of abolitionism and especially as a consequence of the Civil War of 1861–65, it seemed unseemly to associate early America with the slaveholding secessionists of Virginia in particular and of the South in general. Far better to imagine America beginning with people who "had traveled across an ocean to escape tyranny and persecution." No less a figure than Barack Obama's hero Abraham Lincoln helped popularize this myth by permanently inserting the Plymouth Thanksgiving into the national calendar as a public holiday, as he did by Executive Order in October 1863, in the middle of the Civil War. On the last Thursday of every November from then until 1941, and the fourth Thursday of every November since, Americans have remembered the Pilgrims as their archetypal ancestors.[46]

The Puritan origins idea retains credibility today due perhaps to Americans' exceptional religiosity—exceptional compared with that in most other democracies at any rate. But, as popular as it is, it's nonetheless incorrect to connect the New England Puritans of the seventeenth century to the Bible thumpers of our day and age. Modern American religiosity generally originated in the Methodist and Baptist evangelical revivalism of the eighteenth century, rather than in the more inward-looking Calvinist Congregationalism of the seventeenth century. And their respective attitudes to greed and gaud could hardly be more contrasting. There is a world of difference between the humble meeting houses of seventeenth-century Massachusetts and the gilded mega-churches of the modern-day south-western Bible Belt; maybe even more than one world of difference.

Nor should we confuse these versions of Christianity with the distinct practices and preoccupations of other ones in early America, including those of the Catholics and Quakers already mentioned, and including also African American ones that originated in enslavement. Which brings us back to the point that, even if Barack Obama sometimes highlights the pursuits of happiness of certain colonial subjects as precursors to those of American citizens, he does not ignore entirely the unhappiness of others. Obama avoids the trap of seeing enslavement as incidental rather than fundamental in United States history, if not in British American colonial history, because for him the revolution brought slavery and liberty into sharper contrast with each other than had ever previously been perceived.

America's "original sin," he says, "contradicted America's founding principles." And although the Constitution was "stained by this nation's original sin of slavery" and was therefore "unfinished," he also asserts that "the answer to the slavery question was already embedded" in it. It was and is he believes "a Constitution that had at its very core the ideal of equal citizenship under the law; a Constitution that promised its people liberty, and justice, and a union that could be and should be perfected over time." That then is the story we see in the chapters that follow.[47]

CHAPTER 2
THE SUBSTANCE OF OUR COMMON CREED:
THE DECLARATION OF INDEPENDENCE
AND THE AMERICAN REVOLUTION

The substance of our common creed

"WE HOLD THESE truths to be self-evident, that all men are Created equal, that they are endowed by their Creator with certain unalienable Rights, that among these are Life, Liberty, and the pursuit of Happiness." Barack Obama describes these words from the Declaration of Independence as "the substance of our common creed." In some respects this claim is true. As an announcement of abstract principles rather than just a random political action, the Declaration of Independence founded the United States on the basis of shared ideological principles, which certainly seems like a common creed of some sort.[1]

And yet. Barack Obama knows that these ideas are not exclusively American, and even that some of these exact expressions of them originated elsewhere. He also knows that in some ways the words are not "common," or weren't when they were written: most obviously that most of the 20 percent of Americans of African descent in 1776 did not enjoy equality, liberty, or the pursuit of happiness.

For Obama, however, these anomalies were eventually resolved thanks to their relationship to each other. First, it is not the ideas or words themselves that are exclusively American for Obama, but the fact that they were written into the American nation's founding document. Second, in this specifically American context, therefore, these words moved from the realm of abstract concepts to become a kind of official doctrine, a "creed" indeed. Hence perhaps the reference to the "substance" of this "common creed." Sufficient substance in fact to help forge a more "perfect union," first through being "made real" in the Constitution, then through new laws created under that Constitution, and finally through transformations in everyday life. The words thereby gained a unique level of agency in America, becoming an active force animating the eventual abolition of enslavement and the amelioration of other iniquities.[2]

Much of the rest of this book is about this process as Barack Obama sees it. The next chapter concerns how these principles informed the Constitution through which the Declaration was for Obama "made real" and the union thereby made "more perfect." The chapters after that are about how the "deliberative democracy" the Constitution created, in conjunction with popular protest, has gradually helped make the union more perfect still over the subsequent two centuries or so. This chapter, though, is mainly about where the words cited above originally came from and how they came to be America's "common creed" in the Declaration of Independence. Just before we go there, though—"creed"?

Creed

Barack Obama's selection of a quasi-religious description of the ideas in the Declaration helps us see why he sees those ideas as possessing sufficient "substance" to be such powerful agents of change in American history. According to the *Oxford English Dictionary*, a "creed" is "1 a. A form of words setting forth authoritatively and concisely the general belief of the Christian Church, or those articles of belief which are regarded as essential; a brief summary of Christian doctrine: usually and properly applied to the three statements of belief known as the Apostles', Nicene, and Athanasian Creeds." And "1. c. More generally: A formula of religious belief; a confession of faith, *esp.* one held as authoritative and binding upon the members of a communion."[3]

Definition "2 a." is similarly sacred: "An accepted or professed system of religious belief; the faith of a community or an individual, *esp.* as expressed or capable of expression in a definite formula." The word does, though, have a more secular sense: "2 b. *transf.* A system of belief in general; a set of opinions on any subject, *e.g.* politics or science." Although "2 c." is more open and could be either religious or not religious: "Belief, faith (in reference to a single fact). *rare.*" Though there is therefore at least one secular connotation of "creed," the word is nevertheless largely religious in its origins and modern connotations.[4]

You may have noticed that I've thus far missed out meaning "1 b." But here it is: "A repetition of the creed, as an act of devotion." Barack Obama performs this devotion often, and often on the most auspicious of occasions. At the beginning of his keynote address at the Democratic National Convention in Boston in July 2004, for example, he said, "Our pride is based on a very simple premise, summed up in a declaration made over two hundred years ago: 'We hold these truths to be self-evident, that all men are created equal. That they are endowed by their Creator with certain inalienable rights. That among these are life, liberty and the pursuit of happiness.'" In his first inaugural address, in 2009: "The time has come to reaffirm our enduring spirit; to choose our better history; to carry forward that precious gift, that noble idea, passed on from generation to generation: the God-given promise that all are equal, all are free, and all deserve a chance to pursue their full measure of happiness." In his second inaugural address, in 2013: "What makes us exceptional—what makes us American—is our allegiance to an idea articulated in a declaration made more than two centuries ago: 'We hold these truths to be self-evident, that all men are created equal; that they are endowed by their Creator with certain unalienable rights; that among these are life, liberty, and the pursuit of happiness.'" He did this act of devotion on many other occasions too, including every single Fourth of July address from 2009 to 2016. And in his farewell address in January 2017 he spoke of "the conviction that we are all created equal, endowed by our Creator with certain unalienable rights, among them life, liberty, and the pursuit of happiness."[5]

As well as the quasi-devotional terms in which Barack Obama describes these words and the semi-liturgical manner in which he repeats them, there is also the seemingly scriptural way in which he transcribes them in writing. The fashion in which they appear at the beginning of this chapter (and in the last one, the next one, and also in Chapter 7) replicates that in Obama's own typography in *The Audacity of Hope*: with the upper-case opening of WE HOLD THESE, and the capitalizations of Created, Creator, Rights, Life, Liberty, and Happiness. As far as I know, these features are not replicated in this form from any original or even venerably ancient copy of the Declaration, certainly not from any versions produced by or on the authority of the Continental Congress of 1776. They thus appear to be Obama's own invention, or else his own acceptance of his editor's or publisher's suggestion. An imagining perhaps of how they should look that's in line with how he thinks they should be read and how they should reach the heart and mind—with all the portent and power of scripture.[6]

As the historian Pauline Maier brilliantly demonstrated, the Declaration of Independence has indeed become "American Scripture," a written creed. For the first decade or so after 1776, Americans celebrated the fact of independence and the general ideas behind it, but the Declaration itself, as a document, was "all but forgotten," and its precise form of words remained for some time largely unquoted. But in the wake of the War of 1812, in the decade leading up to the semi-centennial celebrations of 1826, Americans began to reinvent the document itself as, in Maier's words, "something akin to holy writ." In 1817, for example, Congress commissioned four paintings of the Revolution from John Trumbull, and the following year he completed the most famous of them; his 12-by-18-foot *The Declaration of Independence* that he exhibited to enormous crowds in Boston, Philadelphia, and Baltimore before delivering it to be hung in the rotunda of the nation's newly completed Capitol. The painting still (mis)educates people in the document as well as the act of declaring independence with all the epical enormity and fantastical inaccuracy of biblical works of art.[7]

When Congress ordered in 1824 that former President Thomas Jefferson be given a gift copy of a new facsimile of the Declaration that he had helped to author almost half a century earlier, he received it "with pleasure" as he saw the reproduction as evidence of "reverence for that instrument, and ... adhesion to its principles and of a sacred determination to maintain and perpetuate them." Which was, he said, "a holy purpose." And when the by then venerable Jefferson and Declaration coauthor John Adams died on the same day—the fiftieth anniversary of July 4, 1776—eulogists went wild at the apparently cosmic significance of the calendrical confluences. One noted: "Had the horses and the chariot of fire descended to take up the patriarchs, it might have been more wonderful, but not more glorious." Another focused his superlatives on the scriptural legacy: "The same venerated instrument that declared our separation from Great Britain, contained also the memorable assertion that 'all men are created equal, that they are endowed by their Creator with certain unalienable rights, and that to secure these rights, governments are instituted among men, deriving their just powers from the consent of the governed.'" This was, the encomium continued, "the text of the revolution—the ruling vital principle—the hope that animated the patriot's heart and nerved the patriot's arm, when he looked forward through succeeding generations, and saw stamped upon all their institutions, the great principles set forth in the Declaration of Independence."[8]

Veneration for the Declaration continued through the next generation. Abraham Lincoln described the doctrine that "all men are created equal" as an "ancient faith" and the "father of all moral principles." He said he "never had a feeling politically that did not spring from the sentiments embodied in the Declaration of Independence." The Founders, Lincoln believed, "meant to set up a standard maxim for free men that would be familiar to all, and revered by all." And indeed the reverential reverberations of the word "creed" connects Barack Obama to his other hero too, an actual preacher who helped put Lincoln's prophecy into practice. On August 28, 1963, Reverend Martin Luther King Jr. began his most famous anaphora by saying that "I have a dream that one day this nation will rise up and live out the true meaning of its creed: 'We hold these truths to be self-evident, that all men are created equal.'"[9]

In her Introduction to *American Scripture*, Pauline Maier described seeing an original copy of the Declaration on display alongside the two other "Charters of Freedom," the Constitution and the Bill of Rights, in what the US National Archives tellingly calls a "Shrine." "The 'shrine' itself," she said, "resembles the awesome, gilded, pre-Vatican II altars of my Catholic girlhood, raised three steps above where the worshippers assembled. The Declaration is its centerpiece, held above the Constitution and the Bill of Rights in what looks like a tabernacle, or perhaps a monstrance, the device used to display the host on special days of adoration. The Constitution and Bill of Rights are spread out beneath, on the altar's surface."[10]

Maier was ultimately unimpressed, however, as all this seemed to her "idolatrous, and also curiously at odds with the values of the Revolution." The Founders had after all pioneered the separation of church and state as part of their mission on behalf of equality, liberty, and the pursuit of happiness. And some were ardent Protestants who were deeply suspicious of what they perceived to be papist idolatry. In any case, the document's message for Maier is "of this world." Hence she concluded her Epilogue by saying (ironically including a line from Isaiah) that: "The vitality of the Declaration of Independence rests upon the readiness of the people and their leaders to discuss its implications and to make the crooked ways straight, not in the mummified paper curiosities lying in state at the Archives; in the ritual of politics, not in the worship of false gods who are odds with our eighteenth-century origins and who war against our capacity, together, to define and realize right and justice in our time."[11]

Yet Barack Obama's veneration of the Declaration is not inconsistent with Professor Maier's final judgement. As we see in the next chapter, Obama is an Enlightenment secularist. He is full-square behind the institutional separation of church and state, but believes that politics is about moral issues, and morality may be conceived of and articulated in religious terms. Or not, as the case may be, but he's perfectly happy for people to campaign for causes and even for office using religious idioms. And it seems he sees the Declaration of Independence in a similar sort of way. For him, it is not a religious document as such, but for religious people like him it carries the force of faith. For nonreligious people it may carry the force if not of faith then of ideological imperative instead. It's its moral force that matters, wherever one may find it. Hence perhaps he calls its most famous words a "creed" but doesn't call them a Credo.

Barack Obama would certainly agree with Pauline Maier's conclusion to the main body of her book. The Declaration is, she said, "a document that spoke both for the revolutionaries and for their descendants, who confronted issues the country's founders had never known or failed to resolve, binding one generation after another in a continuing act of national self-definition." For Obama, that continuing act of national self-definition comprises the making of a "more perfect" union—from the adoption of the Declaration and then the Constitution through the abolitions of slavery and segregation and on to the struggles of today. These are the subjects of the subsequent chapters. The rest of this one is about how Obama sees the abstract concepts of equality, liberty, and the pursuit of happiness come to gain "substance" in the "common creed" articulated in the Declaration of Independence.[12]

A subject of King George

While Barack Obama often quotes the Declaration of Independence, he says very little about how it came about. Perhaps not detailing the causes and events of the American Revolution is a diplomatic kindness attending the sensitivities of a former mother country that needily pleads that it has a "special relationship" with the United States. And for electoral reasons too, as long and detailed historical lectures aren't necessarily the best way to win voters and influence people. The shorthand of "empire" and "tyranny" is therefore best, and as symbols they'll suffice, as most Americans know in more or less detail what these words refer to. And in any case Obama usually uses these terms not to dwell on the American Revolution for its own sake, but to denote what he sees as a longer series of oppressions overcome, collectively illustrating the liberating continuities of American history as a whole. For Obama, these outcomes are more important than the processes that brought them about.

In announcing his bid for the presidency in February 2007, for example, Obama noted that "we've changed this country before." And he went on to list three transformative moments, among which the American Revolution just happened to be one: "In the face of tyranny, a band of patriots brought an Empire to its knees. In the face of secession, we unified a nation and set the captives free. In the face of Depression, we put people back to work and lifted millions out of poverty." And then, without breaking a step, further continuities of overwhelming positives: "We welcomed immigrants to our shores, we opened railroads to the west, we landed a man on the moon, and we heard a King's call to let justice roll down like water, and righteousness like a mighty stream." A very different kind of King of course from the king held responsible for the British tyranny that provoked American independence.[13]

Barack Obama has at least once publicly mentioned this other king. He did so in what was perhaps his most damning indictment of British imperial tyranny in America. But this rare mention was safely made in a commencement address in June 2006, far away from the campaign trail and long before Obama held the responsibilities of American head of state. Urging the graduating class of the University of Massachusetts in Boston—the city of so many revolutionary moments—to "pursue the happiness you hope for," he noted that today "this dream sounds common—perhaps even clichéd—yet for most of human history it's been anything but." And then he once again made a list, this time of oppressed people and oppressive regimes in eras before American freedom and self-government arrived. "As a servant of Rome, a peasant in China," he said, "or a subject of King George, there were very few unlikely futures. No matter how hard you worked or struggled for something better, you knew you'd spend your life forced to build somebody else's empire; to sacrifice for someone else's cause." Or, as he put it even more emphatically in a commencement address at Knox College in Galesburg, Illinois, the year before:

> As a servant of Rome, you knew you'd spend your life forced to build somebody else's empire. As a peasant in eleventh-century China, you knew that no matter how hard you worked, the local warlord might take everything you had—and that famine might come knocking on your door any day. As a subject of King George, you knew that your freedom to worship and speak and build your own life would be ultimately limited by the throne.
> And then America happened.[14]

It seems then that for Obama the essence of the Revolution was not the taxes and other British acts that caused it, or the protests against them, but the transition from colonial subjection to national self-determination, the moment of the Declaration itself. "At that time in human history," he said in Boston, "it was kings and princes and emperors who made decisions. But those patriots knew there was a better way of doing things, that freedom was possible, and that to achieve their freedom they'd be willing to lay down their lives, their fortunes and their honor. And so they fought a revolution." In a July 4 speech on the White House South Lawn in 2013, Obama expressed that feeling this way: "On July 4, 1776, a small band of patriots declared that we were a people created equal, free to think and worship and live as we please; that our destiny would not be determined for us, it would be determined by us." In his weekly radio address the same day the president added that the "small band of patriots declared ... that we were a people created equal—free to think and worship and live as we please ... that we were no longer colonists, we were Americans."[15]

These comments seem perfectly supportable as general critiques of imperialism. But, as mentioned in the previous chapter, they are more accurate characterizations of Britain's later imperialism in Africa and Asia than of earlier colonization in America and Australasia. Nor do they say much about the specific grievances that caused the colonial revolt of 1776—a revolt that actually few colonists imagined or desired until they found themselves swept up in what the Declaration calls "the course of human events." That course of events began of course with the Sugar Act of 1764 and the Stamp Act of 1765, the first direct Parliamentary taxes on the American colonists. These acts were met with resistance in the form of political pamphlets, legislative resolutions, riots in the streets, threats and acts of violence against British agents and their American supporters, and an economic boycott of Britain. These actions forced Parliament to repeal the Stamp Act in 1766 and later to reduce the Sugar duty.

The calls for "no taxation without representation," though, were more about representation than about taxation. The colonists' main complaint was that each colony had its own legislative assembly and only their locally elected representatives had the right to pass laws on local affairs, especially but not only concerning taxation. This colonial threat to British sovereignty prompted Parliament to pass a Declaratory Act in 1766 claiming authority to "legislate for the colonies in all cases whatsoever." And the following year MPs followed up with the Townshend Duties on glass, lead, paper, paint, and tea.

These revenue measures were accompanied by enforcement provisions that empowered the Royal Navy to police the seas for tax evaders and Vice Admiralty Courts to try those thereby caught. The Townshend Duties furthermore introduced into the colonies a notorious bureaucracy in the form of the Board of Customs Commissioners. After these Commissioners were forced to hide in Boston Harbor's Castle William during the Liberty Riot of 1768, British troops arrived to restore order in the Massachusetts capital. The Boston Massacre of March 5, 1770, was the eventual outcome. The shock of the killing of five civilians prompted the repeal of all the Townshend Duties except the one on tea, which MPs kept on point of principle and to maintain legal precedent.

The Tea Act of 1773 then exempted the East India Company from the one remaining Townshend Duty. This attempt to advantage British merchants over American ones prompted protests organized by Sons of Liberty across the colonies, most famously the Boston Tea Party of December 1773. Parliament then passed the Coercive Acts that closed the port of Boston until compensation was paid for the tea dumped into the harbor, provided for trials of Tea Party participants in England, stationed troops in unoccupied dwellings in Boston, and replaced the 1691 Massachusetts charter with what amounted to military rule. Colonists called them the Intolerable Acts.[16]

In response to these escalations, a Continental Congress that sat in September and October 1774 initially attempted reconciliation, sending the Olive Branch Petition to a king who refused to receive it on the grounds, ironically and yet logically enough, that sending it to him rather than to Parliament violated the principles of constitutional and limited monarchy. The Continental Congress, however, also advised colonists to prepare for defense and promised aid from all if any one colony was attacked. Indeed tensions boiled over into the battles of Lexington and Concord in Massachusetts in April 1775, and subsequent armed rebellion finally turned into a revolutionary war with the Declaration of Independence, approved on July 4, 1776 by a Second Continental Congress that had first convened in May 1775 and which as a consequence of Independence became the first government of the United States.

The war was eventually won with combined Franco-American armies and navies and American militias forcing the surrender of British General Charles Cornwallis at Yorktown, Virginia, in September 1781. Although it took until February 1783 for all parties to agree terms and for the British finally to recognize American Independence in the Treaty of Paris (also formerly known as the Treaty of Versailles).

In the year of America's birth

Barack Obama usually uses only the vague references cited previously on the few occasions that he mentions the causes and course of the American Revolution. But there was an occasion on which he actually referred a specific event, without naming it and not in great detail but identifiably so all the same, and it raises a variety of interesting issues. In his first inaugural address, Obama invited his fellow Americans to be inspired by an incident that happened in December 1776. "In the year of America's birth," he said,

> in the coldest of months, a small band of patriots huddled by dying campfires on the shores of an icy river. The capital was abandoned. The enemy was advancing. The snow was stained with blood. At a moment when the outcome of our revolution was most in doubt, the father of our nation ordered these words be read to the people: 'Let it be told to the future world ... that in the depth of winter, when nothing but hope and virtue could survive ... that the city and the country, alarmed at one common danger, came forth to meet [it].'[17]

Obama's words evoke a well-known moment early in the revolutionary war. Newly arriving forces under British General William Howe had driven General George Washington's American ones off Long Island, out of New York, and into Pennsylvania. On Christmas Eve, 1776, however, Washington and his men crossed back over the Delaware River and achieved victories in surprise attacks on British forces and Hessian mercenaries at Princeton and Trenton, New Jersey.

Obama could rely on his listeners' familiarity with these events thanks in part to a famous visual fix on them. This winter campaign later inspired one of the best-known paintings of the War of Independence, *Washington Crossing the Delaware*, Emanuel Leutze's 1851 dramatization of the riverine scene of that Christmas night. It is not surprising that Obama would evoke this image, even without directly mentioning the painting: it is an icon of audacity. Nor is it surprising that he would thereby invite an association between Washington as the first American president and himself as the first African American president: two icons of hope.

Let it be told to the future world

What is possibly more surprising is that the words of the unnamed author that George Washington ordered to be read out and that Barack Obama opted to recall were those of Thomas Paine, then one of the general's *aides de camp*. In December 1776 Paine wrote the first in a series of sixteen pamphlets published before the end of the war in 1783. Collectively known as *The American Crisis*, or just *The Crisis*, the words Obama quoted come from *No. 1*, issued on December 23, 1776, and actually go as follows: "Let it be told to the future world, that in the depth of winter, when nothing but hope and virtue could survive, that the city and the country, alarmed at one common danger, came forth to meet and to repulse it." It is obviously understandable that Obama would excise the most martial parts of the passage to suit the circumstances of his own moment. Also perhaps that he would not wish to overdramatize 2009 with other well-known words Paine used in 1776, although they are perhaps the most magnificent and moving of the many great lines that Thomas Paine mustered and that Obama may have mulled over as he and his speechwriters prepared his historic inaugural address:

> These are the times that try men's souls: The summer soldier and the sunshine patriot will, in this crisis, shrink from the service of his country; but he that stands it now, deserves the love and thanks of man and woman. Tyranny, like hell, is not easily conquered; yet we have this consolation with us, that the harder the conflict, the more glorious the triumph. What we obtain too cheap, we esteem too lightly: it is dearness only that gives every thing its value. Heaven knows how to put a proper price upon its goods; and it would be strange indeed if so celestial an article as FREEDOM should not be highly rated.[18]

The American Crisis was not the first or even the most famous of Thomas Paine's writings, however. On January 10, at the earlier end of the same momentous year, Paine had published *Common Sense*, a call to break from Britain that many have credited as the single most influential inspiration for American independence. *Common Sense* was also a radical pamphlet, monstering monarchy and calling for the simplest possible form of representative government for the new republic that by the end of the year the pamphlet's author was fighting to establish.

Yet for various reasons Paine was an unlikely source for Obama to cite, which is perhaps why he remained unnamed even while his words were quoted. For starters, Thomas Paine was born in England. In Thetford, Norfolk, to be exact, on February 9 1739. As a young man he variously worked as a corset maker, school teacher, excise officer, and occasional writer, living first in his home town and later in London and in Lewes in Sussex. In November 1774, at the age of thirty-seven, after various professional and personal failures, including a divorce, he arrived in Philadelphia carrying letters of introduction from Benjamin Franklin. There he worked as a writer, editor, and printer before finding fame by authoring and publishing *Common Sense*.

It is also a slightly surprising citation because Paine was a notorious radical and wasn't known for the kind of calm, compromising politics that Obama favors. Although Thomas Jefferson was an admirer, the more conservative John Adams was not, once calling *Common Sense* "a poor, ignorant, malicious, short-sighted Crapulous mass." But it was perhaps Paine's post-American Revolution career and in particular his involvement with the French Revolution that secured him a certain notoriety. After Edmund Burke complained of the overturning of French customs and institutions in his *Reflections on the Revolution in France* (1790), Paine celebrated them and elaborated on the same natural rights and social contract theories in *Rights of Man* (1791–92) that he'd briefly summarized earlier in *Common Sense*. Subsequently charged with sedition, he fled to

France, where he took honorary citizenship and a seat in the revolutionary assembly representing the Pas-de-Calais.[19]

Thomas Paine then became a Girondin, and opposed the death penalty for Louis XVI and Marie-Antoinette, as he did as a matter of principle for anyone and everyone, for which offence he was remanded in Paris's Luxembourg Prison and for which indeed the Montagnards judged him worthy of judicial extermination himself. His requests for life-saving assistance fell on the deaf ears of the then President Washington, who now found Paine more a nuisance than useful, and what apparently saved Paine's neck was a momentary inefficiency in the machinery of the Terror. On the appointed day, the executioners missed the mark on Paine's prison door, chalked as it was on the inside rather than the outside on account of it having been open to give the sickly inmate a bit of air. That error stayed his execution long enough for Robespierre to fall from grace on 9 Thermidor An II, better known as July 27, 1794. He was finally freed in November after Ambassador James Monroe proved his American citizenship. Yet Paine never stopped being a pain. During his time in jail, he completed *The Age of Reason* (1794–96), a defense of natural religion that was too Godly for many Jacobins and too ungodly for many Americans. And his advocacy of rights for women did nothing to diminish his reputation as a dangerous extremist, possibly a lunatic.

Despite his tribulations, Thomas Paine's immeasurable but undoubtedly enormous contribution to American independence and the wider Enlightenment nevertheless earned him a pension and a house from the state of New York, where he retired in 1802. His later years were not happy ones, however. In addition to being infamous and occasionally assaulted for his radicalism and supposed irreligion, he was also reputedly drunken, cantankerous, and odiferous. He died on June 8, 1809, and his funeral was attended by six people.[20]

From this time forward forever

Barack Obama also discusses the philosophy and philosophers more directly behind the words of the Declaration of Independence than Thomas Paine was. Before discussing that, though, a few more words about exactly how that Declaration came about, in this case precisely how the document came to be written.

The aforementioned events from the Sugar Act to the outbreak of war finally alienated enough colonists to make the break from Britain possible. The enormous popularity of Paine's *Common Sense* persuaded many members of the Continental Congress that by late spring or early summer there was sufficient support to sustain a bid and win a war for independence. On June 7, 1776, then, Virginia delegate in Philadelphia Richard Henry Lee proposed a resolution to Congress to the effect that "these United Colonies are, and of right ought to be, free and independent States, that they are absolved from all allegiance to the British Crown, and that all political connection between them and the State of Great Britain is, and ought to be, totally dissolved."[21]

Three days later Congress decided that some of their number should "prepare a declaration to the effect of the said first resolution," and the day after that it appointed John Adams of Massachusetts, Benjamin Franklin of Pennsylvania, Thomas Jefferson of Virginia, Robert R. Livingston of New York, and Roger Sherman of Connecticut to what became known as The Committee of Five. Jefferson wrote a first draft of the declaration, and, with a few amendments made, the committee submitted its work to Congress on June 28. Congress made some more alterations before approving an almost final version on July 4.[22]

In the meantime, on July 2, Congress approved the Lee Resolution—meaning that the United States is actually two days older than we're accustomed to thinking, thanks to the tradition of celebrating Independence on the fourth. President Obama mentioned on July 4, 2013 that there "in that hall in Philadelphia, as they debated the Declaration, John Adams wrote to his beloved Abigail." He predicted that independence would be celebrated "from one end of the continent to the other, from this time forward forever," and so it has so far been. But many historians annually amuse themselves by recalling another part of Adams's prediction: "The Second Day of July 1776, will be the most memorable Epocha, in the History of America."[23]

And if Independence was actually decided two days before the fourth, the signing of the Declaration actually happened some weeks after. John Trumbull's aforementioned painting has done a great deal to imprint in our minds the idea that the Declaration was signed on the fourth itself. In fact, Congress ordered production of an engrossed, parchment copy of the Declaration on July 4 to be signed later. It was finally presented to Congress on August 2. That version was also amended to allege that the Declaration was adopted unanimously and to include the Lee Resolution in its conclusion. Many signed on that day, August 2, others did so when they could in the weeks that followed, though some never did, notwithstanding the claim of unanimity, a claim we return to a little later.

Enlightenment thinkers like Hobbes and Locke

In his draft of the Declaration of Independence, Thomas Jefferson's original formulation of the famous phrase that Barack Obama (and everyone) quotes went as follows: "We hold these truths to be sacred & undeniable; that all men are created equal & independant, that from that equal creation they derive rights inherent & inalienable, among which are the preservation of life, & liberty, & the pursuit of happiness." The revisions of this section of the Preamble, made mostly by John Adams and Benjamin Franklin and with a few final ones done in Congress, were thus more stylistic than anything, made in the cause of concision and clarity, and perhaps for the sake of the more pleasing cadences of the clauses we find in the final version. Plus the additional anaphoric "that." But, conceptually speaking, nothing substantial changed, and even in literary terms some key words and phrases, including the concluding triad, remained unchanged. We'll encounter a much more substantial and significant revision of Jefferson's draft later in this chapter.[24]

But much of what Jefferson wrote remained either unaltered in substance or entirely unedited because the men who read and revised the Declaration were already familiar with the ideas and even many of the phrases it contained. As Barack Obama rightly notes, the Declaration's ideas were already old "more than two centuries ago" when Jefferson expressed them and the Second Continental Congress modified and published them. Jefferson himself recollected, in a letter to Henry Lee almost half a century after Independence, that he had intended the Declaration "to be an expression of the American mind." His aim in drafting it therefore was not "to find out new principles, or new arguments … but to place before mankind the common sense of the subject, in terms so plain and firm as to command their assent … All it's authority rests then," he continued, "on the harmonizing sentiments of the day, whether expressed in conversation, in letters, printed essays, or the elementary books of public right, as Aristotle, Cicero, Locke, Sidney, etc."[25]

To James Madison, Jefferson similarly said that he didn't "consider it part of my charge to invent new ideas altogether, and to offer no sentiment that had ever been expressed before." Others concurred. According to Jefferson's letter to Madison, Richard Henry Lee once said that the Declaration was "copied from Locke's treatise on government." And John Adams, possibly jealous that Jefferson's contribution to the Declaration eclipsed his own, wrote that there is "not an idea in" it "but what had been hackneyed in Congress for two years before."[26]

Adams was waspish but wasn't wrong. He and others in Congress and in the colonial legislatures and indeed "out of doors" in the towns and counties had not only been discussing independence, but also debating the very terms in which it should be declared. As Pauline Maier wrote and as Danielle Allen rightly reminded us more recently, the Declaration was in many ways authored "collectively," a product of "democratic writing." A result indeed of the kind of civic conversation Barack Obama favors, even before the Constitution institutionalized America's "deliberative democracy."[27]

Such collective and democratic writing was possible because large numbers of people knew their philosophy. To begin with, the concept of "self-evident" truths was well known to anyone who'd read John Locke's *An Essay Concerning Human Understanding* (1690), or was otherwise acquainted with the contemporary epistemological orthodoxy that the newborn human mind was a tabula rasa that acquires knowledge by experience of the world. The idea, that is, that the truth is out there, an object to be discovered through observation and the application of reason, not something somehow subjectively conceived or constructed in our own minds. The truth is "*self*-evident."

This idea of self-evidence is itself fundamental to the concept upon which the next philosophical claims of the Declaration rest: the "Laws of Nature and of Nature's God," as the Declaration's first paragraph describes the basis of natural rights. Natural rights to these radical Whigs were scientific facts as self-evident, as objectively discoverable, as any other. These ideas about rights were also often attributed to John Locke, this time to his *Two Treatises of Civil Government* (also 1690), or more specifically the *Second*

Treatise, although, like Jefferson and his Declaration, Locke is best known as their chief elaborator rather than their originator. "The state of nature has a law of nature to govern it," Locke wrote, "which obliges everyone; and reason, which is that law, teaches all mankind, who will but consult it, that being all equal and independent, no one ought to harm another in his life, health, liberty, or possessions." Locke also used another phrase to describe rights, one that defined "property" broadly as "life, liberty, and estates." The resemblance of Locke's phrasing to that in the Declaration is unmissable.[28]

The members of Congress would have known equally well the provenance of the next passages of the Declaration of Independence: "That to secure these rights, Governments are instituted among Men, deriving their just powers from the consent of the governed, – That whenever any Form of Government becomes destructive of these ends, it is the Right of the People to alter or to abolish it, and to institute new Government." These ideas—the consent of the governed, government as a trust, and the logically proceeding right to revolt against misgovernment and to form a new government—had all been enunciated often enough in England's seventeenth-century age of revolutions, and once again were distilled in Locke's *Second Treatise*. These ideas remained commonplaces of eighteenth-century radical Whiggism, and were perfectly familiar to any well-schooled and many less well-schooled people in Britain and especially in the colonies at the time.

Barack Obama the constitutional lawyer knows these things well. As he notes in *The Audacity of Hope*, "Enlightenment thinkers like Hobbes and Locke, suggested that free men would form governments as a bargain to ensure that one man's freedom did not become another man's tyranny; that they would sacrifice individual license to better preserve their liberty."[29]

Thomas Hobbes (1588–1679) was the less likely of the two men to be included in Obama's canon. Best known for *Leviathan* (1651), Hobbes indeed propounded the notions of natural equality, individual rights, and the social contract. But, perhaps scarred from his birth near England's southern shores as the Spanish Armada menaced the coasts in 1588, and then by living through the instabilities and dangers of the civil wars of 1642–51, the Regicide of 1649, the Interregnum of 1649–60, the Restoration of 1660, and to the outbreak of the Popish Plot and Exclusion Crisis of 1678–81, he was no admirer of disorder, and his political philosophy was absolutely authoritarian. He saw the State of Nature as a "war of all against all" in which life was "solitary, poor, nasty, brutish, and short." To prevent a descent into such conditions again, the subject must alienate all rights and abjure rebellion and revolution in a social contract offering absolute obedience to authority. For "Covenants without the Sword are but Words," Hobbes wrote, "and of no strength to secure a man at all."[30]

John Locke (1632–1704) was rather more relaxed about human nature and political authority than Thomas Hobbes was. And, with his un-Hobbesian idea of unalienable rights, including the right to revolt, Locke was much more a forebear of America's Founders and indeed of Barack Obama. Locke probably wrote the *Two Treatises* during the Exclusion Crisis of 1678–81, the failed attempts to prevent James, Duke of York from succeeding to the English throne. James inherited the crown in 1685 anyway, but soon became despised for his Catholicism and for an absolutist ideology with which he seemed to act increasingly in accord. In 1688 Queen Mary of Modena bore James a male heir who would be raised a Catholic and would supersede James's Protestant daughter Mary in the line of succession. A temporary inconvenience in the form of an ageing James was thus replaced by the terrifying prospect of a perpetual papist tyranny emanating from his royal loins (notwithstanding rumors that the baby was an imposter brought into the queen's chamber in a warming pan). Leading English politicians therefore invited James's son-in-law, Prince William of Orange, to invade and thereby secure English Protestantism and liberty. He did so and subsequently became King William III and his wife, James's eldest daughter, co-inherited the throne as Queen Mary II.

John Locke, exiled with many others after the 1683 Rye House Plot to assassinate Charles II and the then James, Duke of York, finally published his *Two Treatises* in the aftermath of this Glorious Revolution. Yet only a minority interpreted 1688 as a "real" revolution, or, to put that in more Lockean, radical Whig terms, a dissolution of government in which authority reverts to the people, who, consenting via a social contract, replace the old regime with a new one more suited to their wants and needs. For most English people at the time, moderate Whig and Tory alike, the Glorious Revolution was no such thing. It was not a people's revolution but a parliamentary one. It represented furthermore the restoration of an Ancient Constitution, a return to the proper balance between Crown and Parliament that had been disrupted by the Norman Conquest of 1066 and, after incremental returns to more conciliar government, further upset by Stuart absolutism before being fully restored in 1688. Even Locke, the radical theorist, agreed that this is what had happened in England in practice. And the Glorious Revolution's outcome was the sovereignty of Parliament. Or, technically, of limited, constitutional monarchy institutionalized in the authority of the "crown-in-parliament." This is not the same thing of course as the sovereignty of the people—the much more theoretically Lockean and radical-Whig origin and outcome of the American Revolution that we see expressed in the doctrines of the Declaration of Independence and enacted by "We the people" in the US Constitution.

Its roots in eighteenth-century liberal and republican thought

Barack Obama's acknowledgment of John Locke as a prominent and perhaps the preeminent philosophical proponent of the principles behind the Declaration of Independence is nevertheless significantly qualified. Obama also notes, for instance, that we can "trace the genesis of the Declaration of Independence to its roots in eighteenth-century liberal and republican thought," and thus not exclusively to seventeenth-century Lockean liberalism. As James T. Kloppenberg details, Obama was educated in the historiography of the "republican synthesis"—a wide-ranging challenge made by historians in the last third of the twentieth century to the notion of Lockean liberalism as the single or most significant source of American revolutionary thought.[31]

One pioneer of "republican synthesis" historiography was J. G. A. Pocock, whose *The Machiavellian Moment* (1975) traced the progress of classical republican thought from sixteenth-century Italy through seventeenth-century England to eighteenth-century America. The instabilities of late-medieval Italian city states prompted Niccolo Machiavelli to explore ancient Greek and Roman means of maintaining political stability in the face of crises, and his Renaissance thinking in turn influenced Englishmen in their civil war and colonial Americans in their revolution.[32]

Probably more influential on Obama specifically, however, are works beginning with Bernard Bailyn's *The Ideological Origins of the American Revolution* (1966) and Gordon Wood's *The Creation of the American Republic, 1776–1787* (1969). Books and articles by Bailyn, Wood, and other "republican synthesis" scholars were on Roger Boesche's bibliographies when Barack Obama took that professor's courses at Occidental College in the early 1980s. Obama reread these works and encountered others like them when finishing his undergraduate studies at Columbia and as a graduate student of law at Harvard a little later. We see more of their influence on Obama's historical-Constitutional thinking in the following chapter.[33]

For present purposes though, it is worth noting that for these scholars the "republican synthesis" was just that—a *synthesis* of various older and newer kinds of republican thinking. Some of it originated in ancient Greece and Rome, and some may indeed have come from Renaissance Italy. But these scholars' works focus more closely on how revolutionary Americans synthesized seventeenth-century English liberal individualism with eighteenth-century republican concerns with fending off corruption through the nurturing of civic virtue. The Declaration of Independence can thus be traced to "real Whig" or "country Whig" or "opposition Whig" writings such as John Trenchard and Thomas Gordon's *Cato's Letters* (1720–23) and other works as well as to Locke's *Two Treatises of Government*.[34]

But, crucially, at each stage the ideas changed, adapted by different people to their own differing circumstances. Equally so in America, where various ideas were blended together and where the mix even included a measure of French radicalism, derived in particular from Montesquieu and Jean-Jacques Rousseau. Furthermore, according to this historiography, colonial American material abundance created a more equal society, or at least one in which unprecedented numbers of people and proportions of the population had enough property to participate in the political system. And not as revolting peasants, but as enfranchised subjects, something that possibly predisposed them to independence and perhaps prepared them for subsequent citizenship. The supposedly exceptionally egalitarian social-economic and political circumstances of early America thus gave old ideas new meanings, or at least radically expanded the numbers of people who were equal enough to enjoy such things as property, liberty, and the pursuit of happiness.

Bernard Bailyn and Gordon Wood shy from associating themselves too closely with American exceptionalism, though, although Jack P. Greene has made an explicit case for it. Among historians generally, however, the term tends to be pejorative, suggesting excessive patriotism, even perhaps a nasty nationalism, or at least a parochial ignorance of outside influences on America. Neither Bailyn nor Wood nor Greene is guilty of any of these things. Their exceptionalism, if we can call it that, is historicized: that is, it emanates from an appreciation that ideas change over time and space, something that's as true of America as it is of anywhere else. Barack Obama does identify explicitly as an American exceptionalist, though, but his exceptionalism is nevertheless similarly nuanced and historicized.[35]

What makes us exceptional

If Barack Obama acknowledges that the ideas behind the Declaration of Independence originated elsewhere, how can he identify its sentiments as specifically American, as "*our common creed*," as indeed exceptional? The answer for Obama lies partly, as it does for Bernard Bailyn, Gordon Wood, Jack Greene, and others, in the specifically American synthesis of ideas emanating from Europe and from the particular and more equal and open social-economic and political circumstances of eighteenth-century America that gave these ideas new or different meanings. But Obama says little specifically about this possibility—just the mentions of Hobbes, Locke, and "eighteenth-century liberal and republican thought" noted above. Bailyn, Wood, and Greene are historians of the colonies and revolution and so they do. But, as we saw in the last chapter, Obama's interest in the colonies is minimal, largely limited to what he sees as precocious features of American national character.

What interests Obama more is the Declaration of Independence itself and its legacy. We can see the specificity of this interest in a passage from his second inaugural address, and simultaneously we can see how he sees the Declaration as the source of American exceptionalism. "What makes us exceptional—what makes us American—" he said, "is our allegiance to an idea articulated in a declaration made more than two centuries ago: 'We hold these truths to be self-evident, that all men are created equal; that they are endowed by their Creator with certain unalienable rights; that among these are life, liberty, and the pursuit of happiness.' "[36]

The key word here perhaps is "allegiance." The Declaration of Independence was not just a statement of abstract ideas, not merely a philosophical rumination on political principles. It was also, and was perhaps first and foremost, an event. An event that created a nation to which citizens could indeed have an allegiance. As we've seen, on July 2, 1776, the Second Continental Congress approved Richard Henry Lee's Resolution on independence. The Declaration approved on the fourth was Congress's justification of that Resolution. As its opening paragraph explains:

> When in the Course of human events, it becomes necessary for one people to dissolve the political bands which have connected them with another, and to assume among the powers of the earth, the separate and equal station to which the Laws of Nature and of Nature's God entitle them, a decent respect to the opinions of mankind requires that they should declare the causes which impel them to the separation.[37]

The first lines of the Declaration thus warn the world in no uncertain terms that big things are actually afoot, so big they can be described as "the Course of human events," so big they must be announced and explained to all "mankind."

The first lines of the next paragraph lay out the fundamental philosophical principles that provide the premises for all that follows: "We hold these truths to be self-evident, that all men are created equal, that they are endowed by their Creator with certain unalienable Rights, that among these are Life, Liberty and the pursuit of Happiness." And then "–That to secure these rights, Governments are instituted among Men, deriving their just powers from the consent of the governed." The Declaration then proceeds from philosophical premises toward the practical matter at hand, moving in that direction with the aid of another of the hyphens included in versions of the document sent to the states—another arrow unmistakably indicating the direction of argument: "–That whenever any Form of Government becomes destructive of these ends, it is the Right of the People to alter or to abolish it, and to institute new Government, laying its foundation on such principles and organizing its powers in such form, as to them shall seem most likely to effect their Safety and Happiness."[38]

The men of the Congress were revolutionaries but they weren't reckless, and so (without a paragraph break to interrupt the logical progression) the Declaration cautions: "Prudence, indeed, will dictate that Governments long established should not be changed for light and transient causes; and accordingly all experience hath shewn, that mankind are more disposed to suffer, while evils are sufferable, than to right themselves by abolishing the forms to which they are accustomed. But,"—and it's a really big but—"when a long train of abuses and usurpations, pursuing invariably the same Object evinces a design to reduce them under absolute Despotism, it is their right, it is their duty, to throw off such Government, and to provide new Guards for their future security." And indeed "–Such has been the patient sufferance of these Colonies; and such is now the necessity which constrains them to alter their former Systems of Government."

At this point, and again without a paragraph break, the document completes its transition from philosophical principle to political actuality: "The history of the present King of Great Britain is a history of repeated injuries and usurpations," the Declaration claims, "all having in direct object the establishment of an absolute Tyranny over these States. To prove this, let Facts be submitted to a candid world."

This Preamble thus establishes the philosophical rationales for revolution and introduces the argument that the colonists had practical reasons for revolt. The next section of the Declaration goes on to list the "Facts" alluded to in the Preamble's final line. The details of the accusations need not detain us now, as Barack Obama is more interested in the general philosophy of the Declaration, the relevance of which transcends time in a way that the particular policies of British governments in the 1760s and 1770s do not. But the fact that there were twenty-seven different paragraphs, many encompassing more than one allegation of abomination, reminds us that the Declaration was not just a justification of revolution but a key part of an actual revolution actually happening in the actual world. The members of Congress were withdrawing the colonists' consent to be governed on the grounds of the "long train of abuses and usurpations" then listed. They were thereby themselves beginning "to institute new Government, laying its foundation on such principles and organizing its powers in such form, as to them shall seem most likely to effect their Safety and Happiness."

The Declaration's conclusion returns briefly to the point about prudence by noting that colonists had petitioned British politicians and appealed to the British people to cease the "Oppressions" their rulers had imposed. But all alas to no avail. The Declaration thus continues: "We, therefore … solemnly publish and declare," (and here the Lee Resolution gets a rerun in the August 2 version that members of Congress eventually signed), "That these United Colonies are, and of Right ought to be Free and Independent States; that they are Absolved from all Allegiance to the British Crown, and that all political connection between them and the State of Great Britain, is and ought to be totally dissolved." Then, again without a paragraph break or even this time a period for pause, the Congress added "and that as Free and Independent States, they have full Power to levy War, conclude Peace, contract Alliances, establish Commerce, and to do all other Acts and Things which Independent States may of right do." The document then concludes: "And for the support of this Declaration, with a firm reliance on the protection of divine Providence, we mutually pledge to each other our Lives, our Fortunes and our sacred Honor."

The Declaration of Independence was therefore not describing what men could do theoretically. It was describing what the men who were writing it were actually doing right there and then. In this "speech act" they turned the words of "Enlightenment thinkers like Hobbes and Locke" into actions and transformed "eighteenth-century liberal and republican thought" into what Obama calls "our common creed." In this process, abstract principles gained "substance," and an "idea" became something a people could actually have an "allegiance" to. And so, as President Obama expressed it in one of his Independence Day addresses, "These are not simply words on aging parchment. They are the principles that define us as a nation, the values we cherish as a people, and the ideals we strive for as a society, even as we know that we constantly have to work in order to perfect our union, and that work is never truly done." And that, for Barack Obama, is what makes the United States "exceptional."[39]

What makes us American

Another criticism levelled at the concept of American exceptionalism is that, in emphasizing the extent of American equality, it underemphasizes American economic, social, and political inequalities. This may be fair in some instances, when, for example, people confuse the phrase "all men are created equal" with the idea that "all men are equal," and then assume that these words represent a description of America as it was then rather than a prescription for what it might later become. Barack Obama does not make these mistakes, though, and indeed his appreciation of the qualification created by the word "created" is fundamental to his understanding of American history. He knows well enough that in America men (and women) were not (and are not) always equal according to law or in everyday life. But the idea that they are "created" equal—as inscribed into the nation's founding document—contains and for Obama idealizes the potential for the amelioration if not the eventual elimination of the legal and lived realities of inequality—the "work that is never truly done" but that each generation nevertheless keeps working toward. Far from ignoring inequality, then, Obama's version of American exceptionalism presupposes its existence.

A different though related criticism levelled at American exceptionalism is that, in emphasizing the unique degrees of American consensus, it underemphasizes American economic, social, and political division and conflict. This same accusation is often also applied more broadly to "Whig" historians by "Progressive" ones who focus on economic, social, and ideological division and conflict in the past. Barack Obama's Whiggish preoccupations with what Americans had (and have) in common—not least the "common creed" that's the main subject of this chapter—opens him to this accusation. As does his Whiggish optimism about historical progress that's the main subject of subsequent chapters.

There are some ways in which Obama perhaps really is guilty of understating social and ideological conflict, at least in the period before Independence. The aforementioned lack of interest in events from the Sugar Act of 1764 to the eve of Independence necessarily means that he ignores certain aspects of American revolutionary history. One of the most obvious is Loyalism. From the time of the Sugar Act onwards there were those in the colonies who supported and as well those who opposed British policies. The former were called "Tories," a term of abuse, and they were sometimes tarred and feathered, had their property attacked, and were otherwise harassed and even terrorized at times. When independence came, their property was confiscated and after the war many were displaced to other British colonies or to Britain itself. To places with which in many cases they had no familiarity and where they had no family or friends.

Some Loyalists were indeed Tories, people who believed in loyalty to authority as a matter of principle, or who believed at least in nonresistance to it. Others, though, were actually moderate Whigs, people who believed in the sovereignty and supremacy of Parliament, whether they liked its particular policies or not. Others besides were more radical Whigs who rejected the rule of Parliament but who nevertheless believed there was still the possibility of negotiation and compromise, or who felt too deep a sense of British identity or patriotism to sign up for separation. Others still were enslaved people who thought that siding with the British offered better odds of liberation, as we see later in this chapter. And yet others were Native Americans who believed the British offered them their best chance of keeping their lands, as we see in Chapter 7. Historians disagree on how many Loyalists there were at any given time, but most estimates fall between a fifth and a third of Euro-Americans, with probably higher proportions among African Americans and the highest among Native Americans.

In a way, though, Barack Obama's silence about Loyalists makes sense. Loyalists never subscribed to the Declaration of Independence (or in some cases subscribed and subsequently unsubscribed). They were therefore by Obama's standard simply not American. Barack Obama's colonial American history—essentially a prehistory of the United States rather than a history of British America—is the first thing to suggest that this is his definition. Obama's references to the Declaration of Independence as "*our* common creed" and "*our* starting point as Americans" and the "foundation of *our* government" further show that his "American" history is not a history of America as a place but instead the history of Americans as a people. That is, the history of those who have subscribed to the American "creed," rather than of those who have simply lived in America. Those who never subscribed did not even reach the "starting point" of being American. And, as President Obama put it on July 4, 2013, "a small band of patriots declared that we were a people created equal—free to think and worship and live as we please. It was a declaration heard around the world—that we were no longer colonists, we were Americans." Which is another way of saying that those who didn't agree with the Declaration were not Americans. Loyalists simply have no place in this *American* history, except as part of a shadowy and only occasionally and vaguely mentioned enemy.[40]

If this is so then Barack Obama channels the presumptions of the members of the Second Continental Congress. The first paragraph of the Declaration refers to Americans as "one people": as in "When in the Course of human events, it becomes necessary for *one people* to dissolve the political bands which have connected them with *another* …" Jefferson's definition of the colonists as a "people" originates with his claims that migrants had left British jurisdiction, entered a State of Nature, and formed their own governments before forming alliances with their former king. He thus called the colonies "states" throughout his *Summary View of the Rights of British America*. But that process by Jefferson's own definition created thirteen states and therefore thirteen different peoples from Massachusetts down to Georgia. What he did in the Declaration, however, was call them "one people." The "American" people were thus created by declaring themselves as such.

Moreover, the embossed edition of the Declaration published on August 2 is headed by the title "The *unanimous* Declaration of the thirteen united States of America," which was accurate in as much as all the *states* represented at the Congress agreed to it. But it was certainly not unanimously agreed to among all the delegates of all those states, and even less so among all the people of the former colonies. Its claim for unanimity therefore makes more sense if we think of it as agreed to by all its adherents. If you agreed with it, you were American. If you didn't, you weren't American. Therefore it was unanimously agreed among Americans. The American people were thus a tautological creation.[41]

Farmers and scholars

Consensus of course is not as demanding a standard as unanimity, but it is possible that, even among the "one people" defined by the Declaration of Independence, Barack

Obama exaggerates the extent of social cohesion and of political like-mindedness. In his "A More Perfect Union" speech of March 2008, for example, Obama claimed: "Farmers and scholars; statesmen and patriots, who had traveled across an ocean to escape tyranny and persecution, finally made real their declaration of independence at a Philadelphia convention that lasted through the spring of 1787." I pointed out in the previous chapter that this phrase elides British-American colonial history, or at least folds some of it within the history of the United States by conflating the founders of the colonies with the Founders of the country. But the term "farmers and scholars; statesmen and patriots" also has other interpretative implications for American revolutionary history.[42]

The term "farmers and scholars" is loaded with moral and political significations. In using it Obama depicted revolutionary Americans in virtuous terms. American revolutionaries were, he is saying, producers of food and of food for thought, nourishing bodies and nurturing minds. But at the same time he also depicted social-economic variety, and yet also and simultaneously unity. Variety is symbolized first in the form of farmers who work with their hands and second in the form of scholars who work with their minds; eighteenth-century equivalents of what today we often call blue collar and white collar workers. And yet, in associating them together in a shared endeavor, what Obama emphasized is what these people had in common with each other, not what made them different from each other. Making the claim, in other words, that America was (and is) an essentially egalitarian place where people of different social-economic backgrounds could (and can) work together on equal terms.[43]

And what makes the association of the images convincing perhaps is that Obama was by no means the first to make it. The association dates indeed to the American Revolution itself. As Obama most certainly knew, the term "farmers and scholars" would bring to mind, consciously or unconsciously, one of the most famous American revolutionaries: John Dickinson. And the term might even bring to mind the first words of the first of Dickinson's twelve *Letters from a Farmer in Pennsylvania*, published in 1767–68, in all their carefully constructed virtue-signaling: "I am a *Farmer*," Dickinson claimed, "settled, after a variety of fortunes, near the banks of the river *Delaware*, in the province of *Pennsylvania*. I received a liberal education, and have been engaged in the busy scenes of life; but am now convinced, that a man may be as happy without bustle, as with it. My farm is small; my servants are few, and good; I have a little money at interest; I wish for no more; my employment in my own affairs is easy; and with a contented grateful mind, undisturbed by worldly hopes or fears."[44]

As we saw in the previous chapter, John Dickinson was in fact a London-educated lawyer, and a politician and political writer renowned as the "Penman of the Revolution." In other words, the self-styled farmer was actually a scholar. In Dickinson's image, therefore, or at least his projected image, farmers and scholars are not even a range of people working together, but are one and the same person. What Barack Obama seems to be promoting by evoking the scholarly "Pennsylvania farmer" is the idea that in an egalitarian, revolutionary America a farmer could actually *be* a scholar.

Barack Obama

Farmers and scholars; statesmen and patriots

This egalitarian message about the nature of revolutionary America is reinforced by the fact that Dickinson was not only both an actual scholar and a self-styled farmer, but also a statesman and a patriot. His *Farmer's Letters* and other writings objected to British taxes and other measures that eventually comprised the causes of the American Revolution. He was later a member of the Continental Congress, and although he didn't sign the Declaration of Independence, as he remained for some time in favor of pursuing reconciliation, he later led a Delaware militia unit in the War of Independence, and later still was as a delegate at the Constitutional Convention. In Dickinson's image, therefore, a farmer as well as a scholar could actually *be* a statesman and a patriot. And so perhaps what Obama is saying is that the American Revolution was not only socially and economically egalitarian, but also politically democratic. That this truly was "America's improbable experiment in democracy," as he also puts it in that paragraph in "A More Perfect Union."[45]

Barack Obama's implication that the American Revolution was egalitarian and democratic, however, may obscure the considerable social divisions that existed in America at the time. And not only because of the aforementioned vast numbers of pro-British Loyalists, and not only because of the one-fifth of Americans who were enslaved at the time, and who we return to shortly. But also because there's ample evidence that social-economic inequality was increasing and opportunity was declining for the "middling sort" and "lower sort" of people in late-colonial America (to use the terms of the time). And furthermore that growing class divisions were matched by ideological tensions that manifested themselves in rising revolutionary demands for more democratic government for the lower sorts than many among the "better sort" who comprise the best-remembered revolutionary leaders truly desired. Even among anti-British patriots who were united in opposition to Britain there was therefore considerable division about the future nature of American society and politics.

Many historians argue indeed, to use the much-quoted phrase of the great historian Carl Becker, that the American Revolution was not only about "home rule," but also about "who should rule at home." Protest against Britain thus entailed a process of democratization within America. From the Stamp Act onwards, people who had not previously been customarily involved in politics were suddenly routinely protesting in the streets. Their contributions were often limited to useful riotousness before 1774, but after the Intolerable Acts these people joined Committees of Inspection that Congress established to police the boycott against Britain, and joined Committees of Safety that Congress established to prepare for possible war. Poorer people's participation in politics was thus institutionalized and thereby legitimized to such an extent that from Independence onwards we see extensions of the franchise throughout much of the early United States. Sometimes to all white men who paid taxes, following the logic of the dictum "no taxation without representation," but increasingly to all white men without property as well, following the logic of the dictum that "all men are created equal." Though not far enough yet to include all black men or any women.[46]

Sometimes concessions to a new kind of democratic politics came in the form of symbolism, such as when scholarly lawyers, politicians, and writers fabricated identities as humble farmers in pseudo-eponymous epistles. But John Dickinson did make a more substantial change in his life as well. Notwithstanding his claim that "my servants are few," he was in fact a large slaveholder and indeed the fourth generation of a family that made a fortune from the toil of enslaved people in the tobacco fields of Talbot County, Maryland. In 1777, however, John Dickinson began the process of manumitting his slaves.

Which reminds us that if Barack Obama is uninterested in these internal processes of the American Revolution leading up to 1776, he nevertheless believes in the transformative power of the main event itself: the Declaration of Independence, Americans' "starting point," "common creed," and "the foundation of our government." But in his considerations of the Declaration and its implications, Obama is no simple consensus historian. While he believes that belief in equality, liberty, and the pursuit of happiness was common or unanimous, he knows that different adherents had different ideas about what these words meant and who they should apply to. Ultimately, for Obama, the logic of the Declaration pushed America in a progressive direction, but not without a long struggle and a great deal of strife over the meanings and applications of its principles.

Let's begin to understand Barack Obama's understanding of the transformative power of the Declaration of Independence by looking at those to whom it did not appear to apply.

All men are created equal

It is often assumed, understandably enough, that the "all men" mentioned in the Declaration of Independence did not include black men, or black or any other women. Barack Obama himself notes that the "Declaration of Independence may have been, in the words of historian Joseph Ellis, 'a transformative moment in world history, when all laws and human relationships dependent on coercion would be swept away forever.' But that spirit of liberty didn't extend, in the minds of the Founders, to the slaves who worked their fields, made their beds, and nursed their children."[47]

It is all too terribly true that the vast majority of African Americans in 1776 were enslaved and therefore definitively did not enjoy equality, liberty, and the pursuit of happiness. It is also true that too few members of Congress believed they should. Yet in other ways the principles of the Declaration really did apply to black as well as to white people. First, it was still both biblical and scientific orthodoxy at the time that all men and women, black and white, descended from Adam and Eve, whatever inequalities some believed had developed since the common origins of humankind. In other words, most delegates believed that all men were *created* equal. And, as we'll see, this belief mattered because it affected many people's views on the rights and wrongs of enslaving those who were equal in the eyes of God.

In any case, and even more importantly, the principles of the Declaration did not belong exclusively to the delegates at the Second Continental Congress. Others also expressed its sentiments—the Declaration was, after all and as we've seen, and in its principal author's own words, "an expression of the American mind." And that included African Americans interested in and acting toward their own liberation, whatever Thomas Jefferson and other leaders believed. Before looking at how slaves themselves applied the Declaration's principles in their own behalf, though, let's explore the complex thoughts and deeds of the document's principal author regarding race and slavery.[48]

Thomas Jefferson expressed strong antislavery sentiments, though he also held slaves and therefore had economic interests in the institution, and he held deeply inhibiting fears of the institution's abolition, and those fears were racially motivated. In all these respects, despite his extraordinary privilege and accomplishments, Jefferson represents the dilemmas of many white Americans of his day as they perceived them, so it's worth examining his ambivalences and ambiguities in some detail. Doing so also helps us understand more deeply the origins of the Declaration that Jefferson drafted, and which is so crucial to Barack Obama's understanding of American history. The aim here is emphatically not to undermine Obama's claims for the Declaration as a dynamic force behind eventual African American liberation and other progressive change. On the contrary, it is to understand Obama's understanding of the complexities of that force, including its contradictions and limitations. To understand in particular the time it has taken to translate the creed the Declaration contains into its own logical outcomes.

Born in 1743, Thomas Jefferson grew up at Shadwell Plantation in Goochland County, Virginia. At the age of twenty-one he inherited from his by then deceased father Peter between twenty and forty slaves and 5,000 acres of land where he built and subsequently constantly rebuilt his Monticello mansion. He married Martha Wayles Skelton in 1772 and the following year inherited 11,000 acres of land and 135 slaves at the death of her father, John Wayles.

Yet Jefferson and some other southerners like him learned to detest enslavement. As he put it some years later, "Nursed and educated in the daily habit of seeing the degraded condition, both bodily & mental, of those unfortunate beings, not reflecting that that degradation was very much the work of themselves & their fathers, few minds had yet doubted but that they were as legitimate subjects of property as their horses or cattle. The quiet & onotonous course of colonial life had been disturbed by no alarm, & little reflection on the value of liberty." Jefferson of course implicitly ignores here the fact that many African American minds had reflected very deeply on the value of liberty. British assaults on white American liberties, however, awoke a new and revolutionary consciousness among some white people. As Jefferson continued, "And when alarm was taken at an enterprise on their own, it was not easy to carry them the whole length of the principles which they invoked for themselves."[49]

Accordingly, in the angriest single section of his draft Declaration of Independence, Thomas Jefferson wrote a scathing attack on the slave trade and by implication on slavery itself. In the last of his original accusations at George III, he wrote:

he has waged cruel war against human nature itself, violating it's most sacred rights of life & liberty in the persons of a distant people who never offended him, captivating & carrying them into slavery in another hemisphere, or to incur miserable death in their transportation thither. this piratical warfare, the opprobrium of infidel powers, is the warfare of the CHRISTIAN king of Great Britain. determined to keep open a market where MEN should be bought & sold, he has prostituted his negative for suppressing every legislative attempt to prohibit or to restrain this execrable commerce: and that this assemblage of horrors might want no fact of distinguished die, he is now exciting those very people to rise in arms among us, and to purchase that liberty of which he has deprived them, & murdering the people upon whom he also obtruded them; thus paying off former crimes committed against the liberties of one people, with crimes which he urges them to commit against the lives of another.[50]

In this passage, Thomas Jefferson explicitly refers three times to Africans and their American descendants as "people," and another time in capital letters as "MEN." Given that women were also victims of the slave trade, it seems that Jefferson's declaration used the term in its broadest sense, including all of humankind (not that he thought that women's equal creation entitled them to vote or to engage actively in politics in any way). It is also very clear that to Jefferson these "distant people" possessed "sacred rights of life and liberty" and that therefore the slave trade was a "cruel war against human nature itself."

As Jefferson ruefully recounted some years later, though, the delegates from Georgia and South Carolina wished to keep the slave trade open, at least for a while, and thus insisted on editing his excoriation of the "execrable" enterprise all but out of the final Declaration. All that remained after Congress's redrafting therefore was that "He has excited domestic insurrections amongst us"—a reference to Virginia Governor Lord Dunmore's November 1775 Proclamation offering freedom to the adult, male slaves of rebellious masters if they joined him to assist in suppressing the American insurrection.

There was though one other reference to the slave trade in the Declaration, albeit an indirect one. The first in the list of accusations against George III states: "He has refused his Assent to Laws the most wholesome and necessary for the public good." Which refers to the king's vetoes of colonial legislation in general, but including vetoes of laws to suppress or discourage the slave trade passed by various colonial assemblies, including Virginia's.[51]

It is not surprising then that, as president, Jefferson was happy to encourage and execute the abolition of the slave trade to the United States in 1808—as soon as it became constitutionally permissible to do so. And part of the reason he despised the Atlantic slave trade was that it would slow and perhaps even prevent the abolition of slavery itself, which would in turn he believed threaten the very survival of the United States. In his *Notes on the State of Virginia*, begun in 1781 and finished by 1784, Jefferson asked: "Can the liberties of a nation be thought secure when we have removed their only firm basis, a conviction in the minds of the people that these liberties are of the gift of God? That they are not to be violated but with his wrath?" He seriously doubted it: "Indeed I tremble for my country when I reflect that God is just: that his justice cannot sleep for ever: that considering numbers, nature and natural means only, a revolution of the wheel of fortune, an exchange of situation, is among possible events: that it may become probable by supernatural interference! The Almighty has no attribute which can take side with us in such a context." That's some statement, especially from a deist believer in a nonintervening creator.[52]

So why did such a powerful man as Thomas Jefferson not do more to promote the abolition of slavery? The principal problem was that while he saw Africans and their American descendants as men with natural rights, he did not see them as equal to Europeans and European Americans. Created equal, maybe, but not equal. In those same *Notes on Virginia*, Jefferson asked rhetorically "Why not retain and incorporate the blacks into the state, and thus save the expence of supplying, by importation of white settlers, the vacancies they will leave?"—instead of colonizing freed black Americans in Africa. The first part of his long answer stated that: "Deep rooted prejudices entertained by the whites; ten thousand recollections, by the blacks, of the injuries they have sustained; new provocations; the real distinctions which nature has made; and many other circumstances, will divide us into parties, and produce convulsions which will probably never end but in the extermination of the one or the other race."[53]

But Jefferson then moved on from what he called this "political" consideration to concerns that he called "physical and moral," and under this heading he detailed his beliefs about what he called the "real distinctions which nature has made." Jefferson wrote: "The first difference which strikes us is that of colour," which for him had many implications, and he began with aesthetic ones. "Is it not," he asked, "the foundation of a greater or less share of beauty in the two races?" He wrote of "the flowing hair" of white people and their "more elegant symmetry of form." And of black people's "own judgment in favour of the whites, declared by their preference of them, as uniformly as is the preference of the Oranootan for the black women over those of his own species." Also: "They secrete less by the kidnies, and more by the glands of the skin, which gives them a very strong and disagreeable odour."[54]

Jefferson's aesthetic sensibility soon segued revealingly into unconscious uneasiness about the unknowability of enslaved people: "Are not the fine mixtures of red and white, the expressions of every passion by greater or less suffusions of colour in the one, preferable to that eternal monotony, which reigns in the countenances, that immoveable veil of black which covers all the emotions of the other race?" The enslaved of course had to hide their true feelings from their enslavers, an opacity that Jefferson and others often self-reassuringly mistook for stupidity.[55]

And Jefferson soon indeed moved on to intellectual judgements. "They seem to require less sleep," he observed, so that "a black, after hard labour through the day, will be induced by the slightest amusements to sit up till midnight, or later, though knowing he must be out with the first dawn of the morning." And "They are at least as brave [as whites], and more adventuresome. But this may perhaps proceed from a want of forethought, which prevents their seeing a danger till it be present ..." And "Comparing them by their faculties of memory, reason, and imagination, it appears to me, that in memory they are equal to the whites; in reason much inferior, as think one could scarcely be found capable of tracing and comprehending the investigations of Euclid; and that in imagination they are dull, tasteless, and anomalous."[56]

But at least they have rhythm: "In music they are more generally gifted than the whites with accurate ears fortune and time, and they have been found capable of imagining a small catch." Although "Whether they will be equal to the composition of a more extensive run of melody, or of complicated harmony, is yet to be proved."[57]

Jefferson also felt that black people's distinctions included emotional and moral inferiority: "They are more ardent after their female: but love seems with them to be more an eager desire, than a tender delicate mixture of sentiment and sensation. Their griefs are transient," he continued: "Those numberless afflictions, which render it doubtful whether heaven has given life to us in mercy or in wrath, are less felt, and sooner forgotten with them. In general, their existence appears to participate more of sensation than reflection."[58]

Jefferson ruled out environment as the cause of all this. "Many millions of them have been brought to, and born in America," he wrote, and "many have been so situated, that they might have availed themselves of the conversation of their masters." And "Some have been liberally educated," he added, optimistically. But "never yet," Jefferson claimed, "could I find that a black had uttered a thought above the level of plain narration; never see even an elementary trait, of painting or sculpture." Jefferson reduced the ample evidence there actually was of black intellectual achievement and equality despite adversity to mere sentimentality: "Religion indeed has produced a Phyllis Whately, but it could not produce a poet," he said, of an African-born woman enslaved in Massachusetts who nevertheless became one of early America's great artists in the English language. "The compositions published under her name are below the dignity of criticism," he said, thereby handily exempting himself from responsibility for justifying his opinion. And "Ignatius Sancho," another one-time slave who, despite these circumstances, became an abolitionist and political commentator, "has approached nearer to merit in composition; yet his letters do more honour to the heart than the head ..." His "imagination is wild and extravagant, escapes incessantly from every restraint of reason and taste." Jefferson also implied that Sancho's writings were authored by someone else, as he did with Wheatley; a common accusation aimed at assailing not only the writers themselves, but also the literary and intellectual ability of all black people.[59]

If black people's "inferiority is not the effect merely of their condition of life," then it followed for Jefferson that it must be inherent and racial in origin. Early in this essay he noted: "Whether the black of the negro resides in the reticular membrane between the skin and scarf-skin, or in the scarf-skin itself; whether it proceeds from the colour of the blood, the colour of the bile, or from that of some other secretion, the difference is fixed in nature"—and we see immediately the unspoken assumption that blackness is abnormal and needs explaining while whiteness isn't and doesn't. He later expressed some uncertainty about precisely what was "fixed in nature," because black people "have never yet been viewed by us as subjects of natural history." And so, he wrote, "I advance it therefore as a suspicion only, that the blacks, whether originally a distinct race, or made distinct by time and circumstances, are inferior to the whites in the endowments both of body and mind. It is not against experience to suppose, that different species of the same genus, or varieties of the same species, may possess different qualifications." He thus questioned the then prevailing scientific and religious orthodoxies on the common origins of humankind, though he failed to furnish a final answer.[60]

Jefferson was certain though that these distinctions meant there should be no racial mixing: "Will not a lover of natural history then, one who views the gradations in all the races of animals with the eye of philosophy, excuse an effort to keep those in the department of man as distinct as nature has formed them?" And Jefferson's views on race and racial mixing meant that emancipation was for him impossible without expatriation. "This unfortunate difference of colour, and perhaps of faculty," he explained,

is a powerful obstacle to the emancipation of these people. Many of their advocates, while they wish to vindicate the liberty of human nature, are anxious also to preserve its dignity and beauty. Some of these, embarrassed by the question 'What further is to be done with them?' join themselves in opposition with those who are actuated by sordid avarice only. Among the Romans emancipation required but one effort. The slave, when made free, might mix with, without staining the blood of his master. But with us a second is necessary, unknown to history. When freed, he is to be removed beyond the reach of mixture.[61]

An American family

Except that Thomas Jefferson was really not so certain. In 1802, early in the first term of his presidency, a journalist named James Callender published the rumor that Jefferson had had children with a slave whom Callender called "dusky Sally." Sarah or "Sally" Hemings was born around 1773, the sixth daughter of a slave named Betty Hemings, and of John Wayles, her owner and Jefferson's father-in-law. She was therefore the half-sister of Martha Jefferson, who died in 1783 and left Thomas a widower. Sally Hemings was first pregnant in 1789, but the child died either in or shortly after her return from Paris, where she had joined her master while he was serving as American minister to France. There is no record of the infant's name. She had two other children who also died young. Harriet, who was born on October 3, 1795, and died on December 7, 1797, and another girl, possibly called Thenia, who was born and died in 1799. She also had four children who lived to adulthood. William, better known as Beverley, was born on April 1, 1798, and lived to at least 1873. Then Harriet, May 22, 1801, to at least 1863, Madison, January 19, 1805 to 1877, and Eston, May 21, 1808 to 1856.[62]

The fact that Callender was a known "scandalmonger" provided a pretext for many people for many years for denying Thomas Jefferson's paternity of Sally Hemings's children. As did the fact that Callender was refused a position as postmaster in the Jefferson administration and may have therefore borne a grudge against the president. Also, Jefferson's eldest daughter denied that her father was at Monticello when Hemings became pregnant with the children conceived there. And Jefferson's recorded opposition to racial mixing made many think it impossible that he was personally involved in any such thing, as if he could ever have contradicted himself.

However. Jefferson freed very few of his slaves, and the only ones he freed were closely connected to Sally Hemings. He liberated Sally's brothers James and Robert during his life time. He manumitted her other brother John in his Will, and arranged for her sons Madison and Eston to be apprenticed to John until they reached twenty-one, at which age they would be freed. He also freed two of Sally's nephews, Joseph Fossett and Burwell Colbert. His daughter Martha did not technically manumit Sally Hemings, but gave her "her time" after her father's death, and she went to live with Madison and Eston in Charlottesville until she died in 1835.

Jefferson's other slaves, almost 130 people in all at the time he died, did not receive such special treatment. Many were auctioned after Jefferson's death to pay off his debts, and all remained enslaved for the rest of their lives. The two other surviving children of Sally Hemings had already freed themselves, though. Beverley and Harriet ran away from Monticello as young adults in 1823. Jefferson had given his overseer $50 to give to Harriet, and neighborhood rumor had it that he had thus colluded in their escape to save leaving a public record of his liberating them, with all the questions that would raise. Or, in fact, answer.

The rumors never fully disappeared, but Madison Hemings resoundingly revived them in 1873 by telling the story of his paternity to journalist S. F. Wetmore, who published it in Ohio's *Pike County Republican*. The publication of Thomas Jefferson's Farm Book in 1953 confirmed that, contrary to Martha Jefferson-Randolph's claims, her father was in fact at Monticello nine months before the births of Sally Hemings's children, except the one in Paris, though it had never been possible to deny their presence together in the French capital.

When the historian Fawn Brodie published her findings about Thomas Jefferson's fatherhood of Sally Hemings's children in 1974, they were panned by many established historians. But when another historian and legal scholar, Annette Gordon-Reed, published hers in *Thomas Jefferson and Sally Hemings: An American Controversy* in 1997, they were much better received, and Gordon-Reed's *The Hemingses of Monticello: An American Family* won the Pulitzer Prize for History in 2009. In the same years that interracial relationships became more widely accepted in the United States, it seems that its long-term historical reality became easier to acknowledge.[63]

In any case, for most remaining doubters the clincher came via science. In 1998, DNA tests were done on an unnamed white descendant of Field Jefferson (Thomas's uncle, as

Thomas has no direct white male descendants and no one wanted to exhume the man himself), and a black descendant of Eston Hemings. These tests showed in both parties the presence of a K2 haplotype, common in Egypt but rare in people of either North European or West African descent. It was absent from the DNA of the descendants of Peter Carr and others previously rumored to be responsible for the physical resemblance of Hemingses and Jeffersons. In other words, Jefferson all but certainly fathered Eston Hemings and so most probably all of Sally Hemings's children. No one can deny that Jefferson said what he said about black people and about racial mixing, but nor can anyone sensibly deny that he had black children anyway.

Despite his sexual attraction to and possible personal affection for Sally Hemings, Thomas Jefferson persisted in insisting on expatriation as a condition of emancipation for African Americans, and for the same reasons that he expressed in the 1780s. As he wrote in his brief *Autobiography* forty years later: "Nothing is more certainly written in the book of fate than that these people are to be free. Nor is it less certain that the two races, equally free, cannot live in the same government. Nature, habit, opinion has drawn indelible lines of distinction between them." Jefferson therefore suggested at various points in his life that if slaves were shipped to Africa or the Caribbean before the age of sexual reproduction, then the black population of the United States would slowly die off. Slowly enough for new, white laborers to replace them and to cover the costs of transportation of former slaves and of compensation that Jefferson believed would be owed their former owners. The money would be raised from proceeds from sales of western lands ceded by the states to the federal government.[64]

In the postrevolutionary era, colonization was commonly considered a possible solution to the problem of slavery and the perceived problem of a multi-racial society. Indeed, thousands of African Americans voluntarily made new lives for themselves in places like Sierra Leone and Liberia, despite the racism on which such schemes were predicated, or in many cases to escape from it. Yet colonization was simply too costly, too impractical, and too unpopular among too many slaveholders and black Americans to make more than a small mark on the edifice of enslavement.

Besides, many African Americans had other ideas for securing liberation, often based on the principles of America's Declaration of Independence. This is where we can see how, whatever Jefferson said or others thought, those principles did apply to black people—because black people applied them to themselves. The examples below therefore provide powerful proof for Barack Obama's claims about the common and empowering nature of the creed.

Liberty

Slaves had fought for freedom in various ways throughout the colonial period of American history. There were insurrections by individuals and groups on slave ships sailing from Africa to America, and there were notable uprisings in the form of a rebellion in

New York City in 1712, an apparent conspiracy there in 1741, and the Stono Rebellion in South Carolina in 1739. Slaves also absconded from their masters individually and in groups, both temporarily and in bids for permanent liberation. And enslaved people otherwise disrupted the economic and social arrangements that oppressed them. When direct resistance and rebellion weren't desirable or doable due to the dangers or impossibilities involved, slaves still formed communities and cultures and acted in other ways that asserted their humanity in spite of their inhuman treatment. In the later eighteenth century, though, and especially in the era of the American Revolution, a kind of African American acculturation encouraged the increasing adoption of another means of liberation, one appropriating the ideas of the enslavers. The ideas we find in the Declaration of Independence.[65]

On April 20, 1773, for example, a petition appeared before the General Court of Massachusetts that said "Sir, The efforts made by the legislative of this province in their last sessions to free themselves from slavery, gave us, who are in that deplorable state, a high degree of satisfaction." The petition then continued with a striking assertiveness, similar to that of American revolutionary petitions to King George III, demanding that their masters live up to their own standards with regard to others: "We expect great things from men who have made such a noble stand against the designs of their fellow-men to enslave them. We cannot but wish and hope Sir, that you will have the same grand object, we mean civil and religious liberty, in view in your next session. The divine spirit of freedom, seems to fire every humane breast on this continent." The named petitioners were Peter Bestes, Sambo Freeman, Felix Holbrook, Chester Joie, and they proceeded to request the freedom to leave America to settle in Africa.[66]

The next year, and still two years before Independence, "The Petition of a Grate Number of Blackes of this Province who by divine permission are held in a state of Slavery within the bowels of a free and christian Country" stated that "we have in common with all other men a naturel right to our freedoms without Being depriv'd of them by our fellow men as we are a freeborn Pepel and have never forfeited this Blessing by aney compact or agreement whatever." After this enunciation of natural rights and social contract theory, one as well-informed as any ever given by a free white man, the document described the miseries of the slave trade and slavery itself before requesting consideration of an "act of the legislative to be pessed that we may obtain our Natural right our freedoms and our children be set a lebety at the yeare of twenty one for whoues sekes more petequeley your Petitioners is in Duty ever to pray."[67]

This particular petition was addressed "To his Excellency Thomas Gage Esq. Captain General and Governor in Chief in and over this Province" as well as "To the Honourable his Majestys Council and the Honourable House of Representatives in General Court assembled May 25, 1774." That is, to the British military governor who had assumed power after the Boston Tea Party, and just five days after Parliament had annulled the 1691 Massachusetts charter and replaced it with much more authoritarian government. The willingness of the enslaved to petition British authorities for their freedom reminds us that they would take whatever side in the imperial dispute would offer them the best chance of what they wanted most: their own liberty.

Indeed in late 1775 and early 1776 several thousand slaves took up Virginia Governor Dunmore's invitation to gain their freedom by joining his "Ethiopian Regiment" to fight against revolting white Virginians, and not just adult male slaves of rebels who Dunmore invited but others also ran to what they hoped was a British army of liberation. Many thousands more fought with British forces later, or else acted as auxiliaries, or simply used the disruptions of wartime to escape enslavement. The Patriots had to open up in response to this black Loyalism, and by the end of the War of Independence some 9,000 black people had served in the Continental army and navy, state militias, and on privateers on the seas, with countless others again serving as auxiliaries.

But wherever these bids for liberty took individuals, they were driven by the radical ideas released in revolution. "The petition of A Great Number of Blackes detained in a State of slavery in the Bowels of a free & Christian Country" was submitted to the postindependence legislature "for the State of Massachusitte Bay" on January 13, 1777, six months on from the Declaration of Independence. It "Humbly shuwith that your Petitioners apprehend that thay have in Common with all other men a Natural and Unaliable Right to that freedom which the Grat Parent of the Unavers hath Bestowed equalley on all menkind and which they have Never forfuted by any Compact or agreement whatever." This petition proceeded to echo the complaints of the one of 1774 against the slave trade and slavery, and then expressed "Astonishment that It has Never Bin Consirdered that Every Principle from which Amarica has Acted in the Cours of their unhappy Dificultes with Great Briton Pleads Stronger than A thousand arguments in favowrs of your petioners". The petition therefore asked for "an act of the Legislatur to be past Wherby they may be Restored to the Enjoyments of that which is the Naturel Right of all men—and their Children who wher Born in this Land of Liberty may not be heald as Slaves after they arrive at the age of twenty one years so may the Inhabitance of this Stats No longer chargeable with the inconsistancey of acting themselves the part which they condem and oppose in others Be prospered in their present Glorious struggle for Liberty and have those Blessing to them, &c."[68]

The African American revolution within the American Revolution was not always seen sympathetically by whites. When South Carolinian Sons of Liberty marched in the streets of Charleston protesting the 1765 Stamp Act with chants of "Liberty, Liberty," they were surprised to find themselves joined by slaves singing the same thing. So surprised indeed that they locked the city down for a week. But things were sometimes different elsewhere. In a pamphlet entitled *The Rights of the British Colonies Asserted and Proved*, published as early as 1764, after the passing of the Sugar Act and with the forthcoming Stamp Act already announced and angrily anticipated, James Otis of Massachusetts noted: "The colonists are by the law of nature freeborn, as indeed all men are, white or black." So, he continued:

Does it follow that 'tis right to enslave a man because he is black? Will short curled hair like wool instead of Christian hair, as tis called by those whose hearts are as hard as the nether millstone, help the argument? Can any logical inference in favour of slavery be drawn from a flat nose, or a long or short face? Nothing better can be said in favour of a trade that is the most shocking violation of the law of nature, has a direct tendency to diminish the idea of the inestimable value of liberty, and makes every dealer in it a tyrant ... It is a clear truth that those who barter away other men's liberty will soon care little for their own.[69]

Where the perfection begins

It is not surprising then that in Massachusetts black and white people came together in ways that illustrate Barack Obama's belief in a history of concerted action to advance the common creed, in this instance to end enslavement there. At the end of "A More Perfect Union," Obama told the story of Ashley Baia of Florence, South Carolina. After Ashley's mother contracted cancer and lost her job and therefore health care, the then nine-year-old girl ate mustard and relish sandwiches to save money for medical bills. And later, rather than blame others in similar circumstances for her problems, she became a community organizer and political campaigner to help alleviate other people's hardships, irrespective of race. Asking members in her group why they were supporting Obama's 2008 presidential campaign, one "elderly black man" replied, "I am here because of Ashley." That unity across race, gender, and age, Obama said, "is where the perfection begins."[70]

There are similar stories from earlier times of people uniting idealistically for the betterment of all, and one of them involves another Ashley from another age. John Ashley was a Yale-educated lawyer, landowner, businessman, and patriot of Sheffield, Massachusetts, whose house may have been the scene of the drafting of the Sheffield Revolves, one of many local initiatives that inspired the Second Continental Congress to declare independence in 1776. In 1780, Ashley's slave "Bett" heard the words of the new Massachusetts Constitution read out in the public square and was struck by the phrase: "All men are born free and equal, and have certain natural, essential, and unalienable rights; among which may be reckoned the right of enjoying and defending their lives and liberties; that of acquiring, possessing, and protecting property; in fine, that of seeking and obtaining their safety and happiness." Bett was probably perfectly familiar with these ideas already, but once she knew they were written into the state Constitution she sensed a legal opportunity. She subsequently supposedly told the lawyer Theodore Sedgwick that "I heard that paper read yesterday, that says, all men are created equal, and that every man has a right to freedom. I'm not a dumb critter; won't the law give me my freedom?"[71]

Theodore Sedgwick took on her cause and that of another Ashley slave named Brom. The case came before the County Court of Common Pleas in Great Barrington in August 1781, where Sedgwick and his assistant Tapping Reeve argued that the Constitutional provision that "all men are born free and equal" effectively abolished enslavement in Massachusetts. The court freed both Brom and Bett and awarded them each 30 shillings compensation for the unpaid labor they'd performed in the past. Ashley subsequently offered Bett live-in work for wages, but she was unwilling to work where she'd once been enslaved and had been beaten with a shovel, and she kept her arm uncovered for all to see the scar she sustained. Instead, she lived in her own house in Stockbridge and went to work for the Sedgwicks, who called her "Mum Bett," although she adopted the legal name Elizabeth Freeman. Legend has it that she once said that "any time while I was a slave, if one minute's freedom had been offered to me, and I had been told I must die at the end of that minute, I would have taken it—just to stand one minute on God's airth a free woman—I would."

Elizabeth Freeman's case did not end enslavement in Massachusetts, however. Not quite, anyway. The jury found that "Brom & Bett are not, nor were they at the time of the purchase of the original writ the legal Negro of the said John Ashley." In other words, they were freed on the grounds of a technical problem with Ashley's ownership, rather than because slavery itself was inconsistent with the law. Yet the case was cited in a subsequent and more directly consequential legal action.

Quock Walker, or Kwaku Walker in the form probably given him by his Ghanaian parents, was born enslaved in 1753. His master James Caldwell promised him his freedom when he reached the age of twenty-five, and when Caldwell died his widow repeated the pledge but with the age of manumission reduced to twenty-one. Her new husband Nathaniel Jennison reneged on this agreement, however, so in 1781 Walker took refuge on the farm of Seth and John Caldwell, brothers of the late James. Jennison recaptured Walker and beat him as a punishment for absconding. Walker then sought legal redress against Jennison, while Jennison sought the same against the Caldwells for stealing his property. On June 12, 1781, the Worcester County Court of Common Pleas heard and ruled in the two cases. In *Jennison v. Caldwell* it awarded Jennison £25 for "deprivation of the benefit of his servant, Walker." But in *Walker v. Jennison*, for assault and battery, the Court awarded Walker £50 damages and freed him under the provisions of the Massachusetts Constitution. On appeal, *Walker v. Jennison* was upheld and *Jennison v. Caldwell* overturned on the grounds that Walker was a free man.

The above were civil cases, but the Massachusetts Attorney General brought public charges of assault and battery in the case of *Commonwealth v. Jennison* in 1783. The state's Chief Justice William Cushing said the following in his charge to the jury:

As to the doctrine of slavery and the right of Christians to hold Africans in perpetual servitude, and sell and treat them as we do our horses and cattle, that (it is true) has been heretofore countenanced by the Province Laws formerly, but nowhere is it expressly enacted or established. It has been a usage—a usage which took its origin from the practice of some of the European nations, and the regulations of British government respecting the then Colonies, for the benefit of trade and wealth. But whatever sentiments have formerly prevailed in this particular or slid in upon us by the example of others, a different idea has taken place with the people of America, more favorable to the natural rights of mankind, and to that natural, innate desire of Liberty, with which Heaven (without regard to color, complexion, or shape of noses—features) has inspired all the human race. And upon this ground our Constitution of Government, by which the people of this Commonwealth have solemnly bound themselves, sets out with declaring that all men are born free and equal—and that every subject is entitled to liberty, and to have it guarded by the laws, as well as life and property—and in short is totally repugnant to the idea of being born slaves. This being the case, I think the idea of slavery is inconsistent with our own conduct and Constitution; and there can be no such thing as perpetual servitude of a rational creature, unless his liberty is forfeited by some criminal conduct or given up by personal consent or contract.[72]

Cushing's words did not formally abolish slavery in Massachusetts, but when a state's Chief Justice says that enslavement "is inconsistent with our own conduct and Constitution" then basically it's all over. The power of the state was always essential to the coercion required to enslave people, and so the suddenly disempowered slaveholders of Massachusetts had little choice but to free their enslaved people in the subsequent years. The census of 1790 recorded no slaves in the state of Massachusetts. We'll briefly return to what is commonly called the Quock Walker Case in the next chapter, when discussing why the United States federal Constitution does not say that "all men are created equal" or that they have "unalienable rights to life, liberty, and the pursuit of happiness."

The end of enslavement was similarly engendered judicially in New Hampshire the following year. The other northern states abolished slavery legislatively. Pennsylvania had already done so in 1780, then Rhode Island and Connecticut followed in 1784, and New York in 1799 and New Jersey in 1804—both of the latter symbolically directing that their emancipation laws take effect on July 4 of those years. Slavery was usually abolished only gradually, though, with slaves born after a certain date to be freed when they reached a certain age, so that in 1810 a quarter of northern African Americans were still enslaved. But the passing of time and new immediate and final abolition laws in the 1820s meant that slavery was all but eradicated from the northern states by the 1830s. The 1777 interdiction of enslavement in the constitution of Vermont (which separated from New York before joining the Union in 1791), and in the territories that would later become Ohio, Indiana, Illinois, Michigan, Wisconsin, and part of Minnesota in the Northwest Ordnance ten years later, completed the First Emancipation.[73]

The pursuit of happiness

But only the First Emancipation. For at the same time that slavery disappeared in the North it went from strength to strength in the South. Tobacco cultivation expanded rapidly with the spread of settlement from the Chesapeake into what became the states of Kentucky in 1792 and Tennessee in 1796, and slavery with it. But it was above all else the invention of the cotton gin in 1793 that doomed new generations of African Americans to enslavement by rendering economically viable the cultivation of long-staple or inland cotton. By 1800 there were a million slaves in the United States, by 1830 there were two million, and by 1860 there were four million.

Yet, for Barack Obama, slavery was already done for because of the very founding of the United States. The ideas of equality and liberty elaborated abstractly in early modern Europe were given substance when transformed into a component of American national identity by the Declaration of Independence—a "common creed" as Obama calls it, reflecting what he sees as its quasi-religious moral and ideological imperative. The creed gained even greater energy and agency when codified at least implicitly in the nation's Constitution. Even so, it would take a civil war to eradicate enslavement, a longer struggle still to eliminate segregation, and the battle to make black lives matter equally in custom as well as in law goes on to this day.[74]

So although Barack Obama's story of the progress of the "common creed" is ultimately optimistic, it isn't starry-eyed and unrealistic. The Declaration of Independence was the "starting point" of the American story, but only the "starting point." As Obama says, "a declaration is not a government; a creed is not enough." The next chapter of this book is therefore about how, in Barack Obama's view, the Declaration was "made real" and the Union made "more perfect" by the establishment at least implicitly of the principles of equality, liberty, and the pursuit of happiness as "the foundation of our government." This time in an actual Constitution. And the chapters after that one are about how for Obama the "more perfect union" of 1787 needed to be and eventually was made more perfect still.[75]

CHAPTER 3
THE FOUNDATION OF OUR GOVERNMENT:
THE CONSTITUTION AND THE NEW NATION

The foundation of our government

"WE HOLD THESE truths to be self-evident, that all men are Created equal, that they are endowed by their Creator with certain unalienable Rights, that among these are Life, Liberty, and the pursuit of Happiness." Barack Obama describes these words from the Declaration of Independence as "the foundation of our government." In some respects this claim is true. As a political action rather just a random announcement of abstract principles, the Declaration of Independence created a national polity based on a particular political philosophy, which certainly seems like a foundation of government of some sort.[1]

And yet. These words do not appear in the United States Constitution, the document that defines the nation's system of government and fundamental law. Barack Obama knows this, of course, but believes nonetheless that the spirit of the Declaration inhabits the Constitution. Indeed in calling the Declaration "the foundation of our government," Obama is echoing the words and intentions of many of those most responsible for the Declaration's production and distribution. The Virginia Declaration of Rights, authored by George Mason and adopted on June 12, 1776, and which Thomas Jefferson had to hand as he wrote the Declaration of Independence, described its contents as "the basis and foundation of government" before going on to state first and foremost that "all men are by nature equally free and independent and have certain inherent rights, of which, when they enter into a state of society, they cannot, by any compact, deprive or divest their posterity; namely, the enjoyment of life and liberty, with the means of acquiring and possessing property, and pursuing and obtaining happiness and safety." And just two days after the adoption of the Declaration of Independence in Philadelphia, and over a decade before the Constitution was drafted, the president of the Second Continental Congress, John Hancock, wrote in a letter to state legislators that the Declaration would be "the Ground & Foundation of a future Government."[2]

It nonetheless matters that the explicit enunciations of equality and liberty we find in the Declaration are absent from the Constitution. Had they been present, American history might have been very different. In the last chapter we saw how in August 1781 a slave named Elizabeth Freeman of Massachusetts along with a fellow slave named Brom sued for their freedom on the basis of the state Constitution's assurances that "all men are born free and equal, and have certain natural, essential, and unalienable rights; among which may be reckoned the right of enjoying and defending their lives and liberties; that of acquiring, possessing, and protecting property; in fine, that of seeking and obtaining their safety and happiness." In the event they were freed thanks to technical problems with John Ashley's ownership. But, confronted with the same arguments two years later, Chief Justice William Cushing told the jury in the subsequent Quock Walker case that the Massachusetts "Constitution of Government … sets out with declaring that all men are born free and equal—and that every subject is entitled to liberty, and to have it guarded by the laws, as well as life and property—and in short is totally repugnant to the idea of being born slaves" and so slavery was "inconsistent with our own conduct and Constitution …" Not only Quock Walker, but all his fellow slaves in the state of Massachusetts were subsequently freed.[3]

There was no way the southern delegates at the national Constitutional Convention six years later were going to risk that happening throughout the United States, and the other delegates knew it. Too few wished to abolish enslavement, at least right away or at the cost of not agreeing a new government and new laws. The delegates therefore never seriously discussed whether to write that all men are created equal and have natural rights to life, liberty, and the pursuit of happiness explicitly into the federal Constitution. It simply wasn't going to happen.[4]

Stained by this nation's original sin

This omission was one of the ways in which the US Constitution guaranteed that slavery would survive, for a while anyway. But only one of the ways. Barack Obama concedes that the Constitution was "ultimately unfinished," that "it was stained by this nation's original sin of slavery, a question that divided the colonies and brought the convention to a stalemate until the founders chose to allow the slave trade to continue for at least twenty more years, and to leave any final resolution to future generations." Indeed, many delegates, even many southern ones, hoped that future generations would eventually eliminate enslavement. And they provided for the abolition of the slave trade, seen by some as a step toward emancipation, but only after allowing the transatlantic trafficking of human beings to continue for twenty more years. Individual states abolished the slave trade to their own jurisdictions in the meantime anyway, although South Carolina and Georgia reopened it to theirs in the last few years before the federal ban came into effect from the first day of 1808.[5]

But the Slave Trade Clause was only one of three that directly supported slavery in some way. And, in providing for at least for the possible eventual end of the slave trade, this clause was the least un-benign of them. There was also a Fugitive Slave Clause that stated that runaways shall not be freed but shall instead be "delivered up" to those to whom their "Service or Labour may be due." And another clause allowed that "Representatives and direct Taxes shall be apportioned among the several States which may be included within this Union, according to their respective Numbers," including the "whole Number of free Persons" and "three fifths of all other Persons." Which of course greatly enhanced those slaves' owners' numbers and power in the House of Representatives and in turn in the presidential Electoral College.

Perhaps this is why there is another Obamian elision at the beginning of "A More Perfect Union," the career-saving oration Obama made in Philadelphia in March 2008. He opened the speech with some of the Constitution's opening words: "WE THE PEOPLE, in order to form a more perfect union." A full quotation would have read: "WE THE PEOPLE of the United States, in order to form a more perfect union." It is possible that Obama redacted the words "of the United States" in order to save time— all of the two or three seconds they would have added to an almost forty minute speech. So perhaps he simply preferred the cadence of the shortened sentence. But neither of these possibilities is incompatible with him wishing to subtly signal that the "WE THE PEOPLE" that the Constitution refers to were not *all* the people of the United States. That most African Americans were slaves and were therefore by definition not citizens, legally property rather than people, and subject to the laws the United States imposed, but not participants in their making or beneficiaries of the rights and protections they guaranteed. That in 1787 therefore African Americans were *in* the United States but not *of* the United States. As Obama says, the Constitution was "unfinished" and so, intentionally or not, it's apt that his quotation of it is also unfinished.[6]

We'll explore slavery in relation to the Constitution even further in the next chapter. In this one, though, we examine Barack Obama's contentions in "A More Perfect Union" that, notwithstanding all of the above, the group of men in Philadelphia "launched America's improbable experiment in democracy." And indeed that "the answer to the slavery question was already embedded within our Constitution—a Constitution that had at is very core the ideal of equal citizenship under the law; a Constitution that promised its people liberty, and justice, and a union that could be and should be perfected over time."[7]

But first, how did the Constitution come into being?

Finally made real

If you've been reading this book from the beginning then you'll already be very familiar with the following phrase from Barack Obama's "A More Perfect Union" speech of March 2008: "Farmers and scholars; statesmen and patriots, who had traveled across an ocean to escape tyranny and persecution, finally made real their declaration of independence at a Philadelphia convention that lasted through the spring of 1787." I've discussed in previous chapters how the Philadelphia Convention happened in the summer of 1787 rather than "the spring," as Obama maintained in a metaphorical suggestion of new beginnings. Also, how the elision of those who "had traveled across an ocean to escape tyranny and persecution" with those who "finally made real their declaration of independence at a Philadelphia convention" collapses the time between the founding of the colonies and the founding of the country and thereby creates a mutually valorizing conflation of the founding and founders of each and an enhanced sense of temporal continuity of American pursuits of happiness and liberty. And finally how the insinuation of the unity and even oneness of the farmers and the scholars and the statesmen and the patriots implies that the American Revolution was fundamentally egalitarian and democratic.[8]

But now it's time to examine the words "finally made real," as when "a group of men … finally made real their declaration of independence" at the Philadelphia Convention. As perhaps suggested by that "finally," there's a long and turbulent time between the declaring of independence in 1776 and the drafting of the Constitution in 1787, its ratification in 1788, and its implementation in 1789. Even longer and more turbulent if we consider the constitution-making process as continuing to the adoption of the Bill of Rights, the first ten amendments of the Constitution, finally included in the law of the land in December 1791.[9]

Yet there's another Obamian conflation to consider here that once again elides what are actually quite different events. The conflation in this instance is of the men of the Second Continental Congress who declared independence in 1776 with those who drafted the Constitution in 1787. Implying that they were "a group" of men who made "their" Declaration of Independence "real" in the form of the Constitution in turn infers the ideological concordance of the two different documents, a confluence even more heavily hinted at by the aforementioned idea that the Declaration's proclamations on equality, liberty, and the pursuit of happiness form the "foundation of our government." In fact, however, of the fifty-six men who signed the Declaration of Independence, only eight were among the fifty-five delegates at the Constitutional Convention. Of those eight, furthermore, two declined to sign the Constitution—Elbridge Gerry of Massachusetts and George Wythe of Virginia were among sixteen in total who couldn't consent to the Constitutional Convention's conclusions.

And, furthermore, some of the most famous men attending one event were absent from the other. John Adams and Thomas Jefferson were in Philadelphia in 1776, but were respectively in London and Paris as ministers to England and France in 1787. George Washington presided over the Constitutional Convention, but was otherwise occupied as Commander-in-Chief of the Continental Army in 1776. Alexander Hamilton and James Madison, the main movers of events in 1787, were only respectively twenty-one and twenty-five years old and were not members of the Continental Congress in 1776. Then there was John Dickinson, who was at the Second Continental Congress but hoped for reconciliation and refused to sign the Declaration in 1776, and who was at the Convention in 1787, but missed the later sessions and didn't sign the Constitution due to illness, though he did approve it and got his fellow delegate George Read to sign it for him. Even an entire state was present for one event but absent from the other, as Rhode Island refused to send any delegates to the Constitutional Convention.

Yet Barack Obama's other contentions—that the Declaration was "our starting point as Americans" and that it contains the country's "common creed,"—imply that the document belonged in a wider sense to all Americans. That implication conforms in fact to Danielle Allen's contention that the Declaration represented a kind of "democratic writing." In other words, it wasn't authored so much by Thomas Jefferson, or even the

Committee of Five, or even the Continental Congress in 1776, as by the American people more generally or as a whole. Indeed, as we saw in the previous chapter, Jefferson himself described his work as an "expression of the American mind." And, as we also saw in Chapter 2, many enslaved African Americans believed its words applied equally to them, whatever others might have thought. In these respects, the men of the Convention of 1787 also owned the Declaration every bit as much as those of the Congress of 1776, whether they'd been among them or not. So in this very real sense it was "their" Declaration that they "made real" in Philadelphia. No more than anyone else's, but no less so either.[10]

But what exactly does "made real" mean? On one level it means bringing the states more closely together by forming a federal union. The fact that the Constitution intended to make that union "more perfect" implied that some kind of union, albeit a less perfect one, already existed. And indeed the soon-to-be founders of the country had already formed a union of the colonies. The First Continental Congress's Continental Association of October 20, 1774, created "committees of correspondence and inspection" to enforce the economic boycott of Britain enacted in response to the Intolerable Acts. These organizations evolved into "committees of safety" that mobilized for defense as the likelihood of war loomed ever more. In other words, the Congress created an intercolonial union of varying institutions with quasi-governmental authority, including certain legislative, executive, administrative, and policing powers.

A sense of independence in the individual colonies led to Congress's rejection of Joseph Galloway's more formal Plan of Union in 1774 and of Benjamin Franklin's suggestion of discussion of unification in 1775. However, when Congress called for a day of fasting on June 7, 1775, it used the term "United Colonies" for the first time, and subsequently did so in other official documents directing its actions; actions that were again essentially governmental, such as commissioning George Washington as commander of its Continental Army. And of course the next year this intercolonial body declared independence on behalf of all thirteen colonies and in so doing expressly created the *United* States.

In declaring independence, the Second Continental Congress also became the first government of the United States, instantiating itself as a polity that administered the United States for nearly five years. The growing prospect of independence, however, inspired a sense among many that a future free nation would need a more formally constituted form of government. So on June 12, 1776, just five days after the tabling of Richard Henry Lee's independence resolution, Congress appointed a committee of thirteen, with one member from each colony, that submitted its proposed Articles of Confederation to Congress a month later, ten days after the passing of the Lee Resolution and eight after approval of the Declaration.

Making a more perfect union wasn't easy, though, even at this embryonic stage. Disputes over such difficult issues as determining the number of representatives each state should have in the national government, and the share of the common tax burden each state should shoulder, delayed Congressional approval of the Articles of Confederation until November 15, 1777. They then had to be ratified by each of the states, where similar issues had to be resolved, although further postponement resulted from the refusal of the "landless" states of Delaware, New Jersey, and Maryland to ratify until the "landed" states relinquished their western territorial claims, ones that dated back to their foundings. Virginia, for example, claimed that by its ancient charter its western border was the Pacific coast, but neighboring Marylanders with no such generous territorial provisions were having none of that. Only after the landed states ceded these western land claims to the national government could the Articles of Confederation come into effect, as they finally did on March 1, 1781.

Some already believed, however, that the Articles themselves required revision. The Confederation government comprised little more than a unicameral legislature. There was no independent executive, only a rotating chairmanship of Congress, and no national judiciary. And, above all, the Confederation Congress was subordinate to the states. The Articles indeed defined the United States as a "a firm league of friendship" and a "confederacy," explicitly stating: "Each State retains its sovereignty, freedom and independence, and every power, jurisdiction, and right, which is not by this confederation expressly delegated to the United States, in Congress assembled."[11]

So while Congress was charged with such important tasks as issuing and borrowing money in order to fulfil such weighty responsibilities as maintaining an army and navy, conducting foreign policy, and keeping the domestic peace, it did not have the powers to pursue these purposes effectively. Above all, the Congress had no independent tax-raising powers. It could requisition money from the states, but had no means of coercing the cash from its constitutional superiors. Thus, while the United States won its war for independence, for example, it could not honor its obligations to repay prewar debts to British merchants or compensate Loyalists for confiscated property. The United States also defaulted on its debts to France, the Netherlands, and Spain. In 1786 the latter nation blocked American access to the Mississippi River and the port of New Orleans. Nor could the United States force Britain to keep its Treaty of Paris promises to withdraw its troops from the Northwest Territories or allow free fishing rights in Canadian waters and free trade with the Caribbean islands.

The need for a more perfect union was perceived as even more urgent due to internal issues. A near mutiny of the army over pay, for example, was only averted by George Washington's Newburgh Address of March 15, 1783, in which the general decisively affirmed the supremacy of civil over military authority. But there was no guarantee that the United States armed forces would always be led by such a charismatic and uncompromising champion of that principle. And what if states started raising trade tariffs and navigation fees against the citizens of the other states, or disputing borders on land or water, or restricting the movement of each others' citizens? Would they start European-style wars with each other as a consequence? Those were the potential problems resolved by Maryland and Virginia when they agreed joint sovereignty of and free trade over the Potomac River at the Mount Vernon Conference, held at Washington's plantation home in March 1785.

James Madison led the call from Mount Vernon to hold an Annapolis Convention the following year to try to achieve similar accords among all the thirteen states. At that stage, though, by no means all felt much urgency to respond, and only twelve delegates from five states showed up at Mann's Tavern in the Maryland capital between the eleventh and fourteenth of September 1786. The previous month, however, had seen the beginnings of a rebellion, led by Daniel Shays of Massachusetts, by western farmers impoverished by the state's policy of only permitting payment of debts and taxes in hard-to-come-by gold and silver. Though finally suppressed in February 1787, only Virginia offered its militia to assist that of Massachusetts. The shock of Shays's Rebellion meant that many more were willing to heed Alexander Hamilton's Annapolis Resolution calling for a new convention "to devise such further provisions as shall appear ... necessary to render the constitution of the Federal Government adequate to the exigencies of the Union." Fifty-five delegates from all the states except Rhode Island assembled in Philadelphia the following May for precisely that purpose.[12]

But did the statesmen and patriots of 1787 really make "real" their Declaration of Independence of 1776 when they made their "more perfect union"? For some historians the answer to that is an emphatic no. Some indeed have argued since the time of Charles Beard in the early twentieth century that the egalitarian (though unfulfilled and hypocritical) philosophy of the Declaration represented the opposite of the capitalist cabalism that lay behind the crafting of the Constitution. The fact that Alexander Hamilton, the first Treasury Secretary of the subsequent dispensation, used the new Constitution's provisions to enact pro-banking and pro-manufacturing measures in the 1790s offers no support to those who dismiss this idea as mere conspiracy theory.[13]

But that's a matter to return to in Chapter 6. For now, what kind of political system did the Founders in Philadelphia create? And how far does that accord with Barack Obama's conception of "a Constitution that had at its very core the ideal of equal citizenship under the law; a Constitution that promised its people liberty, and justice, and a union that could be and should be perfected over time"? Were the Founders really the founders of what Obama calls "America's improbable experiment in democracy"?[14]

WE THE PEOPLE

There are certainly some decidedly democratic aspects of the American governmental system, even as established in 1787. The most fundamental is the conceptual foundation of the Constitution—the idea that America's new system of government and law was created by "WE THE PEOPLE."

This invocation of popular sovereignty helps us more fully understand Barack Obama's claim that the Declaration of Independence was "made real" in the Constitution. The Declaration is of course famously couched in the terms of Lockean social contract theory, and it virtually quotes John Locke when it says: "Governments are instituted among Men, deriving their just powers from the consent of the governed," and that if "any Form of Government becomes destructive of these ends"—of securing the rights to life, liberty and the pursuit of happiness, and because those rights are "unalienable"—"it is the Right of the People to alter or to abolish it, and to institute new Government, laying its foundation on such principles and organizing its powers in such form, as to them shall seem most likely to effect their Safety and Happiness." If the Declaration itself was therefore an action abolishing an old government, then the drafting of the Constitution was the next action of instituting a new one. And the Founders in 1787 seemed to be following that principle perfectly precisely when they prefaced their Constitution with the words "We the People of the United States, in Order to form a more perfect Union, establish Justice, insure domestic Tranquility, provide for the common defence, promote the general Welfare, and secure the Blessings of Liberty to ourselves and our Posterity, do ordain and establish this Constitution for the United States of America."[15]

Even if the Founders of 1787 were following the logic of their recent forebears in 1776, they were nonetheless adapting to rapidly developing circumstances and newly perceived needs. And their attachment to principle didn't prevent them from engaging in political machinations to achieve particular ends. James Madison, often called "the Father of the Constitution," set the Convention's early course with his reflections on what he thought was wrong with American government at the time, written up as "Vices of the Political System of the United States." The delegates rejected some of the details of what Madison advocated, but accepted his fundamental reformulation of the American union. Madison wanted the national government to have what he called "concurrent jurisdiction" with the states. That is, for a national government to share authority and power with the state governments over American territory and people, rather than being merely a subordinate agent of the states. In other words, for the United States to be a nation, a federation rather than a confederation. This was perhaps, at least in institutional terms, the most fundamental feature of the "more perfect union."[16]

As well as accruing unprecedented authority to the national government, this initiative would defy the orders of the Confederation Congress, which had limited the remit of the Convention to revising but not revolutionizing the governance of the United States. So how could the Convention claim the right to cast aside these instructions? The answer lay in what some states had already done when abandoning old and adopting new constitutions, beginning with Massachusetts in 1780. That is, to conceive the Philadelphia meeting as a "Convention"—a meeting of "the people." That meant the men there conceiving themselves not as mere representatives acting on their own initiatives in the interests of the people. Instead, they had to see themselves as the actual people, or at least as delegates carrying out the will of the people irrespective of their own opinions: another reason why the Constitution begins with the words "We the people of the United States . . ."

Of course the Philadelphia delegates were in some rather important senses not "the people" of the United States, or not all of them at any rate. There were only fifty-five of them there, of whom only thirty-nine eventually approved the Constitution. Moreover, they were selected exclusively from the nation's wealthy white men, a minority group. But in identifying themselves as "We the people" they nonetheless invoked the principle of popular sovereignty as the fountain of American government and fundamental law.

In taking seriously the idea that the Constitution was a product of "the people," Barack Obama can argue that the American nation is the product of a "social contract." Citing the theories of Thomas Hobbes and John Locke, Obama notes that "free people make a bargain to ensure that one man's freedom did not become another man's tyranny; that they would sacrifice individual license to better preserve their liberty. And," he continues, "building on this concept, political theorists writing before the American Revolution concluded that only a democracy could fulfil the need for both freedom and order—a form of government in which those who are governed grant their consent, and the laws constraining liberty are uniform, predictable, and transparent, applying equally to the rulers and the ruled." And on this matter of "equal citizenship," in addition to evoking the authority of "the people," the Constitution also expressly rules out rule by monarchy and aristocracy, constitutional inequalities that still actually exist in some twenty-first-century western democracies.[17]

In all these ways, then, the Founders created what Abraham Lincoln would later call "government of the people," in the sense that it was founded by the people and belonged to the people. And to that extent—and it's a considerable extent—Barack Obama is right to say that the Founders "launched America's improbable experiment in democracy."[18]

A "deliberative democracy"

But that doesn't necessarily mean that the Founders created a "government by the people." Abraham Lincoln's Gettysburg triad encourages us to think of "government of the people, by the people, for the people" as three inseparable things, or even as one single thing, as does Barack Obama's frequent quotation of the famous phrase. The three together furthermore are often seen as defining American democracy. But their predecessors differed on these matters. First, the term "democracy" then signified an "estate," as did "monarchy" and "aristocracy," and not necessarily a system of government. It was therefore perfectly possible and indeed normal back then to believe that while a system of government might incorporate "the democracy," the system itself did not necessarily have to be democratic. More likely, moreover, a system that incorporated "the democracy" would be representational or "republican" rather than "democratic," for another connotation of "democracy" was the direct rule of the people rather than the representation of them. For many of the Founders indeed, representative rather than democratic government was essential, as the latter equated to or at least could lead to anarchy.

And indeed for quite a few of the Founders in 1787, "mob rule" was a very real and present prospect. Many felt that the democratizing logic of popular protests against British measures from the Stamp Act Riots to the Boston Tea Party, validated by the democratic demotic of Thomas Paine's *Common Sense* and even the Declaration of Independence, was unleashing the unruliness that manifested itself in Shays's Rebellion, and it terrified many of them. So as far as some of the Founders were concerned, a government *of* the people could only be *for* the people if it had the power to protect them from the near-inevitable lawlessness of government *by* the people. As Obama indeed acknowledges when he writes that the "Founders recognized that there were seeds of anarchy in the idea of individual freedom, and intoxicating danger in the idea of equality." In here of course inheres the other meaning of the term "government of the people"—that the people not only founded the government, but must also be governed by it.[19]

And so indeed in the Constitution the Founders created a system of government that incorporated "the democracy" in representative form only, and, furthermore, balanced it by governance by their supposed betters. The original Constitution embedded representation, what we today more loosely or broadly call "democracy," in the House of Representatives, with its directly elected congressmen and in our more democratic nowadays congresswomen. Of course there were many among the people who couldn't vote—poor white men who didn't reach the property qualifications that continued to exist in some states until well into the nineteenth century. Also excluded were almost all black men and absolutely all women, white and black (although some women did vote in New Jersey, thanks to a failure to explicitly exclude them, which many women exploited until that door was closed on them in 1808). Again, though, the fact of representation established a principle that could be and was put into practice more perfectly in the fullness of time.

But the Founders did much else besides, much of it specifically designed to counter the will of the people, or more specifically what they commonly called "the confusion of a multitude" and "the tyranny of the majority." They did so via a complex system of separated and diffused powers among different institutions that acted as checks and balances against each other. Barack Obama eloquently expresses the nature and purpose of the separate but interdependent institutions the Constitution created in writing that "Madison's constitutional architecture" included "not only rule of law and representative government, not just a bill of rights, but also the separation of the national government into three coequal branches, a bicameral Congress, and a concept of federalism that preserved authority in state governments, all of it designed to diffuse power, check factions, balance interests, and prevent tyranny by either the few or the many." But exactly how did the Founders form a working system of government while simultaneously doing all this separating and diffusing and checking and balancing?[20]

The first problem the Founders faced after formulating a federation based on popular sovereignty was that of determining how state representation would work in the national government. The Virginia Plan or Large State Plan proposed representation in proportion to a state's population, but members from less populous states objected that their people would be underrepresented. The New Jersey Plan or Small State Plan accordingly advocated one-state-one-vote, but members from more populous states objected that their people would thereby be underrepresented. Both sides had compelling points. The Convention therefore agreed instead the Connecticut or Great Compromise of July 16, creating a bicameral legislature with a number of congressmen in the House of Representatives in proportion to a state's population and two members from each state in the Senate.

This solution to one problem in turn solved others. While the lower house of Congress was designated as the "democratic" chamber, with congressmen elected by the people every two years, senators would be selected by state legislatures every six years (with one-third of them subject to reappointment every two years). Most states subsequently opted for popular election of senators, though this was not constitutionally guaranteed until the adoption of the Sixteenth Amendment in 1913.

The Constitution gave Congress (the House of Representatives and the Senate together) unprecedented powers. Article I, section 8 includes specific powers to raise taxes, regulate trade, print money, raise an army and navy, and to use the militia to suppress domestic insurrections, among many other things. At the end of these "enumerated powers," though, there's a more open-ended one that gives Congress power "to make all laws which shall be necessary and proper for carrying into execution the foregoing powers." As we'll see, this "necessary and proper" clause (also called the "enabling clause" and the "implied powers clause") would later provide the justification for "loose construction"—a permissive interpretation of what the Constitution allows the government to do based on the idea that what is not explicitly forbidden is permitted. As opposed to "strict construction"—a proscriptive interpretation of what the Constitution allows the government to do based on the idea that what is not explicitly permitted is forbidden.

Some of the checking and balancing is achieved by requiring first that all bills pass both Houses of Congress, though each House has special responsibility in accordance with its particular constituency. So, money bills, for example, originate in the House of Representatives, in keeping with the principle of no taxation without representation. Foreign policy matters, on the other hand, belong first and foremost to the supposedly older, wiser, and worldlier heads of the Senate chamber (and the president). The Founders also allowed that the executive branch could check the legislative one by providing for a presidential veto power, and also that the legislature can countercheck the executive by overriding such a veto with a two-thirds majority of both Houses of Congress.

The Senate also has "advice and consent" powers over presidential patronage. The House of Representatives, furthermore, can impeach and the Senate can try a president for "Treason, Bribery, or other high Crimes and Misdemeanors." If found guilty, a president can be removed from office. And in creating Congress in the Constitution's Article I and the presidency in the much less detailed Article II, the Founders expressed an idea of ultimate legislative supremacy over the executive. Certainly, Barack Obama's exercises of presidential powers, though modest by modern standards, went far beyond what the Founders envisioned. Although, as we will soon see, Obama believes the Founders also deliberately and carefully crafted adaptability into their Constitution.

The president is elected every four years, or in fact selected by an Electoral College comprising as many members per state as a state has in Congress (in keeping with the Connecticut Compromise)—another balance against government by the people. Hence, for example, it's perfectly possible for one candidate to win almost three million more popular votes than another and still lose the election. The original intent was to prevent a cynically divisive, habitually mendacious, potentially tyrannous, and certainly dangerous demagogue from ever becoming president of the United States.

Another and later guard against the will of the people came with presidential term limits. There was initially no restriction on the number of terms a president could serve, although George Washington set a precedent of two. No one broke this informal rule until Franklin Delano Roosevelt went for and won a third term in 1940 and then a fourth one in 1944. The two-term limit was finally made law with the adoption of the Twenty-Second Amendment in 1951, a Grand Old Party backlash against a Democratic president whose New Deal eased poor people's suffering and raised most people's prospects in the Great Depression, and who helped defeat nationalism, imperialism, and racist supremacism in World War II.

The Constitution's Article III concerns the third branch of government, the judiciary, and provides yet more checks and balances. It directs that the chief justice and associate justices of the Supreme Court are not elected but nominated by the president and appointed or not on the say-so of the Senate. Judges also serve on "good behavior," insulating them from political or other pressures that might distract them from exclusive devotion to law and justice, theoretically at any rate. The judiciary also checks the powers of the executive and legislative branches of government. Though the Constitution is silent on this, customarily the Supreme Court exercises "judicial review" of the constitutionality (if and when challenged) of executive actions and Acts of Congress—examples of which we'll return to later.

Article IV protects the rights of citizens across the states, guarantees the mutual protection of republicanism, and defines how new states may be admitted to the Union. Article V describes the procedures for making constitutional amendments, which can be initiated by two-thirds of both Houses of Congress or by two-thirds of state legislatures calling conventions, and which must be approved by three-fourths of the states. Such elaborate procedures and the supermajority votes required by them reflect the specialness of Constitutional law. The Constitution defines the institutions and operations of government, after all, and it is the supreme law, the law by which all lesser law must abide. The legislation of mere politicians is thus appropriately subordinate to the superior will of the sovereign people.

What Barack Obama believes the Founders did therefore, in sum, was create a political system that allows debate but controls conflict by constitutionalizing compromise. This system of checks and balances aims at equilibrium between the legislative, executive, and judicial branches of government, between the rights and interests of the states and the federal government, between government and the people, and ultimately therefore between authority and liberty. This system is, furthermore, the heart of what Obama and others have called a "deliberative democracy." The Constitution's "elaborate machinery is" Obama says, "designed to force us into a conversation, a 'deliberative democracy' in which all citizens are required to engage in a process of testing their ideas against an external reality, persuading others of their point of view, and building shifting alliances of consent."[21]

Compromise is thus crucial to Obama's understanding of the Founders and the Constitution. And not compromise as a necessary evil but compromise as a positive good. "After all," Obama explains, "if there was one impulse shared by all the Founders, it was a rejection of all forms of absolute authority, whether the king, the theocrat, the general, the oligarch, the dictator, the majority, or anyone else who claims to make choices for us." And it was "not just absolute power that the Founders sought to prevent. Implicit in [the Constitution's] structure, in the very idea of ordered liberty, was a rejection of absolute truth, the infallibility of any idea or ideology or theology or 'ism,' any tyrannical consistency that might lock future generations into a single, unalterable course, or drive both majorities and minorities into the cruelties of the Inquisition, the pogrom, the gulag, or the jihad." Barack Obama's constitutional history is thus not just about people and events and what they might teach us about society and politics. It is also about institutions and processes and what they might teach us about civility and democracy.[22]

One of the Founders' central insights

But there was also the matter of finding the right balance between the national and state governments as well as between the branches of the national one. Articles IV and VI of the Constitution thus concern the obligations of the federal and the state governments toward each other and place certain limits on their respective powers. Yet the brevity of these provisions belies the complexity of the issues involved.

As Barack Obama observes, federalism was (and is) not just a problem of balance between levels of government, but a problem of the nature of governance itself. As the delegates gathered in Philadelphia in May 1787, Obama says, "they were faced with a discouraging fact: In the history of the world to that point, there were scant examples of functioning democracies, and none that were larger than the city-states of ancient Greece." Contemporary conditions were equally unpropitious. "With thirteen far-flung states and a diverse population of three or four million," Obama points out, "an Athenian model of democracy was out of the question, the direct democracy of the New England town unmanageable." Even an elective or "republican form of government" was only thought applicable "for a geographically compact and homogenous political community" with "a common culture, a common faith, and a well-developed set of civic virtues" that could limit "contention and strife."[23]

As Obama also says, though: "our history has vindicated one of the Founders' central insights: that republican self-government could actually work better in a large and diverse society, where, in Hamilton's words, the 'jarring of parties' and differences of opinion could 'promote deliberation and circumspection.'" Here, Obama quotes *Federalist* No. 70, one of the famous essays in favor of the Constitution, in which Alexander Hamilton was primarily concerned with the document's proposal for the office of president. As the only elected federal official representing the entire United States, rather than being one of two representing a state in the Senate or one of several representing the people of a smaller district in the House of Representatives, the president was peculiarly placed to mediate the jarring of parties, Hamilton argued. But it was actually James Madison who most fully propounded a new paradigm for perceiving competing interests within an extended polity more generally.[24]

In *Federalist* No. 10, Madison identified the problem of factions in the following way, and the essay's worth quoting at length as it speaks to the heart of Barack Obama's ideas about competing interests and the art of compromise. First, Madison normalized self-interest and factionalism, a radical move in an age in which they were considered highly antisocial (however hypocritically or unrealistically). "The latent causes of faction are thus sown in the nature of man," Madison wrote:

> A zeal for different opinions concerning religion, concerning government, and many other points … an attachment to different leaders ambitiously contending for pre-eminence and power; or to persons of other descriptions whose fortunes have been interesting to the human passions, have, in turn, divided mankind into parties, inflamed them with mutual animosity, and rendered them much more disposed to vex and oppress each other than to co-operate for their common good … But the most common and durable source of factions has been the various and unequal distribution of property. Those who hold and those who are without property have ever formed distinct interests in society. Those who are creditors, and those who are debtors, fall under a like discrimination. A landed interest, a manufacturing interest, a mercantile interest, a moneyed interest, with many lesser interests, grow up of necessity in civilized nations, and divide them into different classes, actuated by different sentiments and views.[25]

When discussing possible solutions to this problem (and it was still a problem, however normal Madison said it was), the philosopher-statesman rejected right away the possible elimination of the freedoms that allowed factions to thrive. Rather, he suggested, "The regulation of these various and interfering interests forms the principal task of modern legislation, and involves the spirit of party and faction in the necessary and ordinary operations of the government."

In describing how such regulation might happen, Madison confronted the then common wisdom concerning the virtues of small and simple states, and once again he confounded the orthodoxies. He contended instead that "a pure democracy, by which I mean a society consisting of a small number of citizens, who assemble and administer the government in person, can admit of no cure for the mischiefs of faction. A common passion or interest," he continued, "will in almost every case, be felt by a majority of the whole," and therefore "there is nothing to check the inducements to sacrifice the weaker party or an obnoxious individual. Hence it is that such democracies have ever been spectacles of turbulence and contention; have ever been found incompatible with personal security or the rights of property; and have in general been as short in their lives as they have been violent in their deaths." However, in further contradiction of contemporary wisdom, he contended: "A republic, by which I mean a government in which the scheme of representation takes place, opens a different prospect, and promises the cure for which we are seeking." Another instance in which government "by" the people was considered incompatible with government "for" the people.[26]

Madison then explained: "The two great points of difference between a democracy and a republic are: first, the delegation of the government, in the latter, to a small number of citizens elected by the rest; secondly, the greater number of citizens, and greater sphere of country, over which the latter may be extended." Madison's next point was the most orthodox in his time, though it is rather more contested today: "The effect of the first difference is, on the one hand, to refine and enlarge the public views, by passing them through the medium of a chosen body of citizens, whose wisdom may best discern the true interest of their country, and whose patriotism and love of justice will be least likely to sacrifice it to temporary or partial considerations." By contrast, his next point after that was much contested in his time, though it is rather more orthodox today: "The question resulting is," he said, "whether small or extensive republics are more favorable to the election of proper guardians of the public weal; and it is clearly decided in favor of the latter."[27]

James Madison then offered "two obvious considerations" to try to prove his point. First, in a small republic "representatives must be raised to a certain number, in order to guard against the cabals of a few." In a larger one, though, "they must be limited to a certain number, in order to guard against the confusion of a multitude." There will therefore be "a greater probability of a fit choice" of "proper guardians of the public weal" in a larger republic. Second, "as each representative will be chosen by a greater number of citizens in the large than in the small republic, it will be more difficult for unworthy candidates to practice with success the vicious arts by which elections are too often carried; and the suffrages of the people being more free, will be more likely to centre in men who possess the most attractive merit and the most diffusive and established characters." This latter point might raise more eyebrows now than it did in Madison's time.[28]

Madison also noted one "other point of difference ... which renders factious combinations less to be dreaded in" larger republics than in smaller ones. "The smaller the society," he said, "the fewer probably will be the distinct parties and interests composing it; the fewer the distinct parties and interests, the more frequently will a majority be found of the same party; and the smaller the number of individuals composing a majority, and the smaller the compass within which they are placed, the more easily will they concert and execute their plans of oppression." However: "Extend the sphere, and you take in a greater variety of parties and interests; you make it less probable that a majority of the whole will have a common motive to invade the rights of other citizens; or if such a common motive exists, it will be more difficult for all who feel it to discover their own strength, and to act in unison with each other." And to make his point explicitly applicable to contemporary debates about the ratification of the Constitution, Madison added "that the same advantage which a republic has over a democracy, in controlling the effects of faction, is enjoyed by a large over a small republic,—is enjoyed by the Union over the States composing it."[29]

Before the ink on the constitutional parchment was dry

These *Federalist Papers* were part of the national debate following the drafting of the Constitution in Philadelphia. The Constitution's Article VII prescribed the process by which the document the Founders drafted was to be ratified. Or not, as the case nearly was. To come into effect it required itself to be ratified by nine of the thirteen states, and, in a further concession to the principle of popular sovereignty, ratification had to be done by specially elected conventions. The resulting debates were often rancorous and a number of states initially rejected what the Constitutional Convention proposed.

As Barack Obama observes, "Before the ink on the constitutional parchment was dry, arguments had erupted, not just about minor provisions but about first principles, not just between peripheral figures but within the Revolution's very core." These arguments concerned "how much power the national government should have—to regulate the economy, to supersede state laws, to form a standing army, or to assume debt." There were also disputes concerning "the president's role in establishing treaties with foreign powers, and about the Supreme Court's role in determining the law" and "such basic rights as freedom of speech and freedom of assembly." And, as Obama ruefully reflects, there were moments when some of the Founders "were not averse to ignoring those rights altogether."[30]

Some of Obama's words here actually apply to the political battles of the 1790s and early 1800s, after the Constitution came into effect, rather than solely to contestation over the Constitution's ratification, and we'll relate them to the disputations of the Washington, Adams, and Jefferson administrations in due course. But some of them were part of or were foreshadowed in the ratification debates of 1787–88. Other than these comments, however, Obama tends to gloss over the often rancorous process of ratification. He portrays *The Federalist Papers* (originally known and published as just *The Federalist*), for example, as masterpieces of applied political philosophy refined in the minds of brilliant thinkers, which they were. But he doesn't portray them as masterstrokes of spin forged in a fiery debate between machinating politicians, which they also were.

The Federalist Papers comprise eighty-five essays recommending ratification and published between October 1787 and August 1788, initially in newspapers before being reissued in book form. They were published under the pseudonym Publius, but fifty-one were authored by Alexander Hamilton, twenty-six by James Madison, three by Hamilton and Madison together, and five by John Jay.[31]

Perhaps these men's signature maneuver is embedded in the papers' collective name. The term "Federalist" is philosophically appropriate for the title of the essays to the extent that it signifies a polity in which power is shared between a central and local governments, which is how the United States as a nation works. The term was also historically correct to the extent that the Constitution would abolish the Articles of Confederation in favor of forming a federation, or a federal nation rather than an alliance of several sovereign states. But the term was also in part inapt. Within the closed doors of the Convention, for example, in the deliberately secret debates that took place, those in favor of the Constitution were known as Consolidators and Nationalists. But calling themselves either of these things in the public ratification debates that followed would have damaged their chances of winning. So the authors called their papers "The Federalist" and called themselves "federalists," with all these terms' abstract implications of sharing power outwards—and all their actual obfuscations of the real-world context of consolidating power inwards. Calling themselves "federalists" also successfully encumbered their opponents with the negative denomination of "anti-federalists."

But this disingenuousness should not obscure the genuine ingeniousness of *The Federalist Papers*. One by one, the eighty-five essays systematically offered positive prognostications of every aspect of the proposed Constitution—executive, legislative, and judicial, as well as of the national-state power-sharing system itself. The essays also answered all allegations of opportunity for abuses of the liberties of individuals and the rights of states that the Constitution potentially provided. All the authors contended that the Constitution's checks and balances provided sufficient protections against attempted abuses of power. And Madison in particular argued that "strict construction" of the Constitution would ensure that any powers not expressly granted to the federal government were implicitly but nonetheless certainly proscribed. *The Federalist* might well have done enough to assure the Constitution's ratification, although not quite enough for a quill drop yet.

A sufficient defense against tyranny

For all the Federalists' efforts, Antifederalists continued to complain about the absence of explicit protections in the Constitution for individual liberties and states' rights. The end result was another compromise: the first ten amendments, collectively called the Bill of Rights.

Barack Obama often speaks and writes of the Constitution and the Bill of Rights as if they were and are one and the same thing. When referring to one of Thomas Jefferson's more radical ruminations, for example, Obama observes that if Americans "have declined to heed Jefferson's advice to engage in a revolution every two or three generations, it's only because the Constitution itself proved a sufficient defense against tyranny." His definition of "the Constitution" here implicitly includes those first ten amendments and their defenses against tyranny. And it is correct to define the Constitution this way in the sense that the document itself says that all amendments "shall be valid to all Intents and Purposes, as Part of this Constitution, when ratified." Yet stating things this way obscures the contemporary context of and contestation over the adoption of the amendments.[32]

At the Constitutional Convention, Elbridge Gerry of Massachusetts and George Mason of Virginia had already called for some sort of bill of rights. Afterwards, several states made their ratifications conditional on the adoption of explicit protections, and Rhode Island and North Carolina refused to ratify until after amendments to that effect were on the road to confirmation. In the first Congress, therefore, starting in March

1789, James Madison collated the various demands, despite his initial concerns that a codification of rights might be seen by some future tyrant as the states' or the people's *only* rights. But, in a proto-Obamian spirit of reasonableness and compromise, Madison proposed twelve amendments to Congress on June 8, 1789, ten of which were finally approved by the states by December 15, 1791.

Eight of those amendments enumerate various liberties and legal immunities for individuals. The first separates church and state and guarantees freedom of religion, speech, assembly, petition, and the press. The second states: "A well-regulated militia, being necessary to the security of a free state, the right of the people to keep and bear arms, shall not be abridged." Whether the first two clauses of that amendment present rationales for the right to bear arms or represent conditions on the right to bear arms remains a matter of urgent and yet apparently unresolvable debate. The third forbids the quartering of soldiers in people's homes without their consent in peacetime and unless in accord with laws made in wartime. The fourth guards against unwarranted searches and seizures. The fifth provides legal guarantees against double-jeopardy, self-incrimination, and the deprivation of life, liberty, and property without due process of law or due compensation. The sixth protects legal rights to a speedy and local trial by jury, to know the charges one is facing, to be confronted by witnesses, and to call witnesses and have the assistance of counsel. The seventh guarantees the right to jury trial in suits at common law over matters worth more than $20, and the eighth guards against excessive bail, fines, and cruel and unusual punishments. The ninth notes that the rights already listed were not the people's only rights, covering Madison's concerns about potential abuses of enumeration. And the tenth reserves the powers not expressly granted to Congress to the states or to the people, a counterpoint to Congress's "necessary and proper" clause and a case-in-point for strict construction.[33]

North Carolina finally ratified the Constitution in November 1789 and Rhode Island did so the following May.

The Supreme Court's role in determining the law

Rhode Island's ratification was not of course the final word on constitutional interpretation. As Barack Obama observes, the Founders argued about, among other things, "the Supreme Court's role in determining the law." In the 1803 case of *Marbury v Madison*, the Court itself established the principle of "judicial review" of the constitutionality of executive actions and legislative acts.[34]

Maryland Federalist and financier William Marbury had petitioned the Supreme Court over his appointment as Justice of the Peace in the new federal city of Washington, DC. This post (and many others) had been created by the outgoing Congress's Judiciary Act of 1801, and Marbury had been appointed one of the "Midnight Judges" by President Adams, who spent his final evening in office making partisan appointments to these new federal positions. But new President Thomas Jefferson's Secretary of State James

Madison failed to deliver or cause to be delivered the commissions of Marbury and others.

Chief Justice John Marshall wrote the unanimous verdict of the Supreme Court that Madison had acted unlawfully as Marbury had "a vested legal right" to his commission. Yet, Marshall further ruled, Marbury would not be given the commission because Congress had unlawfully extended the Supreme Court's jurisdiction in authorizing it to issue writs of mandamus. As the chief justice put it: "the Court held that it lacked jurisdiction because Section 13 of the Judiciary Act passed by Congress in 1789, which authorized the Court to issue such a writ, was unconstitutional and thus invalid." In justifying this decision, Marshall unequivocally asserted the Supreme Court's right to exercise judicial review of the actions of the other branches of government: "It is emphatically the province and duty of the Judicial Department to say what the law is." Those words are inscribed in gold letters on the white marble wall of the Supreme Court building that overlooks the Capitol today.[35]

The Constitution doesn't specify that the Supreme Court has the power of judicial review, so Marshall's ruling was itself an innovative interpretation of the law. Some indeed argued and pointed at the apparent irony that in ruling that Congress had unlawfully extended the Supreme Court's jurisdiction Marshall had unlawfully extended the Supreme Court's jurisdiction. No less a figure than President Jefferson said that judicial review was "a very dangerous doctrine indeed, and one which would place us under the despotism of an oligarchy."[36]

And yet for better and for worse the Supreme Court's constitutional rulings have comprised pivotal moments in American history. One that particularly interests Barack Obama, as it should all of us, is *Dred Scott v Sandford* (1857), which denied that African Americans had any legal rights, laid the grounds for a possible ruling that state abolitions of slavery had no legal standing, and thus played a major part in starting the Civil War. Another, *Plessy v Ferguson* (1896), validated "separate but equal" facilities that legalized segregation while *Williams v Mississippi* (1898) ruled that literacy tests and poll taxes were nonracial and thereby legalized disfranchisement. Equally importantly, though, these Jim Crow decisions were reversed by later generations of Supreme Court justices.

Fundamentalist faith

We'll return to these specific legal-political issues in the next chapter and the one after, but it is worth noting now that the establishment of the principle of "judicial review" was not the final word on constitutional interpretation. To this day some say that the Founders' "original intent" should remain the basis of constitutionalism. Others argue otherwise.

As Barack Obama observes, many contemporary conservative activists insist that in reading rights into the Constitution in recent times "liberal judges" have "placed themselves above the law, basing their opinions not on the Constitution but on their own whims and desired results ... subverting the democratic process and perverting the Founding Fathers' original intent." Conservatives therefore prefer the "appointment of 'strict constructionists'" to the judiciary, jurists who know "the difference between interpreting and making law" and "would stick to the original meaning of the Founders' words." So that when legal disputes happen "we appeal to a higher authority—the Founding Fathers and the Constitution's ratifiers." As Obama notes, some such as "Justice [Antonin] Scalia [since deceased], conclude that the original understanding must be followed and that if we strictly obey this rule, then democracy is respected."[37]

Barack Obama admits to temptation to take this point of view. Kind of. "Maybe I am too steeped in the myth of the founding to reject it entirely," he says. "Maybe like those who reject Darwin in favor of intelligent design, I prefer to assume that someone's at the wheel." He thus declares in an unusual and perhaps therefore suggestive double negative that he is "not unsympathetic to Justice Scalia's position." But then he adds that "in many cases the language of the Constitution is perfectly clear and can be strictly applied. We don't have to interpret how often elections are held, for example, or how old a president must be." Obama thus concedes that conservative originalists are correct about the totally obvious.[38]

Obama similarly bows to the Founders before rounding on their self-styled disciples when saying the following. "I understand," he writes, "the strict constructionists' reverence for the Founders." He confesses that he himself has sometimes "wondered whether the Founders themselves recognized at the time the scope of their accomplishment," and he lists the drafting of "the Constitution in the wake of revolution," the writing of the Federalist Papers, ratification, and the Bill of Rights, all accomplished "in the span of a few short years," to illustrate the scope of their accomplishment. These documents, he furthermore says, "seem so incredibly right that it's easy to believe that they are the result of natural law if not divine inspiration." But then comes a calmly Obamian boom: "So I appreciate the temptation on the part of Justice Scalia and others to assume that our democracy should be treated as fixed and unwavering; the fundamentalist faith that if the original understanding of the Constitution is followed without question or deviation, and if we remain true to rules that the Founders set forth, as they intended, then we will be rewarded and all good will flow."[39]

It seems then that for Obama constitutional literalism is actually about as sensible as biblical literalism. And as a "fundamentalist faith" it may be similarly dangerous.

The freedom of the apostate

Others on the other hand argue that so much time has passed and times have changed so much that the opinions of the patriarchs of the eighteenth century are as applicable in today's world as their penchants for periwigs and slave-ownership.

As Barack Obama observes, some contemporary radical activists insist that "the Constitution itself was largely a happy accident, a document cobbled together not as the result of principle but as the result of power and passion." Or else they think that "we can never hope to discern the Founders' 'original intentions' since the intentions of Jefferson were never those of Hamilton, and those of Hamilton differed greatly from those of Adams." That "the Founders and ratifiers themselves disagreed profoundly, vehemently on the meaning of their masterpiece" and their "shifting alliances and occasionally underhand tactics" mean that it is "unrealistic to believe that a judge, two hundred years later, can somehow discern the original intent of the Founders or ratifiers." Or even "that because the 'rules' of the Constitution were contingent on time and place and the ambitions of the men who drafted them, our interpretations of the rules will necessarily reflect the same contingency, the same raw competition, the same imperatives—cloaked in high-minded phrasing—of those factions that ultimately prevail."[40]

As with the "comfort offered by the strict constructionist," Obama sees "a certain appeal to this shattering of myth, to the temptation to believe that the constitutional text doesn't constrain us much at all, so that we are free to assert our own values unencumbered by fidelity to the stodgy traditions of a distant past." But if strict construction based on original intent is for Obama a "fundamentalist faith," then this other attitude to the Founders is "the freedom of the relativist, the rule breaker … the freedom of the apostate." And, in case readers miss the inference of irreligiosity the first time around, on the next line Obama writes that "such apostasy leaves me unsatisfied." Unsatisfied because of the following question: "why," Obama asks, "if the Constitution is only about power and not principle, if all we are doing is making it up as we go along, has our republic not only survived but served as a rough model for so many successful societies on earth?"[41]

Fidelity to our founding principles

Barack Obama's answer to that question lies in a concept of constitutional evolution. He doesn't reject original intent outright, but instead refashions it into something we might call evolutionary intent. In short, Obama believes that the Founders' original intent was that interpretations of their laws should move with the times.

Let's note first how Obama's grammar when discussing this matter locates the Founders' words and deeds not only in their own time, but also in all time since. As he said in his second inaugural address: "we have always understood that when times change, so must we; that fidelity to our founding principles requires new responses to new challenges …" In saying "we" he appears here to address his audience on the day and all Americans alive today. Yet the word "always" indicates his inclusion of all Americans from the nation's founding, irrespective of death. Obama thereby suggests that the Founders "understood" as well as their descendants would "that when times change, so must we." That the Founders themselves therefore thought that "new responses to new challenges" would be required to maintain "fidelity to" America's "founding principles."[42]

Let's note also that Obama wrote here of "fidelity" to the Founders' "principles" rather than their words. His fidelity is therefore to the spirit of the Constitution, not to its letter, just as he believes the Founders originally intended. By the same token, fidelity to what conservatives believe to be the word of the Constitution can constitute infidelity to "our founding principles," as it would betray the Founders' intention that interpretation of the Constitution should evolve, that successive generations should continue the mission of making a more perfect union.[43]

Barack Obama firmly believes that to this extent at least we can still read the Founders' minds. Recounting his own time teaching Constitutional law at the University of Chicago for over a decade before commencing his political career, he remembers telling students, "We have a record of the Founders' intentions ... their arguments and their palace intrigues. If we can't always divine what was in their hearts, we can at least cut through the mist of time and have some sense of the core ideals that motivated their work." He then specifies the Declaration of Independence, the Federalist Papers, and the Constitution as the legacies they left us, but the reference to "their arguments and palace intrigues" indicates that he means James Madison's notes on the Convention as well. And from these documents Obama divines the following about the Founders' intentions.[44]

Obama's view of the Founders and their work is, in his own words, "one that sees our democracy not as a house to be built, but as a conversation to be had." Therefore "the genius of Madison's design is not that it provides us a fixed blueprint for action, the way a draftsman plots a building's construction. It provides us with a framework and with rules." But, he notes, and here is the point of departure from literalism to a different kind of originalism, from original intent to evolutionary intent, "fidelity to these rules will not guarantee a just society or assure agreement on what's right." Instead, and here is a foundation of Obama's view of how American politics and history work (or should work):

> What the framework of our Constitution can do is organize the way by which we argue about the future. All of its elaborate machinery—its separation of powers and checks and balances and federalist principles and Bill of Rights—are designed to force us into a conversation, a "deliberative democracy" in which all citizens are required to engage in a process of testing their ideas against an external reality, persuading others of their point of view, and building shifting alliances of consent.[45]

As Garry Wills has noted, on this matter Obama has the authority of none other than Abraham Lincoln behind him. Alongside Obama's words Wills quotes Lincoln's speech at New York's Cooper Union on February 27, 1860. The founders' intent was "to set up a standard maxim for free society," Lincoln said, "which should be familiar to all, constantly looked to, constantly labored for, and even though never perfectly attained, constantly approximated." And thus both Lincoln and Obama tell us that the founders intended, in Wills's elegant words, "to make the Constitution a means for its own transcendence."[46]

The context of an ever-changing world

Indeed Barack Obama notes that these ideas are "by no means original to me." And he cites contemporary authorities such as Supreme Court Justice Stephen Breyer who "don't dispute that the original meaning of constitutional provisions matters. But they insist that sometimes the original understanding can take you only so far—that ... we have to take context, history, and the practical outcomes of a decision into account." The Founders thus "told us *how* to think but are no longer around to tell us *what* to think. We are on our own, and have only our own reason and our judgment to rely on." And on this matter Obama says that he sides "with Justice Breyer's view of the Constitution—that it is not a static but rather a living document, and must be read in the context of an ever-changing world."[47]

In support of this view, Obama sometimes recites the familiar argument that the Founders could simply not foresee how the world would change in the future— something we can see in hindsight. But Obama also goes further by arguing that the Founders' great insight was precisely that they did not have that kind of foresight. Hence they provided a framework with rules, but not a blueprint. Moreover, in a fabulously ironic insight of his own, Obama argues that the Founders themselves rejected the kind of "fundamentalist faith" required for belief in originalism. "It's not just absolute power that the Founders sought to prevent," Obama notes in another key passage quoted earlier but worthy of repetition: "Implicit in [the Constitution's] structure, in the very idea of ordered liberty, was a rejection of absolute truth, the infallibility of any idea or ideology or theology or 'ism', any tyrannical consistency that might lock future generations into a single, unalterable course, or drive both majorities and minorities into the cruelties of the Inquisition, the pogrom, the gulag, or the jihad."[48]

The Founders' framework therefore accommodates the possibility of error, including the Founders' own errors, but comprehends the capacity to correct it. "Because power in our government is so diffuse," Obama says, "the process of making law in America compels us to entertain the possibility that we are not always right and do sometimes change our minds; it challenges us to examine our motives and our interests constantly, and suggests that both our individual and collective judgments are at once legitimate and highly fallible."[49]

Obama admits that "this reading of the Constitution and our democratic process ... seems to champion compromise, modesty, and muddling through," and even perhaps "to justify logrolling, deal-making, self-interest, pork barrels, paralysis, and inefficiency—all the sausage-making that no one wants to see and that editorialists throughout our history often labelled as corrupt." Yet he rejects the notion "that democratic deliberation requires abandonment of our highest ideals, or of a commitment to the common good." At its best, he argues, repeating Alexander Hamilton's characterization of the productivity of American political process, it "offers us the possibility of a genuine marketplace of ideas, one in which the 'jarring of parties' works on behalf of deliberation and circumspection: a marketplace in which, through debate and competition, we can expand our perspective, change our minds, and eventually arrive not merely at agreements but at sound and fair agreements." And, furthermore, "we must test out our ideals, vision, and values, against the realities of a common life, so that over time they may be refined, discarded, or replaced by new ideals, sharper visions, deeper values." Thus, he says, "It may be the vision of the Founders that inspires us, but it was their realism, their practicality and flexibility and curiosity, that ensured the Union's survival."[50]

The historian and political scientist James T. Kloppenberg is therefore spot-on in depicting Barack Obama as a "philosophical pragmatist." That is, as continuing an American intellectual tradition propounded most famously by William James (1842–1910) and John Dewey (1859–1952). Obama indeed sees the tradition of philosophical pragmatism in deed if not in name as dating to the Founders themselves. As Kloppenburg quotes Obama describing the Founders: "They were suspicious of abstraction and liked asking questions, which is why at every turn in our early history theory yielded to fact and necessity." Thus Obama writes that "the Constitution envisions a road map by which we marry passion to reason, the ideal of individual freedom to the demands of community."[51]

The "passion" and "individual freedom" as well as "reason" and the "demands of community" distinguish the Founders' and Obama's practicality from a "vulgar pragmatism" that takes political positions or at least administrative lines of least resistance without reference to principle. Philosophical pragmatism by contrast aims to find effective means to implement principled ends. The philosophy may be idealistic, but the pragmatism is grounded in accepting the need to compromise to get good things if not necessarily the best things done, to achieve what's possible if not what's perfect. Indeed, given Obama's (and the Founders') suspicions of dogmatism, pragmatism itself is virtuous in his view. For Obama, then, it is perfectly understandable that the pragmatic Founders did not form a perfect union. But in their philosophical idealism they nevertheless formed a "more perfect" one. And they intended, furthermore, that later generations would in their own ways make it more perfect still.

A term Obama himself prefers to use and indeed puts in quote marks (as mentioned earlier) is "deliberative democracy": a term that perhaps describes perfectly the process by which philosophical pragmatism achieves its ends. The phrase was coined by Joseph M. Bessette in an essay entitled "Deliberative Democracy: The Majority Principle in Republican Government," first published in 1980, and reprinted in Bessette's book, *The Mild Voice of Reason: Deliberative Democracy and American National Government*, from 1994. But again Obama uses a new term to describe what he sees as an old tradition. Hence the Constitution's "elaborate machinery" was "designed to force us into a conversation, a 'deliberative democracy' in which all citizens are required to engage in a process of testing their ideas against an external reality, persuading others of their point of view, and building shifting alliances of consent."[52]

And that's not only how the Founders intended to "organize the way by which we argue about the future," but for Obama it's also how the Founders themselves "brought about the Constitution itself." As he notes, quoting James Madison himself, at the Philadelphia Convention "no man felt himself obliged to retain his opinions any longer than he was satisfied of their propriety and truth, and was open to the force of argument."[53]

A "wall of separation" between church and state

Barack Obama's philosophical pragmatism is also evident in his attitudes to religion and to American religious history, and in his belief in the righteousness of the Constitution's First Amendment provisions for freedom from and freedom of religion.

We saw in Chapter 1 that while Obama finds the Pilgrims' and the Puritans' "escape from tyranny and persecution" inspiring, he is no advocate of their "brand of strict Calvinism" and considers himself no Cotton Mather. Obama's "city on a hill" is for those of all faiths and none, the perfect opposite of John Winthrop's "city upon a hill" that was only for believers in his one-true-religion. Obama's account of the Founders' faith, furthermore, reflects his own eighteenth-century style of secularism—a belief that religion can inform politics but should be separate from government. And Obama's account of religion in the United States since then also suits his Whiggish sense of historical progress.[54]

Obama notes: "The Founders may have trusted in God, but true to the Enlightenment spirit, they also trusted in the minds and senses that God had given them." He's also well aware of the diversity and complexity of the Founders' views on religion and the politics of religion. "Many of the leading lights of the Revolution," Obama observes, "most notably Franklin and Jefferson, were deists who, while believing in an Almighty God, questioned not only the dogmas of the Christian church but central tenets of Christianity itself (including Christ's divinity)." But "Of course, not all the Founding Fathers agreed; men like Patrick Henry and John Adams forwarded a variety of proposals to use the arm of the state to promote religion." And so it was that "Jefferson and Madison in particular argued for what Jefferson called a 'wall of separation' between church and state, guarding the state against sectarian strife, and defending organized religion against the state's encroachment or undue influence."[55]

Obama again uses history here to drive home a contemporary political point. "It was Jefferson," Obama points out, "not some liberal judge in the sixties, who called for a wall between church and state." And he repeats the point later on in *The Audacity of Hope*: "Contrary to the claims of many on the Christian right who rail against the separation of church and state, their argument is not with a handful of sixties judges. It is with the drafters of the Bill of Rights and the forebears of today's evangelical church."[56]

And Obama is completely correct on both counts. Thomas Jefferson took tremendous pride in building that "wall of separation." When the ageing Sage of Monticello designed his own tombstone, he asked for just three of his many achievements to constitute his epitaph. They were, and indeed are, in the chronological order in which they appear on the memorial:

Author of the Declaration of American Independence
of the Statute of Virginia for religious freedom
& Father of the University of Virginia[57]

Jefferson drafted Virginia's "Act for establishing religious Freedom" in 1777, though it was not introduced into the General Assembly until 1779 and it only finally passed into law on January 16, 1786. Nevertheless, pass it eventually did, and it is worth quoting it at some length to remind protagonists at both poles of today's debate on the role of religion in public life that secularism is not about suppression of religion but about freedom of religion. Indeed, the Act begins with the predicate "Whereas, Almighty God hath created the mind free," and proceeds accordingly to state "that all attempts to influence it by temporal punishments or burthens, or by civil incapacitations tend only to beget habits of hypocrisy and meanness, and therefore are a departure from the plan of the holy author of our religion."[58]

After a long preamble detailing why both actively encouraging and discouraging religious practices by the state is wrong, the Act directs:

> that no man shall be compelled to frequent or support any religious worship, place, or ministry whatsoever, nor shall be enforced, restrained, molested, or burthened in his body or goods, nor shall otherwise suffer on account of his religious opinions or belief, but that all men shall be free to profess, and by argument to maintain, their opinions in matters of Religion, and that the same shall in no wise diminish, enlarge or affect their civil capacities.[59]

Interestingly, the Act concludes with a philosophical conundrum concerning the unlimited principle but limitable instantiation of natural rights. The assemblymen agreed that "though we well know that this Assembly elected by the people for the ordinary purposes of Legislation only, have no power to restrain the acts of succeeding Assemblies ... and that therefore to declare this act irrevocable would be of no effect in law; yet we are free to declare, and do declare that the rights hereby asserted, are of the natural rights of mankind, and that if any act shall be hereafter passed to repeal the present or to narrow its operation, such act will be an infringement of natural right." Which makes the original intentions of this particular group of founders fairly clear.[60]

The Constitution's First Amendment is much shorter than the Virginia act for religious freedom and freedom from religion, but is based on the same principles. It contains what's called the Establishment Clause and an accompanying Free Exercise Clause. But what's also interesting is how it's grouped with several other fundamental freedoms, as if they're all inseparable from each other and from the general principles of freedom as a whole. The whole thing goes as follows: "Congress shall make no law respecting an establishment of religion, or prohibiting the free exercise thereof; or abridging the freedom of speech, or of the press; or the right of the people peaceably to assemble, and to petition the Government for a redress of grievances."[61]

Defending organized religion

The Founders were not hostile to theism therefore, only to theocracy. Thomas Jefferson in particular was skeptical about the clergy. "In every country and in every age," Jefferson once wrote, "the priest has been hostile to liberty. He is always in alliance with the despot, abetting his abuses in return for protection to his own." The reference to "the priest" resounds with anti-Catholicism, but Jefferson was if anything yet more damning of puritanical Protestantism. As he wrote to John Adams (of Massachusetts, let's not forget) about John Calvin, the original Genevan puritan: "His religion was demonism. If ever man worshiped a false God, he did. The being described in his five points is … a demon of malignant spirit. It would be more pardonable to believe in no God at all, than to blaspheme him by the atrocious attributes of Calvin."[62]

Yet, in his draft of the Declaration of Independence and in his Virginia Statute for religious freedom, Jefferson defended the right to worship freely. As Barack Obama says, when Jefferson called for "a 'wall of separation' between church and state" he was in part "defending organized religion against the state's encroachment or undue influence." Even more than that, though, Obama credits the "critical role that the establishment clause has played not only in the development of our democracy but also in the robustness of our religious practice."[63]

And as Obama further says, "while it was Jefferson and Madison who pushed through the Virginia statute of religious freedom that would become the model for the First Amendment's religious clauses, it wasn't these students of the Enlightenment who proved to be the most effective champions of separation between church and state. Rather," he explains, "it was Baptists like Reverend John Leland and other evangelicals who provided the popular support needed to get these provisions ratified." "They did so" moreover "because they were outsiders" and "because their style of exuberant worship appealed to the lower classes; because their evangelization of all comers— including slaves—threatened the established order; because they were no respecters of rank and privilege; and because they were consistently persecuted and disdained by the dominant Anglican Church in the South and the Congregationalist orders of the North." Furthermore, "they also believed that religious vitality inevitably withers when compelled or supported by the state. In the words of Reverend Leland, 'It is error alone, that stands in need of government to support it; truth can and will do better without … it.' "[64]

John Leland was born in Grafton, Massachusetts on May 14, 1754, to Congregationalist Puritan parents. But he was baptized in June 1774 and went on to baptize some 1,500 people himself, first in Virginia from 1775 to 1791 and then back in Massachusetts, where he finally died on January 14, 1841. In his *Chronicle of His Time in Virginia*, Leland wrote: "The notion of a Christian commonwealth should be exploded forever. Government should protect every man in thinking and speaking freely, and see that one does not abuse another. The liberty I contend for is more than toleration. The very idea of toleration is despicable; it supposes that some have a pre-eminence above the rest to grant indulgence, whereas all should be equally free, Jews, Turks, Pagans and Christians." The choice of language might be slightly different today, but Barack Obama's sentiments are still very similar. As the latter wrote, "we are no longer just a Christian nation; we are also a Jewish nation, a Muslim nation, a Buddhist nation, a Hindu nation, and a nation of nonbelievers."[65]

In fact, the religious diversity created by the separation of church and state itself makes it all the more essential to maintain this inclusive kind of secularist tradition. As Obama writes, "Jefferson and Leland's formula for religious freedom worked. Not only has America avoided the sorts of religious strife that continue to plague the globe, but religious institutions have continued to thrive—a phenomenon that some observers attribute directly to the absence of a state-sponsored church, and hence a premium on religious experimentation and volunteerism." And "given the increasing diversity of America's population, the dangers of sectarianism have never been greater."[66]

Barack Obama more than hints in the previously mentioned passage at the political radicalism of Baptism, and indeed John Leland frequently preached, for example, against enslavement. Leland also authored the Resolution for the General Committee of Virginia Baptists of 1789, which stated "that slavery is a violent deprivation of rights of nature and inconsistent with a republican government, and therefore, recommend it to our brethren to make use of every legal measure to extirpate this horrid evil from the land; and pray Almighty God that our honorable legislature may have it in their power to proclaim the great jubilee, consistent with the principles of good policy."[67]

We return to the links between religion and abolitionism in the next chapter. But it is worth noting now that Obama sees some American religious traditions as invaluable to the historical progress of the United States. He once spoke, for example, of how "Because of its past, the black church understands in an intimate way the Biblical call to feed the hungry and clothe the naked and challenge powers and principalities. And in its historical struggle for freedom and the rights of man, I was able to see faith as more than just a comfort to the weary or a hedge against death, but rather as an active, palpable agent in the world."[68]

And he sees as well how others' faith can do the same for them. "Evangelical revivalism has repeatedly swept across the nation," he writes, "and swathes of successive immigrants have used their faith to anchor their lives in a strange new world. Religious sentiment and religious activism have sparked some of our most powerful political movements, from abolition to civil rights to the prairie populism of William Jennings Bryan." But if Obama takes a subtle swipe at some on the contemporary religious Right there, subverting their claims for Christianity as a force for conservatism, he also seems to take a swing at the unwitting intolerance of some on the other side. While John Lennon asked us to "Imagine no religion," Barack Obama asks us to "Imagine Lincoln's second inaugural address without reference to 'the judgments of the Lord,' or King's 'I Have a Dream' speech without reference to 'all of God's children.'" Even a nonbeliever can call that one for Obama.[69]

None of this is inconsistent with the constitutional separation of church and state, as far as Barack Obama is concerned. "Surely," he says, "secularists are wrong when they ask believers to leave their religion at the door before entering the public square; Frederick Douglass, Abraham Lincoln, William Jennings Bryan, Dorothy Day, Martin Luther King Jr.,—indeed the majority of great reformers in American history—not only were motivated by faith but repeatedly used religious language to argue their causes." But, ironically, Obama is here using a particular definition of "secularism," one that falsely portrays secularism as intolerance, one promoted by those seeking the kind of privileged place for religion in governance that Obama opposes. Obama is actually a secularist in an older, broader, more open sense, one consistent with the values of the Enlightenment, in believing in the institutional separation of church and state. It is just that, like most of the Founders and like many people who call themselves secularist today, theist and atheist alike, Obama believes: "Not every mention of God in public is a breach in the wall of separation."[70]

But, as Obama further explains, if religion is to be part of the wider political process, then "What our deliberative, pluralistic democracy does demand is that the religiously motivated translate their concerns into universal, rather than religion-specific values. It requires that their proposals must be subject to argument and amenable to reason." It must thus be "accessible to people of all faiths, including those with no faith at all." The arguments for separation of church and state and for the inclusion of religion in public discourse sometimes therefore have the same source.[71]

~~In God We Trust~~ *E Pluribus Unum*

Barack Obama's ecumenicalism is secular as well as religious, and celebrates unity at the same time as diversity. His first speech on the national stage, at the Democratic Convention in Boston, Massachusetts on July 27, 2004, as well as some of his other orations, contained the refrain "*E pluribus unum*. Out of many, one."[72]

These words appear on the Great Seal of the United States, adopted by the Confederation Congress in 1782. They also formed the unofficial motto of the United States, until Congress adopted an official one in 1956: "In God We Trust." Obama has cited "*E Pluribus Unum*" or "Out of many, one" often in order to express what he sees as his own and his country's values. As far as I know, he has never used "In God We Trust" to do either of these things. Nor "One nation under God," which was added to the previously secular Pledge of Allegiance in 1954. Obama's preference for the nonreligious phrase to express national values perhaps reflects his Enlightenment secularism, his belief in the separation of church and state. But it also implies an inclusiveness that reflects his commitment to what unifies Americans even in their religious and other kinds of diversity.

Through the early days of the Union

Besides the role of the Supreme Court in determining the law, and the position of organized religion in public life, Barack Obama identifies other contentions that arose "Before the ink on the constitutional parchment was dry" and that continued "through the early days of the Union." And they were "not just about minor provisions but about first principles, not just between peripheral figures but within the Revolution's very core." The Founders "argued about how much power the national government should have—to regulate the economy, to supersede state laws, to form a standing army, or to assume debt." And "about the president's role in establishing treaties with foreign powers" and even "the meaning of such basic rights as freedom of speech and freedom of assembly, and on several occasions, when the fragile state seemed threatened, they were not averse to ignoring those rights altogether." So how exactly did these arguments arise and which Founders stood where on what?[73]

During the 1789–97 administration of George Washington, Treasury Secretary Alexander Hamilton attempted "to regulate the economy" by creating a National Bank and attempting to impose protective tariffs to promote finance and manufacturing, but we deal with these things in detail in Chapter 6. We'll also discuss Hamilton's assumption of revolutionary war debts, a policy that also benefitted a financier class by repaying "stock jobbers" who'd speculatively purchased government IOUs off ordinary soldiers who'd received them as wages and sold them under par to speculators when short of cash. And in Chapter 7 we explore arguments "about the president's role in establishing treaties with foreign powers" when we encounter Washington's destruction of the alliance with France.[74]

But it is worth noting here that these arguments engendered America's first political party system. Despite a deep-seated feeling that political partisanship represented the displacement of the virtuous pursuit of the public good in favor of personal and factional ambitions and interests—a feeling that persisted despite James Madison's myth-busting *Federalist* No. 10—political parties emerged in the mid-1790s and were fairly fully formed by the end of the century. Washington was a Federalist, for all his claims to be above party "factionalism." Barack Obama validates his presidential predecessor's self-assessment when he writes that John "Adams's idea of a politics grounded solely in the public interest—a politics without politics—was proven obsolete the moment Washington stepped down from office." It was in fact obsolete well before then, but the first president is more venerated now than he was in his own fractious and indeed factious time.

On the other hand, Washington is rightly remembered for setting a tone of executive leadership that was consistent with what Barack Obama sees as the anti-tyrannical ideology of the American Revolution. As Obama recounts, "George Washington declined Caesar's crown because of this impulse, and stepped down after two terms" as president. We've seen already that Washington took two terms and no more, and he did indeed earlier turn down titular laurels. During Congress's 1789 debates on the formal address for the Chief Executive, Vice President John Adams as president of the Senate agitated initially for "Highness." When others suggested what he felt were the unduly lowly alternatives of "Electoral Highness" and "Excellency," Adams upped the ante by suggesting "Majesty." Washington settled for "Mr. President," as suggested by James Madison and others in the House of Representatives, as a more suitably republican ceremonial.[75]

Washington's successor, John Adams, almost always less venerated by others than by himself, also failed to live up to his own antiparty idealism and was, as Obama's comments suggest, a fiercely partisan Federalist both as Washington's vice-president and as president himself from 1797 to 1801. As Washington's first secretary of state, Thomas Jefferson resigned his post in protest at Federalist foreign and domestic policies, and became a leading Democratic-Republican and America's third president from 1801 to 1809. His successor from 1809 to 1817 was James Madison, who as a Congressman first led the emergent Democratic-Republic opposition to Hamilton's original Federalist economic policies in the early 1790s.

Party politics also mixed with the other contentions that Barack Obama mentions. Arguments over "a standing army" originated with English distrust of royal authority in the years before the 1640s Civil War, and many eighteenth-century Americans shared this sentiment. Even George Washington in his Newburgh Address and even Alexander Hamilton in *The Federalist* warned of the dangers of military power to civil authority. The Continental Army was mostly disbanded after the American revolutionary war in deference to the republican preference for civil militia, and all that then remained of the regular army was one western regiment to safeguard settlers and one battery of artillery to protect the West Point arsenal.

In 1791, though, Congress authorized the formation of the Legion of the United States, renamed the United States Army in 1796. When the Whiskey Rebellion erupted in western Pennsylvania and Virginia in 1794, in opposition to a tax on distilled spirits that were easier for western farmers to transport to faraway markets than other grain products were, Hamilton joined President Washington and General Henry "Light Horse" Lee to harry the rebels home with a larger force than any that fought in a single field in the War of Independence. At the outset of the undeclared "Quasi-War" with France of 1798 to 1800, Washington successfully pushed a reluctant President Adams to appoint Hamilton as major general and then inspector general. When Washington died on December 14, 1799, Hamilton thus became the army's senior officer, a post he held for six months and a day.

During the war with France, the Federalist Congress passed and President Adams signed the Alien and Sedition Acts, probably the source of Barack Obama's comments on arguments "about the meaning of such basic rights as freedom of speech and freedom of assembly" and on how some Founders "were not averse to ignoring those rights altogether." The Naturalization Act extended the period of residency required for citizenship from five to fourteen years, the Alien Friends Acts allowed the president to imprison or deport noncitizens deemed dangerous, and the Alien Enemies Act allowed the president to imprison or deport anyone from a hostile nation. Even worse was the Sedition Act, which, in a ludicrously obvious violation of the First Amendment, made it illegal on pain of fines and imprisonment to "write, print, utter, or publish ... any false, scandalous and malicious writing" against the government.[76]

Obama's assessment of these acts is subtly expressed but could hardly be harsher. In discussing modern perceptions "that we live in the worst of political times, that a creeping political fascism is closing its grip around our throats," Obama selected three instances of historical horrors to put matters into perspective. The first and the third were "the internment of Japanese Americans under FDR" and "a hundred years of lynching under several dozen administrations." In between these two, Obama inserts "the Alien and

Sedition Acts under John Adams." At first glance the acts of 1798 may seem out of place between the other such obviously horrific violations of the rights to liberty and even indeed the right to life itself. Yet the Sedition Act in particular could not have been more of a betrayal of the First Amendment right to free speech. And free speech of course is not only a fundamental right in and of itself but is also foundational to the functioning of a "deliberative democracy," which Obama believes is the genus and genius not only of the First Amendment, but also of the entire Constitution and of American democracy itself. Seen by these standards, the administration's attack on free speech was an attack on the American republic itself. The Sedition Act was therefore tantamount to treason.[77]

It is clear enough therefore where Barack Obama's historical sympathies lie. In reference to the Founders' spirit of anti-absolutism, Obama notes that "Hamilton's plans for leading a New Army foundered and Adams's reputation after the Alien and Sedition Acts suffered for failing to abide by this impulse." That said, Obama is much less dogmatic than many of the men at that time were. As we see in Chapter 6, Obama praises Hamiltonian economics, and rather glosses over the Treasury Secretary's laissez-faire attitude to labor exploitation—in contrast to the Jeffersonian agrarians who thought the rise of manufacturing would create an underclass of dependent wage workers who would undermine a republic of small but independent, landowning "yeoman" farmers (mythical as that image may have been, and slaveholders as most of them were).[78]

A testament to Federalist Party cynicism is the fact that the Sedition Act was set to expire when the next president took office. To his credit, President Thomas Jefferson did not request its renewal, and only the Alien Enemies Act survived his administration. Jefferson did not undo Hamilton's economic machinery either, however, and indeed his embargo on British imports probably did more to promote American manufacturing than Hamilton's failed tariffs would have done. Jefferson thus proved himself to be more of a pragmatist than he sometimes sounded before he was president. Furthermore, as Barack Obama observes, "Jefferson helped consolidate the power of the national government even as he claimed to deplore and reject such power." As we see in Chapters 4 and 7, the Louisiana Purchase of 1803 also added vastly to American territory, which extended enslavement and made the United States a trans-Mississippi and indeed a continental nation.[79]

Conservative or liberal, we are all constitutionalists

After the turbulent politics of the 1790s and the tumultuous election of 1800, Thomas Jefferson adopted an emollient attitude. He urged all to "bear in mind this sacred principle, that though the will of the majority is in all cases to prevail, that will to be rightful must be reasonable; that the minority possess their equal rights, which equal law must protect, and to violate would be oppression." He encouraged all to "reflect that, having banished from our land that religious intolerance under which mankind so long bled and suffered, we have yet gained little if we countenance a political intolerance as despotic, as wicked, and capable of as bitter and bloody persecutions." Given these provisos, though, he defended free speech: "If there be any among us who would wish to dissolve this Union or to change its republican form," he said, "let them stand undisturbed as monuments of the safety with which error of opinion may be tolerated where reason is left free to combat it."[80]

But Jefferson also called on his "fellow-citizens" to "unite with one heart and one mind" and to "restore to social intercourse that harmony and affection without which liberty and even life itself are but dreary things." And he felt that they could find that common ground by remembering that differing views over particular policies don't necessarily mean divergences in general politics. For "every difference of opinion," he pointed out, "is not a difference of principle. We have called by different names brethren of the same principle. We are all Republicans, we are all Federalists."[81]

Barack Obama agrees that for all that Americans might differ over certain matters they nevertheless share a more fundamental unity grounded in a creed of equality and liberty "made real" in a constitution. A "careful reading of our founding documents," Obama wrote, "reminds us just how much all of our attitudes have been shaped by them. More than two hundred years later," he added, Americans may disagree over "the meaning of a 'reasonable' search, or whether the Second Amendment prohibits all gun regulation, or whether the desecration of the flag should be considered speech," and also over other issues such as "abortion, or end-of-life care, or homosexual partnerships."[82]

Still, Obama continued, we'd be "hard pressed to find a conservative or liberal in America today ... who doesn't subscribe to the basic set of individual liberties identified by the Founders and enshrined in our Constitution and our common law." He then noted the rights to free speech, religion, peaceful protest and petition, property, legal immunities, and "the right to make our own determinations, with minimal restriction, regarding family life and the way we raise our children. In that sense," he added, "wherever we lie on the political spectrum, we all subscribe to the Founders' teachings" and "we are confident in the fundamental soundness of the Founders' blueprints and the democratic house that resulted." And Obama concluded these Jeffersonian reflections with very Jeffersonian words: "Conservative or liberal, we are all constitutionalists."[83]

Thomas Jefferson was optimistic about America's prospects at the turn of the nineteenth century. "Let us, then," he said in his inaugural address,

> with courage and confidence pursue our own Federal and Republican principles, our attachment to union and representative government. Kindly separated by nature and a wide ocean from the exterminating havoc of one quarter of the globe; too high-minded to endure the degradations of the others; possessing a chosen country, with room enough for our descendants to the thousandth and thousandth generation; entertaining a due sense of our equal right to the use of our own faculties, to the acquisitions of our own industry, to honor and confidence from our fellow-citizens, resulting not from birth, but from our actions and their sense of them; enlightened by a benign religion, professed, indeed, and practiced

in various forms, yet all of them inculcating honesty, truth, temperance, gratitude, and the love of man; acknowledging and adoring an overruling Providence, which by all its dispensations proves that it delights in the happiness of man here and his greater happiness hereafter—with all these blessings, what more is necessary to make us a happy and a prosperous people?[84]

Barack Obama can be similarly sunny when looking back at the time that Thomas Jefferson looked forward to. "IN SUM," Obama says "the Constitution envisions a road map by which we marry passion to reason, the ideal of individual freedom to the demands of community." And "the amazing thing is that it's worked. Through the early days of the Union, through the depressions and world wars, through the multiple transformations of the economy and Western expansion and the arrival of millions of immigrants to our shores, our democracy has not only survived but has thrived."[85]

And yet. Thomas Jefferson knew that all was not well and Barack Obama knows it too. As early as 1784 Jefferson had written of Virginia that "I tremble for my country when I reflect that God is just: that his justice cannot sleep for ever." All but forty years later he wrote that "this momentous question, like a fire bell in the night, awakened and filled me with terror. I considered it at once as the knell of the Union." The momentous question of course was the question of slavery. And, as Barack Obama noted in Philadelphia, the document the Founders drafted there in 1787 "was eventually signed but ultimately unfinished." For it was "stained by this nation's original sin."[86]

CHAPTER 4
A NEW BIRTH OF FREEDOM: SLAVERY
AND THE CIVIL WAR

This nation's original sin

In his speech on "A More Perfect Union" in March 2008, Barack Obama said the following about the Founders, the Constitution, and slavery: "The document they produced was eventually signed but ultimately unfinished. It was stained by this nation's original sin of slavery, a question that divided the colonies and brought the convention to a stalemate until the founders chose to allow the slave trade to continue for at least twenty more years, and to leave any final resolution to future generations."[1]

The specific section of the Constitution to which Obama here refers is the Slave Trade Clause. On the other clauses he was vague that day, but in *The Audacity of Hope* he was perhaps freer to write than he was to speak in the Philadelphia hot spot and at a particularly critical moment in his presidential campaign, following the uncovering of incendiary comments about race that his pastor Reverend Jeremiah Wright had made in the past. In the book, though, Obama identified all three of the original constitutional clauses that clearly if not exactly explicitly, supported enslavement: "The Three-fifths Clause and the Fugitive Slave Clause and the Importation Clause." We'll come back to how the founders left "any final resolution" to the slavery question "to future generations" later in this chapter. For now, though, let's look at the constitutional provisions that favored enslavement. Beginning with "the Importation Clause."[2]

The original Constitution said: "The migration or importation of such Persons as any of the States now existing shall think proper to admit, shall not be prohibited by the Congress prior to the Year one thousand eight hundred and eight." In the years after Independence every state forbade the slave trade, although Georgia and South Carolina reopened it in advance of the anticipated federal ban. It was in deference to these states that the Founders forbade the federal government from forbidding the slave trade for twenty years, though a national interdiction was finally effected from the first of January 1808.[3]

But this provision was arguably more than the "Importation Clause" that Barack Obama calls it. The word "migration"—if distinct from "importation"—implies that after twenty years, Congress could forbid the interstate as well as the international slave trade. And the constitutional power Congress had (and has) "to regulate interstate commerce" further suggests a right to prohibit slave trading across state lines. James Madison would later deny that this was so, arguing that the words "migration" and "importation" referred to a single process and that therefore Congress was only allowed to ban the international and not the internal slave trade. Whatever the case, Congress never interdicted the internal trade, and immeasurable suffering and fear followed from the continuing tearing apart of families, friends, and communities through a trade in human beings that by the 1840s extended for more than a thousand miles from Delaware to Texas.

The Constitution protected another kind of human trafficking in the United States. It directed: "No Person held to Service or Labour in one state, under the Laws thereof, escaping into another, shall, in Consequence of any Law or Regulation therein, be discharged from such Service or Labour, but shall be delivered up on Claim of the Party to whom such Service or Labour may be due." In 1793, Congress passed a Fugitive Slave Act that gave legislative form to the constitutional right of slaveholders or their agents to recover runaways by subjecting anyone who obstructed them to a very sizable fine of $500. Many northerners, black and white, nevertheless responded by constructing the Underground Railroad—a series of safe houses for escapee slaves and a metaphor for the network of fugitives and those who hid and helped them. Some state legislatures passed "personal liberty laws" requiring slaveholders and their agents to produce proof in court that their captors were southern runaways rather than free black northerners. Though perhaps thousands of legally free African Americans were kidnapped in the North and enslaved in the South in the nineteenth century, northern juries ruled with increasing frequency that alleged runaways from the South were in fact free.

Congress thus passed a new Fugitive Slave Act in 1850, doubling the fine for aiding absconders, adding the threat of six months' imprisonment, and requiring northern law-enforcement officials to assist in recapturing runaways or forfeit $1000. It also required claimants to submit nothing more than an affidavit to a federal marshal swearing that their captive was their legal property, and thereby deprived alleged runaways of trial by jury. And judges were rewarded $10 for ruling someone enslaved, but only half that fee for ruling someone free. As horrendous as this act was, it was so hated in the North that it contributed to tensions that eventuated in civil war and abolition.

But civil war did not come until 1861, and enslaved people had to wait until 1865 for constitutional confirmation of their liberation. And that long wait was partly due to another constitutional clause, the one providing that "representatives and direct Taxes shall be apportioned among the several States which may be included within this Union, according to their respective Numbers, which shall be determined by adding to the whole Number of free Persons, including those bound to Service for a Term of Years, and excluding Indians not taxed, three fifths of all other Persons."

This clause is sometimes misunderstood as defining slaves as three-fifths of a person. It was fact worse than that. It rested on the presumption that slaves were legally property—not necessarily people at all, although southern slave codes paradoxically defined slaves both as property and as people, the latter to grant certain though limited legal rights but mostly to authorize the disciplinary necessities arising from defining people as property in the first place. But the constitutional provision's principal purpose was to increase the power of the slave states in the federal government. The counting of three-fifths of the slaves as part of a state's population proportionally increased the number of southern members of the House of Representatives. That in turn inflated southern influence on presidential elections, as the Electoral College comprised (and still comprises) as many members per state as each has in Congress: the House of Representatives and the Senate combined.[4]

The Three-Fifths Clause is perhaps therefore best known by the name given to it by nineteenth-century abolitionists: "the Slave Power" (although the term also applied to the political influence of slaveholders more generally). We see the congressional power the clause gave slaveholders when we look a little later at legislative compromises in favor of enslavement. For now, though, let's see how well the Slave Power worked by exploring slaveholding among the early presidents of the United States.

Of the first five presidents, George Washington, Thomas Jefferson, James Madison, and James Monroe were all Virginia slaveholders. And while each member of the Virginia dynasty served two terms, the single non-slaveholder among the first five chief executives, John Adams of Massachusetts, served only one. So for thirty-two of the thirty-six years between 1789 and 1825, the American presidency was held by southern slaveholders. Non-slaveholding John Quincy Adams was the next president, but was a one-termer like his father. His successor from 1829 to 1837 was Andrew Jackson, a Tennessee slaveholder. Forty years out of forty-eight.

Martin Van Buren of New York had as a young man owned a man named Tom, but made no real effort to recover him when he ran away in 1814. And Van Buren didn't own slaves when he served as president from 1837 to 1841. He was defeated in the next election by Virginia-born William Henry Harrison, who had inherited slaves but had renounced enslavement and moved to Ohio, so 1840 was the first time the presidency was contested by two non-slaveholders. Harrison's, however, was the shortest presidency in American history. Inaugurated on March 4, 1841, he died a month later of what was thought to be pneumonia and was replaced by his Vice President John Tyler (1841–45), another Virginian, who was followed by James K. Polk of Tennessee (1845–49), then Zachary Taylor of Kentucky (1849–50): slaveholders all.

Zachary Taylor was the last to own slaves in office, though two post-Civil War presidents, Andrew Johnson (1865–69) and Ulysses S. Grant (1869–77), held slaves earlier in their lives. But it is notable that Taylor's 1850s successors were lifelong non-slaveholders: Millard Fillmore (1850–53), Franklin Pierce (1853–57), and James Buchanan (1857–61). As was the president from 1861 to 1865, Abraham Lincoln. This was possible because northern population growth had by that time sufficiently outstripped southern, something southerners feared from the start, and which had inspired them to insist on the Three-fifths Clause in the first place.

A house that was built by slaves

On July 25, 2016, at the Democratic National Convention in Philadelphia, Michelle Obama made a point of particular pertinence to the issue of slaveholding presidents and the general importance of enslavement in the early republic. Beginning by lauding

Hillary Clinton's "guts and the grace to keep coming back and putting those cracks in the highest and hardest glass ceiling until she finally breaks through," she continued with words that suggest that she shares her husband's views on struggle and progress in the American past:

> That is the story of this country, the story that has brought me to this stage tonight, the story of generations of people who felt the lash of bondage, the shame of servitude, the sting of segregation, but who kept on striving and hoping and doing what needed to be done so that today I wake up every morning in a house that was built by slaves.[5]

And the White House, occupied by so many slaveholders, was indeed built by slaves. Construction of the Executive Mansion in the purpose-built capital city of Washington DC began in 1792. The District of Columbia Commissioners appointed by President George Washington to oversee public construction initially hoped to rely mainly on European immigrant workers. They recruited some, and also engaged white laborers from neighboring Maryland and Virginia. But, according to the White House Historical Association, "response to recruitment was dismal and soon they turned to African Americans—both enslaved and free—to provide the bulk of labor that built the White House, the United States Capitol, and other early government buildings."[6]

Enslaved and free African Americans worked in all aspects of the capital's construction, but did a disproportionate share of the hardest labor. Slaves cut the White House stones from a quarry in Aquia, Virginia, for example, and felled the trees and dredged the swamp of the site where those stones were laid. As for the legislature, Congress's 2005 report on the "History of Slave Laborers in the Construction of the United States Capitol" found that between 1795 and 1801 the Commissioners made 385 payments for "Negro hire." That is, paying owners for leasing their slaves.[7]

None of this should surprise us in the slightest. Slave labor was commonly used in public projects as well as private enterprise, and Washington DC spans the Potomac River, laid on land donated by the slave states of Maryland and Virginia. And we saw in Chapter 1 how every colony allowed slavery, how the institution was only finally widely questioned by white people during the revolutionary era, and how the slow process of abolition was only just beginning as the early American republic took shape. Yet Michelle Obama's comments still caused something of a stir, provoking the discomfort of the likes of Bill O'Reilly, prompting articles in the *Washington Post* and other publications to point out that the First Lady was incontrovertibly correct according to mainstream and easily accessible sources.

If some of us are still thus squeamish about slavery, then we are perhaps not as far from the Founders as we might think. Not one of the constitutional clauses noted earlier, for example, is explicit about enslavement, even though most of the Founders held slaves. Each of the clauses employs a euphemism, even though their purposes were obvious to all. The Slave Trade Clause refers to "such Persons as any of the States now existing shall think proper to admit." The Fugitive Slave Clause defines a slave as a "Person held to Service or Labour." The Slave Power Clause refers to "three fifths of all other persons." James Madison's Notes on the Convention confirm in a self-referential detail that a certain squeamishness prevailed in Philadelphia in the summer of 1787: "Mr. MADISON thought it wrong to admit in the Constitution the idea that there could be property in men."[8]

Others obviously agreed. So the first time the Constitution mentions the word slavery explicitly is in the Thirteenth Amendment, the one that finally abolished the institution in 1865.

The answer to the slavery question

We've also seen already another kind of silence in the US Constitution. Although Barack Obama calls the principles of equality, life, liberty, and the pursuit of happiness "the foundation of our government," these words were not included in the federal Constitution. Yet they might well have been. They were after all included in the Massachusetts state Constitution of 1780, which declared: "All men are born free and equal, and have certain natural, essential, and unalienable rights; among which may be reckoned the right of enjoying and defending their lives and liberties; that of acquiring, possessing, and protecting property; in fine, that of seeking and obtaining their safety and happiness."[9]

As we saw in preceding chapters, in 1781 a slave named Elizabeth Freeman sued for her freedom on the basis of this constitutional embodiment of her natural rights. She and a fellow slave named Brom won their freedom due to a technical problem with their master's titles, and thereby failed to attain a legal ruling that enslavement was inconsistent with the law. But in the *Quock Walker Case* of 1783, in which *Brom and Bett v. Ashley* was cited, Chief Justice William Cushing advised the jury that the state's Constitution "sets out with declaring that all men are born free and equal—and that every subject is entitled to liberty, and to have it guarded by the laws, as well as life and property—and in short is totally repugnant to the idea of being born slaves." Therefore, he concluded, "slavery is inconsistent with our own conduct and Constitution." Enslavement consequently quickly expired in Massachusetts.[10]

No doubt some of the Founders would have happily seen the same words included in the federal Constitution—and with the same effect on enslavement throughout the nation. But they knew that this would have destroyed any chance of a deal in Philadelphia in 1787. Southern delegates were never going to allow the very real legal risk to slavery across the country that these words would have represented had they been included in the federal Constitution. Equality and unalienable rights to life, liberty, and the pursuit of happiness would thus remain part of America's "common creed," but would not be admitted in the law of the land.

And yet Barack Obama says, "Of course, the answer to the slavery question was already embedded within our Constitution—a Constitution that had at its very core the ideal of equal citizenship under the law; a Constitution that promised its people liberty, and justice, and a union that could be and should be perfected over time." We explored Obama's belief in the Constitution's promises of equal citizenship, liberty, and justice in the previous chapter. But, as Obama readily observes, these promises originally only applied to "members of America's political community" and the document drafted in 1787 "provided no protection to those outside the constitutional circle." Enslaved people were very much outside the circle, and so the Constitution remained "unfinished."[11]

Which is why Barack Obama's claim in the previous quotation is so important a part of his understanding of American history: that the union "could be and should be perfected over time." And indeed the union was finally made much more perfect by the Thirteenth Amendment abolishing enslavement in 1865. That, however, didn't happen through the normal operations of what Obama and others have called America's "deliberative democracy." As Obama also said in Philadelphia: "words on a parchment would not be enough to deliver slaves from bondage, or provide men and women of every color and creed their full rights and obligations as citizens of the United States. What would be needed," he continued, "were Americans in successive generations who were willing to do their part—through protests and struggle, on the streets and in the courts, through a civil war and civil disobedience and always at great risk—to narrow that gap between the promise of our ideals and the reality of their time."[12]

As Obama thus suggests, it was largely popular pressure rather than politicians' words or deeds that advanced the abolitionist agenda. And it was military force rather than reasoned compromise that finally brought abolition about. In the meantime, the kind of constitutional compromises Obama normally praises served to sustain slavery for almost eighty more years, first with the concessions contained in the original Constitution's proslavery clauses, then, enabled by those clauses, through a series of political compromises that postponed Civil War until 1861 and full emancipation until 1865.

Before analyzing these admitted aberrations from Barack Obama's general rules of American history, though, we need to explore his opinions on a different but closely related issue: the institution of slavery itself—the social rather than the political history of slavery.

The hope of slaves

The social and political histories of slavery are closely related because part of the social history of slavery was a political struggle against it by the slaves themselves. We've seen already that emancipation was not a gift given by newly enlightened white people. Many whites on the contrary owed their enlightenment to black abolitionists, initially in particular to the courage and sacrifices of black soldiers during the War of Independence. In addition, Quock Walker, Elizabeth Freeman, Brom, and the slave petitioners, runaways, and rebels we met in Chapter 2 exhibited in abundance the audacity and hope that Barack Obama believes has driven Americans toward fulfilling the promises of the nation's common creed. These of course were just a few of the millions of American slaves who aspired to freedom, whether they were able to attain it or not. And Obama summoned the spirit of all of them when he spoke of "the hope of slaves sitting around a fire singing freedom songs."[13]

Of course slaves couldn't sing freedom songs openly, so they sang them in code. In the fields and in the "hush harbors" where the "invisible institution" of the African American church evolved, slaves sang songs such as "Roll, Jordan Roll":

Went down the River Jordan,

Where John baptized three,

When I walked the Devil in Hell,

Said John ain't baptized me,

I said, roll, Jordan, roll,

Roll, Jordan, roll,

My soul ought to rise in heaven, Lord,

For the year when Jordan rolls,

Well, some say John was a Baptist,

Some say John was a Jew,

Well, I say John was a preacher,

And my bible says so too,

I said, roll, Jordan, roll,

Roll, Jordan, roll,

My soul ought to rise in heaven, Lord,

For the year when Jordan rolls, Hallelujah.[14]

A white Methodist preacher named Charles Wesley wrote "Roll, Jordan, Roll" in the early eighteenth century, and it was adopted by slaveholders who hoped that Christian messages would encourage subservience among slaves. Instead of that, however, slaves adopted Christianity as a liberation theology, and in the process turned many gospel songs and stories into subversive commentaries on enslavement. The River Jordan, for example, was where John baptized, preached, and prepared people for the coming of the Christ, as the song says. But it was also where the Jews crossed into the Promised Land after the Exodus from Egyptian slavery, as the singers knew. And thus the River Jordan represented the Mississippi and Ohio rivers, where runaway slaves crossed into the Free States if and when they could. Slaves sang a lot of songs about rivers.

There is also something about how these songs were sung that resounds in Barack Obama's image of "slaves sitting around the fire." That is, the songs were often sung communally, and frequently in the call-and-response style still seen in the antiphonal interactions of African American preachers and congregations today. These phenomena reflected the strength of the "slave community"—whether the local community in the quarters on a single plantation or the larger community of African Americans across the South or even nationwide. That community helped slaves survive by providing a sense of self-worth both for individuals and for a people besieged by oppression and racism. All too often, slave communities provided a new home for those sold away from their old homes. But it also helped slaves escape, providing food, shelter, and hiding places for those on the run. And for those who never escaped, the slave community helped sustain the hope required to keep on "singing freedom songs."

Barack Obama has felt the power of these communal songs and stories of suffering and survival on the deepest possible personal level. In his autobiography he recalled his first visit to Trinity United Church of Christ in Chicago and the first sermon he heard Reverend Jeremiah Wright preach about the "audacity to hope." Years later it still inspired feelings that he expressed in his most sublime eloquence, in prose and yet in a poetry of Christian imagery imbued in African American idiom:

And in that single note—hope!—I heard something else; at the foot of that cross, inside the thousands of churches across the city, I imagined the stories of ordinary black people merging with the stories of David and Goliath, Moses and Pharaoh, the Christians in the lion's den, Ezekiel's field of dry bones. The stories—of survival, and freedom, and hope—became our story, my story; the blood that had spilled was our blood; the tears our tears.[15]

Of course slavery was not all about singing and resisting, hoping and escaping. It was also a system of extreme and extensive violence. The violence of masters, overseers, and drivers on the farms and plantations, the violence of the patrollers policing the larger localities, the violence of the state slave codes, and of the federal Fugitive Slave Act and the federal constitutional provision it was based upon. Michelle Obama alluded to this violence when she spoke of "generations of people who felt the lash of bondage." Barack Obama has also spoken of those who "endured the lash of the whip" and who shed "blood drawn by lash," the latter phrase borrowed from Abraham Lincoln's second inaugural address and included in Obama's own second inaugural address.[16]

In speaking and writing of slaves' hopes of freedom, of their resistance, religion, and community, and of the institution's inherent violence, Barack Obama has distilled what historians generally identify as the essences of the social history of slavery. And yet Obama has only written or spoken publicly about these things on rare occasions. And even when he's done so he's done so only briefly and in passing, placing them in rhetorical processions of various and often positive historical phenomena. What follows by way of illustration are the passages of the speeches that the quotes mentioned previously come from, with italics added to identify the mentions and to highlight how Obama's social history of slavery is placed within his history of everything else. The first is from

"The Audacity of Hope," Obama's address to the Democratic National Convention in July 2004.

> John Kerry calls on us to hope. John Edwards calls on us to hope. I'm not talking about blind optimism here—the almost willful ignorance that thinks unemployment will go away if we just don't think about it, or the health care crisis will solve itself if we just ignore it.
>
> That's not what I'm talking about. I'm talking about something more substantial. *It's the hope of slaves sitting around a fire singing freedom songs*; the hope of immigrants setting out for distant shores; the hope of a young naval lieutenant bravely patrolling the Mekong Delta; the hope of a millworker's son who dares to defy the odds; the hope of a skinny kid with a funny name who believes that America has a place for him, too.[17]

Next, from President Obama's first inaugural address, in January 2009:

> Our journey has never been one of short-cuts or settling for less. It has not been the path for the faint-hearted—for those who prefer leisure over work, or seek only the pleasures of riches and fame. Rather, it has been the risk-takers, the doers, the makers of things—some celebrated but more often men and women obscure in their labor, who have carried us up the long, rugged path towards prosperity and freedom. For us, they packed up their few worldly possessions and travelled across oceans in search of a new life. For us, they toiled in sweatshops and settled the West; *endured the lash of the whip* and ploughed the hard earth. For us, they fought and died, in places like Concord and Gettysburg; Normandy and Khe Sahn.[18]

And finally, from the president's second inaugural address, January 2013: "Through *blood drawn by lash* and blood drawn by sword, we learned that no union founded on the principles of liberty and equality could survive half-slave and half-free. We made ourselves anew, and vowed to move forward together."[19]

Why would Barack Obama mention slavery as a social institution only infrequently? And why even then would he place it alongside other historical phenomena, perhaps thereby obscuring the uniquely horrific nature of what people in the abolitionist era called "the peculiar institution," and what historians since have generally considered a singularly horrendous iniquity? Slaves after all were legally defined as property, and as such could be bought and sold, and they lived their lives and could be killed with few if any legal protections. Slaves' families were legal nonentities and husbands and wives and parents and children could be torn away from each other, and all other bonds could be similarly broken at any time and for any reason the owners chose. An enslaved woman could be raped by her enslaver with total impunity, and her rape by another was legally speaking merely a trespass on her owner's property. A slave could be killed and again with impunity by his or her owner or an authorized other, an overseer or a patroller, for offering the slightest resistance or defiance. Could be and were—all these horrors happened every single day for the two-and-a-half centuries of enslavement's existence in British America and the United States.

Yet there are compelling reasons, some political, some historical, why Barack Obama would mention these things only infrequently and often only alongside other phenomena. One regrettably obvious one is that to talk more fully about slavery would have been politically risky, especially for an African American. Already alleged to be Kenyan-born and a Muslim during his electoral campaign, he needed if he could to avoid stereotyping ascription as a single-interest candidate, or as playing the "race card," or as an "angry black man." As we saw before, Reverend Jeremiah Wright's outspoken condemnations of historical racism almost derailed Barack Obama's presidential campaign. Obama distanced himself from Wright because he genuinely disagreed with some of what Wright said, but he also had to do so to save his presidential campaign.[20]

But a less lamentable reason is Barack Obama's wish for racial reconciliation through common remembrance. Most fundamentally, that means including African American history in the popular perception of American history, even if inclusion risks implication of equivalence. In a speech of February 2012, marking the breaking of the ground for the groundbreaking National Museum of African American History and Culture (NMAAHC), Obama said, for example, "When future generations hear these songs of pain and progress and struggle and sacrifice, I hope they will not think of them as somehow separate from the larger American story. I want them to see it as central—an important part of our shared story." And, as he said in his weekly address after the museum's opening in September 2016: "this museum tells a story of America that hasn't always taken a front seat in our national narrative. As a people, we've rightfully passed on the tales of the giants who built this country. But too often, willful or not, we've chosen to gloss over or ignore entirely the experience of millions upon millions of others." And "All of that," he added, "isn't simply the African-American story; it's part of the American story."[21]

In these speeches President Obama added to his account of the social history of slavery by giving examples of how the construction of American democracy was in many key ways a common endeavor, even when done by people from such opposite ends of the social spectrum as slaveholders and slaves. He explained in 2012 that he found it "fitting that this museum has found a home on the National Mall" because "it was on this ground long ago that lives were once traded, where hundreds of thousands once marched for jobs and for freedom." Although any mention of enslavement implicitly recognizes that enslaved people were legally property, this was Obama's first explicit public acknowledgment of this most fundamental feature of the institution's uniqueness in the history of iniquity. Even then, though, Obama linked slavery quickly to freedom by moving within the same sentence from the slave markets in Washington to the Civil Rights March on Washington.[22]

Another such Obamian acknowledgment came a few years later. When commemorating a century-and-a-half since the passing of the Thirteenth Amendment, Barack Obama spoke of how slavery was "wrong in every sense. Stealing men, women, and children from their homelands. Tearing husband from wife, parent from child; stripped and sold to the highest bidder; shackled in chains and bloodied with the whip. It's antithetical not only to our conception of human rights and dignity, but to our conception of ourselves—a people founded on the premise that all are created equal."[23]

Yet rather than seeing this history as divisive, Obama strives to see it as something shared, even finding common ground between those who freed themselves and those whom they enslaved. "It was here," Obama continued at the NMAAHC groundbreaking ceremony, "that the pillars of our democracy were built, often by black hands." Michelle Obama was making much the same point, as well as a point about progress, when she mentioned that "generations of people who felt the lash of bondage, the shame of servitude" had nevertheless "kept on striving and hoping and doing what needed to be done so that today I wake up every morning in a house that was built by slaves." Her husband used precisely the same words, "a house that was built by slaves," just two months later, on September 23, 2016, in his White House address marking the opening of the NMAAHC.[24]

We're the slaves who built the White House

And Barack Obama used something close to those words over a year earlier as well, on March 7, 2015, in a speech marking the semicentenary of a bloody Sunday in Selma, Alabama: "We're the slaves who built the White House and the economy of the South." Though he was remembering the violence of the state troopers against voting rights marchers half-a-century before, he was again reaching for reconciliation through remembrance of collective endeavor in the name of equality. And that Selma speech is probably Obama's most powerful single exposition of what we might call his American syncretism. The oration's title is "For We Were Born of Change," the "We" encompassing all Americans alike even while specifying a particular constituency. In the same section of the speech cited earlier, each sentence commences with "We are" or "We're," suggesting continuities and commonalities that transcend time and transcend all distinctions of race, gender, and categorization of any kind.[25]

"We are," Barack Obama said, "Sojourner Truth and Fannie Lou Hamer, women who could do as much as any man and then some. And we're Susan B. Anthony, who shook the system until the law reflected that truth." The struggle for freedom for slaves and the subsequent one for equality for freed people are thus represented respectively in the persons of the runaway slave and abolitionist activist Sojourner Truth and the early civil rights campaigner Fanny Lou Hamer. But, even more than that, African American struggles are linked to those of white women through the person of women's suffrage campaigner Susan B. Anthony, a particularly telling inclusion, given Anthony's later opposition to the enfranchisement of black men before black or white women.

Barack Obama began these stanzas of this speech with "We are Lewis and Clark and Sacajawea, pioneers who braved the unfamiliar, followed by a stampede of farmers and miners, and entrepreneurs and hucksters." And so he continued, to an audience of all races, sexes, religions, birth places, and political parties: "We're the immigrants who stowed away on ships to reach these shores, the huddled masses yearning to breathe free—Holocaust survivors, Soviet defectors, the Lost Boys of Sudan. We're the hopeful strivers who cross the Rio Grande because we want our kids to know a better life." And then "We're the slaves who built the White House and the economy of the South." And then "We're the ranch hands and cowboys who opened up the West, and countless laborers who laid rail, and raised skyscrapers, and organized for workers' rights," GIs, Tuskegee Airmen, Navajo code-breakers, Japanese Americans, the firefighters of 9/11, and soldiers in Afghanistan and Iraq. And "We're the gay Americans whose blood ran in the streets of San Francisco and New York" and "We are storytellers, writers, poets, artists ... the inventors of gospel and jazz and blues, bluegrass and country, and hip-hop and rock and roll." And "We are Jackie Robinson" and "the people Langston Hughes wrote of" and "the people Emerson wrote of."[26]

And as Obama acknowledges on other occasions, the common endeavor is not only manifest in a metaphorical community imagined in a flight of rhetorical fancy. It was and is much more than that, made real as it was in a phenomenon dating to the days and the interracial relations of Sally Hemings and Thomas Jefferson, Elizabeth Hemings and John Wayles, the original African woman and Captain Hemings, and those of many generations before them. And to the Obamas as to many African Americans, this is personal. As Barack Obama has pointed out, "I am married to a black American who carries within her the blood of slaves and slaveowners, an inheritance we pass on to our two precious daughters." And, as he has also said, he is himself the son of a black man and a white woman respectively from Kenya and Kansas and has "brothers, sisters, nieces, nephews, uncles and cousins of every race and every hue, scattered across three continents." And some of his own mother's ancestors also once enslaved African Americans.[27]

There is therefore substance, even literally consanguinity, in Barack Obama's American syncretism, for all that slavery was certainly a "peculiar institution." And in any case Obama's emphasis on continuity and collectivity in America's long march to freedom doesn't shroud oppression. When recounting slavery and freedom, Obama sometimes situates the two together, rhetorically positioning them as historical antitheses. Rather than slighting the former in favor of the latter, his juxtaposing perhaps deepens our appreciation of the costs of enslavement and of the value of freedom. The one looks worse and the other one better when placed in relation to each other. To see how Obama rhetorically situates slavery and freedom and other tragedies and triumphs in the African American and therefore the American past we can return to the speech at the 2012 groundbreaking ceremony for the NMAAHC:

> When our children look at Harriet Tubman's shawl or Nat Turner's bible or the plane flown by Tuskegee Airmen, I don't want them to be seen as figures somehow larger than life. I want them to see how ordinary Americans could do extraordinary things; how men and women just like them had the courage and determination to right a wrong, to make it right.

I want my daughters to see the shackles that bound slaves on their voyage across the ocean and the shards of glass that flew from the 16th Street Baptist church, and understand that injustice and evil exist in the world. But I also want them to hear Louis Armstrong's horn and learn about the Negro League and read the poems of Phyllis Wheatley. And I want them to appreciate this museum not just as a record of tragedy, but as a celebration of life.[28]

And, finally, the rarity of Barack Obama's mentions of the social history of slavery and his tendency to place it in a story of progress are not just about the political positioning of himself or the cultural reconciliation of the races today, but are in fact also consistent with other aspects of his American history. As we saw earlier, for example, Obama's colonial and revolutionary America are primarily about religious freedom, homespun virtues, the democracy of the New England town meeting, the Declaration of Independence, and the Constitution. His interest in colonies and empire is therefore largely limited to understanding them as the contexts or pretexts of liberation. And, so, similarly, his interest in enslavement is largely limited to understanding it as the context or even the pretext of emancipation. Barack Obama's history of slavery is therefore, like the rest of his American history, ultimately a history of freedom.

There are three other notable Obamian mentions of the social history of slavery, made on a single occasion in reference to the persons of Denmark Vesey, Frederick Douglass, and Harriet Tubman. But Obama mentions these people in connection with the political history of slavery, specifically in reference to enslavement's eventual and overdue abolition. But before exploring that, we need to examine Obama's reflections on enslavement's extended and undue survival.

Any final resolution

Although Barack Obama doesn't portray slavery as a singular social system, he does portray it as a peculiar political problem. As he said when commemorating the Constitution's Thirteenth Amendment, "for decades, America wrestled with the issue of slavery in a way that we have with no other, before or since." He nonetheless once again focused more on the eventual winning of the campaign against slavery than on the compromises that allowed it to survive and even thrive as it did for many years. Obama's American history thus moves pretty hastily from the constitutional convention's proslavery compromises mentioned previously to the antislavery endeavors of Abraham Lincoln examined later, with only a few allusions to the many concessions made in favor of slavery in the meantime. To understand Obama's history more completely, though, and his concept of the Constitution more fully, we need to explore the compromises of the pre-Civil War years. Because if the "answer to the slavery question" was "already embedded within our Constitution," as Obama claims, the "deliberative democracy" the Constitution created nevertheless protected enslavement for almost eighty years, as indeed Obama admits.[29]

We've already seen how abolition by the non-plantation states created a North and South on either side of the Pennsylvania-Maryland border—the Mason-Dixon Line, so-called after surveyors Charles Mason and Jeremiah Dixon who in the 1760s settled the long-running boundary dispute between the two colonies, as they then were. The free state/slave state divide was then extended westwards, by way of the northwest and southwest ordnances of 1787, along the Ohio River as far as the Mississippi. And we've also seen how that same year the Founders provided for the slave trade to be ended in 1808, but left "any final resolution to future generations."[30]

Congressman James Tallmadge Jr. of New York was born in 1778 and was therefore a member of the next generation. When the territory of Missouri applied for statehood in 1819, he attempted to append a gradual abolition amendment to the admission bill that would have freed slaves born in the new state at the age of twenty-five. For sure, other new slave states had already been admitted to the Union: Kentucky in 1792, Tennessee in 1796, Louisiana in 1812, Mississippi in 1817, and Alabama was joining just as the Missouri Bill hit the floor of the House. But Missouri was the first territory to apply for statehood from fully inside the Louisiana Purchase region, the vast swathe of land west of the Mississippi River bought by President Thomas Jefferson from France in 1803.

Northerners like Tallmadge were determined to stop slavery spreading there, some of them openly describing the institution as evil in the debates over Missouri's admission. Some southerners responded darkly with early talk of secession and war. Thomas Jefferson wrote prophetically in April 1820 that "this momentous question, like a fire bell in the night, awakened and filled me with terror. I considered it at once as the knell of the Union. It is hushed indeed for the moment, but this is a reprieve only, not a final sentence. A geographical line, coinciding with a marked principle, moral and political, once conceived and held up to the angry passions of men, will never be obliterated; and every new irritation will mark it deeper and deeper."[31]

The previous month, though, Senator Henry Clay of Kentucky had indeed hushed the issue for the moment by brokering the Missouri Compromise, wherein slavery was forbidden in the purchase territory north of parallel 36°30′, the southern boundary of Missouri—except that slavery was allowed in Missouri itself. Maine was also separated from Massachusetts and joined the Union in its own right, rebalancing the number of slave and free states at twelve of each. Deliberative democracy had saved the Union, for the time being, but the price for that was the westward expansion of enslavement.

The next sectional crisis was not explicitly about slavery. When Congress passed a new Tariff Act in 1828, some used the occasion to advance arguments for states' rights. South Carolinians in particular pointed out that this "Tariff of Abominations" meant they had to pay higher prices for goods to subsidize the economic evolution of northern manufacturing. But, with the First Emancipation nearing completion and with wider abolitionism on the rise, they were also concerned with how they might use the Constitution to protect their increasingly peculiar institution.

In 1828, John C. Calhoun published his *South Carolina Exposition & Protest*, though he did so anonymously as he was hoping to retain his status as vice president after the election that year. In it, he advanced a "State Compact Theory" according to which the Constitution comprised a "compact" in which each state retained its sovereignty and the federal government was their "agent." If the federal government exceeded its jurisdiction, any state could "interpose" its sovereign authority to nullify a law within its boundaries or even by seceding from the Union. And when Congress renewed the tariff in 1832, South Carolina correspondingly declared it "void and no force." President Jackson sent gunboats into Charleston harbor to enforce federal law if needs be, but once again Henry Clay ended the Nullification Controversy with a compromise in which South Carolina would accept a tariff that would be gradually reduced until by 1842 it reached the level it was at in 1816.[32]

Government of the people, by the people, for the people

A little earlier in the Nullification Crisis, however, South Carolina Senator Robert Hayne had repeated the case for State Compact Theory. In turn, in 1830 and in what became known as the Hayne-Webster debate, Massachusetts Senator Daniel Webster made a proto-Obamian case for a nationalist interpretation of the Constitution: that the Constitution was not formed by the states but by "We the people." So the states were not nations, and could not nullify a federal law or secede from the Union, as such actions would defy the sovereignty of the ultimate authority: the people of the United States.

Barack Obama is famously fond of quoting or paraphrasing Abraham Lincoln on this matter of the sovereignty of the people. In his own acceptance speech on November 4, 2008, the new president-elect celebrated how his campaign "drew strength" from many sources, including "the millions of Americans who volunteered and organized and proved that more than two centuries [after the founding], a government of the people, by the people and for the people has not perished from the Earth." Those last words of course come from the last line of Abraham Lincoln's Gettysburg Address, his dedication of November 19, 1863 to those who fought and died on the Pennsylvania battleground that July. It is worth quoting in full because Barack Obama uses several phrases from it that we encounter again a little later. But also just because.[33]

> Fourscore and seven years ago our fathers brought forth, upon this continent, a new nation, conceived in liberty and dedicated to the proposition that "all men are created equal."
>
> Now we are engaged in a great civil war, testing whether that nation, or any nation so conceived and so dedicated, can long endure. We are met on a great battlefield of that war. We have come to dedicate a portion of it, as a final resting place for those who died here, that the nation might live. This we may, in all propriety do. But in a larger sense, we cannot dedicate, we cannot consecrate, we cannot hallow, this ground. The brave men, living and dead, who struggled here, have hallowed it, far above our poor power to add or detract. The world will little note, nor long remember what we say here; while it can never forget what they did here.

It is rather for us the living, we here be dedicated to the great task remaining before us—that from these honored dead we take increased devotion to that cause for which they here gave the last full measure of devotion—that we here highly resolve that these dead shall not have died in vain, that this nation shall have a new birth of freedom, and that government of the people, by the people, for the people shall not perish from the earth.[34]

But both Barack Obama and Abraham Lincoln owe a great deal of the credit for that final line to Daniel Webster. In his Second Reply to Hayne in January 1830, Webster addressed the issues of "the origin of this government and the source of its power." He asked, "Whose agent is it? Is it the creature of the State legislatures, or the creature of the people?" And he answered, "It is, Sir, the people's Constitution, the people's government, made for the people, made by the people, and answerable to the people."[35]

We all indeed owe an enormous debt to a brilliant orator who's less well-remembered now than he was in Lincoln's day. Webster concluded his Second Reply with the following words:

When my eyes shall be turned to behold for the last time the sun in heaven, may I not see him shine on the broken and dishonored fragments of a once glorious Union; on States dissevered, discordant, belligerent; on a land rent with civil feuds, or drenched, it may be, in fraternal blood! Let their last feeble and lingering glance rather behold the gorgeous ensign of the republic, now known and honored throughout the earth, still full high advanced, its arms and trophies streaming in their original lustre, not a stripe erased or polluted, not a single star obscured, bearing for its motto, no such miserable interrogatory as "What is all this worth?" nor those other words of delusion and folly, "Liberty first and Union afterwards"; but everywhere, spread all over in characters of living light, blazing on all its ample folds, as they float over the sea and over the land, and in every wind under the whole heavens, that other sentiment, dear to every true American heart—Liberty *and* Union, now and for ever, one and inseparable![36]

In Daniel Webster's final phrase there—"Liberty *and* Union, now and for ever, one and inseparable!"—we can find three meanings. First, it was a riposte to a toast reputedly given by John C. Calhoun as a riposte to a toast reputedly given by Andrew Jackson at the Jefferson Day dinner of April 13, 1830, which was itself a riposte to the *The South Carolina Exposition and Protest*. As the Nullification Crisis was escalating, the formidable former duelist Jackson made his hostility to Calhoun clear by saying "Our Union. It must be preserved." The supposedly shaking and no-longer-so-anonymous South Carolinian author responded by saying, "The Union, next to our liberty, most dear. May we all remember that it can only be preserved by respecting the rights of the States and by distributing equally the benefits and burdens of the Union."[37]

But Webster's "Liberty *and* Union" was much more than an intervention in a transitory Washington tiff. Webster's second meaning was that the Union itself was one and inseparable, unbreakable—no state could secede on its singular initiative. And that was because of the third and the most significant meaning of Webster's phrase: that the Union, founded as it was by the sovereign people, was the political embodiment of liberty itself. Webster thereby did more than rehearse and refine the constitutional case for perpetual union that the Civil War would be fought on. His eloquent association of the abstract concept of "Liberty" with the actual reality of the "Union" helps us understand how so many gave "the last full measure of devotion" to the Union's preservation.[38]

The self-imposed gag rule

In the years from 1830 to the Civil War—the antebellum era—the constitutional politics of slavery became ever more complicated, and compromises over it ever harder to contrive. One of the few constitutional compromises of the nineteenth century that Barack Obama mentions, perhaps because it betrayed the particular principles of a deliberative democracy as well as the general principle of liberty itself, is "the self-imposed gag rule that the Twenty-fourth Congress would place on all debate regarding the issue of slavery."[39]

From the early 1830s, the growing abolitionist movement began petitioning Congress against slavery—a tactic that British abolitionists successfully deployed against the slave trade before its abolition by that nation in 1807 and against slavery itself before its abolition in British dominions in 1834. (That their former imperial masters abolished enslavement before the land of the free did was a matter of national shame to many Americans at the time, but was thereby something else that helped promote the American abolitionist cause.) In 1836 the House of Representatives (of indeed the twenty-fourth Congress of 1835–37) passed the first in a series of "gag rules" that would table these petitions without discussion. And in 1840 Congress passed the Twenty-first Rule, a Standing Order that didn't require biennial renewal and that prevented the House not only from discussing, but even from receiving abolitionist petitions. In 1844, though, former president and then leading antislavery Congressman John Quincy Adams finally managed to assemble a large enough coalition to defeat this obvious and egregious violation of the Constitution's First Amendment. Just in time for the next sectional crisis over slavery in the western territories.

The 1820 Missouri Compromise had resolved the issue of slavery's expansion within the US territories that existed at the time. But new controversies arose over slavery in the vast region from east Texas to the California coast acquired by the United States via the Mexican American War of 1846 to 1848. Americans in the Mexican state of Coahuila y Tejas declared their independence in 1836 after General Antonio Lopez de Santa Anna built a metaphorical wall against American immigration. Texas applied to join the American Union immediately, but admission was impeded by northern congressmen anticipating war with Mexico and fearing the further spread of slavery. The Republic of Texas was an independent nation for the next eight years. In 1844, however, President

James K. Polk asked Congress for a Joint Resolution on annexation, requiring a simple majority rather than the supermajorities normally required for admission to statehood.

Although Texas thus joined the Union as a slave state, Polk still needed money for the war with Mexico that annexation provoked. In 1846, Congressman David Wilmott of Pennsylvania proposed that slavery be barred from any territories acquired in the conflict. And northern congressmen proposed and saw the Wilmott Proviso defeated several times in subsequent years, among them Abraham Lincoln, member of the US House of Representatives from Illinois' Seventh District from 1847 to 1849. They defended the action under the Constitution's provision that "Congress shall have power to dispose of and make all needful rules and regulations respecting the territory or any other property belonging to the United States."[40]

Southerners responded with the Calhoun Resolutions of February 1847, named after the ageing but still-active author of *The South Carolina Exposition and Protest*. In accord with State Compact Theory, the Calhoun Doctrine, as the Resolutions also came to be called, argued that western territories were the common property of all the states and therefore not under the exclusive authority of the federal government. Also, no territory could ban slavery until it applied to join the Union. And Congress couldn't ban slavery in any territory or state because citizens could not, under the Fifth Amendment, "be deprived of life, liberty, or property, without due process of law." Thus was the Bill of Rights deployed in defense of enslavement.

So President Polk got his money anyway, and in the 1848 Treaty of Guadalupe Hidalgo the United States secured not only Texas, but also all those other territories westwards to the Pacific. But that of course set the scene for further sectional crises. These crises might have taken longer to arise, except for the discovery of gold in California early in 1848. The subsequent arrival there of over 80,000 "49ers" entitled the territory to apply for statehood. It did so in October 1849 and New Mexico followed in May the next year. The now elderly Henry Clay cemented his ambiguous reputation as "The Great Compromiser" by brokering yet another one. The Compromise of 1850 admitted California to the Union as a free state and abolished slave trading (but not slavery) within Washington DC. But it allowed slavery in New Mexico and the Utah territory. And it included the aforementioned Fugitive Slave Act, greatly angering a growing army of abolitionists.

A lawmaker was beaten unconscious on the Senate floor

One of those most instrumental in the passing of the Compromise of 1850 was Stephen Douglas, one of Barack Obama's predecessors as US senator from Illinois, who divided Henry Clay's original omnibus bill into separate parts to manufacture a majority in the chamber for each. But it was the 1854 Kansas-Nebraska Act that secured Douglas's notoriety. As chairman of the Senate Committee on Territories, he ensured that southerners could take slaves into these lands and that the people would decide whether slavery would be allowed when they applied for statehood. Kansas and Nebraska are both north of parallel 36°30′, so the Kansas-Nebraska Act cast aside the Missouri Compromise and its restriction on the spread of enslavement north of that state's southern border.

Douglas defended the measure on the grounds of "popular sovereignty," appropriating American democratic tradition for the purposes of the peculiar institution, though he assured northerners that these territories were unsuited to slavery anyway, alienating the southern allies he'd sold his soul to gain. He also argued that leaving matters to local decisions would avert further national crises over the issue. He could not possibly have been more wrong about that. Proslavery "Jayhawkers" and antislavery "Free Soilers" poured into Kansas, set up rival capitals at Lecompton and Topeka, and respectively applied for statehood with separate constitutions. Kansas was unable to enter the Union until January 1861, though it finally did so as a free state. Statehood had proved an insoluble problem until then because in the summer of 1856 settlers began fighting a mini civil war in which up to 200 people died before the bigger Civil War.

And "Bleeding Kansas" in the meantime led to bloodshed in Washington. As Barack Obama once said, "Tensions ran so high, so personal, that at one point, a lawmaker was beaten unconscious on the Senate floor." Indeed militant abolitionist Senator Charles Sumner of Massachusetts made a speech called "The Crime against Kansas" on May 19 and 20, 1856—it was a long speech. In one of the more exciting parts of it, Sumner alluded metaphorically and generally to southerners' sexual exploitation of slaves by referring to the institution's Kansan expansion as the "rape of a virgin Territory." But he also got particular and personal. Of Andrew Butler, one of the sponsors of the Kansas Act, Sumner said "The senator from South Carolina has read many books of chivalry, and believes himself a chivalrous knight with sentiments of honor and courage. Of course he has chosen a mistress to whom he has made his vows, and who, though ugly to others, is always lovely to him; though polluted in the sight of the world, is chaste in his sight—I mean the harlot, slavery." Which was an allusion to Butler's sexual exploitation of slaves specifically and was not merely a metaphor for slavery generally.[41]

South Carolina Congressman Preston Brooks, Butler's younger second cousin, also considered himself a man of honor and so on, and on May 22 he entered the Senate chamber and beat Sumner unconscious and then beat him some more with his gold-headed gutta-percha walking cane. Sumner's physical injuries and mental trauma were so severe that he didn't return to the Senate chamber permanently until 1859. It was not the most edifying illustration of Barack Obama's ideal of deliberative democracy.

Yet Charles Sumner was lucky, in a way. Preston Brooks' and his friends decided that their chivalric code defined the Massachusetts senator as insufficiently gentlemanly to deserve the honor of being challenged to and possibly killed in a duel. Sumner thus survived to see the passing of the Thirteenth, Fourteenth, and Fifteenth Amendments that abolished slavery and acknowledged equal citizenship and voting rights regardless of race. Sadly, Brooks didn't. He contracted croup and died of an inflamed windpipe in January 1857.[42]

Stephen Douglas's term as senator was in its later stages as these events unfolded, and he was due to face reelection in 1858. In the meantime, one of the most consequential legal cases in American history would reach the Supreme Court. And Douglas would have to debate its implications with "a tall, gangly, self-made Springfield lawyer."[43]

Who would walk into the Supreme Court a free man and leave a slave

The Dred Scott case is another example of the constitutional struggles over slavery mentioned, if only briefly, by Barack Obama. As Obama says, the "Constitution's exquisite machinery would secure the rights of citizens, those deemed to members of America's political community. But it provided no protection to those outside the constitutional circle," including "the black man Dred Scott, who would walk into the Supreme Court a free man and leave a slave."[44]

Dred Scott was born in Virginia in 1795 and in 1818 moved to Alabama with his owner Peter Blow. Twelve years later Blow moved to St. Louis, Missouri, where he sold Scott to an army surgeon named John Emerson. Emerson took Scott first to Fort Armstrong in Illinois and then to Fort Snelling in a part of the Wisconsin Territory that would later be in Minnesota. The former was free territory under the 1787 Northwest Ordnance and the Illinois state constitution of 1819, and the latter was a free land according to the Missouri Compromise. Scott might have sued for his freedom and that of his wife Harriet and daughter Eliza on this basis after they moved back to the slave states, first to Louisiana then back to St Louis. But in 1846 he attempted to purchase his freedom from Emerson's widow, another Eliza. When she refused, with the help of abolitionists (including the now antislavery family of Peter Blow), he finally sued for his and his wife's freedom on the grounds that they'd been liberated by being in free territories, and that of his daughter as she was born on a steamboat on the Mississippi River.

The case worked its way through the justice system before reaching the ultimate court of appeal, and Eliza Emerson transferred ownership of Scott to her brother John, so the case was recorded as *Dred Scott v Sandford*. Scott was not technically legally free when he walked into the Supreme Court. The previous federal appeal court had returned the same verdict as the Supreme Court of Missouri: that Scott was in fact Sandford's slave, but allowed that he would be hired out and his earnings placed in escrow and presented either to Scott or to Sandford on final resolution of the case. Yet in 1850 Eliza Emerson married Calvin C. Chaffee, a Massachusetts abolitionist and US congressman, and after the Dred Scott case was resolved the Chaffees deeded Scott and family to Henry Taylor Blow, son of Peter, who manumitted them on May 26, 1857, suggesting that all sides were in fact colluding in an antislavery legal test case. If so, then Scott had been free in all but name. Whatever the circumstances, Scott finally became fully free after the Supreme Court verdict, though not alas for long, as he died of tuberculosis in September 1858.[45]

That verdict, however, had found against Dred Scott, and Chief Justice Roger B. Taney, a proslavery Marylander, delivered a 7–2 majority ruling that had profound implications for African Americans and for enslavement as an institution. Taney ruled that the Scott suit should never have happened and none like it should ever happen again. And not on the grounds of any technicality but because of what he argued was the long-accepted doctrine that Africans and their descendants were "so far inferior, that they had no rights which the white man was bound to respect." Taney directly addressed the questions raised by the words of the Declaration of Independence, quoting them as follows in his ruling, "that all men are created equal; that they are endowed by their Creator with certain unalienable rights; that among them is life, liberty, and the pursuit of happiness; that to secure these rights, Governments are instituted, deriving their just powers from the consent of the governed." He answered as follows:

> The general words above quoted would seem to embrace the whole human family … But it is too clear for dispute, that the enslaved African race were not intended to be included, and formed no part of the people who framed and adopted this declaration; for if the language, as understood in that day, would embrace them, the conduct of the distinguished men who framed the Declaration of Independence would have been utterly and flagrantly inconsistent with the principles they asserted.

As for the Constitution, Taney argued that the Slave Trade and Fugitive Slave clauses proved that the phrase "We the people" was also never intended to apply to those of African heritage. Black people thus could not be citizens and therefore had no constitutional rights.

Judge Taney also added an ominous *ober dictum*. That is that, according to the Fifth Amendment, no citizen can be deprived of property without due process of law, which of course is true. But Taney drew the same conclusions as the Calhoun Resolutions, that all the agreements concerning slavery in the western territories were therefore unconstitutional. Certainly that meant the Northwest Ordnance and the Missouri Compromise, but it may also have meant every law restricting slavery anywhere, even the abolition acts of the First Emancipation in the northern states.[46]

A house divided against itself

For the popular-sovereignty-supporting and election-facing Stephen Douglas, the Dred Scot verdict was awkward, and his challenger for the Senate seat aimed to exploit all of the awkward. Abraham Lincoln was a part of a growing movement that was bringing antislavery into the political mainstream, to the point that in the early 1850s parties were splitting on sectional grounds and reconstituting behind sectional lines. There had been Democratic Republicans and Federalists from both North and South in the first party system from the 1790s to the 1820s, and the same was so among the Democrats and Whigs of the second party system from the 1830s to the 1850s. But the Republican Party emerged after the Kansas-Nebraska Act as an exclusively northern one, dedicated to ending the expansion of enslavement. The Republican Party was peopled mostly by antislavery Whigs, although the rump of that party continued to argue forlornly for unity before finally dying in the Civil War. The Democratic Party for its part was becoming an increasingly southern one as more and more of its northern members joined the Republicans.

Accepting the Republican nomination for the Illinois Senate seat at the State Capitol in Springfield on June 16, 1858, Abraham Lincoln made his famous "A House Divided" speech—one of his greatest orations. Beginning with the words of Jesus according to the Gospels of Matthew and Mark, he said:

> "A house divided against itself cannot stand." I believe this government cannot endure, permanently half slave and half free. I do not expect the Union to be dissolved—I do not expect the house to fall—but I do expect it will cease to be divided. It will become all one thing, or all the other. Either the opponents of slavery, will arrest the further spread of it, and place it where the public mind shall rest in the belief that it is in course of ultimate extinction; or its advocates will push it forward, till it shall become alike lawful in all the states, old as well as new—North as well as South.[47]

And Lincoln cited "the Nebraska doctrine, and the Dred Scott decision" as indications of the direction in which things were heading. Lincoln also referenced the anticipated Supreme Court consideration of *The Lemmon Slave Case*, concerning whether Jonathan and Juliet Lemmon had lost legal title to their eight slaves by taking them into the free state of New York while travelling from Virginia to Texas. Would the Supreme Court declare the New York abolition act unconstitutional, as Roger B. Taney's Dred Scott *ober dictum* had heavily hinted?

In the event, the case never came to Washington because of the outbreak of war in 1861, but its prospect loomed menacingly over the nation in 1858. And so Abraham Lincoln characteristically mixed his famous folksiness and his formidable forensic skills by pondering the following. "Put this and that together," he said, "and we have another nice little niche, which we may, ere long, see filled with another Supreme Court decision, declaring that the Constitution of the United States does not permit a State to exclude slavery from its limits." So "We shall lie down pleasantly dreaming that the people of Missouri are on the verge of making their State free, and we shall awake to the reality instead, that the Supreme Court has made Illinois a slave State."[48]

Abraham Lincoln lost the senatorial election of 1858, but between the "House Divided" speech and the seven head-to-heads of the Lincoln-Douglas Debates between August 21 and October 15, 1858, he became a national name. But of course his name signified different things in the northern and southern sections of the nation. He won the Republican nomination for the presidency in 1860 and, in a four-way race with Democrat Stephen Douglas, Southern Democrat John C. Breckinridge, and the Constitutional Union Party's John Bell, he won the White House on almost entirely northern vote.[49]

The southern states then started seceding from the Union. First to go was South Carolina on December 20, 1860. The other Deep South states of Mississippi, Florida, Alabama, Georgia, Louisiana, and Texas followed soon after and formed the Confederate States of America on February 4, 1861. Lincoln was inaugurated exactly a month later, and a month after that the president attempted to resupply Fort Sumter, the federal military facility in Charleston Harbor. The American Civil War began as the Confederates fired at and captured it on April 12 and 13, 1861. The president began mobilizing for war, and the upper south states of Virginia, Arkansas, Tennessee, and North Carolina subsequently seceded, bringing the total number of Confederate states to eleven.

What does this say about our democracy?

For Barack Obama, the peculiar genius of American politics is that progress is made by the "deliberative democracy" created by the Constitution, even if sometimes slowed by the needs for compromise and consensus. But, as Obama admits, "Democratic deliberation might have been sufficient to expand the franchise" to poor white men and eventually to women, and to "lessen religious and class tensions," but "deliberation alone could not provide the slave his freedom or cleanse America of its original sin. In the end, it was the sword that would sever his chains." And so he asks the obvious question with regard to slavery and the Civil War: "What does this say about our democracy?"[50]

And Obama began his reflections on that question in classically scholarly style. "There's a school of thought," he rightly wrote, "that sees the Founding Fathers only as hypocrites and the Constitution only as a betrayal of the grand ideals set forth by the Declaration of Independence." These historians agree, at least metaphorically, "with early abolitionists that the Great Compromise between North and South was a pact with the Devil." Obama further notes that others on the other hand argue that all the compromises on slavery were necessary for the formation and survival of the Union and that "the Founders only sought to postpone what they were certain would be slavery's ultimate demise." Indeed "the genius of the Constitution" was that it "permitted the space for abolitionists to rally and the debate to proceed, and provided the framework by which, after the Civil War had been fought, the Thirteenth, Fourteenth, and Fifteenth Amendments could be passed, and the Union finally perfected."[51]

But Obama then abandons all attempts at objective analysis and adopts a more ambivalent and atavistic attitude, although the resulting reflections are equally insightful. "How can I," he asks, "an American with the blood of Africa coursing through my veins, choose sides in such a dispute? I can't. I love America too much, am too invested in what this country has become, too committed to its institutions, its beauty, and even its ugliness, to focus entirely on the circumstances of its birth. But neither can I brush aside the magnitude of the injustice done, or erase the ghosts of generations past, or ignore the open wound, the aching spirit, that ails this country still."[52]

Yet he actually does do some very complex and intriguing choosing of sides.

The cranks, the zealots, the prophets, the agitators, and the unreasonable

As Obama knows, the most determined and determining struggle against slavery before the Civil War didn't happen in Washington. And the struggle was not led by politicians, but by ordinary men and women, black and white. In his speech commemorating the hundred and fiftieth anniversary of the passing of the Thirteenth Amendment, Obama showed where the heart and soul of abolitionism really was. "Preachers, black and white," he said,

> railed against this moral outrage from the pulpit. Former slaves rattled the conscience of Americans in books, in pamphlets, and speeches. Men and women organized anti-slavery conventions and fundraising drives. Farmers and shopkeepers opened their barns, their homes, their cellars as waystations on an Underground Railroad, where African Americans often risked their own freedom to ensure the freedom of others. And enslaved Americans, with no rights of their own, they ran north and kept the flame of freedom burning, passing it from one generation to the next, with their faith, and their dignity, and their song.[53]

"The best I can do in the face of our history," Obama therefore writes, "is remind myself that it has not always been the pragmatist, the voice of reason, or the force of compromise, that has created the conditions for liberty." In fact, the "hard, cold facts remind me that it was unbending idealists like William Lloyd Garrison who first sounded the clarion call for justice; that it was slaves and former slaves, men like Denmark Vesey and Frederick Douglass and women like Harriet Tubman, who recognized power would concede nothing without a fight. It was the wild-eyed prophecies of John Brown, his willingness to spill blood and not just words on behalf of his visions, that helped force the issue of a nation half slave and half free." He concludes therefore that "I'm reminded that deliberation and the constitutional order may sometimes be the luxury of the powerful, and that it has sometimes been the cranks, the zealots, the prophets, the agitators, and the unreasonable—in other words, the absolutists—that have fought for a new order."[54]

So who exactly were these cranks, zealots, prophets, agitators, and absolutists, and what unreasonable things did they do?

William Lloyd Garrison

It wasn't actually William Lloyd Garrison who "first sounded the clarion call for justice." We've seen that antislavery ideas had existed from the late seventeenth century, though they only became widespread among whites in the era of the American Revolution. And Garrison wasn't even the first of the more militant abolitionist activists of the antebellum age. In 1829, a North Carolina-born black Bostonian named David Walker published *An Appeal to the Colored Citizens of the World* and with it inaugurated a new era of abolitionism that called for immediate liberation, equal citizenship, and no compensation for the "man-stealers" whose enslavement of others was never legitimate and should therefore never be rewarded.[55]

David Walker died in 1830, but William Lloyd Garrison (1805–79), a white radical from Massachusetts, continued his cause. Garrison republished Walker's writings in early editions of *The Liberator*, the abolitionist magazine he began editing and publishing in 1831. That year Garrison also cofounded the New England Anti-Slavery Society, later reorganized as the Massachusetts Anti-Slavery Society, an affiliate of the American Anti-Slavery Society that Garrison also cofounded in 1833.

Though opposed to violence, William Lloyd Garrison was indeed an ideological "zealot." In the first issue of *The Liberator*, he wrote that

> I am aware that many object to the severity of my language; but is there not cause for severity? I will be as harsh as truth, and as uncompromising as justice. On this subject, I do not wish to think, or to speak, or write, with moderation. No! no! Tell a man whose house is on fire to give a moderate alarm; tell him to moderately rescue his wife from the hands of the ravisher; tell the mother to gradually extricate her babe from the fire into which it has fallen;—but urge me not to use moderation in a cause like the present. I am in earnest—I will not equivocate—I will not excuse—I will not retreat a single inch—AND I WILL BE HEARD.[56]

An "unbending idealist" indeed. Garrison also called the Constitution, with all its compromises on slavery, "a covenant with death" and "an agreement with hell," the comments recalled by Obama's characterization of those who thought constitutional compromises comprised "a pact with the Devil." And so Garrison called for "No Union with Slaveholders" and argued repeatedly for northern secession: a most un-Obamian position, for sure, but that's precisely Obama's point. It perhaps took such an "absolutist" to push the cause so hard that by the 1850s a US Senator and former New York governor could say that there was a "higher law" than the Constitution and speak of an "irrepressible conflict" over slavery. In the 1860s the same man who spoke these unreasonable words, William Henry Seward, would be President Lincoln's Secretary of State.[57]

Denmark Vesey

Denmark Vesey is a particularly interesting choice of illustrative historical figure by Barack Obama. Born around 1767 on the Danish Virgin Island of St. Thomas, he was purchased in his adolescence by a Bermuda sea captain and slave trader named Joseph Vesey, for whom the multilingual Telemaque (Denmark Vesey' original name) worked as an assistant specializing in interpreting French and Spanish. The two later resettled in Charleston, South Carolina, where the slave was hired out as a carpenter.

On November 9, 1799, Telemaque won $1500 in a lottery and subsequently bought his freedom for $600: an unusual and unexpected turn of events. He afterwards started his own carpentry business, and became a preacher in the African Methodist Episcopal

Church that he helped found in 1818. Besides slavery and discrimination against free black people, Vesey was angered by his former master's refusal to permit him to purchase the freedom of his wife Susan and their sons Sandy and Robert. Inspired by the Haitian revolt from 1791 and independence from 1804, and then by congressional debates over Missouri, he and a network of coconspirators began plotting a rebellion that they planned would commence on July 14, Bastille Day, 1822.

The size of the conspiracy was obviously a strength but also a weakness, the latter as it was betrayed from within. Vesey and five coconspirators were hanged on July 2, and over the course of the month twenty-nine more men were hanged with thirty-one others transported, including Sandy. Susan migrated to Liberia and Robert was eventually freed in 1865. Proceedings against the alleged conspirators were aided by torture and death threats. South Carolina Attorney General Robert Hayne, later the unequal oratorical opponent of Daniel Webster, ruled that the state constitution's guarantee of right of *habeas corpus* didn't apply to black people. Four white men were also found guilty of conspiracy, but suffered no worse punishment than a year in jail and a $1000 fine.

Denmark Vesey's was not the only attempt to rebel against enslavement in the United States. Gabriel's Conspiracy of 1800 in and around Richmond, Virginia, was first delayed by a storm and then betrayed by some involved. There was also Nat Turner's Rebellion in August 1831 in Southampton County, Virginia, in which around sixty whites, including children, were killed before a retaliatory rampage resulted in the deaths of around 200 blacks, some undoubtedly uninvolved in the insurrection. Another fifty-six African Americans were executed after trials without juries, including Turner, who was hanged and then flayed, beheaded, and quartered. Barack Obama has pretty much sidestepped this especially controversial and complicated episode, though he hasn't ignored it completely. In reference to historical artifacts to be housed in the NMAAHC, Obama listed Nat Turner's bible, a source of his apocalyptic preaching, alongside Harriet Tubman's shawl.[58]

Frederick Douglass

Born in early 1818 in Talbot County, Maryland, Frederick Douglass (originally Bailey) spent much of his childhood in Baltimore. His "mistress" Sophia Auld first taught him to read, and it was when her husband Hugh forbade her on the grounds that, according to his autobiography, "If you teach that nigger (speaking of myself) how to read, there would be no keeping him," that Douglass himself decided there would be no keeping him. He learned to write as well as to read by goading white children into proving their literary prowess by chalking letters on pavements. And he also acquired and repeatedly devoured a copy of *The Columbian Orator*, a schoolbook that required pupils to read and copy out its digests of virtuous republican poetry and prose. From these beginnings Douglass went on to become one the greatest American thinkers, writers, and speakers of the nineteenth century.

Frederick Douglass escaped enslavement on his third attempt on September 3, 1838, travelling by rail, ferry, steamboat, and foot, arriving in New York City after twenty-four hours. On September 15 the same year he married Anna Murray, a free black woman he knew from Baltimore, and they adopted the name Douglass to avoid attention—he was a fugitive, after all. They settled in New Bedford, Massachusetts, and in 1839 he became a licensed preacher with the African Methodist Episcopal Zion Church, honing his own oratorical abilities. He first heard William Lloyd Garrison speak in Bristol, Massachusetts, in 1841, and soon after became an abolitionist lecturer himself. Acclaim arrived with publication in 1845 of *Narrative of the Life of Frederick Douglass, an American Slave*, but his newfound fame meant he had to travel in England and Ireland to evade slave catchers. Abolitionist admirers there raised the money to pay off his former master and free him from fear of recapture.

Douglass returned to the United States in 1847 and wrote and spoke relentlessly against slavery, publishing an updated autobiography, *My Bondage and My Freedom*, in 1855, and another one, *The Life and Times of Frederick Douglass*, in 1881, revised in 1892. During and after the Civil War he campaigned for equal roles and pay for black soldiers in the Union Army and for equal suffrage and citizenship afterwards—and not only for black men, but also for all women. The motto of his abolitionist newspaper *The North Star* was "Right is of no sex, Truth is of no color, God is the Father of us all, and we are all Brethren." He spoke for women's equality many times, including at the landmark Seneca Falls Convention "to discuss the social, civil, and religious condition and rights of woman" in 1848.

Anna Murray Douglass died in 1882, and two years later Frederick Douglass married the white feminist activist Helen Potts. When criticized for his interracial relationship, Douglass responded that he was the same color as his mother and his wife was the same color as his father. He was also the first black man to contest a presidential election, as Victoria Woodhull's running mate for the Equal Rights Party in 1872, although as an ally of President Ulysses S. Grant he neither acknowledged his nomination nor campaigned on the ticket. But at the 1888 Republican Party National Convention he became the first African American to receive a nominating vote for the Presidency of the United States. He died on February 20, 1895, after attending a meeting of the National Council of Women in Washington, DC.

There are profound parallels between the lives of Frederick Douglass and Barack Obama. Another one besides some of those previously noted is that after sometimes stormy intellectual journeys both men finally found themselves at home with American political traditions and institutions. Douglass initially agreed with William Lloyd Garrison's condemnation of slavery's Constitution, but changed his mind after reading Lysander Spooner's *The Unconstitutionality of Slavery* (1846). Spooner glossed over the Constitution's proslavery clauses but argued in any case that the document's original meaning (whatever the Founders' intentions) lay in natural rights theories of equality and liberty.

Like Spooner before him and Obama after, Douglass was a great interpolator of the complexities and contradictions of the American founding. On July 5, 1852, he gave to the Ladies' Anti-Slavery Sewing Society of Rochester, New York, an untitled speech that has since gained the name "What to the Slave is the Fourth of July?" Douglass powerfully expressed the obvious contrast between the professions of the Declaration of Independence and the conditions of slaves: "What, to the American slave," he asked, "is your 4th of July?"

> I answer: a day that reveals to him, more than all other days in the year, the gross injustice and cruelty to which he is the constant victim. To him, your celebration is a sham; your boasted liberty, an unholy license; your national greatness, swelling vanity; your sounds of rejoicing are empty and heartless; your denunciations of tyrants, brass fronted impudence; your shouts of liberty and equality, hollow mockery; your prayers and hymns, your sermons and thanksgivings, with all your religious parade, and solemnity, are, to him, mere bombast, fraud, deception, impiety, and hypocrisy—a thin veil to cover up crimes which would disgrace a nation of savages.[59]

Yet, as for Barack Obama, none of that for Frederick Douglass invalidated the Declaration in terms of theory, or at least in terms of the promises inherent in its theory. Whatever practices prevailed in the American nation, he praised the "great principles of justice and freedom" of its founding document and implied their redemptive potential by calling them "saving principles." "Stand by those principles," he urged his audience, "be true to them on all occasions, in all places, against all foes, and at whatever cost."[60]

Douglass declined to detail arguments on the Constitution, as "The subject has been handled with masterly power by Lysander Spooner" and others, who "have, as I think, fully and clearly vindicated the Constitution from any design to support slavery for an hour." And he asked his listeners "if the Constitution were intended to be, by its framers and adopters, a slave-holding instrument, why neither slavery, slaveholding, nor slave can anywhere be found in it?" The imperatives of the age demanded that Douglass deny the clear intentions of the proslavery clauses, whereas the relative luxury of historical reflection means Barack Obama doesn't have to.[61]

But on other aspects of the Constitution's character the two men are as one. "On the other hand," Douglass said, "it will be found to contain principles and purposes, entirely hostile to the existence of slavery." If "interpreted as it ought to be interpreted, the Constitution is a GLORIOUS LIBERTY DOCUMENT. Read its preamble, consider its purposes." And Douglass ended his oration with a Whiggish flourish of Obamian optimism. "There are forces in operation, which must," he foretold, "inevitably work the downfall of slavery. 'The arm of the Lord is not shortened,' and the doom of slavery is certain. I, therefore, leave off where I began, with hope. While drawing encouragement from the Declaration of Independence, the great principles it contains, and the genius of American Institutions, my spirit is also cheered by the obvious tendencies of the age."[62]

It is remarkable how much Barack Obama's oratory echoes that of Frederick Douglass. Not only the sentiments, but also the references and even the cadences. Of course, some of those rhetorical characteristics are commonly inherited from Greek technique, American tradition, and African American idiom. But others are individual to each man, and yet each man is similar to the other—either because Obama borrows from Douglass's rhetoric or because their other similarities result in rhetorical confluences. There is the note of "hope," for example, in the earlier quote. But also, remember Obama on the War of Independence in his first inaugural address: "The capital was abandoned. The enemy was advancing. The snow was stained with blood." And Douglass: "The country was poor in the munitions of war. The population was weak and scattered, and the country a wilderness unsubdued." In his first inaugural address, Obama also quoted Thomas Paine's *American Crisis*, as we saw in Chapter 2. And Douglass: "there was a time when to pronounce against England, and in favor of the cause of the colonies, tried men's souls." Obama described the Founders as "Farmers and scholars; statesmen and patriots." For Douglass they were "statesmen, patriots and heroes." And when Obama says that Vesey, Douglass, and Harriet Tubman "recognized power would concede nothing without a fight," we recall Douglass's dictum: "Power concedes nothing without a demand."[63]

Harriet Tubman

Although the politics of both Frederick Douglass and Barack Obama rose and rise above race, both also belonged to networks of African American activists and their allies. In 1868, Douglass was asked to write a letter for a forthcoming biography of a famous black woman long of his acquaintance. He responded by writing,

> You ask for what you do not need when you call upon me for a word of commendation. I need such words from you far more than you can need them from me, especially where your superior labors and devotion to the cause of the lately enslaved of our land are known as I know them. The difference between us is very marked. Most that I have done and suffered in the service of our cause has been in public, and I have received much encouragement at every step of the way. You, on the other hand, have labored in a private way. I have wrought in the day— you in the night ... The midnight sky and the silent stars have been the witnesses of your devotion to freedom and of your heroism. Excepting John Brown—of sacred memory—I know of no one who has willingly encountered more perils and hardships to serve our enslaved people than you have.[64]

The woman, also lauded by Barack Obama, was Harriet Tubman. Araminta "Minty" Ross was born, probably early in the 1820s, in Dorchester County, on Maryland's Eastern Shore, just south of Talbot County, the birthplace of Frederick Douglass. Her mother, Harriet, also called "Rit," lost her eldest three children—Linah, Mariah Ritty, Soph— to slave sales, but adopted a deadly determination that a Georgia slave trader would not get his hands on her ninth and youngest. With the help of fellow slaves and free blacks, she hid Moses for a month. When finally confronted by the trader and her master

Edward Brodess, she told them "the first man comes into my house, I will split his head open." They backed off, and the incident instilled in her daughter a hope that escaping enslavement would somehow be possible.[65]

Harriet Tubman suffered a head injury as a young woman when an overseer hurled a two-pound weight at another slave and hit her instead. The trauma left her with seizures and headaches for the rest of her life, though it also gave her visions and dreams that she understood as divine inspirations. Her master attempted to sell her after she again became ill from her injuries in 1849, though. Angry at that and at her family's continued enslavement despite a previous promise to free them, she prayed for her master to mend his ways. But, when one of Brodess's attempts to sell her appeared to approach completion, "First of March I began to pray, 'Oh Lord, if you ain't never going to change that man's heart, kill him, Lord.'"[66]

His unexpected death a week later only increased the likelihood of her family being broken by the division of his estate, however, so she resolved to run. Her first escape attempt came that September with her brothers Ben and Henry, but they returned as Ben had just had a son, and they made her go back too. She soon absconded again, though, alone this time, and this time she made it, 120 miles by foot across eastern Maryland, through Delaware and New Jersey, to Philadelphia, Pennsylvania.

Many slaves escaped from slavery, but no one else did what Harriet Tubman did. Between December 1850 and December 1860 she returned to Maryland thirteen times or more and helped at least seventy other people find freedom via the Underground Railroad, including members of her own family. During the Civil War, furthermore, she was a nurse and helped wartime fugitives escape. On June 2, 1863, she led an armed raid on the plantations along the Combahee River in South Carolina, liberating at least 750 more people. She was also an army scout whose reconnoitering and intelligence work helped win the Battle of Cedar Creek with the consequent capture of Jacksonville, Florida, on March 1, 1864.

William Lloyd Garrison fittingly styled Harriet Tubman "Moses," and the nickname became a popular one. She suffered financial struggles after the war, and didn't receive a public pension for her wartime service until 1899. Yet she found some personal happiness and married Nelson Davis in 1869—she had first married John Tubman in 1844, and took her mother's first name at the same time, but he later left her for someone else and declined to be rescued by her. And she enjoyed her late renown, especially after publication of *Scenes in the Life of Harriet Tubman* in 1869 (which Frederick Douglass did write a tribute for) and *Harriet, the Moses of her People* in 1886, both by admirer Sarah Hopkins Bradford, and for her role in the women's suffrage movement. She died of pneumonia on March 10, 1913, at around ninety years of age.[67]

John Brown

Harriet Tubman met John Brown in April 1858. She schooled him in the geography of the Upper South and tried to recruit from among her many connections for his 1859 attack on the federal armory at Harper's Ferry, Virginia (now West Virginia). She said of him that "he done more in dying than 100 men would in living."[68]

John Brown was born on May 9, 1800, in Torrington, Connecticut, but never stayed anywhere very long. His family moved to Ohio in 1805 where his tanner father Owen supported Oberlin Institute (now College), a progressive school that admitted African Americans and women. Though thus raised in a radical household, Brown committed to militant abolitionism after the 1837 assassination of abolitionist preacher Elijah P. Lovejoy. After mixed fortunes in his father's trade in Pennsylvania and Ohio, he moved to Springfield, Massachusetts, in 1846, where as a white member of the African American-founded but mixed-race congregation of the Sanford Street Free Church he heard and talked with Frederick Douglass. He was also involved in the Underground Railroad, and the Fugitive Slave Act inspired him to found The League of Gileadites, dedicated to harboring runaways. He then moved to the predominantly black settlement of North Elba, New York, founded on abolitionist Gerrit Smith's Adirondack land grants.

Frustrated by pacifist abolitionists, he claimed: "These men are all talk. What we need is action—action!" And in 1855 he went to Kansas to defend with firearms the cause of "free soil." On May 21 Sheriff Samuel J. Jones led 800 proslavery "Border Ruffians" in the sack of Lawrence, destroying two printing presses and the Free State Hotel. Only one man died, a proslavery posse member killed by falling masonry, but this event and the attack on Charles Sumner the following day prompted some of Brown's followers to hack five proslavery settlers to death at Potawatomie Creek on May 24. That incident inspired a spiral of violence in "Bleeding Kansas." Brown, nine of his own men, and twenty locals saved the town of Palmyra from a proslavery onslaught at the Battle of Black Jack on June 2, 1856. Then Brown and forty supporters were scattered by a force ten times their number at the August 30 Battle of Osawatomie, but not before leaving twenty dead and forty wounded.

In September 1856 John Brown went back east and began planning and raising funds for what he wished would be a war to end enslavement. Due to various complications, including others' reservations about the unlawful use of violence, Brown's projected force of 4,500 ultimately only numbered twenty-one. On October 16, 1859, they attacked Harper's Ferry anyway, hoping to capture arms and then march South, inspiring slave insurrections and recruiting from them along the way. In the event, they got pinned down by local people at the armory itself, until federal forces arrived under Colonel Robert E. Lee and Lieutenant J. E. B. Stuart, both of whom would later turn traitor against their own nation as Confederate generals. Brown refused to surrender, but on October 18 he and six others were captured, ten were killed, and the others escaped. Brown and his men killed four and wounded nine.

John Brown and four others were hanged on December 2 for murder, conspiracy, and treason against the Commonwealth of Virginia, as were two more the following year. Opinion on Brown varied then and has done since, some commending him as a martyred hero, others condemning him as a terrorist, others acquitting him on the grounds of insanity. Others still have been ambivalent. The woman he called "General Tubman" helped him in advance and appeared to agree to assist in the attack on Harper's

Ferry, but then disappeared when the time came. Yet we've seen her admiring eulogy. Similarly, Frederick Douglass frankly told Brown he opposed the Harper's Ferry plan and flatly refused to join in. But in a speech in 1881 Douglass said that Brown's "zeal in the cause of my race was far greater than mine—it was as the burning sun to my taper light—mine was bounded by time, his stretched away to the boundless shores of eternity. I could live for the slave, but he could die for him."

Barack Obama is perhaps ambivalent and certainly ambiguous about John Brown. His references to Brown's "wild-eyed prophecies" and "visions" are only slightly less medicalized echoes of Abraham Lincoln's assessment of Brown as "insane." But Obama's description of Brown's "willingness to spill blood and not just words" recalls Douglass's later validation, Tubman's valediction, and Brown's own assessment of himself. And Obama also notes that Brown's visions and actions, alongside those of William Lloyd Garrison, Denmark Vesey, Frederick Douglass, and Harriet Tubman, "helped force the issue of a nation half slave and half free."[69]

I'M LEFT THEN with Lincoln

But if the cranks, the zealots, the prophets, the agitators, and the unreasonable forced the issue of a nation half slave and half free, they were ultimately unable to bring it back together again all free. So Barack Obama concluded his reflections with the following words: "I'M LEFT THEN with Lincoln, who like no man before or since understood both the deliberative function of our democracy and the limits of such deliberation." Obama could hardly be more complimentary, considering his own political predilections.[70]

Obama also praised "the firmness and depth of his convictions" and "his unyielding opposition to slavery and his determination that a house divided could not stand." He nevertheless concedes that Lincoln's "presidency was guided by a practicality that would distress us today, a practicality that led him to test various bargains with the South in order to maintain the Union without war; to appoint and discard general after general, strategy after strategy, once war broke out; to stretch the Constitution to the breaking point in order to see the war through to a successful conclusion."[71]

The comments regarding the firing of generals may refer to Lincoln's 1862 dismissal of George B. McClellan, who seemed more intent on a Virginia vacation than on fighting secession. It is certainly true that Lincoln's subsequent appointment of Ulysses S. Grant at the head of Union forces was more effective in seeing the war "through to a successful conclusion." Obama may also have been referring to the 1861 firing of John C. Frémont and the revocation of the general's orders to free slaves in Missouri. Lincoln was calculating of course that keeping the Union in the war required keeping Missouri in the Union. But we examine Lincoln's views on race in the next chapter, and there's no question that some of them should indeed "distress us today." Lincoln also used emergency powers to suspend habeas corpus in Missouri, and in Delaware, Maryland, and Kentucky, stretching "the Constitution to the breaking point."

But, at least concerning Lincoln's consistency and determination regarding slavery and the Union, Obama's analysis is ultimately laudatory. He argues that "for Lincoln, it was never a matter of abandoning conviction for the sake of expediency. Rather, it was a matter of maintaining within himself the balance between two contradictory ideas— that we must talk and reach for common understandings, precisely because all of us are imperfect and can never act with the certainty that God is on our side; and yet at times we must act nonetheless, as if we are certain, protected from error only by providence." And, as Obama says in *The Audacity of Hope*, using one of Lincoln's own most famous phrases, "That self-awareness, that humility, led Lincoln to advance his principles through the framework of our democracy, through speeches and debate, through the reasoned arguments that might appeal to the better angels of our nature."[72]

Power in words

The Audacity of Hope is not the only place where Barack Obama has referred to the rhetorical brilliance of Abraham Lincoln. When announcing in Springfield, Illinois, in 2007 his bid to become Lincoln's successor, the would-be forty-fourth president said the following of the sixteenth: "He tells us that there is power in words. He tell us that there is power in conviction." Words indeed were the means Lincoln used to exercise power, even when that meant using words to conceal his convictions in the cause of achieving his objectives.[73]

Occasionally Obama's case for Lincoln rests on shifting temporal sands. As Obama said on the aforementioned occasion, "As Lincoln organized the forces arrayed against slavery, he was heard to say: 'Of strange, discordant, and even hostile elements, we gathered from the four winds, and formed and fought to battle through.'" But Lincoln in fact said these words in his "House Divided" speech of June 16, 1858, long before he could organize American armed forces as the country's Commander-in-Chief: another Obamian elision. But Obama is maybe making three subtle and related points here, each of which relates to historical debates about Lincoln's intentions. First, Obama seems to be hinting that Lincoln's determination to destroy slavery came from long-held convictions, implying that he intended to become president to do something about slavery, rather than being forced by being president to do something about slavery. Second, that when Lincoln was able he indeed "organized" forces and so, far from being harried by others or carried by events, he was always an active agent of emancipation. Third, and again, that Lincoln's "forces" were not only martial, but also rhetorical.[74]

Abraham Lincoln continued to marshal his rhetorical powers behind his convictions even when he did have the powers of commander-in-chief. But subtly. In his inaugural address of March 4, 1861, Lincoln spoke with spine-tingling eloquence about unity. He said at the end, "I am loath to close. We are not enemies, but friends. We must not be enemies. Though passion may have strained it must not break our bonds of affection. The mystic chords of memory, stretching from every battlefield and patriot grave to every living heart and hearthstone all over this broad land, will yet swell the chorus of the Union, when again touched, as surely they will be, by the better angels of our nature."[75]

That apparently placatory pronouncement had a probably intentionally pyrrhic sort of substance. Earlier in the speech, Lincoln had reiterated his campaign promise that "I have no purpose, directly or indirectly, to interfere with the institution of slavery in the States where it exists. I believe I have no lawful right to do so, and I have no inclination to do so." And he repeated the Republican Party platform provision "That the maintenance inviolate of the rights of the States, and especially the right of each State to order and control its own domestic institutions according to its own judgment exclusively, is essential to that balance of power on which the perfection and endurance of our political fabric depend; and we denounce the lawless invasion by armed force of the soil of any State or Territory, no matter what pretext, as among the gravest of crimes." Lincoln also said that "a proposed amendment to the Constitution ... to the effect that the Federal Government shall never interfere with the domestic institutions of the States" was already "implied constitutional law," but "I have no objection to its being made express and irrevocable."[76]

Lincoln even apparently endorsed the Constitution's Fugitive Slave Clause, though he thought it right for northern courts to require proof that a captive was legally enslaved. After all, he noted, quoting the Constitution, "the citizens of each State shall be entitled to all privileges and immunities of citizens in the several States so that a free man be not in any case surrendered as a slave." That comment was in part a tart retort to Chief Justice Roger B. Taney's claim that black people could not be citizens and had no constitutional or even any other kind of rights. Yet Lincoln still expressed this willingness to support a constitutional clarification of the oppression of African Americans.

Lincoln's compromises may indeed distress us, as Obama confesses. But they were not a commitment to enslavement. At most they were a concession to preexisting laws and a confession of his own incapacities as the president of a constitutional democracy of checks and balances, one very much including checks on executive power. But Lincoln's comments also need to be seen in the context of his attempts to shape events in the long term. To begin with, as well as laying down the law on himself, he laid the law down on the secessionists—very much including laws he knew they wouldn't and couldn't accept. In so doing he left them with little choice but to step into the trap he set for them.

First, he made the historical case for the perpetuity of the Union. "I hold that in contemplation of universal law and of the Constitution the Union of these States is perpetual," Lincoln said in his first Inaugural. "Perpetuity is implied if not expressed," he professed, "in the fundamental law of all national governments. It is safe to assert that no government proper ever had a provision in its organic law for its own termination." And he added the following repudiation of State Compact Theory: "If the United States be not a government proper, but an association of States in the nature of contract merely, can it, as a contract, be peaceably unmade by less than all the parties who made it?"

And then we find some of Abraham Lincoln's American history. And it is very similar indeed to Obama's own. Lincoln clearly believed as Obama does, for example, in an exceptional American facility for turning philosophy into practice and ideas into institutions. And he articulated the constitutional concept of modifiable perfection in a most Obamian manner. "Descending from these general principles," Lincoln said,

> we find the proposition that in legal contemplation the Union is perpetual confirmed by the history of the Union itself. The Union is much older than the Constitution. It was formed, in fact, by the Articles of Association in 1774. It was matured and continued by the Declaration of Independence in 1776. It was further matured, and the faith of all the then thirteen States expressly plighted and engaged that it should be perpetual, by the Articles of Confederation in 1778. And finally, in 1787, one of the declared objects for ordaining and establishing the Constitution was "to form a more perfect Union."
>
> But if destruction of the Union by one or by a part only of the States be lawfully possible, the Union is less perfect than before the Constitution, having lost the vital element of perpetuity.[77]

And the relevance of Abraham Lincoln's American history to matters of his own moment was "that no State upon its own mere motion can lawfully get out of the Union; that resolves and ordinances to that effect are legally void, and that acts of violence within any State or States against the authority of the United States are insurrectionary or revolutionary." To all his own intents and purposes, then, secession hadn't happened. Indeed Lincoln was so set on denying its legality that he didn't explicitly acknowledge its existence, speaking instead of "A disruption of the Federal Union."

Lincoln thus used the past to define the present as it was in 1861. And then he proceeded to use both to try to shape the future. "I therefore consider," he continued, "that in view of the Constitution and the laws the Union is unbroken, and to the extent of my ability, I shall take care, as the Constitution itself expressly enjoins upon me, that the laws of the Union be faithfully executed in all the States . . . I trust this will not be regarded as a menace, but only as the declared purpose of the Union that it will constitutionally defend and maintain itself." Of course Lincoln knew perfectly well that secessionists would rightly regard this promise as the "menace" he pretended it wasn't. They simply could not accept him doing his constitutional duties in their states if their secessions were to have any meaning. They would have no option but to see his actions as invasions of their self-proclaimed sovereignty and then respond accordingly. They would therefore start the war—they would have to—at least in the sense of firing the first shots.

And Lincoln further pleaded innocence regarding the premeditated consequences of his actions by saying that "there needs to be no bloodshed or violence, and there shall be none unless it be forced upon the national authority. The power confided to me will be used to hold, occupy, and possess the property and places belonging to the Government and to collect the duties and imposts; but beyond what may be necessary for these objects, there will be no invasion, no using of force against or among the people anywhere." Lincoln was thus able to put the full onus on his enemies when concluding that "in your hands, my dissatisfied fellow-countrymen, and not in mine, is the momentous issue of civil war. The Government will not assail you. You can have no conflict without being yourselves the aggressors. You have no oath registered in heaven to destroy the Government, while I shall have the most solemn one to 'preserve, protect, and defend it.' "[78]

Lincoln then allowed the events he set in motion to play back into his hands—that is, into the interpretative context he'd prepared for them in his inaugural address and previous speeches. On April 12 he attempted to resupply Fort Sumter in Charleston Harbor, and the South obligingly attacked and two days later captured it. That allowed Lincoln on April 15 to call for 75,000 volunteers and on April 19 to proclaim a blockade of southern ports, later deemed the de facto declaration of war. As we've seen, another four slaves states then seceded from the Union and joined the Confederacy—Virginia, Arkansas, Tennessee, and North Carolina. But Lincoln had ensured that the war had started on his terms, and he would ensure that it would end that way as well.[79]

We unified a nation and set the captives free

When announcing his own presidential candidacy in 2007, Barack Obama lauded and simultaneously laid a current and collective claim to Abraham Lincoln's two greatest achievements by proclaiming: "We unified a nation and set the captives free." Yet some have argued that Lincoln cared more for the Union than he did for the slaves. Lincoln himself said in a seemingly self-incriminating and frequently quoted letter to Horace Greeley of the *New York Tribune*, responding to an editorial impatiently urging him to abolish enslavement: "If I could save the Union without freeing any slave I would do it, and if I could save it by freeing all the slaves I would do it, and if I could save it by freeing some and leaving others alone I would also do that." The paper published the letter on August 24, 1862.[80]

The previous month, though, Lincoln had discussed a possible Emancipation Proclamation with his cabinet, and by late August preparations for it were well under way. He signed it on September 22, to go into effect the next New Year's Day, unless the Confederates surrendered first, which Lincoln knew they wouldn't do. In other words, by the time he wrote to the *Tribune*, he was actively preparing to save the Union by freeing some of the slaves. Whatever Lincoln said in that letter then, it seems that Obama was quite right to list Lincoln's two great achievements in tandem. The issues of saving the Union and freeing the slaves were already inseparable in Lincoln's estimation.

Some of the slaves. The Emancipation Proclamation had its weaknesses, as Abraham Lincoln was acutely aware. One was that it freed slaves in rebel-held areas only. Those enslaved in the four Union slave states and in already captured areas remained enslaved. And it freed them not on the grounds of natural or civil rights but by defining them as contraband, thus conceding, albeit for sake of expediency, the slaveholders' concept of people as property. And it was merely a war measure, and only an Executive Order, not congressional legislation, much less a constitutional amendment. But the Emancipation Proclamation nonetheless changed the nature of the war. From the moment it came into effect on January 1, 1863, even from the moment of its preannouncement the previous September, saving the Union and freeing the slaves were not only inseparable in Lincoln's estimation, but were also inseparable in a reality of his own creation.

The Emancipation Proclamation and its reinvigorating effect on the Union war effort also raised the possibility of freeing the slaves on the grounds of natural rights and by constitutional means. Immediately after his reelection in November 1864, President Lincoln threw his personal political capital behind attempts to amend the Constitution to end enslavement. When the House of Representatives passed the Thirteenth Amendment on January 31, 1865, Lincoln showed his commitment to it by signing it, though there was no legal requirement that he do so or even any legal meaning in him doing it. The meaning was symbolic, importantly so. He said in a speech the next day that he "thought all would bear him witness that he had never shrunk from doing all that he could to eradicate slavery by issuing an emancipation proclamation." And Obama gives Lincoln full credit on this account. "President Lincoln understood," Obama said when commemorating of the Thirteenth Amendment, "that if we were ever to fully realize that founding promise, it meant not just signing an Emancipation Proclamation, not just winning a war. It meant making the most powerful collective statement we can in our democracy: etching our values into our Constitution. He called it 'a King's cure for all the evils.' "[81]

Of course African Americans themselves did all they could to expedite Emancipation. Slaves, by their always potentially and often actually troublesome presence on the plantations, inspired laws directing that for every twenty of them there had to be an overseer to ensure order, depriving the Confederate armies of many thousands of potential fighting men. And slaves anyway abandoned the plantations during the wartime disruptions, doing so in droves as Union troops advanced on their localities. In late 1862, furthermore, Lincoln's War Department sanctioned black regiments that had already formed to fight for freedom in Louisiana and South Carolina. And once the Emancipation Proclamation transformed a war for the Union into the war against slavery that it always implicitly was, African Americans started joining the army. Though initially confined to noncombat roles and only later allowed equal pay and officer status, by the end of the conflict between 180,000 and 200,000 African Americans, northern and southern, had fought for freedom.

Barack Obama says very little about the military conduct of the war. This diffidence is itself Lincoln-like. As Obama wrote in *The Audacity of Hope*, it was Lincoln's "humility that allowed him, once the conversation between North and South broke down and war became inevitable, to resist the temptation to demonize the fathers and sons who did battle on the other side, or to diminish the horror of war, no matter how just it might be." And indeed "Lincoln, and those buried at Gettysburg, remind us that we should pursue our own absolute truths only if we acknowledge that there may be a terrible price to pay." His comment added in between these observations: "The blood of slaves reminds us that our pragmatism can sometimes be moral cowardice," illustrates the importance of principle in Obama's mind. But his pursuit of principle, like Lincoln's, is tempered by humility and decency.[82]

Otherwise, one of Obama's few comments on the war itself is the one relayed before the one relayed just above: "In the face of secession, we unified a nation and set the captives free." That may seem a rather stark abbreviation of a very bloody conflict, but the shortness of the phrase shouldn't disguise the fullness of its meanings. As we've seen previously, Obama is almost always more interested in the outcomes of historical processes than he is in those processes themselves. Thus his history of the American Revolution says little about tyranny but much about liberty, and is really a history of the "creed" contained in the Declaration of Independence and of the "more perfect union" formed by the Constitution. And so in turn his history of the Civil War is ultimately a history of victory. And a victory of enormous importance. As he said in another brief comment on this conflict, this time when speaking against the then putative war in Iraq but prefacing by saying that he was not against all wars: "The Civil War was one of the bloodiest in history, and yet it was only through the crucible of the sword, the sacrifice of multitudes, that we could begin to perfect this union, and drive the scourge of slavery from our soil."[83]

And in the final analysis Barack Obama's history of slavery is also really a history of liberty. "At its heart," he said, "the question of slavery was never simply about civil rights. It was about the meaning of America, the kind of country we wanted to be—whether this nation might fulfill the call of its birth: 'We hold these truths to be self-evident, that all men are created equal, that they are endowed by their Creator with certain unalienable rights, that among those are life and liberty and the pursuit of happiness.' "[84]

And yet, as Barack Obama knows and shows, if the fight for freedom was finally won, the struggle for equality had only just begun.

CHAPTER 5
WE SHALL OVERCOME: RECONSTRUCTION, JIM CROW, AND CIVIL RIGHTS

. . .

Barack Obama began his oration on "A More Perfect Union" on March 18, 2008 in Philadelphia in the following way: " 'WE THE PEOPLE, in order to form a more perfect union.' " These words are from the opening of the United States Constitution—but they are not all of the words of the opening line of that document. The Constitution actually begins as follows: "We the People of the United States, in order to form a more perfect union."[1]

It is obviously perfectly possible that Obama redacted "of the United States" simply to save time, although that would have cut out only a few seconds from an almost forty-minute speech. So perhaps he simply preferred the cadence of the shortened sentence. Even if that's so, though, the redaction may still be meaningful. As Obama said on this and other occasions, the Constitution forbade the federal government from forbidding the slave trade for twenty years, directed that the representation of the slave states be augmented by counting three-fifths of enslaved people as part of their populations, and provided that runaway slaves be returned to their owners. The Constitution therefore secured "the rights of citizens, those deemed to members of America's political community," but offered "no protection to those outside the constitutional circle," as Obama wrote in *The Audacity of Hope*. So, while enslaved people lived in the United States, they were by definition not citizens. They were therefore subject to the nation's laws but were neither makers nor beneficiaries of them. In short, enslaved Americans were among the people but were not "of the United States." The document the Founders signed was, therefore, as Obama put it, "ultimately unfinished." And his quotation from it was correspondingly incomplete.

The Philadelphian oration of 2008 was not the only occasion on which Barack Obama has edited the Constitution's opening words. He also did so in a speech on March 7, 2015, marking the fiftieth anniversary of the "Bloody Sunday" attack on voting rights marchers by state troopers on the Edmund Pettus Bridge in Selma, Alabama. But this time his formulation differed, altered in a way that reflected how the Constitution had been amended between the days of slavery and the days of segregation and yet also how those amendments had been violated. How things had changed and not changed.

The Thirteenth Amendment says: "Neither slavery nor involuntary servitude, except as a punishment for crime whereof the party shall have been duly convicted, shall exist within the United States, or any place subject to their jurisdiction." This Thirteenth Amendment passed Congress on January 31, 1865, and was ratified by the states by December 6 of the same year. The Fourteenth, passed by Congress on June 13, 1866, and ratified on July 9, 1868, directs: "All persons born or naturalized in the United States, and subject to the jurisdiction thereof, are citizens of the United States and of the State wherein they reside." So "No State shall make or enforce any law which shall abridge the privileges or immunities of citizens of the United States; nor shall any State deprive any person of life, liberty, or property, without due process of law; nor deny to any person within its jurisdiction the equal protection of the laws." And the Fifteenth, passed by Congress on February 26, 1869, ratified February 3, 1870, provides that "the right of citizens of the United States to vote shall not be denied or abridged by the United States or by any State on account of race, color, or previous condition of servitude." Although that applied to men only until the adoption of the Nineteenth Amendment in 1920.[2]

These provisions are perfectly clear. In Barack Obama's words, the Thirteenth Amendment aimed "to deliver slaves from bondage" and the Fourteenth and Fifteenth aimed to guarantee "full rights as citizens of the United States" to the freedmen (literally men only until 1920). These three "Reconstruction Amendments" were thus the signal achievements of an era of very real effort to create racial equality and therefore fuller democracy in the South. Yet the last quarter of the nineteenth century and the first two-thirds of the twentieth were the years when Jim Crow ruled. Segregation and disfranchisement, though clearly violations of the Fourteenth and Fifteenth Amendments, were instituted by southern states, enforced by government agencies, and supported by terrorism, sometimes state-sponsored terrorism. If the Constitution was finally finished after the Civil War, then, its promises nevertheless remained unfulfilled for several generations more. As Obama said in "A More Perfect Union": "words on a parchment would not be enough to ... provide men and women of every color and creed their full rights and obligations as citizens of the United States." And as he said when commemorating the hundred and fiftieth anniversary of the Thirteenth Amendment in 2015: "For another century, we saw segregation and Jim Crow make a mockery of these amendments." With these words Obama echoes the great African American scholar and early civil rights leader W. E. B. Du Bois, who famously said: "The slave went free; stood a brief moment in the sun; then moved back again toward slavery."[3]

It may be for this reason that in the 2015 speech in Selma—"For We Were Born of Change"—Barack Obama again cited *some* of the opening words of the US Constitution: "We the People ... in order to form a more perfect union." The phrase sounded the same on the day as it did in the earlier speech in Philadelphia. But the transcription of the 2008 oration had no grammatical indication of any redaction, just a comma where "of the United States" would be, while the one in 2015 replaced those words with ellipses. This difference may be due to nothing more than the distinctive habits of different transcribers. Even if that's so, though, the ellipses may still be meaningful.

They symbolize perhaps that the Reconstruction Amendments acknowledged African Americans as being "of the United States" in a way that the original Constitution of 1787 had not. They thus represent a measure of progress toward "a more perfect union." Yet, at least as read, these little apparitions of empty promises hauntingly remind us that the Constitution may have been finished on paper but remained very much unfinished in practice. Obama's quotation from it is therefore once again appropriately incomplete.[4]

How is it then that Jim Crow made a mockery of these amendments? And how did America eventually overcome? But, first, how did the amendments initially come about?

The Nation's Second Founding

Barack Obama has said little in his speeches and books about Reconstruction and so-called Redemption. His favoring of a fuller accounting of the tribulations of Jim Crow and especially the triumphs of Civil Rights shows once again his preference for the positive narrative of overcoming injustice rather than dwelling on the details of the injustices overcome.

But that doesn't mean that Obama doesn't care about this immensely important earlier era. Indeed he cared enough that, in one of his last acts as president, he created the first National Parks Service monument dedicated to Reconstruction. The idea was first proposed in the 1990s by President Bill Clinton's Interior Secretary Bruce Babbitt, with Eric Foner, the foremost historian of Reconstruction and one of the foremost of all of American history, suggesting a siting at Beaufort, South Carolina. Unfortunately the project was blocked by Congress after lobbying organized by the non-forward-looking Sons of Confederate Veterans. Obama, however, created the monument under the Antiquities Act of 1906 that allows the president "to declare by public proclamation historic landmarks, historic and prehistoric structures, and other objects of historic or scientific interest that are situated upon the lands owned or controlled by the Federal Government to be national monuments."[5]

The preamble of the president's "Proclamation for the Establishment of the Reconstruction Era National Monument" comprises a 2,186-word essay written by Obama himself. In it he details events in and around Beaufort during and after the Civil War, and places them in the contexts of the wider Reconstruction Era and the longer-run of American history. In an interview with the American Historical Association online magazine, Gregory Downs and Kate Masur, two leading Reconstruction historians and the chief academic campaigners for the reinvigorated monument movement, described the Proclamation as "a remarkable piece of history writing" that represents "a complete break with the old 'Dunning School'/*Birth of a Nation* narrative" of Reconstruction. That is, a break with an interpretation initiated by historian William A. Dunning, imitated by Woodrow Wilson and others, and indeed popularized by D. W. Griffith's monstrous movie that denigrated Reconstruction efforts to create an interracial democracy. Not coincidentally, this historiographical tradition served to justify the white supremacist regimes and Jim Crow policies subsequently established throughout the South.

Instead, as Downs and Masur say, Obama aligns himself with "the version of Reconstruction that academic historians have been writing about for years but that has so rarely made its way into public consciousness." One that "places slavery's abolition at the center of the story and recognizes Reconstruction as the 'Nation's Second Founding' and the era in which the federal government, for the first time, promised to protect the rights of all individuals living within the nation." This rather different historiographical tradition commenced with W. E. B. Dubois's *Black Reconstruction in America* (1935) and culminated perhaps with Eric Foner's magisterial *Reconstruction: America's Unfinished Revolution* (1988). Downs and Masur are rightly "gratified," furthermore, that Obama "mentioned by name the historian Willie Lee Rose and her book *Rehearsal for Reconstruction*," the brilliant scholar's seminal work on Reconstruction in general and on Beaufort in particular.[6]

While the Civil War raged in the background

Barack Obama's essay begins, as most historical articles do, by establishing its own historiographical perspective, the one described above. Obama then notes that Reconstruction "began when the first United States soldiers arrived in slaveholding territories." In Beaufort and surrounding Low Country South Carolina the process commenced early, as Admiral Samuel F. DuPont bombarded Port Royal Sound in November 1861, forcing slaveholders to flee. As Obama also notes, though, "More than 10,000 African Americans—about one-third of the enslaved population of the Sea Islands at the time—refused to flee the area with their owners." Beaufort thus "became one of the first places in the United States where formerly enslaved people could begin integrating themselves into free society. While the Civil War raged in the background," Obama adds, "Beaufort County became the birthplace of Reconstruction, or what historian Willie Lee Rose called a 'rehearsal for Reconstruction.'"[7]

Locating the commencing of Reconstruction in "the early Civil War years," as Obama thus does and as post-Dunning historians do, makes an important point. That is, as Downs and Masur say, that both were parts of the same effort behind liberation—the Civil War was about freeing the slaves (de facto from the start if only de jure later on)— not just a so-called war between the states—and Reconstruction was about establishing a meaningful freedom for those thereby liberated—not just a continuation by other means of a so-called war of northern aggression. Both together, in fact, comprised a single moment when, in Obama's words, "Americans abolished slavery and struggled earnestly, if not always successfully, to build a nation of free and equal citizens."[8]

Obama reinforces this point later in the essay when he comments on the "historic ceremonies on January 1, 1863, to announce and celebrate the issuance of the Emancipation Proclamation" at Camp Saxton, when General Rufus B. Saxton himself invited "everyone, African American and white, 'to come to the camp ... on New Year's Day, and join in the grand celebration.'" He was indeed joined by "Over five thousand people" for a three-hour jubilee "by a grove of live oaks near the Smith plantation house," one of which still lives to this day and goes by the name of "the Emancipation Oak."[9]

Yet, despite acknowledging this early beginning of Reconstruction and its relationship with the war effort, Barack Obama barely mentions President Abraham Lincoln in his essay. This may be because what Obama described elsewhere as the sixteenth president's "unyielding opposition to slavery and his determination that a house divided could not stand" was not visibly matched by an unyielding support for equality when the house was being reconstructed. Lincoln certainly supported Congress's 1861 Confiscation Acts that emancipated slaves and commandeered the property of Confederates as contraband. But he placed military personnel in charge of captured southern localities such as Beaufort, and their plantations and indeed human property, who were of course under the president's control as commander-in-chief. The idea was in part to secure the freedom and safety of the liberated, but it was also to ensure that political policies pertaining to these places and people were not determined by radical Republicans in Congress.[10]

As Obama is aware, that sometimes meant Lincoln's actions fell far short of radical abolitionist expectations, first for Emancipation and then for Reconstruction. Such was certainly the case in late 1861 when the president ordered John C. Frémont to rescind his emancipation of enslaved Missourians and then fired the general for refusing to carry out the order. Lincoln was aiming to keep Missouri within the Union, and indeed losing this and the other three non-Confederate slave states to secession might have dealt a fatal blow to the Union, which in turn would have guaranteed the indefinite extension of enslavement. It nevertheless may be this that Barack Obama obliquely referred to when he described Lincoln as being "guided by a practicality that would distress us today," including discarding "general after general."[11]

In one of the great debates of the Illinois Senate race of 1858, moreover, Abraham Lincoln had assured his opponent Stephen Douglas, and by extension the large audience present on the day and the even larger one who would read his words later, that "I am not, nor have ever been in favor of bringing about in any way the social and political equality of the white and black races." During the war, furthermore, Lincoln's active support for colonizing freed people in Central America and Haiti, and his lack of action on equal roles and pay for black Union troops, prompted a frustrated Frederick Douglass to complain powerfully of the president's "inconsistencies, his pride of race and blood, his contempt for Negroes and his canting hypocrisy." At the end of the war Lincoln proposed African American voting rights for the "the very intelligent, and especially those who have fought gallantly in our ranks." Progress, for sure, but hardly a wholehearted endorsement of equality.[12]

On the other hand, Abraham Lincoln was often either genuinely ambivalent or deliberately ambiguous about things, the latter as a matter of political calculation, as we saw in relation to war and Emancipation. So what can we tell from his actual actions about his real intentions for Reconstruction and for African Americans?

Although Reconstruction in effect began, as Obama says, "when the first United States soldiers arrived in slaveholding territories," it didn't begin officially until nearly a year after the issuing of the Emancipation Proclamation. Partly designed to bring an early end to fighting, Lincoln's December 1863 Proclamation on Amnesty and Reconstruction pardoned all but the highest-ranking Confederates and permitted southern states to start the process of readmission to Congress once 10 percent of voters registered in 1860 had pledged allegiance to the United States, and provided they abided by abolition. Radical Republicans believed this to be too lenient, however, and too permissive, and countered with the Wade-Davis Bill that would have required a majority to pledge allegiance, and to pledge an "ironclad oath" of never having fought for or otherwise supported the Confederacy to be able to vote in subsequent elections. Lincoln pocket vetoed it.[13]

The radicals conceived the southern states as conquered provinces akin to territories, and as such they could be constitutionally subject to federal enforcement of racial equality. Lincoln on the other hand felt that punitive policies could be counterproductive, and he had in any case a philosophical and political problem with the radicals' constitutionalism. He believed the southern states could not be conquered territories because, from the point of view of constitutional law, they had never left the Union. As we saw in Chapter 4, this perspective was useful at the beginning of the war, allowing the political positioning Lincoln did in order to be able to blame secessionists for the opening of armed conflict, thereby paving the way to saving the Union and eventually to Emancipation. But it left Lincoln limited scope to reshape the South at the end of the war. He nevertheless described secession as situating the southern states in an "improper relationship" with the Union, which may have given the inscrutable manipulator some room for reforming maneuver.

But we will never know what might have come of Lincoln's Ten Percent Plan because of the murderous actions of John Wilkes Booth in Ford's Theater on the night of April 14, 1865. Lincoln died of gunshot wounds early the next morning, six days after southern General Robert E. Lee surrendered to Union General Ulysses S. Grant at Appomattox Courthouse in Virginia. It is worth remembering, though, that Booth's fatal rage was roused by Lincoln's suggestion of enfranchising at least some African Americans.

The United States fiercely debated

This modest but brilliant American president was succeeded in office by his opposite, a man whose self-righteousness and self-regard were inverse measures of his moral rectitude and administrative aptitude. Andrew Johnson was in fact a Tennessee Democrat, and his appeal to certain southerners alongside his antislavery and anti-secession credentials got him onto the Lincoln ticket in the election of 1864. Not completely horrendous, Johnson seemed to favor at least limited voting rights for African Americans, albeit for the political advantages that might afford him over his adversaries. He wrote in 1864: "The better class of them will go to work and sustain themselves, and that class ought to be allowed to vote, on the ground that a loyal negro is more worthy than a disloyal white man." And when president in 1865 he recommended that the governor of Mississippi "extend the elective franchise to all persons of color who can read the Constitution in English and write their names, and to all persons of color who own real estate valued at least two hundred and fifty dollars, and pay taxes thereon, [so] you would completely disarm the adversary, and set an example the other states will follow."[14]

Even then though Johnson was unwilling to offer freed people the protection they needed from their former enslavers. As far as he was concerned, secession had never happened, so Reconstruction wasn't needed, and he wasn't interested in reform, so didn't make any effort as Lincoln had done to finesse a vague but potentially effective justification of federal interference in the internal affairs of the southern states. Instead, Johnson restored confiscated land to pardoned owners rather than leaving it with the Freedmen's Bureau or allowing it to be given or sold to former slaves, or for that matter to poor and displaced whites, who the Bureau also aimed to assist. And with little more sympathy for former slaves than he had for their erstwhile enslavers, he vetoed Congress's Civil Rights Act of 1865.

The political vacuum Johnson created permitted a period of "Self-Reconstruction" in which southern state legislatures passed the "Black Acts" that deprived African Americans of such basic civil rights as voting, serving on juries in cases involving white people, and owning firearms to protect themselves from the kind of people who supported the Black Acts. Limiting freedom of movement and imposing certain conditions in work contracts furthered the cause of restoring enslavement as closely as possible after emancipation. Fortunately, the Freedman's Bureau, established by Abraham Lincoln in March 1865 to help provide housing, clothing, fuel, and food for freed black people and displaced white people, and to offer advice about labor contracts, ensured that the effects of the Black Acts were minimized in most places.

Barack Obama acknowledges the divisions and dangers that existed during early Reconstruction. "In the years immediately following the end of the Civil War," Obama observes, "the United States fiercely debated issues critical to Reconstruction. Southern Democrats tried to regain the power they held before the Civil War. The Republican majorities in the US Congress rebuffed them, and proceeded to pass legislation and constitutional amendments to implement the principles of the Union victory. In 1867, Congress passed the Military Reconstruction Acts that called for military administration of southern states and new state constitutions." There is no explicit identification of Andrew Johnson here, just that mention of "Southern Democrats" that may include the president alongside the politicians in the southern states who passed the Black Acts. And it was both Johnson's non-Reconstruction and southern "Self-Reconstruction" that radical Republicans started responding to from the winter of 1865.[15]

And as Obama said when commemorating the hundred and fiftieth anniversary of the Thirteenth Amendment, "Progress proved halting, too often deferred. Newly freed slaves may have been liberated by the letter of the law, but their daily lives told another tale. They couldn't vote. They couldn't fill most occupations. They couldn't protect themselves or their families from indignity or from violence." And so, he continued, "abolitionists and freedmen and women and radical Republicans kept cajoling and kept rabble-rousing, and within a few years of the war's end at Appomattox, we passed two more amendments guaranteeing voting rights, birthright citizenship, equal protection under the law."[16]

Indeed radicals led by Thaddeus Stevens in the House of Representatives and Charles Sumner in the Senate rejected Andrew Johnson's recommendation of readmission of former secession states, and in December 1865 they formed a Joint Committee on Reconstruction to wrestle control of the process from the hands of the president. Congress, furthermore, repassed the Civil Rights Act and overrode Johnson's veto, ensuring the bill became law in April 1866. That act declared: "All persons born in the United States ... are hereby declared to be citizens of the United States; and such citizens of every race and color, without regard to any previous condition of slavery ... shall have the same right in every State ... to make and enforce contracts, to sue, be parties, and give evidence, to inherit, purchase, lease, sell, hold, and convey real and personal property, and to full and equal benefit of all laws and proceedings for the security of person and property, as is enjoyed by white citizens, and shall be subject to like punishment, pains, and penalties and to none other, any law, statute, ordinance, regulation, or custom to the Contrary notwithstanding." And that year, 1866, congressional Republicans also attempted to impeach Johnson for obstruction, failing by one vote on that occasion but finally succeeding two years later.[17]

After the 1866 elections and with the president's power all but broken, Republicans pressed ahead with Congressional or Radical Reconstruction. It is also called Military Reconstruction, as the 1867 "Military Reconstruction Acts" that Barack Obama mentions, which were repassed over Johnson's vetoes, divided the South into five districts overseen by 20,000 US soldiers. The purpose was to protect black people's rights, and they were deployed accordingly by President Ulysses S. Grant (1869–77), for example, to suppress the Ku Klux Klan. Although no former secessionists were tried for treason, "proscription" prevented thousands of whites from voting until an Amnesty Act in 1872 pardoned all but the foremost 500 ex-Confederates. By the middle of 1870, however, all the former secession states were restored to the Union, each one guaranteeing to all men the right to vote and providing integrated schooling and other public services, and all supported by federal Enforcement Acts in 1870–71 and a new Civil Rights Act in 1875.

Robert Smalls, came to prominence

One of the great achievements of Reconstruction therefore was the participation in politics of the previously enslaved. African American men voted, joined the Republican Party, and formed the Union League and other institutions that organized political action, and many held public office. As Barack Obama says in his essay on Reconstruction, Beaufort was where "many of the Reconstruction Era's most significant African American politicians, including Robert Smalls, came to prominence."[18]

Robert Smalls was born in Beaufort in 1839, "the son of slaves of the Henry McKee family," yet went on to be a South Carolina delegate at the Republican National Convention in Baltimore in 1864 and at the state Constitutional Convention in Charleston in 1868.

Smalls and others failed to get African American rights onto the Republican national manifesto in 1864, but the state constitution he subsequently worked on did deliver "universal male suffrage and racial, political, and legal equality" in South Carolina in 1868, making the state that had most dogmatically defended slavery and secession suddenly one of the most democratic in the country. As Obama says, Smalls was "elected to the South Carolina General Assembly from 1868 to 1874, first as a representative and then as a senator." He was then "elected to the U.S. House of Representatives, where he served five terms" from 1875 to 1887. In all, some 1,500 African American men held public office in the decade between 1867 and 1877, not an equal proportion of the black population as for the white population, but obviously more than before and, more surprisingly, more than would do so again for a century after. Some 633 African Americans served as state legislators during Reconstruction, fifteen others as US congressmen, four from Alabama and six from South Carolina, including Robert Smalls. Two more served as US senators, both from the state of Mississippi.[19]

The achievements of black politicians, however, are often invisible to those who are blinkered by long-held habits of racist hostility. As Obama says, "The success of Smalls and other African American lawmakers who had been enslaved only a handful of years before infuriated South Carolina's Democrats. Some of them turned to violence, carried out by the Ku Klux Klan and others. On more than one occasion, a home-grown vigilante group known as the Red Shirts terrorized Robert Smalls." Indeed across the South terrorist groups and individuals intimidated and even assassinated black voters and office holders and their "Scalawag" (southern white Republican) and "Carpetbagger" (northern migrant) allies. They also targeted African American women for sexual attacks in all-too-real reversals of their imaginings of attacks by black men against white women.[20]

The southern "Conservative Party," increasingly integrating into the national Democratic Party, benefitted from the frequently febrile and fearful atmosphere they created by winning increasing numbers of elections for the white supremacist movement. Growing divisions among Republicans in the Grant administration and in the South itself didn't help. Neither did the Panic of 1873 and the economic depression that followed. Conservatives and Democrats, furthermore, increasingly championed a "New Departure" in politics, emphasizing economic development, attacking Republican corruption, and allying with alienated or co-opted scalawags and carpetbaggers, though they also styled themselves "Redeemers" to signal their continued intention to put an end to Reconstruction. One southern state after another fell to the "Redeemers" in the early 1870s, leaving only Florida, Louisiana, and South Carolina "unredeemed" by the time of the elections of 1876. Democrats had won a majority in the federal House of Representatives in 1874, but it was the quadrennial elections two years later that finally killed the attempt to create a lasting democracy in the South.

As Barack Obama explains, "As a result of the contested Presidential and South Carolina gubernatorial elections of 1876, deals were made that effectively ended political and military Reconstruction in 1877." Indeed in 1876 business-minded Bourbon Democrats captured the Senate, and Democratic presidential candidate Samuel J. Tilden won the popular vote for the presidency, though not without the benefit of white supremacist intimidation, violence, and ballot stuffing in the southern states. But, at the end of the election, twenty Electoral College votes remained disputed: three in Oregon and the others in as yet "unredeemed" Florida, Louisiana, and South Carolina. The Compromise of 1877, also called the Great Betrayal, finally gave all twenty votes to the Republican Rutherford B. Hayes, who thereby won the election with 185 electoral votes to Tilden's 184. Hayes then did his part of the deal and pulled the remainder of the already diminished number of federal soldiers from the final Reconstruction states. Southern conservatives hailed the end of Reconstruction as "Redemption." Which, for all its Christian connotation, is just another way of saying "moved back again toward slavery."[21]

The political progress of Reconstruction could not always be reversed right away in every southern state, though. Robert Smalls, for example, "continued to serve in Congress until 1886," as Barack Obama points out, before returning to work "for many years as the Presidentially appointed customs collector for the Port of Beaufort." As Obama also says, however, while "Smalls spoke eloquently" for "democracy and representative government" as a delegate at another state constitutional convention in 1885, "Democrats had regained control of the State government" and "had figured out how to take back African Americans' rights as citizens." And so "South Carolina voters ratified a new constitution that effectively eliminated African Americans from electoral politics and codified racial segregation in law for decades to come."[22]

We will return to the details of disfranchisement and segregation in due course, but it needs noting first that although Reconstruction ignominiously ended with the increasing exclusion of African Americans from electoral politics, there were nevertheless other important achievements in this era.

To build a nation of free and equal citizens

As we've previously seen, Emancipation was not just a gift given by white people but was something black people fought for. In the previous chapter we saw that slaves disrupted farms and plantations during wartime, undermining the Confederate effort. They also absconded more than ever before, especially as Union troops neared their neighborhoods, and up to 200,000 fought for freedom in the Union army. Barack Obama duly acknowledges African Americans' active agency in their own emancipation when he says that "enslaved people on plantations and farms and in cities escaped from their owners and sought refuge with Union forces or in free states." And indeed "In and around Beaufort County during Reconstruction, the first African Americans enlisted as soldiers. . ."[23]

As early as August 1862 General Saxton received permission to recruit African American troops and from that November to January the next year trained some 5,000 men for the First South Carolina Regiment Volunteers at "Camp Saxton in Port Royal—formerly the site of a plantation owned by John Joyner Smith." He selected former abolitionist activist Colonel Thomas Wentworth Higginson of the 51st Massachusetts Infantry to train them. The runaway and rescuer Harriet Tubman served as a nurse at the camp from May 1862.[24]

One African American war hero was the aforementioned Robert Smalls. In 1851, when he was twelve years old, "his owner" Henry McKee "hired him out to work in Charleston, where he learned to sail, rig, and pilot ships," as Barack Obama explains. But Smalls put his skills to unexpected use when the opportunity arose. As Obama tells it, "In May 1862, Smalls navigated the CSS Planter, a Confederate ship, through Charleston harbor, past the guns of Fort Sumter, and turned it over to Union forces. This courageous escape made him an instant hero for the Union, and he soon began working as a pilot for the U.S. Navy." And in a measure of how the world turned upside down, at least for a while, "Smalls and his family used prize money awarded for the Planter to purchase the house in Beaufort once owned by the family that had owned him."[25]

Obama further acknowledges African American agency in Reconstruction when he notes that 10,000 people, "about one-third of the enslaved population of the Sea Islands at the time—refused to flee the area with their owners." For once, slaves freed themselves by staying put while the slaveholders ran away. And Obama does the same when he says that Beaufort County was one of the first places "where formerly enslaved people could begin integrating themselves into free society." As this subtly worded comment suggests, though, African Americans could not realistically destroy the slave system and subsequently reform southern society on their own. They were not passive victims of slavery by any measure, but the impoverishment the enslaved endured for two centuries and more inevitably had its effects. "To build a nation of free and equal citizens" therefore required the combined efforts of the Union Army, the federal government and its agencies, and black and white volunteers from the North, as well as the former slaves themselves.[26]

Barack Obama powerfully portrays the combined nature of the effort in Beaufort. "With Federal forces in charge of the Sea Islands," Obama says, "the Department of the Treasury, with the support of President Lincoln and the War Department, decided to turn the military occupation into a novel social experiment, known as the Port Royal Experiment, to help former slaves become self-sufficient. They enlisted antislavery and religious societies in the North to raise resources and recruit volunteers for the effort. Missionary organizations headquartered in the Northeast established outposts in Beaufort County." The conclusion of Obama's essay on Reconstruction notes—with a hyphen pointing to a lesson from the age—that the monument testifies to "the enormous contributions of those who made it possible—in our shared history."[27]

With some help from outsiders, then, former slaves forged two kinds of institutions that were vital for the future of the African American community: educational ones and religious ones. As Obama explains, "Freed people hungered for education, as South Carolina had long forbidden teaching slaves to read and write." From 1862 and for the next four decades, white women like Laura M. Towne and Ellen Murray, and black women like Charlotte Forten, all from Pennsylvania, taught at the Penn School on St. Helena Island. They began educating former slaves at the Oaks plantation house, the army headquarters, and then in the Brick Baptist Church. Construction of dedicated school buildings began in 1864, with financial donations from the people of Philadelphia and on fifty acres donated by African American landowner Hastings Gantt. As Obama explains, "Penn School helped many African Americans gain self-respect and self-reliance and integrate into free society. Towne and Murray strove to provide an education comparable to that offered in the best northern schools. The faculty also provided other support, including medical care, social services, and employment assistance." Similar efforts helped educate the formerly enslaved all across the former slave states. And, elected "to the Beaufort County School Board in 1867," Robert Smalls also "began his advocacy for education as the key to African American success in the new political and economic order."[28]

One of the great achievements of Reconstruction was indeed the founding of Howard University in 1867, where Barack Obama gave the commencement address on May 7, 2016. The president spoke that day of a "spirit of achievement and special responsibility" that "has defined this campus ever since the Freedman's Bureau established Howard just four years after the Emancipation Proclamation; just two years after the Civil War came to an end. They created this university with a vision—a vision of uplift; a vision for an America where our fates would be determined not by our race, gender, religion or creed, but where we would be free—in every sense—to pursue our individual and collective dreams." And he acknowledged the university's role since then as "a centerpiece of African-American intellectual life and a central part of our larger American story," a "home of many firsts," including producing the "first black Nobel Peace Prize winner" and the first "black Supreme Court justice," as well as "Countless scholars, professionals, artists, and leaders from every field who received their training here."[29]

And the Brick Church, near the center of St. Helena Island, was originally built by slaves for their owners in 1855, but, as Obama says, "When the white population fled from the Sea Islands in 1861, the suddenly freed African Americans made the church their own." Slaves had formerly been forbidden from worshiping without supervision in case they interpreted Christ's affinity with the poor and oppressed as Christ's affinity with the poor and oppressed. Although, as we saw before, slaves congregated in secret and used religion subversively anyway, regarding Christianity as a liberation theology. Not surprisingly, then, "Once freed from their owners, African Americans in Beaufort County" and indeed across the South "wanted to worship in churches and join organizations they controlled." And, as Obama adds, "The Brick Church has been a place of worship and gathering ever since, and continues to serve the spiritual needs of the community to this day."[30]

Penn School especially has had an interesting history since Reconstruction. It "would evolve into the Penn Center in the 20th century," Obama relates, "and remain a crucial place for education, community, and political organizing for decades to come." Darrah Hall in particular, Obama also notes, "is the oldest standing structure on the site of the Penn School grounds. Students and community members built it around 1903, during the transition in the South from the Reconstruction Era to an era of racial segregation and political disenfranchisement." And yet, "As a meeting place in the 1950s and 60s for civil rights leaders, including Dr. Martin Luther King Jr., and the staff of the Southern Christian Leadership Conference," the school "links the democratic aspirations of Reconstruction to those of the modern civil rights movement." There are of course equivalents of Beaufort's Baptist Brick Church all across the southern states. Such as

Ebenezer Baptist Church in Atlanta, Georgia, where Dr. Martin Luther King Jr. grew up, and Dexter Avenue Baptist Church in Montgomery, Alabama, from where he launched his career as a civil rights activist.[31]

Schools and churches established during Reconstruction therefore helped sustain African American individuals and communities during the trials to come and in turn helped lay the ground for the triumphs that followed. In a more general sense, as Obama says, "Even as Jim Crow laws and customs limited political participation and access to public accommodations, African Americans maintained visions of freedom and built strong community institutions. Ownership of land, access to education, and churches and civic organizations that took root during the Reconstruction Era laid the foundation for the modern civil rights movement."[32]

Barack Obama thus mentions more widespread African American ownership of land as one of the signal achievements of Reconstruction. The confiscation policies of some Union Army officials during the Civil War and the Freedmen's Bureau's sales of some confiscated lands during Reconstruction certainly led to significant advances. There was, however, no systematic or sustained effort to reform the southern economy after the abolition of slavery, not even to compensate the formerly enslaved for their years of unpaid labor, or two-and-a-half centuries of unpaid labor if we include all the forebears of the Emancipation generation, and all the wealth they created and that their descendants in different circumstances would have inherited. Few former slaves received even the fabled "forty acres and a mule."

So, although African Americans escaped enslavement and refused to return to the gang-labor system of Old South slavery, most were nevertheless forced into tenancy and many into unrewarding sharecropping, with others unable to get ahead because of the credit trap of crop liens, and even sinking into the permanent dependency of debt peonage or exploited even more egregiously and impoverished even more extremely by the chain gang "justice" of the legal system. As the bittersweet saying with its double-meaning has it, the slaves wanted "Nothing but Freedom," and that's pretty much what they got.

African Americans were therefore unable to employ economic bargaining as a means of resisting the racist reaction that came with "Redemption." And thus it is that Eric Foner describes Reconstruction as "America's Unfinished Revolution." And Barack Obama appears to agree with that assessment. As we've seen, Obama said explicitly that, even after the nation's founding, the Constitution was "unfinished" because of America's "original sin" of slavery. And those ellipses in the speech in Selma seem to say implicitly that, even after the "Nation's Second Founding," the Constitution remained unfinished because of America's residual sin of racism.[33]

To vote here in Selma and much of the South

One of the main means by which "Redemption" was realized and by which white supremacy was subsequently sustained was through extralegal violence. "Extralegal" as it was often perpetrated either with the direct assistance of those in authority or with their indirect assistance in providing many dark places with their willfully averted attention. Sometimes such violence was spontaneous and ad hoc, other times it was organized by groups such as the Ku Klux Klan and the South Carolina Red Shirts mentioned in Barack Obama's essay on Reconstruction. The Klan was first formed in 1866 with the specific purpose of disciplining black people in the sudden absence of the slave codes. After this group was suppressed by the Grant administration in the early 1870s, other "White Liners" like the Red Shirts and various "Rifle Clubs" took their place, although the Klan enjoyed a revival after being glorified in Griffith's gruesome *Birth of a Nation* in 1915.

A recent report by the Equal Justice Initiative, a southern legal pressure group, showed that some 3,959 black southerners were lynched in the years between 1877 and 1950. The early perception was that lynching victims had committed sex crimes, a propaganda claim that both exploited and extended racist stereotypes about black men's sexuality and violence. But the journalist and activist Ida B. Wells first showed as far back as the 1890s that many black people were murdered for being what some white people felt was economically uppity. Lynching peaked indeed when agricultural prices fell and consumer prices rose, and when it came time for landlords to settle accounts with tenants.[34]

The annual number of lynchings, furthermore, was 50–100 during Reconstruction, before peaking at 161 in 1892 and then gradually declining to an average of around ten a year by the 1930s. The rate of decline is partly explained by negative publicity produced by the likes of Wells, by the National Association for the Advancement of Colored People (NAACP) after it formed in 1909, and by many others, including black women petitioners in the South, appalled politicians in the North, and horrified observers overseas. But it is also notable that lynching rose as white supremacists pushed for "Redemption" and then Jim Crow laws, and fell after these were safely in place. In other words, lynching was not just extrajudicial law enforcement, bad as that was, but was demonstrably about securing a political, social, and economic regime of white supremacy by means of terrorism. As Barack Obama noted in 2015, for a century after slavery, "we saw justice turn a blind eye to mobs with nooses slung over trees. We saw bullets and bombs terrorize generations."[35]

Legalized disfranchisement, however, began with a Georgia poll tax of 1877 that prevented many black and poorer white people from voting. It then spread somewhat slowly across the South as African American democratic advancements during Reconstruction could not be instantly undone. But the persistent war of attrition against black voters and office-holders allowed a quickening of iniquity with Mississippian adoption of a new constitution in 1890, including a poll tax and literacy test as requirements for registering to vote. Between then and 1908 all the former Confederate states plus Oklahoma imitated the "Mississippi Plan" by means of new constitutions, constitutional amendments, and legislation, some adding residency requirements and other measures that excluded the vast majority of black southerners from voting, as Barack Obama notes was the case with South Carolina in 1895. The non-Confederate Border States didn't adopt disfranchisement, though they did impose segregation.

Some disfranchisement measures excluded many poor whites from the polls as well, in some states in the tens of thousands, because making these laws explicitly race-based would have violated the Fifteenth Amendment too obviously to survive judicial scrutiny. But interpretations of literacy tests results, understanding clauses, and grandfather clauses that exempted those whose family forebears could vote before Emancipation ensured that disfranchisement was increasingly racially discriminatory. And while the racial motivations of election laws were formally hidden from federal officialdom, they were nonetheless flaunted before their victims. Barack Obama highlighted the adding of insult to injury in the methods used in qualifying for voting when he spoke at the semicentennial of the 1965 Voting Rights march in Selma, Alabama. "Fifty years ago," Obama noted, "registering to vote here in Selma and much of the South meant guessing the number of jellybeans in a jar or bubbles on a bar of soap. It meant risking your dignity, and sometimes, your life."[36]

By such means was a solidly Democratic South engineered, and White Primaries further guaranteed that party candidates and elected officials walked the White Line.

"Separate but equal"

Historians have long debated the degree of de facto segregation during Reconstruction, but there's no doubt that afterwards the de jure kind became part of everyday life in the South and beyond. As with disfranchisement, some states mandated racial separation in their constitutions, others through legislation. By the early twentieth century legalized segregation existed in every former slave state, including the non-Confederate ones, and some Border States, in all kinds of public facilities from schools to cemeteries (although in churches many African Americans preferred to worship their own way anyway). In spaces that had to be shared, black people were forced to perform demeaning acts of deference, especially toward white women, including avoiding eye contact, hat-tipping, and stepping aside on and even stepping off of pavements.

Segregation wasn't a singularly southern phenomenon, though. Powers in Washington colluded with it and even increasingly practiced it in the public spaces of the nation's capital. The Civil Rights Act of 1875 provided that "all persons within the jurisdiction of the United States shall be entitled to the full and equal enjoyment of the accommodations, advantages, facilities, and privileges of inns, public conveyances on land or water, theaters, and other places of public amusement; subject only to the conditions and limitations established by law, and applicable alike to citizens of every race and color, regardless of any previous condition of servitude." Yet, in a set of legal battles collectively called the *Civil Rights Cases*, the Supreme Court ruled in 1883 that the federal government had no power to regulate the private sphere, and the Thirteenth Amendment didn't set a precedent for doing so as it had "merely abolished slavery."[37]

Segregation laws, however, were passed by state legislatures—public bodies, which was a different matter. And, explicitly race-based, those laws were transparent violations of the Constitution and clearly open to legal challenge under the terms of the Fourteenth Amendment. In 1890, Louisiana, the one state with a tri-racial rather than the usual biracial system, legislated separate train carriages for "colored" as well as "black" and "white" people. A multiracial action group called Citizens of New Orleans decided to subject segregation to legal examination. Homer Plessy, one-eighth African American and therefore legally "colored," was the agent at the center of the action that followed. In 1892, as planned, he bought a first-class ticket in New Orleans on the East Louisiana Railway, informed the guard of his racial status, sat in the whites-only carriage, defied instructions to move to the one for coloreds, and was arrested. However, the Supreme Court subsequently ruled in *Plessy v. Ferguson* (1896) that Louisiana law was constitutional because the facilities provided were "separate but equal."[38]

Plessy v. Ferguson ranks alongside the previously examined Dred Scott Case in the annals of shame of the Supreme Court, but there were alas other ignominious instances besides. In addition to the 1883 *Civil Rights Cases*, *Williams v. Mississippi* (1898) sanctioned the state's judicial violence at the same time as its disfranchisement. Henry Williams was indicted for murder by an all-white grand jury and convicted of this capital crime by an all-white petit one. His counsel argued that he was denied a fair trial as African Americans were excluded from voting and therefore from jury service, meaning he was not tried by a jury of his peers. However, the Supreme Court unanimously ruled that the Mississippi poll tax and literacy laws were nonracial.[39]

In another case, Jackson W. Giles, on behalf of 5,000 black citizens of Montgomery County, challenged a 1901 Alabama law restricting voting to persons "of good character and who understand the duties and obligations of citizenship," criteria that were subjectively assessed according to the racist biases of officials. However, the Supreme Court ruled in *Giles v. Harris* (1903) that federal courts had no jurisdiction over states' voter registration requirements, revealing a low estimation of the value of African Americans' fundamental freedoms, as well as ruling out further recourse to the Fifteenth Amendment.[40]

Each of the Reconstruction Amendments contained the provision that "Congress shall have power to enforce" them "by appropriate legislation." But it didn't do so extensively until the 1960s. Deliberative democracy didn't fail in this instance just because of overeagerness to compromise. It failed mainly because white supremacist abuse of democracy reached into the highest levels of federal government. While southern states deprived most black citizens of the right to vote, they nevertheless benefitted from full population counts in the apportionment of seats in the US House of Representatives. Northern outrage at the increasing disfranchisement evident in the 1900 census prompted Indiana Republican Congressman Edgar D. Crumpacker to propose diminished apportionment in proportion to disfranchisement. But the Solid South voting bloc defeated his and later efforts of the same sort, along with numerous initiatives to investigate abuses by election officials. And they stymied several legislative efforts to make lynching a federal crime and thereby have it investigated by national agencies rather than colluded in by southern state ones. In addition to voting solidarity, the one-party system of the South also gradually gained their representatives disproportionate seniority in the congressional committee system and therefore awesome power over federal budgets and projects.

Southern electioneering and the Solid South in Congress and in the Electoral College pressured even Republicans to welcome Jim Crow to Washington. President Theodore Roosevelt (1901–09) took advice from and even publicly invited Booker T. Washington to dinner at the White House. Yet he also promoted the "lily-white movement" to ensure nonblack leadership among southern Republicans, and began the resegregation of federal government offices and capital city facilities that were first desegregated by President Ulysses S. Grant some thirty years previously. William Howard Taft continued these reversals during his tenure from 1909 to 1913. Roosevelt's Progressive Party challenge to Taft, however, helped swing the 1912 election for Democrat Woodrow Wilson, although Wilson won outright in 1916 thanks to support in the South as well as substantial success in the northern states. Though resident in New Jersey, Wilson was the first southern-born politician to win a presidential election since James Buchanan in 1856 and the first to hold the office since Andrew Johnson's unelected tenure ended in 1869. Segregation in Washington accelerated throughout Wilson's two terms, extending from government department offices into their restaurants and rest rooms.

How far we've come

In line with his general preference seen in previous chapters for positive long-term historical developments over often negative long-gone institutions and events, Barack Obama doesn't dwell often or for long on disfranchisement, segregation, or the violence that enforced these iniquities. And when he does mention them, it is often in the context of the coming of the Civil Rights Movement. On February 21, 2005, for example, at a Gala celebrating the sixty-fifth birthday of civil rights hero John Lewis, Obama referenced disfranchisement distinctly obliquely while pointing at the future much more directly: "there was once a time," he said, "when John Lewis might never have guessed that he'd be serving in Congress. And there was a time not long before that when people might never have guessed that someday, African-Americans would be able to go to the polls, pick up a ballot, make their voice heard, and elect that Congress." And Obama spoke in a similar way on the same day about segregation: "How far we've come from the days when the son of sharecroppers would huddle by the radio as the crackle of Dr. King's dreams filled his heart with hope. He was often forced to leave school to work in the fields and the public library was off-limits to his kind, and yet young John Lewis sought knowledge."[41]

Obama's emphasis on "How far we've come" rather than on how bad things were is similar to his telling of the stories of the American Revolution and of slavery: the overcoming of injustice and oppression is more worthy of focus than the fact that they once existed. That may frustrate those historians who feel that passing quickly over such matters might imply that they don't matter. But I think that would misunderstand the nature and intent of Barack Obama's American history. Obama is after all a narrative historian above all and therefore more interested in the passing of time rather than in any single moment, in the dynamics of change rather than in the operations of long-gone institutions. In any case, moreover, Obama's story of how we got where we are does not allow us to forget where we were before. Quite the contrary in fact, when framed in such terms as "how far we've come." How far we've come necessarily implies that we were once a long way from where we are. The phrase therefore shows that injustice and oppression are intrinsic parts of Obama's narrative, starting points perhaps, but as such they give the story its direction. Overall, Obama's narrative of the making of a "more perfect union" would make no sense unless that union was previously less perfect, and so his story of change presupposes preexisting imperfection.

This particular kind of Obamian perspective is illustrated best by his words in his commemoration of the Thirteenth Amendment, when he bridged the gap between America's first and second reconstructions as follows: "And yet, through all this, the call to freedom survived. 'We hold these truths to be self-evident.' And eventually, a new generation rose up to march and organize, and to stand up and to sit in with the moral force of nonviolence and the sweet sound of those same freedom songs that slaves had sung so long ago ... Calling out for basic justice promised to them almost a century before." Or perhaps in his Reconstruction essay, in both its rapid panning over of the Jim Crow era but also in its point that progress is preceded by pain. "Ultimately," Obama concluded, "the unmet promises of Reconstruction led to the modern civil rights movement a century later."[42]

A long line of heroes

This general tendency and these particular comments may again seem on the surface to slight another phenomenon: the civil rights movement before the Civil Rights Movement. Yet Barack Obama does acknowledge the forebears of John Lewis, Martin Luther King, and the many others involved, as he did in his speech at the semicentenary of Bloody Sunday. "As is true across the landscape of American history," Obama said, "we cannot examine this moment in isolation. The march on Selma was part of a broader campaign that spanned generations; the leaders that day part of a long line of heroes."[43]

Indeed post-enslavement racist injustice and oppression were earnestly resisted from their earliest days. Booker T. Washington founded the vocational Tuskegee Institute and urged fellow African Americans to practice economic self-reliance before campaigning for equality, yet he also privately funded civil rights litigation. But perhaps the most lasting legacy was left by the likes of W. E. B. Du Bois. Following a 1905 meeting of black activists on the Canadian side of the famous falls, he and William Monroe Trotter led the Niagara Movement, denouncing segregation and calling for equal voting rights and extended education. In 1909 he and others founded the NAACP, which made several successful legal challenges to Jim Crow, including winning *Guinn v. United States* (1915), a Supreme Court ruling on the unconstitutionality of a grandfather clause exempting anyone descended from anyone who could vote in Oklahoma up to January 1, 1866, from a literacy law that thereby exclusively disfranchised African Americans. The NAACP also campaigned against the racism that Jim Crow was based on, including organizing protests against D. W. Griffith's 1915 film *Birth of a Nation* for its glamorization of the Ku Klux Klan and its grotesque representations of African Americans by white actors in blackface.

And Du Bois, like Ida B. Wells, drew attention to and inspired action against the violence that supported oppression. In May and June 1917 possibly as many as 250 African Americans were murdered in the "East St. Louis massacres" by whites who resented economic migrants. There was an unusual level of outrage at this incident because many black Americans had moved there not only to escape racial oppression further south, but also to work in industries providing military and other supplies for the war that the United States had entered that April. Further encouraged by Du Bois's "The Massacre of East St. Louis" in the September issue of the *The Crisis*, the NAACP's journal, some 9,000 African Americans marched in a Silent Parade along New York's Fifth Avenue. Also indicative of increasing African American anger, though, was the August 17 Houston riot that followed the harassment and beating of black soldiers stationed at Camp Logan and in which over 100 mutinied and killed sixteen whites. Nineteen people were hanged and sixty-seven more imprisoned.

The NAACP nevertheless campaigned for the commissioning of African Americans as officers in World War I, and, in a rare concession from Woodrow Wilson, hundreds fought in the war in such positions. W. E. B. Du Bois himself was due to receive an army commission, but failed his physical. The fighting in and the winning of World War I had the opposite effect of calming things down, though. Experiencing the generally more relaxed racial attitudes of Europeans, or at least the noninstitutionalization of racism, and the idealism inspired by the end of the war to end all wars, including President Wilson's efforts at Versailles to construct the peace as a victory for freedom and self-determination, civil rights optimism and activism increased. Union leader and civil rights advocate A. Philip Randolph coined the term "the New Negro" in 1917 to personify a renewed determination, a denomination that resonates historically with *Novus Homo*, the name given to Romans leaving their families for the first time to serve in the ancient Senate. And closer to home and in more recent times it echoed as well J. Hector St. Jean de Crevecoeur's "New Man," the economically independent, socially equal, and politically free American of the 1780s, a partly mythical figure but nonetheless an American ideal that African Americans felt equally entitled to aspire to be.[44]

The white supremacist war against African American independence, equality, and freedom nevertheless raged on. The October 1919 Elaine Race Riot in Arkansas, for example, saw more than 200 black tenant farmers murdered for trying to form a union, which some opponents constructed as a conspiracy to kill white people. Twelve more were sentenced to death for involvement in the mayhem, but the NAACP aided their appeals on the grounds that confessions had been extracted through torture. The case eventuated in *Moore v. Dempsey* (1923) in which the Supreme Court finally extended federal oversight of the administration of justice in the states. That of course didn't stop assassins killing civil rights activists, including NAACP organizer Elbert Williams, lynched on June 20, 1940 for trying to register black voters in Brownsville, Tennessee. Nor did it change the Jim Crow laws.

But things did change after World War II. Though idealized by some, many others, especially African Americans, had regarded World War I as an imperialist conflict and a rich man's war and a poor man's fight. But the struggle against Nazism was much more clearly a fight against injustice abroad, and correspondingly more inspiring of a fight against injustice at home, one aiming for a "double V"—victory over Germany and Japan and another one over Jim Crow. After more than a million African Americans fought against racist regimes overseas, as well as again experiencing nonsegregated public facilities abroad, many were simply no longer willing to tolerate second-class citizenship in the country they fought for and for which many had laid down their lives. Barack Obama acknowledged the ironic tragedy and real idealism in African American sacrifice at the 2016 opening of the National Museum of African American History and Culture (NMAAHC) in 2016, noting "the men and the women who rushed to the warfronts to secure all of our freedom, understanding that when they came home they might not yet be free." Perhaps it is not surprising then that one of the first victories of the dawning civil rights era was Executive Order 9981, with which President Harry S. Truman desegregated the American military in 1948.[45]

Furthermore, around 700,000 black people moved from the South to the North and West seeking wartime work, accelerating the Great Migration that began during World War I. While white resentment resulted in race riots such as those recounted previously, a newly consolidated and largely urban black population developed new expectations and new means of expressing them. African Americans were initially excluded from skilled and higher-paid work, until a call by the leader of the Brotherhood of Sleeping Car Porters A. Philip Randolph for a march on Washington in 1941 prompted President Franklin Delano Roosevelt to issue Executive Order 8802, banning discrimination in defense work and founding the Fair Employment Practices Commission. Though the Commission had no enforcement powers, it uncovered and discouraged unjust practices, so that within three years over a million African Americans, almost a third of them women, found manufacturing jobs. These new diplomatic and new social-economic circumstances had profoundly energizing political effects. Between 1940 and 1946, NAACP membership grew from 50,000 to 450,000. America was preparing for a Second Reconstruction.

The students who walked passed angry crowds

In 1947, when Harry Truman's Commission on Civil Rights published a report entitled *To Secure These Rights* calling for equality, and indeed the abolition of segregation, the president hailed it as "an American charter of human freedom." The next year he called on Congress to pass an extensive civil rights program. The federal legislators demurred, but things were changing outside of Washington. In the six years following the war's end, eleven states and many more cities in the North and West banned racial discrimination in employment and in the use of public facilities. But of course the most dramatic transformations came in the southern and border states.[46]

It was in this context that the NAACP adopted a new line of legal attack on Jim Crow. The organization had previously confined itself to arguing that "separate but equal" institutions were unequal because black people's facilities were less well funded and cared for than ones for white people. But in the early 1950s the NAACP legal department leaders Charles Hamilton Houston and Thurgood Marshall insisted instead that they were unequal because they were separate. As with Homer Plessy, the lawyers picked their litigants carefully in order to maximize public sympathy. The Topeka, Kansas, branch chose an assistant pastor named Oliver Brown to try to enroll his three daughters at a white school, and they were rejected as expected. Not wanting to single out the South, furthermore, the NAACP used this Mid-West case as the lead one in a group of five that reached the Supreme Court under the name of *Brown v Board of Education* (although it was also necessary to have one with a B at the beginning as class actions are named alphabetically after the first individual concerned).

After failing to reach a decision in December 1952, the Court allowed the protagonists a year to investigate the intentions of the framers of the equal protection clause of the Fourteenth Amendment, an unusual move that signaled the magnitude of the decision being made. Then contingency kicked in. In September 1953, Chief Justice Fred M. Vinson, thought to be hostile to overturning the "separate but equal" doctrine, had a heart attack and died. The case was heard again in December, and the following May 17 the new Chief Justice, Earl Warren, after engineering unanimity with the help of southern Justice Stanley Reed, delivered a verdict that said that "segregation of white and colored children in public schools has a detrimental effect upon the colored children. The impact is greater when it has the sanction of the law; for the policy of separating the races is usually interpreted as denoting the inferiority of the Negro group." The ruling thus concluded that "separate educational facilities are inherently unequal." The next year, in *Brown II*, the Court ordered that desegregation take place "with all deliberate speed." In the autumn of 1955, Cheryl Brown entered an integrated school in Topeka, Kansas. Twelve years later Thurgood Marshall started a period of twenty-four years as the first African American Associate Justice of the United States Supreme Court.[47]

There were protests against the Brown decisions of course, not least *The Southern Manifesto*, signed by eighty-two of 106 southern congressmen and all but three southern senators (the exceptions being Albert Gore and Estes Kefauver of Tennessee and Lyndon Johnson of Texas). It promised to resist "forced integration" by "any lawful means," whatever that meant. Other southern citizens and state officials promised "massive resistance," some of it of dubious legality, some of it indubitably illegal. Arkansas Governor Orval Faubus even deployed the National Guard to prevent the desegregation of Little Rock Central High School in the fall of 1957. Though not keen on change, President Dwight David Eisenhower felt obligated to enforce the law laid down by the Supreme Court, and so federalized the Arkansas National Guard and sent them back to barracks. The D-Day mastermind then found himself ordering the 101st Airborne Division to protect nine children from protesters who were screaming at them day after day because they thought them unworthy of an equal education. These are the events that Barack Obama referred to at the opening of the NMAAHC when he spoke of "The students who walked passed angry crowds [to] integrate our schools": understated words that mirror the moving calm of the "Little Rock Nine" as they ignored and out-adulted their outrageously abusive elders.[48]

The military also had to accompany James Meredith to ensure his right to enroll at the University of Mississippi on September 20, 1962. And again on September 25 and 26 after Governor Ross Barnett and Lieutenant Governor Paul B. Johnson Jr. refused his right to register and had to be held in contempt by the Fifth US Circuit Court and fined $10,000 until they desisted. Meredith finally enrolled under the guard of federal marshalls. Even then, a white riot resulted in twenty-eight marshalls suffering gunshot wounds, ninety-seven others were otherwise injured, and two other people killed. Meredith began classes under the protection of the United States Army.

As a consequence of this violence, the same James Meredith later set off from Memphis, Tennessee, on a solo March Against Fear, this time targeting disfranchisement. On day two, however, June 7, 1966, he was shot and wounded by a white supremacist terrorist. Yet some 15,000 people then hit the road to continue the march, and after his spell in hospital Meredith rejoined them before they reached Jackson, 220 miles and twenty days later. During the march more than 4,000 African Americans registered to vote, and still more did so afterwards.

On June 11, 1963, Governor George Wallace attempted to prevent the entry of Malone Jones and James Hood to University of Alabama, and President John F. Kennedy sent guards to get them in too. That evening the president made his much noted TV and radio speech about a "rising tide of discontent," urging the country to embrace civil rights as "a moral issue ... in our daily lives," and appealing to Congress to pass new civil rights legislation. Even then it took more violence to see things through, and this time of the deadly kind.

Medgar Evers had fought for his country against fascism, including in the Battle of Normandy in 1944, and was one of those veterans who was no longer willing to tolerate racism at home. As an agent of the Mississippi Regional Council of Negro Leadership and the NAACP, he applied for and was refused a place at the University of Mississippi Law School after the Brown verdict, the beginning of the legal campaign that eventually got James Meredith through the door. Evers had previously helped organize the "Don't Buy Gas Where You Can't Use the Rest Room" antisegregation campaign and had been involved in the investigation into the kidnapping, torture, and murder of fourteen-year-old Emmet Till in August 1955 for speaking supposedly flirtatiously to a white woman. There had been attempts on Evers's life before, but in the early hours of June 12, 1963, the night of President Kennedy's speech, he was shot and killed outside his home by Byron De La Beckwith, a member of the White Citizens' Council and later of the Ku Klux Klan. White juries failed to agree a verdict at the time, but Beckwith was finally convicted of the murder in 1994. The president presented a civil rights bill to Congress one week later, though it didn't pass into law until over seven months after Kennedy's own assassination in Dallas, Texas, in November 1963.

Dr. King's mighty cadence

Brown v. Board of Education stated: "In the field of education, the doctrine of 'separate but equal' has no place." It did not state that it had no place anywhere else, however; although it implied it and thereby inspired a continuing fight against injustice everywhere. One famous battle began on December 5, 1955 when Rosa Parks was arrested for refusing to relinquish her seat on an Alabama bus. People then boycotted the buses, simply walking to work instead, often inspired by a stunningly articulate and charismatic local preacher whose name soon became widely known, Dr. Martin Luther King Jr. After a little over a year, the combination of organization and protest succeeded in desegregating public transport in Montgomery.

The courts were also involved, illustrating Barack Obama's point that organized actions by ordinary citizens can change the law. In February 1956, civil rights attorney Fred Gray filed a court case on behalf of several African American women, including Claudette Colvin, a fifteen-year-old who had been arrested some months before and for the same violation as Rosa Parks, but was named *Browder v Gayle* after the main plaintiff Aurelia Browder and the defendant W. A. Gayle, the mayor of Montgomery. In June the local US District Court delivered the verdict that segregated public transport in Montgomery "violates the Constitution and laws of the United States" by denying the "equal protection" clause of the Fourteenth Amendment. The US Supreme Court upheld the verdict in November and federal marshals delivered the desegregation order to Mayor Gayle on December 20.[49]

Furthermore, a series of Supreme Court cases beginning with *Morgan v. Virginia* (1946), then *Sarah Keys v. Carolina Bus Company* (1955), and culminating with *Boynton v. Virginia* (1960) had declared segregation on buses crossing state lines and at terminals serving them to be illegal and that equal treatment of customers was enforceable under the Constitution's clause allowing Congress to regulate interstate commerce. Southern states had ignored these rulings, however, and the Interstate Commerce Commission had done little to uphold the law, so the Congress of Racial Equality (CORE) and the Student Non-Violent Coordinating Committee (SNCC) organized the Freedom Rides. The first Freedom Riders, mixed-race groups of protesters travelling together, departed from Washington DC for New Orleans, Louisiana, on March 4, 1961. In the course of the summer over 400 people went on at least sixty separate Freedom Rides, until, after hundreds of attacks and arrests, the ICC announced in September that it would enforce the desegregation of public transport facilities throughout the South.

CORE and the Fellowship of Reconciliation had been organizing sit-ins aimed at desegregating lunch counters since the 1940s, but consistent and concerted protests began on February 1, 1960, when four black students from the North Carolina Agricultural and Technical State University sat down at a whites-only lunch counter at a Woolworth's store in Greensboro and refused to move until closing time. Then the next day they came back, and the next day, and the day after that, and others in increasing numbers joined them, white as well as black, until July, when Woolworth's finally agreed to serve all its customers equal respect. The sit-in movement spread, with some 70,000 people participating in them at lunch counters and all kinds of other private and public facilities across the South.

Yet, for all the protests, there was still massive resistance, including state violence, and the terrorism that helped to install Jim Crow in the first place was deployed in the effort to defend it. The successful desegregation of Birmingham, Alabama, in 1963 was achieved after public revulsion at television pictures of the police using night sticks, fire hoses, and attack dogs on children. It was followed by the September 15 bombing of the 16th Street Baptist Church that killed Addie Mae Collins, Carole Robertson, and Cynthia Wesley, all aged fourteen, and Carol Denise McNair, aged eleven.

The shock and horror at this act of terror, added to that at the murder of Medgar Evers, and at the assassination of President Kennedy, helped convince many of those who once thought that things were moving too quickly that, in fact, things were moving too slowly. The immense success of the quarter-million-strong March on Washington of August 28, 1963, further contributed to the sense that the time for change had arrived. Martin Luther King's "I Have a Dream" speech, made that day from the steps of the Lincoln Memorial, contributed to the feeling that a better future beckoned. And, as we've seen, Barack Obama has often echoed what he called "Dr. King's mighty cadence" from that day and others. All this added to increasing impatience with the southern voting bloc that had long held up progress and thereby paved the way for the fuller interdiction of segregation by the Civil Rights Act of July 2, 1964.[50]

The culmination of it all

This and a previous Civil Rights Act of 1957 had also supposedly outlawed practices associated with disfranchisement, but as the acts lacked sufficient enforcement provisions these practices continued anyway, and so once again it required people power to push politicians into effective action. The NAACP had demanded the end of disfranchisement since the organization's founding, and it renewed its voter registration drives alongside its own and other groups' struggles against segregation in the aftermath of World War II. Alongside CORE and SNCC, the NAACP also organized the 1964 Freedom Summer, a voter registration movement in Mississippi during which James Chaney was arrested by Neshoba County deputy sheriff and Ku Klux Klan member Cecil Price, then released, but only to be ambushed and murdered by Price's fellow Klansmen. Chaney was one of around twenty-five African American civil rights activists murdered between 1961 and 1965, but what caught many people's particular attention on this occasion was that he was kidnapped and murdered alongside Michael Schwerner and Andrew Goodman, white civil rights volunteers from New York. Yet, in the face of such danger, people persisted. As Barack Obama put it, "there was struggle and sacrifice, discipline and tremendous courage. And," he said, "there was the culmination of it all one Sunday afternoon on a bridge in Alabama."[51]

What happened at that bridge in Selma illustrates almost everything Barack Obama believes about the Civil Rights Movement in particular and about American history in general, which is perhaps why he called it "the culmination of it all." As Obama put it in 2015 in a speech entitled "For We Were Born of Change" given half a century on: "In one afternoon 50 years ago, so much of our turbulent history—the stain of slavery and anguish of civil war; the yoke of segregation and tyranny of Jim Crow; the death of four little girls in Birmingham; and the dream of a Baptist preacher—all that history met on this bridge."[52]

Politicians and civil servants in Selma had managed to maintain disfranchisement despite Civil Rights to the degree that in January 1965 only 355 out of 15,000 African American citizens there were registered to vote. This and local judge James Hare's 1964 ban on civil rights gatherings of three or more people perhaps represent in miniature the massive abuse of constitutional democracy that means that Barack Obama's making of "a more perfect union" has always been a work-in-progress. Yet for Obama the problem is not in the system itself; it is in the implementation, in the actions of individuals. And the Alabama authorities' actions appear to vindicate that view, as with brutal blatancy they violated the right to peaceful protest, the right to equality under the law, and the right of all to vote—rights that are all clearly stated in the Constitution's First, Fourteenth, and Fifteenth Amendments.

But, as Obama said in his speech in Philadelphia, and it's a point he's frequently repeated and reformulated: "words on a parchment would not be enough to deliver slaves from bondage, or provide men and women of every color and creed their full rights and obligations as citizens of the United States. What would be needed were Americans in successive generations who were willing to do their part—through protests and struggle, on the streets and in the courts, through a civil war and civil disobedience and always at great risk—to narrow that gap between the promise of our ideals and the reality of their time." It was in exactly this spirit that Martin Luther King organized a new voter register drive and a march to draw attention to violations of voting rights that still occurred, even after the Civil Rights Act, in Selma and across the South.[53]

On the morning of March 7, 1965, some 600 people assembled for a planned march to the Alabama capital of Montgomery, but they didn't even make it across the bridge heading out of Selma before being beaten back and bloodied by state troopers. In "For We Were Born of Change," President Obama used all his historical and rhetorical skills to evoke the scenes of Bloody Sunday, including the courageous but law-abiding audacity and hope of people confronting the lawless violence of the state. "Young folks with bedrolls and backpacks were milling about," he said,

> Veterans of the movement trained newcomers in the tactics of non-violence; the right way to protect yourself when attacked. A doctor described what tear gas does to the body, while marchers scribbled down instructions for contacting their loved ones. The air was thick with doubt, anticipation and fear. Selma—the strength and courage of non-violence … The courage of ordinary Americans willing to

endure billy clubs and the chastening rod; tear gas and the trampling hoof; men and women who despite the gush of blood and splintered bone would stay true to their North Star and keep marching towards justice.[54]

Martin Luther King organized a second march to the bridge two days later, and then another one on March 21, for which 3,000 gathered and which this time made it to Montgomery. As Obama noted on an earlier occasion, in 2005 and when marking the sixty-fifth birthday of John Lewis, one of the organizers and marchers, and one of those beaten and bloodied, "They marched again. They crossed the bridge. They awakened a nation's conscience, and not five months later, the Voting Rights Act of 1965 was signed into law." And as Obama said in Selma itself in 2015, "In time, their chorus would well up and reach President Johnson. And he would send them protection, and speak to the nation, echoing their call for America and the world to hear: 'We shall overcome.' "[55]

Indeed in a speech to Congress on March 15, just over a week after "Bloody Sunday," President Lyndon Johnson used those words: "We Shall Overcome." They come from a hymn originally written by Charles Albert Tindley and first published in 1900 as "I'll Overcome Some Day," but which was then adapted during a Charleston, South Carolina, tobacco workers strike in 1945 to the tune of an old slave song called "No More Auction Block for Me," also known as "Many Thousands Gone." As "We Shall Overcome," the song became an anthem of the Civil Rights Movement that connected the struggle for equality back to the struggles against slavery. Its popularity was extended by its use by Pete Seeger and other members of the Highlander Folk School. Joan Baez, for example, led a rendition of it at the March on Washington in 1963. These and President Johnson's use of the words of a black gospel song illustrate Barack Obama's belief that popular protest can help build a broad coalition and then touch politics at the highest level. On August 6, President Johnson signed the Voting Rights Act, finally adding effective enforcement measures to the outlawing of disfranchisement.

The strength and courage of nonviolence

Though subtly done, and rendered in narrative form, Barack Obama's semicentenary speech in Selma has a clear perspective on three particular issues of historiographical debate. These same perspectives also inhere consistently in Obama's other speeches and writings. The first of the three is that it was nonviolence, the peaceful protest pioneered by King that ultimately led to success, not the more sectarian strands of the civil rights effort. Second, that the civil rights movement was a people's movement, not merely one led by great campaigners like Dr. King and certainly not one led by presidents. And these two points of interpretation support a third one—that the Civil Rights Movement (and indeed all of African American history) is part of the mainstream of American history, and is not an "outlier."[56]

Let's look first at Barack Obama's views on different strands of the Civil Rights Movement. As noted earlier, in the Selma speech of 2015, Obama spoke of "Veterans of the movement" training "newcomers in the tactics of non-violence," of "the strength and courage of non-violence," and of "the courage of ordinary Americans willing to endure" the brutalities they knew they'd encounter. Obama was even more explicit about the power and the effectiveness of nonviolent protest when he spoke at John Lewis's sixty-fifth birthday celebrations ten years earlier. "And if there's anything we can learn from this living saint sitting beside me," he said, "it is that change is never easy, but always possible. That it comes not from violence or militancy or the kind of politics that pits us against each other and plays on our worst fears; but from great discipline and organization, from a strong message of hope, and from the courage to turn against the tide so that the tide eventually may be turned."[57]

These reflections align with Barack Obama's philosophies of political action—with both his practical, everyday philosophical pragmatism and his principles of constitutionalism. "You see," Obama said in a commencement address at Howard University in 2016, "change requires more than righteous anger. It requires a program, and it requires organizing." And he gave the following historical example involving one the greats of the Civil Rights Movement. "At the 1964 Democratic Convention," he recounted, "Fannie Lou Hamer—all five-feet-four-inches tall—gave a fiery speech on the national stage. But then she went back home to Mississippi and organized cotton pickers. And she didn't have the tools and technology where you can whip up a movement in minutes. She had to go door to door." So, he concluded, "Passion is vital, but you've got to have a strategy."[58]

In any case, Obama further noted, "democracy requires compromise, even when you are 100 percent right." And he added,

> This is hard to explain sometimes. You can be completely right, and you still are going to have to engage folks who disagree with you. If you think that the only way forward is to be as uncompromising as possible, you will feel good about yourself, you will enjoy a certain moral purity, but you're not going to get what you want. And if you don't get what you want long enough, you will eventually think the whole system is rigged. And that will lead to more cynicism, and less participation, and a downward spiral of more injustice and more anger and more despair. And that's never been the source of our progress. That's how we cheat ourselves of progress.[59]

And again he cited examples from the past of how impassioned campaigning had to combine with the ordinary drudgery of constitutional process in order to make a more perfect union. "We remember Dr. King's soaring oratory, the power of his letter from a Birmingham jail, the marches he led. But he also sat down with President Johnson in the Oval Office to try and get a Civil Rights Act and a Voting Rights Act passed." As ever, not a perfect one, but a more perfect one. "And those two seminal bills were not perfect," Obama added, "just like the Emancipation Proclamation was a war document as much as it was some clarion call for freedom. Those mileposts of our progress were not perfect. They did not make up for centuries of slavery or Jim Crow or eliminate racism or provide for 40 acres and a mule. But they made things better. And you know what, I will take better every time. I always tell my staff—better is good, because you consolidate your gains and then you move on to the next fight from a stronger position."[60]

All this is essential for Obama because constitutional process accommodates both the right and the wrong that exist in the world as it is. "Another Howard alum, Zora Neale Hurston, once said," Obama said: " 'Nothing that God ever made is the same thing to more than one person.' Think about that. That's why our democracy gives us a process designed for us to settle our disputes with argument and ideas and votes instead of violence and simple majority rule." And he related this point to the sometimes painful necessities that freedom of speech entails. "So don't try to shut folks out," he urged the graduates,

> don't try to shut them down, no matter how much you might disagree with them. There's been a trend around the country of trying to get colleges to disinvite speakers with a different point of view, or disrupt a politician's rally. Don't do that—no matter how ridiculous or offensive you might find the things that come out of their mouths. Because as my grandmother used to tell me, every time a fool speaks, they are just advertising their own ignorance. Let them talk. Let them talk. If you don't, you just make them a victim, and then they can avoid accountability.[61]

"That doesn't mean you shouldn't challenge them," Obama added, "Have the confidence to challenge them, the confidence in the rightness of your position. There will be times when you shouldn't compromise your core values, your integrity, and you will have the responsibility to speak up in the face of injustice. But listen. Engage. If the other side has a point, learn from them. If they're wrong, rebut them. Teach them. Beat them on the battlefield of ideas." Here of course Obama sounds positively Jeffersonian. As the third president said in his inaugural address: "error of opinion may be tolerated where reason is left free to combat it."[62]

It is not that Obama disregards or disrespects the legacies of more radical leaders from the 1960s and other times. In the last chapter we saw how he acknowledged the contributions to abolitionism of "unbending idealists" such as William Lloyd Garrison, Denmark Vesey, Harriet Tubman, Frederick Douglass, and even John Brown, noting that "it has sometimes been the cranks, the zealots, the prophets, the agitators, and the unreasonable—in other words, the absolutists—that have fought for a new order." Perhaps in a similar way Obama credits the likes of Malcolm X with a role in the Civil Rights Movement and certainly with a role in his own intellectual development. Obama's *Dreams from my Father* famously charts his own personal journey, including his encounters in his earlier days with the works and even the persons of numerous radical black thinkers. But, as the elder Obama put it in *The Audacity of Hope*, "I'm left, then, with Lincoln." And so he is similarly left with King.[63]

It is worth noting here, though, as Thomas J. Sugrue has pointed out, that Obama's representation of the strands of civil rights obscures how those strands overlapped and intertwined. For one thing, mainstream activists were sometimes more radical than the aforementioned representations suggest. John Lewis, for instance, the "living saint" who is Obama's own hero and close friend—though very much in the nonviolent and integrationist wing of the Movement, had to be persuaded to tone down the speech he originally intended to deliver at the 1963 March on Washington.

Indeed it is often forgotten today how mainstream civil rights leaders were perceived by many at the time. Martin Luther King was denounced by FBI Director J. Edgar Hoover as "the most dangerous Negro in America," and even relatively reasonable people felt he was moving too far, too fast. In his later career, furthermore, King campaigned against the Vietnam War and launched the Poor People's Campaign as President Johnson's Great Society and War on Poverty collapsed under the weight of internal and international conflict. Yet King's reconstruction was completed when President Ronald Reagan represented him as nonradical after reluctantly conceding to the creation of Martin Luther King's birthday as a national holiday in 1984. To give a sense of the revisionist effort made to moderate King: Reagan and others portrayed him as opposed to affirmative action when, in fact, he was in favor of affirmative action.[64]

It is also worth noting how onetime member of the Nation of Islam and separatist Malcolm X genuinely moved toward the mainstream in his own later years, finally embracing an orthodox Islam that was much more politically inclusive. And Barack Obama knows all this. In his early writings he acknowledged the synergies of the different strands of the Civil Rights Movement. "From W. E. B. Du Bois to Booker T. Washington to Marcus Garvey to Malcolm X, to Martin Luther King," he wrote in 1988, "this internal debate has raged between integration and nationalism, between accommodation and militancy, between sit-down strikes and boardroom negotiations." But, he continued, "The lines between these strategies have never been simply drawn, and the most successful black leadership has recognized the need to bridge these seemingly divergent approaches." Yet by the time he wrote *Dreams from My Father* in 1995, Obama was saying that "nationalism dissipated into an attitude rather than any concrete program, a collection of grievances and not an organized force, images and sounds that crowded the airwaves but without any corporeal existence." Something that "shattered into a thousand pieces."[65]

Which brings us to our next point—about how nonviolence and nonsectarianism allowed for that most Obamian of things, synergy, and it is where Obama's obscuring of the particulars of radicalism nevertheless contains a general historical truth—that the mainstream Civil Rights movement comprised an inclusive coalition that created a popular political movement.

The folks whose names you never heard of

Barack Obama pays due respect and does so frequently to the famous names of Civil Rights Movement, in particular to Martin Luther King and also of course to his friend John Lewis. But in Selma in 2015 Obama spoke also of "Young folks with bedrolls and backpacks" and of the "courage of ordinary Americans." He also noted that day: "The

Americans who crossed this bridge, they were not physically imposing. But they gave courage to millions. They held no elected office. But they led a nation."[66]

Similarly, in his speech marking John Lewis's sixty-fifth birthday, Obama said "I've often thought about the people on the Edmund Pettus Bridge that day. Not only John and Hosea Williams leading the march, but the hundreds of everyday Americans who left their homes and their churches to join it. Blacks and whites, teenagers and children, teachers and bankers and shopkeepers—a beloved community of God's children ready to stand for freedom." And it was this community collectively that won the day in his view because of the inclusive breadth of its coalition. And, relating the Civil Rights Movement to American historical tradition more generally, Obama said in 2015 that "Selma shows us that America is not the project of any one person. Because the single-most powerful word in our democracy is the word 'We.' 'We The People.' 'We Shall Overcome.' 'Yes We Can.' That word is owned by no one. It belongs to everyone."[67]

Obama repeated these points at the opening of the NMAAHC: "It's the maids who decided, you know what, I'm tired of segregation and I'm going to walk for my freedom," he said. "It's the porters who not only worked tirelessly to support their families, but ultimately helped bring about the organization that led to better working conditions for all Americans here in the United States. It's about our moms and grandparents and uncles and aunts who just did the right thing and raised great families, despite assaults on their dignity on every single day." And again Obama aligned his thoughts on that occasion with his thoughts on African American and indeed all of American history more generally. The museum is about, he said on that same occasion, "more than just telling stories about the famous. It's not just about the icons. There's plenty of space for Harriet Tubman and Dr. King and Muhammed Ali. But what makes the museum so powerful and so visceral is that it's the story of all of us—the folks whose names you never heard of, but whose contributions, day after day, decade after decade, combined to push us forward and the entire nation forward."[68]

Like separating the strands of the Civil Rights Movement, however, the drawing of too sharp a distinction between regular people and political activists can be somewhat historically distorting, manifestly so given Obama's faith in the political engagement of ordinary citizens. If we take the example of Rosa Parks, we can see how an ordinary individual can at the same time be a political icon, and indeed in some respects the much-promoted ordinarity is a part of the iconography. Parks has often been portrayed as "just" a "maid" who just got tired one day—physically tired from her labor and tired of her demeaning treatment. Even Barack Obama has promoted this idea, referring to her in *The Audacity of Hope* as a "black seamstress," even though he knows she was a political activist also.[69]

It is true that Rosa Parks was a tailor's assistant in a Montgomery, Alabama, department store. But it is also true that as far back as the early 1930s, long before she found fame, she had protested against the conviction of the Scottsboro Boys, nine African American teenagers falsely accused and unfairly convicted of rape after humiliating some white boys who tried to force them off a train travelling between Chattanooga and Memphis, Tennessee. In the 1940s she was three times denied the right to register to vote.

Nevertheless, she persisted, and on the fourth time of trying she became one of the few enfranchised African Americans in Alabama. She was longtime secretary to E. D. Nixon, leader of Montgomery chapter of the NAACP. She attended training sessions for political activists at Highlander School, Tennessee, in 1954, the year before she refused to be moved off her seat on the bus. She kept her seat and sparked the boycott just over a month after the acquittal of the killers of Emmett Till, tortured and lynched after speaking to a white woman. It is also true that Montgomery activists had been planning a bus boycott for over a year before it started. The local NAACP and the Montgomery Improvement Association put the boycott into full effect the very day after Parks's gesture, in line with plans long prepared by the Montgomery Women's Political Council.

But the characterization of Rosa Parks as a "black seamstress" who almost accidentally ignited a peaceful revolution was constructed at the time for those who were then uncomfortable with "agitators" and their perceived political militancy, and for public relations reasons the myth was therefore one that civil rights leaders understandably allowed to be believed. As Obama noted in the Selma speech of 2015, "we are well-served to remember that at the time of the marches, many in power condemned rather than praised them. Back then, they were called Communists, half-breeds, outside agitators, sexual and moral degenerates, and worse—everything but the name their parents gave them. Their faith was questioned. Their lives were threatened. Their patriotism was challenged."[70]

It is much more widely accepted today that the aims of the mainstream Civil Rights Movement were in accord with the traditional American creed of equality and liberty, and the mainstream Movement's methods were equally in accord with the First Amendment's guarantee of "the right of the people peaceably to assemble, and to petition the Government for a redress of grievances." That's certainly Barack Obama's view, so his characterization of Rosa Parks as a "seamstress" and other women like her as "maids who decided" they were "tired of segregation" and were "going to walk for my freedom" was not about pretending that "the people" were apart from the political process, but more about confirming, in Jeffersonian and indeed Obamian fashion, that they were and are rightfully a part of it.[71]

That certainly seemed to be the case when Obama spoke of "the porters who not only worked tirelessly to support their families, but ultimately helped bring about the organization that led to better working conditions for all Americans here in the United States." The profession of "porters" brings to mind A. Philip Randolph, founder and leader of the Brotherhood of Sleeping Car Porters who celebrated the arrival of "the New Negro" as early as 1917, whose plans for a March on Washington pressured President Franklin Roosevelt into forbidding discrimination in defense work and into founding the Fair Employment Practices Commission in 1941, who similarly pressured President Harry Truman to end segregation in the US armed forces in 1948, and who finally did formally lead the March on Washington in 1963.[72]

Yet Obama's use of the plural "porters" also reminds us that Randolph was not alone, that the members of his Union and many others besides stood alongside him as he could not have stood alone. These porters and these maids, the "moms and grandparents and uncles and aunts" were among those who Obama celebrated in *The Audacity of Hope* as "the faceless, nameless men and women, slaves and soldiers and tailors and butchers, constructing lives for themselves and their children and grandchildren, brick by brick, rail by rail, calloused hand by calloused hand."[73]

And we can see in Obama's words that it was these people, "the folks whose names you never heard of," who were the most powerful agents of change, not presidents. As Obama said, "In time, their chorus would well up and reach President Johnson." *In time*—they led, he followed. *Their chorus would well up and reach President Johnson*—they sang, he heard. And "he would send them protection, and speak to the nation, echoing their call for America and the world to hear: 'We shall overcome.'" It was the people's song the president sang.[74]

As old as our beginnings and as timeless as our hopes

Barack Obama's history of the Civil Rights Movement—of peaceful, popular protest in accord with the principles of the Declaration of Independence and the processes of the Constitution and the rights it guarantees—is not only an African American history, but also a quintessentially American history. In his 2005 valediction to John Lewis, Obama said "And so it was, in a story as old as our beginnings and as timeless as our hopes, that change came about because the good people of a great nation willed it so." And ten years later at a bridge in Alabama Obama observed, in a rhetorical mapping of geographical landmarks to mark the path of historical time, that "there are places and moments in America where this nation's destiny has been decided. Many are sites of war—Concord and Lexington, Appomattox, Gettysburg. Others are sites that symbolize the daring of America's character—Independence Hall and Seneca Falls, Kitty Hawk and Cape Canaveral. Selma is such a place."[75]

And Obama added: "What greater expression of faith in the American experiment than this, what greater form of patriotism is there than the belief that America is not yet finished, that we are strong enough to be self-critical, that each successive generation can look upon our imperfections and decide that it is in our power to remake this nation to more closely align with our highest ideals?" This acknowledgment that protest is American, not anti-American, allows Obama to associate Selma directly with his larger theme of America as historically a product of protest. "That's why Selma," he said next, "is not some outlier in the American experience … It is instead the manifestation of a creed written into our founding documents: 'We the People … in order to form a more perfect union.' 'We hold these truths to be self-evident, that all men are created equal.'"[76]

Barack Obama has been repeatedly determined to stress these connections and continuities between African American and the rest of American history, to the point in fact of seeing them as inseparable from each other. As noted in the previous chapter, there is a danger therein of drawing false equivalences between the oppressions that were particular to African Americans and the hardships suffered by others. But the benefits of Obama's approach are the preservation and popularization of the memory of

African American history, and its incorporation into a gradually more inclusive popular version of American history. Just as Obama has often stressed that he sees America as one society, one people—"out of many, one"—so he sees the American people as having one common history, even in the midst of conflict. In any case, Obama deftly avoids the pitfall of false equivalence by honoring the particularities of suffering while still stressing the commonalities of aims and values.

Obama, for example, took the opportunity of the 2012 groundbreaking ceremony for the NMAAHC to advance these ideas about remembrance and about the simultaneity of particularity and commonality. On the point of remembrance, he noted that one reason the Museum was being built was "Because just as the memories of our earliest days have been confined to dusty letters and faded pictures, the time will come when few people remember drinking from a colored water fountain, or boarding a segregated bus, or hearing in person Dr. King's voice boom down from the Lincoln Memorial." And on the point of inclusion he said on the same occasion that thanks to the Museum future "generations will remember the sometimes difficult, often inspirational, but always central role that African Americans have played in the life of our country." And "When future generations hear these songs of pain and progress and struggle and sacrifice, I hope they will not think of them as somehow separate from the larger American story. I want them to see it as central—an important part of our shared story. A call to see ourselves in one another."[77]

In remarks at the actual opening ceremony in September 2016 Obama noted that the museum existed "so that the story of the African American experience could take its rightful place in our national memory." And the online written introduction of the president's weekly address at the time of the opening said: "The National Museum of African American History and Culture not only tells the African American story—it tells the American story."[78]

Yet the inclusion of African American history in American history does not for Obama necessitate the exclusion of the unique tragedies of the former. In fact it means incorporating those tribulations into the latter. This means, first, balancing the ghastly and the great. At the NMAAHC groundbreaking ceremony, for example, Obama said "I want my daughters to see the shackles that bound slaves on their voyage across the ocean and the shards of glass that flew from the 16th Street Baptist church, and understand that injustice and evil exist in the world. But I also want them to hear Louis Armstrong's horn and learn about the Negro League and read the poems of Phyllis Wheatley. And I want them to appreciate this museum not just as a record of tragedy, but as a celebration of life."[79]

And then at the opening ceremony: "It's a story that is full of tragedy and setbacks, but also great joy and great victories." And in his weekly address on the same subject:

This museum chooses to tell a fuller story. It doesn't gauze up some bygone era or avoid uncomfortable truths. Rather, it embraces the patriotic recognition that America is a constant work in progress; that each successive generation can look upon our imperfections and decide that it is within our collective power to align this nation with the high ideals of our founding. That's what you'll see inside. You'll see it in the shackles of an enslaved child and in the hope of Harriet Tubman's gospel hymnal. You'll see it in the tragedy of Emmett Till's coffin and in the resilience of a lunch counter stool and in the triumph of a Tuskegee Airplane. You'll see it in the shadow of a prison guard tower and in the defiance of Jesse Owens' cleats and in the American pride of Colin Powell's uniform.[80]

"All of that," Obama said, "isn't simply the African-American story; it's part of the American story. And so it is entirely fitting that we tell this story on our National Mall, the same place we tell the stories of Washington and Jefferson and our independence; the story of Lincoln who saved our union and the GIs who defended it; the story of King who summoned us all toward the mountaintop." And, he concluded, "That's what we'll celebrate not just this weekend, but in the years and generations ahead—a fuller account of our glorious American story."[81]

For we were born of change

One of the corollaries of Barack Obama's history of the making of "a more perfect union" is that it is perfectly patriotic to be critical. As he asked rhetorically at the Selma semicentenary, "what could be more American than what happened in this place? What could more profoundly vindicate the idea of America than plain and humble people—unsung, the downtrodden, the dreamers not of high station, not born to wealth or privilege, not of one religious tradition but many, coming together to shape their country's course?" Obama thus saw the protesters at Selma as having the same "idea held by generations of citizens who believed that America is a constant work in progress; who believed that loving this country requires more than singing its praises or avoiding uncomfortable truths. It requires the occasional disruption, the willingness to speak out for what is right, to shake up the status quo. That's America."[82]

In this way as well, African American struggles for liberty and equality are again an American tradition, part of an American narrative, inspired by other American moments, and finally inspiring other American moments. "Because of what they did," Obama said of the Selma marchers, "the doors of opportunity swung open not just for black folks, but for every American. Women marched through those doors. Latinos marched through those doors. Asian Americans, gay Americans, Americans with disabilities—they all came through those doors." And he spoke similar words when commemorating the Thirteenth Amendment: "And doors of opportunity swung open, not just for the black porter, but also for the white chambermaid, and the immigrant dishwasher, so that their daughters and their sons might finally imagine a life for themselves beyond washing somebody else's laundry or shining somebody else's shoes. Freedom for you and for me. Freedom for all of us."[83]

Barack Obama has never said or written much in detail about the histories of these other Americans, at least not as much as he's said and written about African Americans and their history. Women appear in Obama's American history, for example, and do so frequently, but he has never done any Women's History per se. Like most historians, he's interested in everything, but he has his specialties. In any case, African American history is for Obama analogous of the history of all Americans, and indeed for the history of the United States itself. As David Remnick astutely noted, in "A More Perfect Union" in 2008 Obama cast the Civil Rights Movement not "in terms not of national guilt but of national progress; the rise of the Joshua generation, black and white, red and yellow." And so "The black freedom struggle became, in Obama's terms, an American freedom struggle."[84]

Nowhere is this sentiment expressed more clearly or more fully in Obama's oeuvre though than in his speech at Selma on March 7, 2015, fittingly entitled "For We Were Born of Change." In perhaps the greatest passage in possibly his greatest speech, even greater maybe than "A More Perfect Union," Obama used an anaphoric "We are" to express rhetorically an essential unity of the American people and American history, in all of their and all of its diversity—Obama's American syncretism again. He established the context for that unity of endeavor as he so often does and we've seen throughout this book by reference to the founding of the nation. "For we were born of change," he said. "We broke the old aristocracies, declaring ourselves entitled not by bloodline, but endowed by our Creator with certain inalienable rights. We secure our rights and responsibilities through a system of self-government, of and by and for the people. Look at our history," Obama urged. And then:

We are Lewis and Clark and Sacajawea, pioneers who braved the unfamiliar, followed by a stampede of farmers and miners, and entrepreneurs and hucksters. That's our spirit. That's who we are.

We are Sojourner Truth and Fannie Lou Hamer, women who could do as much as any man and then some. And we're Susan B. Anthony, who shook the system until the law reflected that truth. That is our character.

We're the immigrants who stowed away on ships to reach these shores, the huddled masses yearning to breathe free–Holocaust survivors, Soviet defectors, the Lost Boys of Sudan. We're the hopeful strivers who cross the Rio Grande because we want our kids to know a better life. That's how we came to be.

We're the slaves who built the White House and the economy of the South. We're the ranch hands and cowboys who opened up the West, and countless laborers who laid rail, and raised skyscrapers, and organized for workers' rights.

We're the fresh-faced GIs who fought to liberate a continent. And we're the Tuskegee Airmen, and the Navajo code-talkers, and the Japanese Americans who fought for this country even as their own liberty had been denied.

We're the firefighters who rushed into those buildings on 9/11, the volunteers who signed up to fight in Afghanistan and Iraq. We're the gay Americans whose blood ran in the streets of San Francisco and New York, just as blood ran down this bridge.

We are storytellers, writers, poets, artists who abhor unfairness, and despise hypocrisy, and give voice to the voiceless, and tell truths that need to be told.

We're the inventors of gospel and jazz and blues, bluegrass and country, and hip-hop and rock and roll, and our very own sound with all the sweet sorrow and reckless joy of freedom.

We are Jackie Robinson, enduring scorn and spiked cleats and pitches coming straight to his head, and stealing home in the World Series anyway.

We are the people Langston Hughes wrote of who "build our temples for tomorrow, strong as we know how." We are the people Emerson wrote of, "who for truth and honor's sake stand fast and suffer long;" who are "never tired, so long as we can see far enough."[85]

Barack Obama brought these points together—about Martin Luther King's reconciliatory approach, the inclusiveness of the Movement, and the American-ness of it all, in remarks recorded by David Remnick in the Oval Office in early 2010. And in these comments we see once again, as we saw with Obama's story of the American Revolution and of slavery, a story of tyranny that is ultimately a history of liberty. At "the core of the civil-rights movement," Obama said, "even in the midst of anger, despair, Black Power, Stokely Carmichael, Huey Newton ... there is a voice that is best captured by King, which is that we as African-Americans are American, and that our story is America's story, and that by perfecting our rights we perfect the Union—which is a very optimistic story in the end."[86]

We know the march is not yet over

In some ways the march from Selma to Montgomery and the Civil Rights Movement as a whole vindicate Barack Obama's radical Whig idea of historical progress toward more expansive and more extended equality and liberty. "We do a disservice to the cause of justice by intimating that bias and discrimination are immutable," he said in Selma in 2015, "that racial division is inherent to America. If you think nothing's changed in the past 50 years," he challenged his audience, "ask somebody who lived through the Selma or Chicago or Los Angeles of the 1950s. Ask the female CEO who once might have been assigned to the secretarial pool if nothing's changed. Ask your gay friend if it's easier to be out and proud in America now than it was thirty years ago. To deny this progress, this hard-won progress—our progress—would be to rob us of our own agency, our own capacity, our responsibility to do what we can to make America better."[87]

Yet Obama is far from naively Whiggish, and the above is part of a sophisticated analysis of where America is on the long journey from where it has been to where it still needs to go. As he said in his 2016 commencement address at Howard, balancing the good and the bad in the here and now on the line of historical time, "No, my election did not create a post-racial society. I don't know who was propagating that notion. That was not mine. But the election itself—and the subsequent one—because the first one, folks might have made a mistake. (Laughter.) The second one, they knew what they were getting. The election itself was just one indicator of how attitudes had changed." And he noted further that

> In my inaugural address, I remarked that just 60 years earlier, my father might not have been served in a D.C. restaurant—at least not certain of them. There were no black CEOs of Fortune 500 companies. Very few black judges. Shoot, as Larry Wilmore pointed out last week, a lot of folks didn't even think blacks had the tools to be a quarterback. Today, former Bull Michael Jordan isn't just the greatest basketball player of all time—he owns the team. (Laughter.) When I was graduating, the main black hero on TV was Mr. T. (Laughter.) Rap and hip hop were counterculture, underground. Now, Shonda Rhimes owns Thursday night, and Beyoncé runs the world. (Laughter.) We're no longer only entertainers, we're producers, studio executives. No longer small business owners—we're CEOs, we're mayors, representatives, Presidents of the United States. (Applause.) I tell you all this because it's important to note progress.
>
> Because to deny how far we've come would do a disservice to the cause of justice, to the legions of foot soldiers; to not only the incredibly accomplished individuals who have already been mentioned, but your mothers and your dads, and grandparents and great grandparents, who marched and toiled and suffered and overcame to make this day possible.[88]

Obama added nevertheless that "I tell you this not to lull you into complacency, but to spur you into action—because there's still so much more work to do, so many more miles to travel." And he noted the remaining "racial gap in economic opportunity" where "the overall unemployment rate is 5 percent, but the black unemployment rate is almost nine." And "Harriet Tubman may be going on the twenty, but we've still got a gender gap when a black woman working full-time still earns just 66 percent of what a white man gets paid." The "achievement gap when black boys and girls graduate high school and college at lower rates than white boys and white girls." And the "justice gap when too many black boys and girls pass through a pipeline from underfunded schools to overcrowded jails." And he pointed out indeed that this "is one area where things have gotten worse. When I was in college, about half a million people in America were behind bars. Today, there are about 2.2 million. Black men are about six times likelier to be in prison right now than white men."[89]

In Selma the year before, furthermore, Obama referred to the Department of Justice report into the shooting of a young black man, Michael Brown, by a white police officer in a St. Louis suburb in August 2014. "Just this week," Obama said, "I was asked whether I thought the Department of Justice's Ferguson report shows that, with respect to race, little has changed in this country. And I understood the question; the report's narrative was sadly familiar. It evoked the kind of abuse and disregard for citizens that spawned the Civil Rights Movement. But I rejected the notion that nothing's changed. What happened in Ferguson may not be unique, but it's no longer endemic. It's no longer sanctioned by law or by custom. And before the Civil Rights Movement, it most surely was."[90]

And then he added: "Of course, a more common mistake is to suggest that Ferguson is an isolated incident; that racism is banished; that the work that drew men and women to Selma is now complete, and that whatever racial tensions remain are a consequence of those seeking to play the 'race card' for their own purposes. We don't need the Ferguson report to know that's not true. We just need to open our eyes, and our ears, and our hearts to know that this nation's racial history still casts its long shadow upon us." And by way of example Obama made the very prescient point that "Right now, in 2015, fifty years after Selma, there are laws across this country designed to make it harder for people to vote. As we speak, more of such laws are being proposed. Meanwhile, the Voting Rights Act, the culmination of so much blood, so much sweat and tears, the product of so much sacrifice in the face of wanton violence, the Voting Rights Act stands weakened, its future subject to political rancor."[91]

And thus Obama also said: "We know the march is not yet over. We know the race is not yet won. We know that reaching that blessed destination where we are judged, all of us, by the content of our character requires admitting as much, facing up to the truth." And indeed "If Selma taught us anything, it's that our work is never done. The American experiment in self-government gives work and purpose to each generation." And so "Fifty years from Bloody Sunday, our march is not yet finished, but we're getting closer. Two hundred and thirty-nine years after this nation's founding our union is not yet perfect, but we are getting closer."[92]

In his farewell address, President Obama repeated his rejection of the notion that his own elevation to the White House meant that America is now postracial. "After my election," he said, "there was talk of a post-racial America. And such a vision, however well-intended, was never realistic. Race remains a potent and often divisive force in our society. Now, I've lived long enough to know," he continued, "that race relations are better than they were 10, or 20, or 30 years ago, no matter what some folks say," he added. "But," he pointed out, "we're not where we need to be."[93]

And in Philadelphia eight years earlier, he spoke of why we're not where we need to be. In "A More Perfect Union," Obama said that we "need to remind ourselves that so many of the disparities that exist in the African-American community today can be directly traced to inequalities passed on from an earlier generation that suffered under the brutal legacy of slavery and Jim Crow." One of those inequalities is economic, the legacy of many generations of unpaid and underpaid labor. Which brings us to Barack Obama's history of America's economy and society, where the relationship between property and liberty may be more complicated and conflicted than we may wish to believe.[94]

CHAPTER 6
THE CHIEF BUSINESS OF THE AMERICAN PEOPLE: PROPERTY AND LIBERTY

She touched her finger to a screen and cast her vote

On the evening of November 4, 2008, in his presidential election victory speech in Grant Park in Chicago, Illinois, Barack Obama spoke of a 106-year-old woman named Ann Nixon Cooper. "She was born just a generation past slavery," he said, "a time when there were no cars on the road or planes in the sky; when someone like her couldn't vote for two reasons—because she was a woman and because of the color of her skin." He then recounted many of the momentous events of her lifetime. First the suffrage movement and women gaining a guaranteed right to vote with the Nineteenth Amendment, then "the dust bowl and depression" and "a New Deal," then World War II, Civil Rights, and the fall of the Berlin Wall. Obama also noted that a "man touched down on the moon" and that "a world was connected by our own science and imagination." And then, "in this election," he said, returning to the person of Ann Nixon Cooper, "she touched her finger to a screen and cast her vote, because after 106 years in America, through the best of times and the darkest of hours, she knows how America can change."[1]

As we've seen in the course of this book, for Barack Obama, the making of "a more perfect union" entails the extension of the "creed" of the Declaration of Independence—that all men are created equal and endowed with unalienable rights to life, liberty, and the pursuit of happiness—more and more effectively to more and more men and women. And for Obama it seems that this kind of social and political progress brings another kind of progress with it. Just "a generation past slavery" there were, he said, "no cars on the road or planes in the sky." After the Civil Rights Movement, on the other hand, "A man touched down on the moon" and "a world was connected by our own science and imagination." And, when a black woman could finally vote for a black man as the winning candidate in a presidential election, she "touched her finger to a screen." Political progress thus arrives with the most spectacular symbols of technological advancement. The march of equality and liberty apparently leading to new and more pursuits of happiness: we drive our cars and fly in planes, we reach the moon and explore a virtual universe. The touch screen is perhaps Obama's most perfect symbol of progress in this speech, though—one in which democracy, technology, and people concord around a single article of electoral machinery; equality and modernity in concert, coordinated by a simple human touch.[2]

A little over eight years later, and back in Chicago, Barack Obama gave his farewell address to the American people as the end of his era in office approached. One of the problems facing the nation was climate change, he pointed out, although he didn't associate the phenomenon too directly on this occasion with all the cars on the road and the planes in the sky. On the contrary, Obama argued that an American spirit of enterprise was the source of the solution rather than the cause of the problem, and he related that spirit directly to American political tradition. "Now, we can and should argue about the best approach to solve the problem," he said. "But to simply deny the problem not only betrays future generations, it betrays the essential spirit of this country—the essential spirit of innovation and practical problem-solving that guided our Founders." And he reinforced this association of political with technological and economic innovation as follows:

> It is that spirit, born of the Enlightenment, that made us an economic powerhouse—
> the spirit that took flight at Kitty Hawk and Cape Canaveral; the spirit that cures
> disease and put a computer in every pocket.
>
> It's that spirit—a faith in reason, and enterprise, and the primacy of right
> over might—that allowed us to resist the lure of fascism and tyranny during the
> Great Depression; that allowed us to build a post-World War II order with other
> democracies, an order based not just on military power or national affiliations but
> built on principles—the rule of law, human rights, freedom of religion, and speech,
> and assembly, and an independent press.[3]

It is certainly the case that the United States has been an economic powerhouse in both philosophical and practical terms, and Obama knows he is by no means the first to say so. "Calvin Coolidge once said," he said, "the chief business of the American people is business," and to a degree Obama agrees. It "would be hard to find a country on earth," he continued, "that's been more consistently hospitable to the logic of the marketplace." And again he related political liberty and economic freedom directly together. "Our Constitution," he contended, "places the ownership of private property at the very heart of our system of liberty." He even related Godliness to gain. "Our religious traditions," he said next, "celebrate the value of hard work and express the conviction that a virtuous life will result in material reward." The rich are, furthermore, regarded "as role models, and our mythology is steeped in stories of men on the make—the immigrant who comes to this country with nothing and strikes it big, the young man who heads West in search of his fortune."[4]

An active national government

So important indeed is economic development to the rest of the history of the United States that Obama has narrated it in much the same way that he has other aspects of the American story. The basis of his analysis is the correlation he sees between property and liberty and economy and society—how economic freedoms bring about both material improvement and social and political progress, as he says they eventually did for Ann Nixon Cooper.

And yet, as with Obama's American social and political history, his economic history is symbolized like this but is in fact more complicated than this. And there is a critical angle (if not a critical theory) to it.

First, while Obama uses the term "free market" to describe the nature of American economic thought and activity, and does so generally approvingly, he also implicitly critiques this concept, at least in its fundamentalist form. He believes that government and economic enterprise are and should remain separate spheres, public and private. For him, government has no place as an economic player. But it does have a place as a sponsor and as a referee. As he points out, "government has been called upon throughout our history to build the infrastructure, train the workforce, and otherwise lay the foundations necessary for economic growth." Also, "Aside from making needed investments that private enterprise can't or won't make on its own, an active national government has also been indispensable in dealing with market failures" and "regulating the marketplace." And, furthermore, "government has helped structure the social compact between business and the American worker." In other words, for Obama, the chief business of the American people may indeed be business, but business does not thrive or even necessarily survive in a vacuum. His economic history is not just a history of private enterprise, therefore. It is, quite rightly, political and social history too.[5]

Second, these three foundational features of the United States economy—with government as entrepreneurial enabler, economic regulator, and social mediator—allow Obama to divide the country's economic history into two distinct eras, or possibly three. The first one and by far the longest dates from the 1790s to the 1930s, when government built the infrastructure, trained the workforce, and otherwise laid the foundations necessary for economic growth, but did little else. The second era came with the Wall Street Crash of 1929, the Great Depression, and the New Deal, during which government added "regulating the marketplace" and structuring "the social compact between business and the American worker" to its original portfolio.

For about a half a century, Obama argues, there was a broad consensus about the rightness of government economic regulation and social mediation. Since the days of Barry Goldwater, however, that consensus has gradually crumbled, and from the presidency of Ronald Reagan onwards the regulatory and mediational apparatuses that distinguished the second era from the first have slowly but surely been eroded. Besides internal ideological hostility, globalization's effects on the ability of national governments to regulate business and protect workers also threaten the post-1929 settlement. We may even already be in a third and very uncertain era.[6]

But before we look at Barack Obama's ideas about these eras of United States economic history, we should look at another period that he largely passes over, but which actually matters a lot to what matters to him. As we saw in Chapters 1 and 2, the British American colonies are not entirely absent from Barack Obama's American history, but they're present in ways that sometimes inadvertently obscure our view of the development of the economy, society, and politics of the nation to be. We need to unobscure.

Our starting point as Americans

Barack Obama describes the Declaration of Independence as "our starting point as Americans." In some respects this claim is true. In declaring and achieving national sovereignty, Americans freed themselves from such imperial regulations as the Navigation Acts, which, from the 1650s onwards, directed that the American colonies' most profitable products had to be transported on English or English American ships only and traded with English or English American merchants alone (British or British American after the 1707 Act of Union that joined England and Scotland). The Declaration and War of Independence also freed the former colonists from the direct taxation that the British parliament had imposed from the 1760s onwards. With Independence, Americans could tax themselves and trade with whom they pleased, which certainly seems like a starting point of some sort.[7]

And yet. An American "spirit of innovation" did not suddenly spring to life with national sovereignty. The aforementioned Navigation Acts and British taxes were themselves signs of thriving American colonial economies that the "mother country" had tried to its cost to exploit for itself. Those colonies were as eminently "hospitable to the logic of the marketplace" as the later United States would be. Indeed the process of colonization itself was what first placed "the ownership of private property at the very heart of" America's "system of liberty." Colonists also celebrated "the value of hard work and" expressed "the conviction that a virtuous life will result in material reward." The first western migrants came from England, the British Isles, and other parts of Europe, and were men and sometimes women "on the make," with colonial settlers hoping to strike it big by sailing rather than trekking "West" in search of their fortunes.[8]

This idea of colonial America as a land of individual opportunity, however, is precluded by Barack Obama's preconceptions about monarchy and imperialism. As we saw in Chapter 1, he believes that before the American Revolution "it was kings and princes and emperors who made decisions." And that as "a servant of Rome, a peasant in China, or a subject of King George, there were very few unlikely futures. No matter how hard you worked or struggled for something better, you knew you'd spend your life forced to build somebody else's empire; to sacrifice for someone else's cause."[9]

This, though, would be a better description of the second British Empire, the one comprising such colonies as Kenya, the land of Barack Obama's paternal heritage. But the earlier English and British state did not have the monetary or military resources to impose that kind of direct imperial rule over its earlier empire. Rather than founding "colonies of exploitation," therefore, the earlier English and British state established "colonies of settlement." Settlement, actually resettlement of course, came at terrible cost to Native Americans and Africans and their descendants, as we see in more detail later. Even some European settlers lived grim lives and suffered grisly ends in early America. But many individual Britons and other Europeans there found themselves to be, to borrow the words of historian John M. Murrin, "beneficiaries of catastrophe."[10]

Initially, British kings and parliaments licensed private businesses such as the Virginia Company or private proprietors such as William Penn to do the work of colonization, granting charters that gave them extraordinary economic as well as political freedom as rewards for their efforts. Yet, to make these colonies work, these companies and proprietors needed settlers. To entice those settlers, they had to devolve their economic and political privileges as rewards for the settlers' efforts. We can look at a classic of the genre of colonial promotional literature to see how those enticements included, above all else, promises of individual economic opportunity, religious freedom, and political liberty—and how these three things were presented as interrelated.

In 1698, a lifetime before the Declaration of Independence, Gabriel Thomas published "An Historical and Geographical Account of Pensilvania and of West-New-Jersey" that specifically aimed to attract settlers to these Middle-Atlantic Colonies. It claimed that "the present Encouragements are very great and inviting, for Poor People (both Men and Women) of all kinds, can here get three times the Wages for their Labour than they can in England or Wales." And indeed Thomas specified a great variety of laborers and the exact gains each could expect for their endeavors, starting with "a Black-Smith (my next Neighbour), who himself and one Negro Man he had, got Fifty Shillings on one Day, by working up a Hundred Pound Weight of Iron ..." And, he went on:

> the Carpenters, both House and Ship, Brick-layers, Masons, either of these Trades-Men, will get between Five and Six Shillings every Day constantly. As to Journey-Men Shooe-Makers, they have Two Shillings per Pair both for Men and Womens Shooes: And Journey-Men Taylors have Twelve Shillings per Week and their Diet. Sawyers get between Six and Seven Shillings the Hundred for Cutting of Pine Boards. And for Weavers, they have Ten or Twelve Pence the Yard for Weaving of that which is little more than half a Yard in breadth. Wooll-Combers, have for combing Twelve Pence per Pound. Potters have Sixteen Pence for an Earthen Pot which may be bought in England for Four Pence. Tanners may buy their Hides green for Three Half Pence per Pound, and sell their Leather for Twelve Pence per Pound. And Curriers have Three Shillings and Four Pence per Hide for Dressing it; they buy their Oyl at Twenty Pence per Gallon. Brick Makers have Twenty Shillings per Thousand for their Bricks.[11]

And on:

> Felt-Makers will have for their Hats Seven Shillings a piece, such as may be bought in England for Two Shillings a piece; yet they buy their Wooll commonly for Twelve or Fifteen Pence per Pound. And as to the Glaziers, they will have Five Pence a Quarry for their Glass. Coopers ... are now reckon'd in Pensilvania, by a modest Computation to be worth some Hundreds (if not Thousands) of Pounds.

The Bakers make as White Bread as any in London … The Butchers for killing a Beast, have Five Shillings and their Diet; and they may buy a good fat large Cow for Three Pounds … The Brewers sell … half Ale and half Stout for Fifteen Shillings per Barrel … And for Silver-Smiths, they have between Half a Crown and Three Shillings an Ounce for working their Silver, and for Gold equivalent.[12]

And on:

Plasterers have commonly Eighteen Pence per Yard for Plastering. Last-Makers have Sixteen Shillings per dozen for their Lasts. And Heel Makers have Two Shillings a dozen for their Heels. Wheel and Mill-Wrights, Joyners, Brasiers, Pewterers, Dyers, Fullers, Comb-Makers, Wyer-Drawers, Cage-Makers, Card-Makers, Painters, Cutlers, Rope-Makers, Carvers, Block-Makers, Turners, Button-Makers, Hair and Wood Sieve-Makers, Bodies Makers, Gun-Smiths, Lock-Smiths, Nailers, File-Cuters, Skinners, Furriers, Glovers, Patten-Makers, Watch-Makers, Clock Makers, Sadlers, Coller-Makers, Barbers, Printers, Book Binders, and all other Trades-Men, their Gains and Wages are about the same proportion as the fore-mentioned Trades in their Advancements, as to what they have in England.[13]

There was even ample opportunity for the less highly skilled, Thomas claimed: "Labouring Men have commonly here, between 14 and 15 Pounds a Year, and their Meat, Drink, Washing and Lodging; and by the Day their Wages is generally between Eighteen Pence and Half a Crown, and Diet also; But in Harvest they have usually between Three and Four Shillings each Day, and Diet." And for women as well: "The Maid Servants Wages is commonly betwixt Six and Ten Pounds per Annum, with very good Accommodation. And for the Women who get their Livelihood by their own Industry, their Labour is very dear, for I can buy in London a Cheese-Cake for Two Pence, bigger than theirs at that price when at the same time their Milk is as cheap as we can buy it in London, and their Flour cheaper by one half."[14]

Migrants could also easily save up the money they made because "Corn and Flesh, and what else serves Man for Drink, Food and Rayment is much cheaper here than in England, or elsewhere …" But, he said, "the chief reason why Wages of Servants of all sorts is much higher here than there, arises from the great Fertility and Produce of the Place; besides, if these large Stipends were refused them, they would quickly set up for themselves, for they can have Provision very cheap, and Land for a very small matter, or next to nothing in comparison of the Purchase of Lands in England." Furthermore, colonial American farmers "can better afford to give that great Wages than the Farmers in England can" because "their Land costs them … little or nothing in comparison, of which the Farmers commonly will get twice the encrease of Corn for every Bushel they sow, that the Farmers in England can from the richest Land they have." And because "they have constantly good price for their Corn, by reason of the great and quick vent into Barbadoes and other Islands."[15]

Gabriel Thomas tied prosperity to liberty, as Barack Obama would do three centuries later. Thomas's third reason for good wages, for example, was that the farmers paying them "pay no Tithes, and their Taxes are inconsiderable; the Place is free for all Persuasions, in a Sober and Civil way; for the Church of England and the Quakers bear equal Share in the Government." And so "They live Friendly and Well together; there is no Persecution for Religion, nor ever like to be; 'tis this that knocks all Commerce on the Head, together with high Imposts, strict Laws, and cramping Orders." And he hinted at the religious values of hard work and reward that Obama would also refer to, albeit in the sterner terms of the seventeenth century. "Here," Thomas said, "are no Beggars to be seen (it is a Shame and Disgrace to the State that there are so many in England) nor indeed have any here the least Occasion or Temptation to take up that Scandalous Lazy Life."[16]

Gabriel Thomas assured his readers, furthermore, that:

what I have here written, is not a Fiction, Flam, Whim, or any sinister Design, either to impose upon the Ignorant, or Credulous, or to curry Favour with the Rich and Mighty, but in meet Pity and pure Compassion to the Numbers of Poor Labouring Men, Women, and Children in England, half starv'd, visible in their meagre looks, that are continually wandering up and down looking for Employment without finding any, who here need not lie idle a moment, nor want due Encouragement or Reward for their Work, much less Vagabond or Drone it about.[17]

Which was partly true. Colonial promotional literature like this understated the risks and hardships of migration and settlement, and overstated the opportunities for and the ease of reaping rich reward. But such accounts appealed effectively all the same to the entrepreneurial attitudes and economic aspirations of potential colonists. Hence just over half a million Europeans migrated to Britain's North American mainland colonies between the founding of Jamestown in 1607 and the declaring of Independence in 1776, or over three-quarters of a million if we include the British colonies in the Caribbean. Most arrived as indentured servants, some died as such and did so soon after their arrival. But among those who survived were many who managed to better themselves economically, many more than would have done so had they stayed at home. In many colonies more than half of adult white men owned land at any one time, and considerably more than half would do so at some point in their lives. Economic betterment in America was therefore a real possibility for many European migrants.

But that only tells one side of the economic history of early America. Another is that the large numbers of colonial migrants settling and taking up land entailed the dispossession, removal, and often the murder of vast numbers of Native Americans—an issue we return to in the following chapter. Another side still is that colonization entailed the enslavement of enormous numbers of Africans and their descendants. We see hints of this phenomenon in Gabriel Thomas's mention of his Blacksmith neighbor's "one Negro Man," and in Thomas's reference to selling corn to Barbados and other islands where planters bought it to feed their slaves. For Thomas, however, slavery was nothing more than an economic fact, a source of labor or of consumption. He was entirely uninterested in slavery as a social or political issue, as were most white Europeans and Euro-Americans of the seventeenth century.

Barack Obama, however, is the opposite. For him, America's "original sin" is an interesting social and especially political issue. But he's not particularly interested in slavery as an economic fact. One reason for that may be his reluctance to adopt a critical theory of economic behavior, something we return to at the end of this chapter. In the meantime, though, another reason may be Obama's characterization of Pilgrims and Puritans as archetypal colonial Americans and of "farmers and scholars" as archetypal revolutionary Americans. Characterizations that inadvertently draw attention away from the enslaved and their enslavers as actual colonial and revolutionary Americans.[18]

The earliest settlers

At his University of Massachusetts commencement address in Boston on June 2, 2006, Barack Obama said that it was "right here, in the waters around us, where the American experiment began. As the earliest settlers arrived on the shores of Boston and Salem and Plymouth, they dreamed of building a City upon a Hill. And the world watched, waiting to see if this improbable idea called America would succeed." Obama thereby identified those he also called "the first settlers" as the Pilgrims who founded Plymouth Colony in 1620 and the Puritans who founded the Massachusetts Bay Colony in 1630. And in calling this founding the beginning of "the American experiment" he associated the origins of all the colonies with persecuted people building religious communities in the New World.[19]

While this remains a popular myth, the first permanent English colony was in fact founded in Jamestown in 1607. And it was founded for the commercial purposes of the Virginia Company, itself founded the year before by London merchants who had previously made their fortunes by financing the plundering of Spanish ships and colonies peopled by those who plundered and murdered Native Americans. The Jamestown settlers' initial mission was to feed off the presumed hospitality of local Amerindians while finding gold and other treasures in the manner of Spanish Conquistadors. When that didn't work out, they experimented in agricultural products and eventually found an economically viable staple in the form of tobacco. Tobacco is both a land- and labor-intensive crop, and, while planters long relied largely on white indentured servants, the first enslaved laborers nevertheless arrived in Virginia in 1619—also predating the Pilgrims and the Puritans. From the 1660s slavery became the principal labor system in the Chesapeake colonies of Virginia and Maryland, and by the time the Revolution began, the mostly enslaved black population of the Chesapeake was 200,000, 40 percent of a total regional population of half a million.[20]

A similar spirit of innovation led to the creation of a rice economy in the Lower South. North Carolina's black population was 33,000 of 110,000 in 1760, but South Carolina had a two-thirds black-majority by the early eighteenth century, which reached 57,000 of 94,000 people on the eve of Revolution. Georgia was at first free of slavery, intended as it was as an experiment in creating an ideal society of small (white) farmers who would also rebalance the alarmingly large black population in the region and provide a buffer zone against Spanish Florida. The Georgia proprietors eventually succumbed to demand for slave labor from farmers and planters who wanted to compete with their South Carolinian neighbors, however, and by 1760 the enslaved population of Georgia was 3,500 of 9,500.[21]

The northern non-plantation colonies were not "slave societies" as the southern plantation colonies were, but they were still "societies with slaves." Of 430,000 people in the Middle Colonies of New York, New Jersey, Pennsylvania, and Delaware in 1760, some 30,000 were black, most of whom were enslaved. And there were just under 13,000 black people in a total population of a little under half a million in the New England colonies of Massachusetts, New Hampshire, Connecticut, and Rhode Island.[22]

And these societies with slaves had close connections with their fellow British American slave societies. In 1764, for example, the British parliament passed a three pence per gallon tax on molasses imported into mainland North America, most of it imported from the Caribbean by the rum manufacturers of Massachusetts, replacing a six pence per gallon duty that was instituted in 1733 to deter importation from the French West Indies. The Sugar Act of 1764 was of course the first of the direct taxes and other measures passed by the British Parliament that eventually led to American independence. But it and its predecessor also remind us that the American colonies did not exist in self-sufficient economic isolation, but depended on trade networks that extended far and wide, in this case to the heavily slave-dependent sugar islands. In the British Caribbean in 1760 slaves formed a massive majority of 313,000 out of a total population of 356,000. We can also take note of 7,200 slaves in the 15,400 population of the British Atlantic islands of Bermuda and the Bahamas.[23]

The slave populations of British America not only produced sugar, rice, tobacco, and other commodities for vast and lucrative commercial markets, but also were products of the same Atlantic trade networks themselves. Of the 785,400 people who crossed the Atlantic to British North America between 1607 and 1775, 522,200 were European migrants and 263,200 were African victims of the slave trade. Of the 1.8 million who migrated to the British islands to which the mainland was closely connected, just over a quarter million were European migrants while over one and a half million were African victims of the slave trade.[24]

Some of these people were kidnapped, transported, and sold at first under the aegis of the Company of Royal Adventurers Trading into Africa, founded in 1660 and revamped as the Royal African Company in 1672, with slave-trading monopoly-status guaranteed by government-granted charter from 1663. Under the chairmanship of James, Duke of York, who was also king James II from 1685 until overthrown in the Glorious Revolution of 1688, these companies actively encouraged demand for enslaved laborers in the Chesapeake in order to broaden their consumer base beyond the Caribbean. After the effective end of the monopoly in 1688 and its formal discontinuation in 1698, the government supported independent slavers, known as "free traders"—indirectly so through its ties to financiers in such businesses as banking and insurance, and more directly so by negotiating the *Asiento*, the right to trade slaves to Spanish America from 1713. These, plus the laws made to create and then regulate race and slavery in the southern mainland and Caribbean colonies, were the main ways in which British imperial and local colonial governments laid the foundations necessary for economic growth before the American Revolution.

The slave trade and slavery were more important than anything else in generating the wealth of the British colonies and therefore also of the American nation to be. The slave trade was a hugely lucrative business in its own right. And the slave populations that the trade created cultivated and harvested America's most lucrative crops. And Gabriel Thomas's comment that farmers in Pennsylvania and West Jersey "have constantly good price for their Corn, by reason of the great and quick vent into Barbadoes and other Islands" reminds us that even northern food producers, some of them slaveholders, some of them not, gained a great deal either way from the enslavement of others near and far.[25]

Farmers and scholars

Which brings us back to Barack Obama's characterization of colonial and revolutionary Americans as "Farmers and scholars; statesmen and patriots, who had traveled across an ocean to escape tyranny and persecution." As we saw before, that characterization is possibly personified by John Dickinson, who authored "Letters from a Farmer in Pennsylvania" (1767–68) among other writings, and thereby gained another moniker as "The Penman of the American Revolution." The term "Farmers and scholars" also resonates with "those homespun virtues that Benjamin Franklin first popularized in *Poor Richard's Almanack*," another characterization of colonial American values given by Barack Obama.[26]

Even if John Dickinson was just the "Pennsylvania Farmer" he claimed to be, he would most likely have profitably vented his corn in Barbados and other islands. As we also saw before, though, there was even more to him than that. He was the great-grandson of Walter Dickinson, a Quaker "who had traveled across an ocean to escape tyranny and persecution" in 1654. But in 1659 the original American Dickinson established a family seat at Croisadore, a tobacco-slave plantation in Talbot County, Maryland, where John Dickinson was born in November 1732. The great-grandson subsequently moved to another family property at Poplar Hall in Kent County, Delaware, and divided most of his adult life between there and Philadelphia, Pennsylvania. John Dickinson certainly advanced the cause of liberty alongside other "statesmen and patriots" with his revolutionary writing, his work as legislator and governor in Delaware, his service in the Continental Congress, the War of Independence, and the Constitutional Convention, and also by manumitting his slaves, as he began to do in 1777. He was, nevertheless, a onetime planter and slaveholder and always a beneficiary of catastrophe.[27]

Given Barack Obama's entirely understandable antipathy to imperialism, it is ironic that his lack of interest in the British Atlantic World seems to leave Britain blameless as far as enslavement is concerned. And as he sees the Declaration of Independence as "our starting point as Americans," so enslavement becomes "this nation's original sin" rather than British America's sin. The point is reinforced when one bears in mind that "sin" can only exist in the context of scripture, and the "creed" that all men are created equal and endowed by their creator with unalienable rights to life, liberty, and the pursuit of happiness is for Obama an "American Scripture."[28]

Even more ironically perhaps, it was a slaveholder from colonial Virginia who tried the hardest to blame the British for enslavement in America. In his draft of the Declaration of Independence, Thomas Jefferson wrote of George III that:

he has waged cruel war against human nature itself, violating it's most sacred rights of life & liberty in the persons of a distant people who never offended him, captivating & carrying them into slavery in another hemisphere, or to incur miserable death in their transportation thither. this piratical warfare, the opprobrium of infidel powers, is the warfare of the CHRISTIAN king of Great Britain. determined to keep open a market where MEN should be bought & sold, he has prostituted his negative for suppressing every legislative attempt to prohibit or to restrain this execrable commerce: and that this assemblage of horrors might want no fact of distinguished die, he is now exciting those very people to rise in arms among us, and to purchase that liberty of which he has deprived them, & murdering the people upon whom he also obtruded them; thus paying off former crimes committed against the liberties of one people, with crimes which he urges them to commit against the lives of another.[29]

All that remained of all of this after the Continental Congress did its revisions and produced the final version of the Declaration was the accusation that the king, represented by Virginia Governor, John Murray, Lord Dunmore, had incited slaves to rebel against their revolting masters. The revisions were made in part because of the unsound nature of Jefferson's supply-side argument. Most members of Congress by contrast acknowledged the importance of American demand for and not just British supply of slave labor. And continuing demand was the main reason for the editing of Jefferson's tirade, for while tobacco colonies such as Virginia had enough slaves to fulfil their economic needs by the time of the American Revolution, the rice colonies of South Carolina and Georgia wished to keep importing more. And indeed they imported about a quarter of a million more before the federal government finally forbade the slave trade to the United States in 1808.[30]

But even that didn't mean an end to American demand for enslaved labor. Right after the Revolution tobacco cultivation and slavery spread from Maryland and Virginia into Kentucky and Tennessee. Moreover, Eli Whitney's 1793 invention of the cotton gin—even the most basic version of which could separate seed from lint some fifty times faster than the average human hand—revolutionized the American economy in the first half of the nineteenth century. Cotton then became the next great staple crop of the New World, spreading as it did across the southwest territories that became the states of Florida, Mississippi, Alabama, Louisiana, Missouri, and Texas. And slavery spread with it, as technological development and economic growth don't always serve the purposes of political liberty and social justice.[31]

As we've seen, Barack Obama has much to say of great value about slavery as a social institution and especially as a political issue in the early history of the United States. He has referred to slavery as an economic institution also, but only rarely and only ever briefly. At the 2012 groundbreaking ceremony for the National Museum of African American History and Culture, Obama said that it was "fitting that this museum has found a home on the National Mall" because "it was on this ground long ago that lives were once traded, where hundreds of thousands once marched for jobs and for freedom." Obama thus acknowledged the commodification of human beings, but we can also see how quickly he moved on from the lives "once traded" to the marching and the jobs and the freedom, reminding us again of his preference for the positive narrative over immersion in the negative aspects of long-gone institutions.[32]

In December 2015, furthermore, in celebrating the hundred and fiftieth anniversary of the Thirteenth Amendment that finally ended enslavement in the United States, Barack Obama made another reference to slave trading as he spoke of "Stealing men, women, and children from their homelands. Tearing husband from wife, parent from child; stripped and sold to the highest bidder; shackled in chains and bloodied with the whip." Obama spoke on this occasion in the powerfully stark and unsparing idiom of abolitionism. Yet once again it is telling that rather than dwelling on the economic implications of slave trading, Obama immediately attended instead to its ideological implications. "It's antithetical," he said next, "not only to our conception of human rights and dignity, but to our conception of ourselves—a people founded on the premise that all are created equal."[33]

Obama has mentioned at least once the historical importance of slavery itself as well as the slave trade to American economic development. In March 2015, at the semicentenary of Bloody Sunday in Selma, Alabama, he said "We're the slaves who built the White House and the economy of the South," although once again he moved quickly on, this time to saying that "we're the ranch hands and cowboys who opened up the West, and countless laborers who laid rail, and raised skyscrapers, and organized for workers' rights."[34]

But those slaves did more than build the economy of the South. When Barack Obama writes and speaks of the economic history of the United States he focuses on the rise of manufacturing industry in the North, as first promoted by President George Washington's Treasury Secretary Alexander Hamilton. But the northern manufacturers who finally thrived from the eighteen-teens onwards often did so in textile production, most especially in cotton—sourced of course from the slave South. Slaves therefore built the economy of the North as well. And those nineteenth-century northern manufacturers were as connected to enslavement as were the earlier Massachusetts rum makers who imported molasses from the West Indies, as were the Pennsylvania farmers who sold their corn to Caribbean planters, and as was a "Farmer from Pennsylvania" who was in fact a tobacco-planting slaveholder from Maryland via Delaware.[35]

Government has been called upon

As Barack Obama says, in a historical analysis that vividly exposes the myth of self-sufficiency that free market fundamentalists enjoy promoting, "government has been called upon throughout our history to build the infrastructure, train the workforce, and otherwise lay the foundations necessary for economic growth." As we saw previously, this was true in the colonial era. In fact it was in the very nature of imperialism and colonialism. But it is nonetheless true too of the economic history of the United States.[36]

It is even true of the very founding of the nation. As Obama rightly says, "All the Founding Fathers recognized the connection between private property and liberty." Their Declaration of Independence alluded indeed to the idea that colonial liberties had originated with the very processes of migration and settlement. The final version of the Declaration briefly summarized the point by saying that colonists had reminded the British people "of the circumstances of our emigration and settlement here." But in his original draft Thomas Jefferson had added that colonial settlements "were effected at the expence of our own blood & treasure, unassisted by the wealth or the strength of Great Britain ..." And in his *Summary View of the Rights of British America*, published two years previously, Jefferson had further argued that the British crown had no feudalist territorial or private rights to American land, and that in going overseas, migrants had therefore left the jurisdiction of the mother country and settled in what was effectively a State of Nature. He also argued in turn that settlers had then mixed their labor with the land and other resources and had thereby created property that was therefore theirs and theirs alone. All these points accorded with John Locke's accounts of the origins of and natural rights to property.[37]

This appears to vindicate free-market fundamentalists' ideas of individual economic self-suffiiciency. Yet Jefferson's account of colonial history also accorded with Lockean accounts of the origins of government, called upon as it originally was as the best means of protecting life, liberty, and property. As Barack Obama says in *The Audacity of Hope*, "Enlightenment thinkers like Hobbes and Locke, suggested that free men would form governments as a bargain to ensure that one man's freedom did not become another man's tyranny; that they would sacrifice individual license to better preserve their liberty." Again, this is what the Declaration of Independence refers to where it says "that all men are created equal, that they are endowed by their Creator with certain unalienable Rights, that among these are Life, Liberty and the pursuit of Happiness" and "–That to secure these rights, Governments are instituted among Men, deriving their just powers from the consent of the governed." Whatever else it might have meant, Jefferson's "pursuit of Happiness" undoubtedly encompassed the right to property, what Locke referred to as "possessions" or "estates."[38]

The Declaration of Independence says next "–That whenever any Form of Government becomes destructive of these ends, it is the Right of the People to alter or to abolish it, and to institute new Government, laying its foundation on such principles and organizing its powers in such form, as to them shall seem most likely to effect their Safety and Happiness." The colonists argued in the Declaration, however, as they had since 1764, that such measures as the Sugar Act, the Stamp Act, and the Townshend Duties represented "taxation without representation," the appropriation of their property without their consent—a clear violation of their natural rights and liberties.

If the purpose of the Declaration of Independence was to "abolish" one form of government, then the purpose of the Constitution was "to institute new Government, laying its foundation on such principles and organizing its powers in such form, as to them [its founders] shall seem most likely to effect their Safety and Happiness." The Constitution's founders at least nominally were "We the People," and with this evocation of popular sovereignty, the Constitution validated natural rights theory, implicitly including the natural right to property. The Founders also organized the new government's powers in such form as to protect people's liberties, with checks and balances that would prevent such abuses as taking people's property without their consent.

Some felt, though, that the original Constitution provided insufficient protections from such abuses, and therefore insisted on various amendments amounting to the Bill of Rights. Those most directly and explicitly protecting property are, first, the fourth, which says that "the right of the people to be secure in their persons, houses, papers, and effects, against unreasonable searches and seizures, shall not be violated, and no Warrants shall issue, but upon probable cause, supported by Oath or affirmation, and particularly describing the place to be searched, and the persons or things to be seized." And second the fifth, which, among other things, says that "no person shall be deprived of life, liberty, or property, without due process of law; nor shall private property be taken for public use, without just compensation." And then the seventh, which says: "In Suits at common law, where the value in controversy shall exceed twenty dollars, the right of trial by jury shall be preserved …" And finally the eighth, which says: "Excessive bail shall not be required, nor excessive fines imposed …" Thus it is that Obama says: "Our Constitution places the ownership of private property at the very heart of our system of liberty."[39]

But the role of government in American history has gone beyond the fundamental purpose of protecting people's property and liberty to a further one of promoting the economy. As Barack Obama says, "government has been called upon throughout our history to build the infrastructure, train the workforce, and otherwise lay the foundations necessary for economic growth." And so indeed it has.[40]

Hamilton understood

One of those who helped found that government, one of the leading lights indeed at the Constitutional Convention of 1787, was Alexander Hamilton. And, as Barack Obama says, "it was Alexander Hamilton who also recognized the vast potential of a national economy—one based not on America's agrarian past but on a commercial and industrial future. To realize this potential, Hamilton argued, America needed a strong and active national government, and as America's first Treasury secretary he set about putting his ideas to work." As Obama also adds, Hamilton "nationalized the Revolutionary War debt, which not only stitched together the economies of the individual states but helped spur a national system of credit and fluid capital markets," and he "promoted policies—from strong patent laws to high tariffs—to encourage American manufacturing, and proposed investment in roads and bridges needed to move products to market."[41]

The national public debt, unpaid off under Articles of Confederation that gave Congress no direct tax-raising powers, stood in 1789 at $52 million, $40 million of it domestic and the rest of it owed to lenders overseas. In addition to that, state governments owed another $25 million. The total of $77 million was an enormous sum for an agricultural nation of just under four million people to sustain or pay off, and many of those people had considerable private debt of their own. Almost all agreed that something had to be done, and in September 1789 Congress requested that the new treasury secretary propose measures to that effect. Alexander Hamilton put his First Report on Public Credit to Congress in January 1790. Its main proposals were federal "assumption" of state debts and "funding" of the national and nationalized debt through "redemption," whereby the government would pay current holders of the government bonds either the full amount of their old "certificates of indebtedness" or "securities" at full face value, or else pay 4 percent annual interest on newly issued government bonds. The government and the nation would thus have sustainable finances.

Later the same year Hamilton's Second Report on Public Credit proposed the creation of a national bank, or rather a mostly private bank chartered to do public business. The government would appoint five of its twenty-five directors, provide a fifth of its $10 million original capital, and hold a quarter of its stock. The bank would store government gold and silver and give bounties and interest-free loans to inventors and investors in economic "improvements." It would also supply currency in the form of coin and paper money, which it guaranteed to accept at face value for payment of taxes and debts, meaning that the money would hold its value relative to specie—gold or silver—preventing its depreciation and therefore price inflation. And it would make state and private banks do the same. The business of the nation would thus expand with plenty of incentives and with an easily available but also stable medium of exchange.

Finally, a Report on Manufactures delivered to Congress in December 1791 was supposed to be the capstone of Hamilton's plan by proposing import tariffs enabling American manufacturers to establish themselves and compete with British ones. There would also be government-funded bounties and premiums to encourage certain manufacturing enterprises, government encouragement of inventions and discoveries (Barack Obama's "strong patent laws"), and, most important after tariffs, the encouragement of internal improvements through government planning and funding of building of roads, bridges, and canals—the creation of a transport infrastructure to assist commerce and industry. Hamilton thus aimed at nothing less than kick-starting an American industrial revolution.

Barack Obama

Barack Obama is undoubtedly right therefore that Hamilton "recognized the vast potential of a national economy." But he also says that "Hamilton understood that only through the liberation of capital from local landed interests could America tap into its most powerful resource—namely, the energy and enterprise of the American people. This idea of social mobility constituted one of the great early bargains of American capitalism; industrial and commercial capitalism might lead to greater instability, but it would be a dynamic system in which anyone with enough energy and talent could rise to the top." These claims are considerably more contestable.[42]

Jefferson ... feared

Barack Obama's language about what Alexander Hamilton "recognized" and "understood" contrasts with his descriptions of Thomas Jefferson's opinions. As Obama puts it, "Hamilton encountered fierce resistance from Thomas Jefferson, who feared that a strong national government tied to wealthy commercial interests would undermine his vision of an egalitarian democracy tied to the land." So, while Jefferson's opposition was fierce, it was nonetheless based on fear. Implicitly, furthermore, Jefferson did not recognize things, or even understand them. And Obama's language is further loaded when he writes of Hamilton's "commercial and industrial future" as opposed to Jefferson's "agrarian past."[43]

What Jefferson feared, and in fact recognized and understood, was that many Americans would pay a high price for Hamilton's programs. And he was far from alone. The main political opposition to Hamilton's reports on public credit could not in fact come from inside the Cabinet, where Jefferson sat as secretary of State, so it came instead from Congressman James Madison. Madison was concerned that Hamilton's "redemption" method of paying the debt at full value to current holders of securities defrauded the "battle-worn veterans of the war for independence" who had originally been given them in lieu of pay for military service. Many of these men were poorer farmers who in need of cash had subsequently sold their securities, usually well below par—as low indeed as 10 cents on the dollar—to wealthy speculators, or "stock-jobbers" as Madison styled them. The "Madison Plan" proposed instead funding the debt by "discrimination," paying current holders what they paid for securities and paying the difference to original recipients.

Madison was far from alone. A growing coalition of "democratic-republican" allies who would by the mid-1790s become the Democratic-Republic Party organized opposition to the Washington-Adams-Hamilton-led Federalist Party. And outside the capital, besides the former soldiers set to lose out to speculators, there was a growing army of angry farmers. Hamilton aimed to raise revenue for his schemes by taxing the distilled spirits many farmers made from grain crops, the former being easier and cheaper to transport in western regions where marketplaces were distant and access to riverine transport was limited or nonexistent. The Whiskey Rebellion broke out in western Pennsylvania late in 1791 and soon spread far and wide. In 1794 George

Washington himself led 13,000 militiamen to suppress the insurrection. They arrested twenty men who were later pardoned, although the whiskey tax continued to be avoided and unenforceable.

Funding and assumption were approved by Congress anyway, partly thanks to the "dinner table bargain" at Thomas Jefferson's residence where deliberative democracy delivered a deal in which Alexander Hamilton got his way in return for the locating of a new capital on the banks of the Potomac River, in the South and therefore far from the financial heart of the nation in the urban North. The National Bank was also chartered for twenty years, despite the democratic-republican "strict construction" objection that creating a bank is not a congressional power enumerated in the Constitution. Hamilton persuaded a hesitating President Washington to sign the bill on the basis of the "implied powers" clause that allows Congress to pass laws that are "necessary and proper" to fulfilling its "enumerated powers"—the basis of a permissively "loose construction" of the Constitution.

Strict construction objections were also employed against the Report on Manufactures and to Hamilton's explicit intention to tie the economic interests of powerful financial elites to the preservation of the federal government. But the tariff and its accompanying proposals were at least temporarily defeated because of the ways they seemed to threaten the foundations of American society as well as its economy. We can see how "Thomas Jefferson feared that a strong national government tied to wealthy commercial interests would undermine his vision of an egalitarian democracy tied to the land" by looking at a famous passage from his 1784 *Notes on the State of Virginia*. "Those who labour in the earth," he wrote,

> are the chosen people of God, if ever he had a chosen people, whose breasts he has made his peculiar deposit for substantial and genuine virtue. It is the focus in which he keeps alive that sacred fire, which otherwise might escape from the face of the earth. Corruption of morals in the mass of cultivators is a phaenomenon of which no age nor nation has furnished an example. It is the mark set on those, who not looking up to heaven, to their own soil and industry, as does the husbandman, for their subsistance, depend for it on the casualties and caprice of customers. Dependance begets subservience and venality, suffocates the germ of virtue, and prepares fit tools for the designs of ambition ... [T]he proportion which the aggregate of the other classes of citizens bears in any state to that of its husbandmen, is the proportion of its unsound to its healthy parts, and is a good-enough barometer whereby to measure its degree of corruption. While we have land to labour then, let us never wish to see our citizens occupied at a work-bench, or twirling a distaff.[44]

Jefferson genuinely feared then that a mass wage-labor force, inevitably engendered by industrialization, would undermine the American republic, possibly fatally. Only the kind of economically enfranchised citizenry comprising a landowning yeomanry would have the necessary virtues to allow the republic to survive and thrive. And such an agrarian republic could be maintained he believed because in America, as opposed to Europe, "we have an immensity of land courting the industry of the husbandman."[45]

Jeffersonian Virginia and neighboring Maryland was dominated by a small but powerful coterie of large planters, of whom Thomas Jefferson was one. It also had large numbers of white tenant farmers and hundreds of thousands of slaves, who together vastly outnumbered the idealized landowning yeoman farmer of the Jeffersonian-agrarian imagination. All of these people in their different ways depended heavily, furthermore, on the caprice of customers of a tobacco-staple, cash crop economy. Jefferson's world was far from the agrarian utopia Jefferson depicted.[46]

Yet Jefferson, James Madison, and many others had a point about Alexander Hamilton's plans. Those plans may have encompassed, as Obama puts it, "the energy and enterprise of the American people," but they didn't envision a great deal of "social mobility." Hamilton may have believed in "a dynamic system in which anyone with enough energy and talent could rise to the top." He himself had been born out of wedlock on the Caribbean island of Nevis in 1757, and yet an extraordinary combination of ability, serendipity, and patronage had seen him rise to the top of the Treasury Department. But, in the industrial society Hamilton envisioned, few would have the opportunity to follow in his footsteps.[47]

Among the advantages of manufacturing that Alexander Hamilton imagined, for example, was that "women and Children are rendered more useful and the latter more early useful by manufacturing establishments, than they would otherwise be." As he further explained, "Of the number of persons employed in the Cotton Manufactories of Great Britain, it is computed that 4/7 nearly are women and children; of whom the greatest proportion are children and many of them of a very tender age." One doesn't need to romanticize a "green and pleasant land" to fear the "dark Satanic Mills" so poetically regretted by William Blake just a few years later.[48]

For all his fears, however, as president from 1801 Thomas Jefferson didn't dismantle the Hamiltonian apparatus. "Some things may perhaps be left undone, from motives of compromise ... and not to alarm too sudden a reformation," President Jefferson pronounced in a proto-Obamian passage in his first inaugural address. And the following year he even elevated manufacturing to a status alongside agriculture, commerce, and navigation as one of the four pillars of the American republic. He promoted internal improvements too with his 1806 approval of the building of a national road into the American interior, commencing in Cumberland, Maryland. And his economic boycott of Britain and France, furthermore, had the same effect as a tariff in encouraging manufacturing, albeit incidentally. Some in his own party angrily accused him of having "Outfederalized Federalism."[49]

President James Madison outfederalized federalism even more, with the support of a new generation of western members of Congress advocating an "American System" of protective tariffs and internal improvements, and also advocating a new national bank to replace the one that wasn't rechartered in 1811. The War of 1812 convinced many of the desirability of greater American economic independence, and in his seventh Annual Message to Congress in 1815 Madison recommended a thoroughly Hamilton economic program. Congress obliged the following year with a second national bank, this time capitalized at $35 million, a protective tariff of 20 percent on manufactured imports, and a host of internal improvement initiatives.

Some still had reservations about government's role in laying the foundations necessary for economic growth, however. James Madison himself vetoed a bill that would have diverted money from the national bank into the national road and other internal improvements. Transport infrastructure then remained mostly in private hands until the Federal Highways Act of 1916, when constitutional scruples made way for the arrival of the horseless carriage. Even so, a consensus in favor of some government sponsoring of economic development and other matters was so prevalent that President James Monroe declared that "an era of good feelings" had broken out during his administration of 1817–25. The 1824 presidential election was even fought by four men of the same Democratic-Republican Party, the Federalists having died out following barely veiled threats of New England secession at the Hartford Convention, just as the War of 1812–15 ended in a good enough result to be called a victory for the United States.[50]

The government's vital role in regulating the marketplace

Andrew Jackson won 43 percent of the popular vote in 1824, to John Quincy Adams's 31 percent, with 13 percent each for Henry Clay and William Henry Crawford. Jackson won the Electoral College too, with 99 votes compared Adams's 84, Crawford's 41, and Clay's 37. With no majority for anyone, however, the result was decided in the House of Representatives, which duly delivered the White House to . . . Adams. Which was perfectly legal as the Constitution didn't direct then that the winner of the popular vote should necessarily become president, and it doesn't do so now. And it made political sense in any case, as many congressmen agreed with Adams's neo-federalism. In his inaugural address indeed he advocated "laws promoting the improvement of the agriculture, commerce, and manufactures, the cultivation and encouragement of the mechanic and of the elegant arts, the advancement of literature, and the progress of the sciences, ornamental and profound."[51]

Andrew Jackson was undisputedly elected president in 1828, however, and vetoed the Maysville Road Bill, partly because the Constitution doesn't directly permit federal funding of roads, and in any case as the road lay entirely in Kentucky it was not even an interstate project, and partly because it was a piece of "pork barrel" politics for the benefit of Henry Clay and his constituents. Jackson hated Clay for supporting Adams in what he called the "corrupt bargain" of 1825, although he would have reason to thank him for brokering the Compromise of 1833. South Carolina had presented Jackson with a dilemma when it nullified the "Tariff of Abominations" that raised import duties to as high as 50 percent in 1828 and was largely renewed in 1832. The agrarian president was no friend of aid to manufacturers, but felt compelled nonetheless to uphold federal authority by sending gunboats into Charleston harbor. Clay's Compromise Tariff ended the crisis by gradually lowering duties to the level of 1816. But then the president declared war on another institution favored by Clay: what he called the "Monster Bank," and Jackson acted with an uncompromising intemperance that led to economic disaster.

As Barack Obama says, "it was during the stock market crash of 1929 and the subsequent Depression that the government's vital role in regulating the marketplace became fully apparent," and for half a century or so afterwards a consensus on the necessity of regulation survived. But, as Obama's open-ended statement suggests, the government's vital role in regulating the economy had previously been at least partly apparent. We saw that the first bank kept and made other banks keep sufficient specie reserves to redeem their notes and loans, and the second bank did the same, at least under the leadership of Nicolas Biddle after the Panic of 1819 showed, again, how under-regulation results in ruination. Jackson thus very much missed the point when he said to Biddle in 1829 that "ever since I read the history of the South Sea Bubble, I have been afraid of banks."[52]

Vendetta-minded Andrew Jackson's ire only increased when Henry Clay challenged him for the presidency in 1832 and tried to use the impending matter of the bank's recharter against him. Jackson the masterful demagogue, however, managed to persuade many that regulations protecting the public interest were against the public interest, and he won with 55 percent of the popular vote to Clay's 38, and with an Electoral College landslide of 219 to forty-nine. Jackson vetoed a recharter bill in 1836, but even before then he disestablished the national bank by withdrawing government revenue and placing it in private "pet banks" instead, and by stripping it of regulatory powers anyway. Other banks then began issuing of loans and paper money as they wished—a practice known then as "wildcat financing." Suddenly seeing what the problem was, Jackson ordered that the federal government deal only in specie, only to accelerate the collapse of boom into bust by triggering the Panic of 1837.

Jackson's former Vice President Martin Van Buren's faith in laissez-faire economics did little to combat the consequence crisis. The 1840 election of William Henry Harrison, of a Whig Party that emerged after 1824, seemed to augur a new Hamiltonian era. But his death a month after taking office was followed by vetoes of Congress's tariff, internal improvements, and bank bills by President John Tyler, a Democrat so disaffected by Jackson's attack on the South Carolina nullifiers he gave his name to the "Tippecanoe and Tyler too" ticket. After that, in any case, national politics became more and more immersed in the slave controversy, eventuating in the emergence of a new Republican Party in the mid-1850s and the election of Abraham Lincoln as president in 1860.[53]

The transition from an agricultural to an industrial society

As Barack Obama says, the "tradition ... of government investment in America's physical infrastructure and in its people, was thoroughly embraced by Abraham Lincoln and the early Republican Party." At the same time, though, Lincoln "also saw how the transition from an agricultural to an industrial society was disrupting lives and destroying communities." And in saying that in this way it is clear that Obama sees it too, notwithstanding his niceties about Hamilton. "For Lincoln," though, and apparently for Obama too, "the essence of America was opportunity, the ability of 'free labor' to advance in life" and he "considered capitalism the best means of creating such opportunity."[54]

One way Lincoln put that philosophy into practice was in the efforts he made and that we saw in Chapter 4 to transform slave labor into free labor. But another was "a series of policies that not only laid the groundwork for a fully integrated national economy but extended the ladders of opportunity downward to reach more and more people." Lincoln thus supported "the construction of the first transcontinental railroad," the National Academy of Sciences' efforts to promote technology and commerce, and "the landmark Homestead Act of 1862, which turned over vast amounts of public land across the western United States to settlers from the East and immigrants from around the world, so that they, too, could claim a stake in the nation's growing economy." And "rather than leave these homesteaders to fend for themselves" he "created a system of land grant colleges to instruct farmers on the latest agricultural techniques, and to provide them the liberal education that would allow them to dream beyond the confines of life on the farm."[55]

True. But at this point in the American economic history presented in *The Audacity of Hope*, Barack Obama skips straight from Abraham Lincoln to such government-sponsored accomplishments as "The Hoover Dam, the Tennessee Valley Authority, the interstate highway system, the Internet, the Human Genome Project," adding that "time and again" therefore "government investment has helped pave the way for an explosion of private economic activity." He also adds that "through the creation of a system of public schools and institutions of higher education, as well as programs like the GI Bill that made a college education available to millions, government has helped provide individuals the tools to adapt and innovate in a climate of constant technological change." All true too. But in the seventy-year elision from the Homestead Act to the Hoover Dam, Obama edits out "The Gilded Age," sarcastically so-called in Mark Twain's and Charles Dudley Warner's 1875 novel of the same name.[56]

The years between 1860 and the end of the century stand in some contrast to the impression created by Barack Obama's metaphorical associations of economic and technological development with political and social progress. From the still mostly agricultural nation of the Civil War era, America became an industrial behemoth by the time of World War I. By 1913 the United States made a third of the world's industrial produce, more than Britain, France, and Germany combined, and by 1929 it made two-fifths. Of course such growth generated enormous wealth, but many paid a terrible price.

Some of this massive increase in productivity had to do with the "spirit of innovation" and "enterprise" that Barack Obama describes, from Andrew Carnegie's "vertical integration" of steelworks at Homestead, Pennsylvania, in the 1870s, to Henry Ford's system of moving assembly-line production thirty years later. But a lot of innovation involved eliminating enterprise. J. D. Rockefeller's "horizontal integration" meant that his Standard Oil Company swallowed up so many competitors that by the 1880s it controlled 90 percent of the nation's production. In 1901, John Pierpont Morgan's United

States Steel Corporation consolidated eight companies into the world's first billion-dollar business. Morgan's banking interests, furthermore, controlled 40 percent of financial and industrial capital by 1912.[57]

Industrialization also entailed enormous social change. As early as 1880 and for the first time in American history more than half the labor force was involved in nonfarm work, and by 1920 more people lived in towns and cities than in the country. Eleven million Americans moved from rural to urban areas between 1870 and 1920, including half a million black southerners who moved north in the Great Migration of 1910–20. In the same half century, 25 million immigrants arrived in America, increasingly from Italy, Eastern Europe, Russia, Asia, and Mexico. The US population as a whole rose from just under 40 million in 1870 to over 120 million in the 1920s.

The "robber barons" created enormous wealth, but kept a great deal of it for themselves, even as they tapped "the energy and enterprise of the American people." From 1873 to 1897, millions lost their jobs during what was known as "The Great Depression" before the one that began in 1929. And as Barack Obama notes as a general point, but one that certainly applies to the Gilded Age, there was little sympathy before the 1930s "for workers left impoverished by capitalism's periodic gales of 'creative destruction'—the recipe for individual success was greater toil, not pampering from the state. What safety net did exist came from the uneven and meager resources of private charity."[58]

Inequality was such that in 1890 the income of America's wealthiest 1 percent was equal to that of its poorest 50 percent, and the one percenters owned as many assets as the remaining 99 percent. They paid their workers poverty wages for twelve-hour days in dangerous conditions. "Workers," as Obama observes, "had almost no protections from unsafe or inhumane working conditions, whether in sweatshops or meatpacking plants," and indeed at the turn of the twentieth century an annual average of 35,000 workers died in mining and manufacturing accidents, most of them preventable. A hundred people, for example, burned or choked to death in the Great Triangle Shirtwaist Company Fire in New York's Greenwich Village on March 25, 1912, and forty-six more jumped to their deaths from the upper stories of the building, the stairwells being blocked to prevent the unauthorized taking of bathroom breaks.[59]

Indeed the law sometimes seemed keener on protecting corporate profits than people's lives, even to the point of defining corporations as people in order to do so. In the case of *Consolidated Silver Mining Co. v. Pennsylvania* in 1888, the Supreme Court ruled that "under the designation of 'person' there is no doubt that a private corporation is included" in the "equal protection" clause of the Fourteenth Amendment of the Constitution. Although the Court has never ruled that corporations are full citizens, "corporate personhood" remains a legal fiction with real implications to this day.[60]

The triumph of a real democracy

Yet people—real ones—pushed back. As Barack Obama says, "During America's first 150 years ... workers were prevented by law and by violence from forming unions that would increase their own leverage." Some formed them nevertheless, and the Great Railroad Strike of 1877 was the first nationwide industrial action. Civil militia units eventually forced the strikers back to work, and for the lower pay that caused the strike in the first place, but not before twenty were killed in Pittsburgh, Pennsylvania. The killing of four workers by police during a strike against pay-cuts and de-unionization among iron workers at the McCormick agricultural machinery plant in Chicago on May 3, 1886, resulted in the Haymarket Rally the next day. A bomb killed a policeman, causing his colleagues to fire into the crowd and at each other, injuring many others. Despite a paucity of evidence, four "Haymarket martyrs" were hanged, another died in jail, and three more were imprisoned until freed by Illinois Governor John Peter Altgeld in 1893. The Homestead Strike of 1892 saw a pitched battle between workers and the private policemen of the Pinkerton Agency in which seven of the former and three of the latter died. The Pullman Strike saw thirty-four railroad workers killed in clashes with federal troops and US marshalls in clashes across the country in 1894.[61]

Strife was also rife in rural places. A Farmers' Alliance was formed at first in Texas in the 1870s but spread to forty-three states by 1890, and that year farmers formed the People's or Populist Party. James Weaver won more than a million popular votes as the Populist presidential candidate in 1892. This "Populist Revolt" was sometimes interracial. Georgia's Tom Watson (whose newspaper was called *The Jeffersonian*) stated that "You are kept apart that you may be separately fleeced ... This race antagonism perpetuates a monetary system which beggars both." Democrats alas responded with appeals to white supremacy, as northern Republicans similarly opiated many industrial workers with anti-immigrant nativism.

Working people's own organizations gradually came to accept change. The Knights of Labor reached its peak of popularity and power in the 1880s, with up to 800,000 members in 1886, and, although it looked back like Tom Watson did to a Jeffersonian concept of individual economic autonomy, it simultaneously looked forward in embracing not only skilled, white, male laborers, but also less skilled, black, and female ones too, though it excluded Asians. The American Federation of Labor (AFL), however, with a membership of 1.6 million in 1904, accepted the industrial and wage-labor environment more readily, and focused instead on the idea of a "corporate commonwealth" in which unions would negotiate to ameliorate pay and conditions, rather than articulate radical social-economic criticism or engage in strike action. AFL leader Samuel Gompers accepted the concept of "freedom of contract" that had been used in politics and law against government regulation of working hours and conditions, though he also used it to defend the rights of workers to organize. His "business-unionism" is best illustrated by his teaming up with Republican Party activist Mark Hanna and J. P. Morgan financier George Perkins to form the National Civic Federation in 1900. In 1905, some AFL members split away to form the International Workers of the World, a more radical and inclusive union, even welcoming Asians, but it failed to change the course of the mainstream.

Similarly, a Socialist Party achieved extensive electoral validation, though not enough to gain effective political power. It reached its peak when Eugene V. Debs won 900,000 votes in the presidential election of 1912, 6 percent of the popular vote. But it took the enormous if amorphous force of the "progressive" movement to effect significant change.

Barack Obama draws some interesting parallels between these times and our time. When his own attempts as president to orchestrate a recovery from yet another bust in capitalism's seemingly endless cycle ran into inevitable resistance, he made a speech in Osawatomie, Kansas, comparing such complacency then and now. "You see," he said, "this isn't the first time America has faced this choice. At the turn of the last century, when a nation of farmers was transitioning to become the world's industrial giant, we had to decide: Would we settle for a country where most of the new railroads and factories were being controlled by a few giant monopolies that kept prices high and wages low? Would we allow our citizens and even our children to work ungodly hours in conditions that were unsafe and unsanitary? Would we restrict education to the privileged few? Because there were people who thought massive inequality and exploitation of people was just the price you pay for progress."[62]

Then, as now, a great range of people thought we should and could do better than this, and their views coalesced into the "Progressive movement" in the late nineteenth and early twentieth centuries. There were novelists such as Edward Bellamy, whose *Looking Backward* (1888) imagined a utopian socialist future. And Upton Sinclair, who's *The Jungle* (1906) caused such revulsion at slaughterhouse practices that it inspired the Pure Food and Drug Act and the Meat Inspection Act of 1906. Academic and journalistic social critics produced such works as Henry Demarest Lloyd's *Wealth Against Commonwealth* (1894) and Ida Tarbell's *History of the Standard Oil Company* (1904) that raised awareness of the ill-doings of the "robber barons." Henry George's *Progess and Poverty* (1879), Thorstein Veblen's *The Theory of the Leisure Class* (1899), and Lincoln Steffens's *The Shame of the Cities* (1904) drew attention to what they called "industrial slavery" and to the more general enormity and enormities of inequality and poverty.

Others were activists such as Jane Addams, who founded Hull House in Chicago in 1889 and began a movement that encompassed over 400 "settlement houses" by 1910, all helping innumerable immigrants integrate into American life. Other progressives focused on reforming people's characters, such as those who campaigned for the Eighteenth Amendment of the Constitution, which banned the production and consumption of alcohol, a political victory that as social policy met with predicable long-term success.

There were even three "Progressive" Presidents: the Republican Theodore Roosevelt, who took office after the assassination of William McKinley in 1901 and served to 1909; his Republican successor William Howard Taft (1909–13); and Democrat Woodrow Wilson (1913–21). As Barack Obama observes, "Teddy Roosevelt recognized that monopoly power could restrict competition, and made 'trust busting' a centerpiece of his administration." His "Square Deal" indeed took on J. P. Morgan's Northern Securities Company under the Sherman Antitrust Act and saw it dissolved by the Supreme Court in 1904. The 1906 Hepburn Act gave the Interstate Commerce Commission the power to examine railroad company records and set fair prices, more authority than it had since its founding in 1887. And, as Obama also notes, his administration also oversaw the passing of America's "first consumer laws—the Pure Food and Drug Act, the Meat Inspection Act—to protect Americans from harmful products."[63]

William Howard Taft did some trust-busting too, but was a more conservative Republican and found himself challenged in 1912 not only by the Democrat Woodrow Wilson, but also by the Socialist Party's Eugene Debs and by Theodore Roosevelt's short-lived Progressive Party. While Wilson's campaign focused on opposing "bigness," Roosevelt's "New Nationalism" advocated practical federal solutions to the problems "bigness" caused, including proposing eight-hour days, a living wage, social insurance, medical care, and pensions—a welfare state being a real proposition following the Sixteenth Amendment of 1913 that authorized a federal income tax.

The Wilson administration, though, was more progressive in practice than expected. The 1914 Clayton Act exempted labor unions from antitrust prosecutions and anti-strike court orders, the Keating-Owen Act outlawed child labor in products involved in interstate commerce, the Adamson Act applied an eight-hour day in the railroad industry, and a Warehouse Act offered credit to farmers using government storage facilities. Wilson also, as Obama notes, "instituted the Federal Reserve Bank, to manage the money supply and curb periodic panics in the financial markets" in 1913, as well as the Commission on Industrial Relations in 1912 and the Federal Trade Commission in 1914. And mobilization for World War I saw unprecedented state intervention in the economy.

Barack Obama is certainly an admirer of the achievements of this era. In Osawatomie he noted that "in 1910, Teddy Roosevelt came here ... and he laid out his vision for what he called a New Nationalism. 'Our country,' he said, '... means nothing unless it means the triumph of a real democracy ... of an economic system under which each man shall be guaranteed the opportunity to show the best that there is in him.' Now, for this," Obama continued, "Roosevelt was called a radical. He was called a socialist—even a communist. But today, we are a richer nation and a stronger democracy because of what he fought for in his last campaign: an eight-hour work day and a minimum wage for women—insurance for the unemployed and for the elderly, and those with disabilities; political reform and a progressive income tax."[64]

It was not, however, enough to prevent a return to the "normalcy" of boom and bust in which the poor pay a terrible price for the recklessness of the rich.

"The chief business of the American people is business"

The war years and their aftermath saw a revival of radicalism and a strike involving over 4 million workers. But also extraordinary suppression as manifested, for example, in a wartime "Sedition Act" under which over 2,000 people were charged and over 1,000 prosecuted for bringing the "form of government" or the war effort into "contempt, scorn, or disrepute." Under the cover of the Red Scare of 1919–20, Attorney General A. Mitchell Palmer oversaw unconstitutional searches of premises and the arrest and detention without charge of scores of radicals and labor leaders, all orchestrated by J. Edgar Hoover at the Radical Division of the Justice Department.[65]

Warren G. Harding promised a return to "normalcy" when elected president in 1920, which turned out to be the start of a decade of extraordinary financial and governmental decadence. Harding's Interior Secretary Albert Fall was the first cabinet member to be convicted of a felony for accepting bribes for favors with government oil reserves in Teapot Dome, Wyoming. During this decade federal regulatory agencies were headed by men who turned blind eyes as speculators ran amok. Harding's death in 1923 saw the elevation to the presidency of Calvin Coolidge, who said, as Barack Obama says, that "the chief business of the American people is business." But perhaps no one personified the complacency of laissez-faire more than Herbert Hoover, elected president in 1928 and whose administration oversaw what Barack Obama mentions next: "the stock market crash of 1929" and the early years of the "subsequent Depression."[66]

On Black Thursday, October 31, stocks lost over $10 billion in value in five hours, near $150 billion in today's money. About 26,000 businesses failed in the next year, and, in the three years following the crash, national productivity fell by a third, prices by 40 percent, and in 1932, eleven million people were jobless—a quarter of the labor force. Even Hoover created a Reconstruction Finance Corporation to lend money to banks and other businesses, a Federal Home Loan Bank System to save people from foreclosure, and extended $2 billion into relief. But it was all too-little-too-late, and Franklin Delano Roosevelt won the presidential election of 1932 with 57 percent of the popular vote and had substantial Democratic majorities in both houses of Congress.[67]

FDR understood

It was in the "First New Deal" of 1933–34 and especially in its first "Hundred Days" that FDR, as Barack Obama says, "engineered a series of government interventions that arrested further economic contraction" and "experimented with policies to restart the economy." He even left "behind a regulatory structure that helps limit the risk of economic crisis." An Emergency Banking Act protected people's savings and a further Banking Act barred commercial banks from stock speculation. This Glass-Steagall Legislation also created the Federal Deposit Incorporation that provided insurance "to provide confidence to bank depositors." A Securities and Exchange Commission regulated trading in stocks and bonds. An Economy Act reduced federal spending, although FDR also took the United States off the Gold Standard, allowing him to inject much-needed cash into the economy. These kinds of measures, as Obama says, aimed "to ensure transparency in the financial markets and protect smaller investors from fraud and insider manipulation." And "countercyclical fiscal and monetary policies," including "tax cuts, increased liquidity, or direct government spending," aimed to "stimulate demand when business and consumers" lose confidence. It was thus in these early days that "the government's vital role in regulating the marketplace became fully apparent" and far more fully articulated than ever before.[68]

It was partly in the First New Deal but mostly in the Second one of 1935–38 that FDR created the third manner in which government has involved itself in the economy—in structuring "the social compact between business and the American worker." A National Industrial Recovery Act had already created a National Recovery Administration to work with the private sector to establish standards for productivity, prices, and working conditions. But "FDR also initiated laws that fundamentally changed the relationship between capital and labor," including "the forty-hour workweek, child labor laws, and minimum wage laws" included in the Fair Labor Standards Act of 1938. Obama also notes that "the National Labor Relations Act … made it possible to organize broad-based industrial unions and forced employers to bargain in good faith." Indeed this 1935 Wagner Act banned such "unfair labor practices" as firing and blacklisting union leaders, and it created a National Labor Relations Board that acted as an honest broker between business and labor. The old and exclusivist AFL gave way as well to the new Congress of Industrial Organizations (CIO), an umbrella for new unions such as United Auto Workers and which was better able to represent a more inclusive and industries-wide constituency in dealing with business and government. Union membership doubled in course of the decade, reaching nine million by 1940.[69]

The New Deal also helped keep people in and even put people back in work. The Agricultural Adjustment Act (AAA) set quotas and paid farmers to grow less and thereby raise food prices and therefore farm incomes. The Tennessee Valley Authority not only built dams and provided jobs, but also made the government an actual economic actor in the energy industry. The early Civil Works Administration ran into practical and political difficulty, but the Civilian Conservation Corps (CCC) not only made environmental improvements, but also employed some three million people between 1933 and 1942. The Works Progress Administration (WPA) employed three million more from 1934 to 1943, in work varying from building valuable transport infrastructure to making invaluable recordings of music, literature, and memoires.

The Home Owners Loan Corporation extended mortgage insurance and Federal Housing Administration (FHA) provided low-rent accommodation for the poor. The Federal Emergency Relief Administration from 1933 assisted local organizations assisting the destitute, but it was the Social Security Act of 1935 that was "the centerpiece of the new welfare state," as Barack Obama describes it, "a safety net that would lift almost half of all senior citizens out of poverty, provide unemployment insurance for those who had lost their jobs, and provide modest welfare payments to the disabled and the elderly poor."[70]

It is true that the New Deal was less beneficial for some than for others. Government jobs went first to husbands as heads of household, and the higher skilled and better paid ones usually went to white people. At the behest of southern Democrats, the Social Security and Fair Labor Standards acts excluded agricultural and domestic workers, who were disproportionately black and female. The AAA and other programs paid farm owners rather than tenants, and in fact many tenants lost their farms as owners were paid to produce less. The CCC had segregated camps, and the FHA rigorously reinforced segregated housing policies.

Even so, as Barack Obama says, the "shock of the Great Depression, with a third of all people finding themselves out of work, ill housed, ill clothed, and ill fed" finally forced government to act to protect the innocent victims of those Obama doesn't call the profligate and irresponsible rich. And even if 15 percent were still unemployed in 1940, and it would take World War II to fully reenergize the economy, "the impulse behind this New Deal compact" nevertheless "involved a sense of social solidarity: the idea that employers should do right by their workers, and that if fate or miscalculation caused any one of us to stumble, the larger American community would be there to lift us up."[71]

Historians have debated whether or to what extent the New Deal was driven by the politics of expediency or by the principles of economic and social justice. For Obama it was both, and for him that's a good thing. "FDR understood," Obama says, employing the same approvingly affirmative word he used in relation to Alexander Hamilton, "that capitalism in a democracy required the consent of the people, and that by giving workers a larger share of the economic pie, his reforms would undercut the potential appeal of government-managed, command-and-control systems—whether fascist, socialist, or communist—that were gaining support all across Europe." And he quoted Roosevelt's words from 1944: "People who are hungry, people who are out of a job are the stuff of which dictatorships are made." FDR was therefore indeed "saving capitalism from itself" as a matter of political expediency.[72]

At the same time, though, "Part of FDR's rationale in passing these laws came straight out of Keynesian economics." This is partly a merely demand-side economic theory that "one cure for economic depression was putting more disposable income in the pockets of American workers." Indeed John Maynard Keynes's *The General Theory of Employment, Interest, and Money* was published in 1936, although the idea that "under-consumption" was a cause of the Great Depression had already informed some earlier New Deal policies.[73]

It was, therefore, a theory of economic efficiency, but one that entailed a good deal of humanity. As Obama explains, the New Deal "compact also rested on an understanding that a system of sharing risks and rewards can actually improve the workings of the market." And "FDR understood," Obama says again, "that decent wages and benefits for workers could create the middle-class base of consumers that would stabilize the U.S. economy and drive its expansion. And FDR recognized," he further says, "that we would all be more likely to take risks in our lives—to change jobs or start new businesses or welcome competition from other countries—if we knew that we would have some measure of protection should we fail." It was also therefore a fundamentally just and humane theory.[74]

Of course the New Deal consensus was not unanimous. Even at the time, Obama explains, there "were those on the right who complained of creeping socialism, and those on the left who believed FDR had not gone far enough." Nonetheless, the New Deal settlement brought "a broad consensus" behind the idea of "an activist federal government that invests in its people and infrastructure, regulates the marketplace, and protects labor from chronic deprivation." And this "new social compact" provided a "bargain between government, business, and workers that resulted in widespread prosperity and economic security for more than fifty years." Its "three pillars" were "the ability to find a job that paid enough to support a family and save for emergencies; a package of health and retirement benefits from his employer; and a government safety net—Social Security, Medicaid and Medicare, unemployment insurance, and to a lesser extent federal bankruptcy and pension protections" that "could cushion the fall of those who suffered setbacks in their lives."[75]

This "model of the American welfare state" was adopted by Republicans and Democrats alike, thanks in part to the general and unprecedented wealth it generated. Hence, Obama says, "the creation of the Great Society programs, including Medicare, Medicaid, and welfare, under" the Democratic President Lyndon Johnson, and "the creation of the Environmental Protection Agency and Occupational Health and Safety Administration under" the Republican President Richard Nixon.[76]

The era of big government is over

Yet a conservative reaction had already begun. Even during the First New Deal the Supreme Court started declaring some of its legislation unconstitutional, although FDR's threat to pack the Court with pliable justices ensured a quieter time thereafter (a frankly startling assault on constitutional checks and balances about which Barack Obama maintains a discreet silence). Some New Deal legislation was rolled back right after the World War II, though. The Taft-Hartley Act of 1947, for example, allowed executive authorities to issue injunctions against strikes and restricted "unfair labor practices" such as secondary picketing. The Twenty-Second Amendment of 1951 ensured there would never be another FDR by limiting presidents to two full terms in office. Even so—and notwithstanding the two terms of Republican Dwight David Eisenhower, the presidential personification of the conservatism of the 1950s—the Civil Rights Movement, the Great Society, and the War Against Poverty seemed to represent continuing validations of New Deal liberalism. And the trouncing of Barry Goldwater by Lyndon Johnson in the presidential election of 1964 seemed to be a rejection of right-wing reaction. Yet Goldwater's appeal to conservatives found a home in Nixon's successful Southern Strategy in 1968 and 1972, and, following the Watergate fallout that saw Jimmy Carter elected in 1976, an antigovernment ideology found its greatest communicator in the person of Ronald Reagan.

As Barack Obama says, "Reagan tended to exaggerate the degree to which the welfare state had grown over the previous twenty-five years," but "the conservative revolution that Reagan helped usher in gained traction." If Reagan never achieved all the federal funding cuts he hoped for, he nevertheless "fundamentally changed the terms of the political debate." As Obama explains, "The middle-class tax revolt became a permanent fixture in national politics and placed a ceiling on how much government could expand. For many Republicans, noninterference with the marketplace became an article of faith."[77]

And indeed Reagan's rhetoric and politics crossed party lines when, as Obama reminds us, Bill Clinton declared "the era of big government over" and "signed welfare reform into law, pushed tax cuts for the middle class and working poor, and worked to reduce bureaucracy and red tape." Yet Clinton also "put a progressive slant on some of Reagan's goals" by "putting the nation's fiscal house in order even while lessening poverty and making modest new investments in education and job training." It thus "appeared as if some equilibrium had been achieved—a smaller government, but one that retained the social safety net FDR had first put into place."[78]

Obama brought the story up-to-date at his time of telling it by noting that "the Bush Administration and its congressional allies have responded by pushing the conservative revolution to its logical conclusion—even lower taxes, even fewer regulations, and an even smaller safety net." As Obama explains, "the basic idea behind the Ownership Society" is that if "we free employers of any obligations to their workers and dismantle what's left of New Deal, government-run social insurance programs, then the magic of the marketplace will take care of the rest."[79]

And he clearly disagrees. On a practical level, as Obama says, "If you are healthy or wealthy or just plain lucky, then you will become more so." But "If you are poor or sick or catch a bad break, you will have nobody to look to for help. That's not a recipe for sustained economic growth or the maintenance of a strong American middle class." And it doesn't work for Obama on a philosophical level either. "If the guiding philosophy behind the traditional system of social insurance could be described as 'We're all in it together,'" he says, "the philosophy behind the Ownership Society seems to be 'You're on your own.'" That, he points out, is "certainly not a recipe for social cohesion." It "runs counter to those values that say we have a stake in each other's success." And it is therefore "not," he pointedly says, "who we are as a people."[80]

But an ideological backlash against "big government" isn't the only reason for recent economic and social change. Barack Obama blames an earlier absence of international competition for the fact that "by the seventies, U.S. productivity growth, the engine of the postwar economy, began to lag." At the same time, though, "The increased assertiveness of OPEC allowed foreign oil producers to lop off a much bigger share of the global economy, exposing America's vulnerability to disruptions in energy supplies." In addition to that, "U.S. companies began to experience competition from low-cost producers in Asia, and by the eighties a flood of cheap imports—in textiles, shoes, electronics, and even automobiles—had started grabbing big chunks of the domestic market." And also "U.S.-based multinational corporations began locating some of their production facilities overseas—partly to access these foreign markets, but also to take advantage of cheap labor." Some US corporations responded by finding "ways to improve productivity through innovation and automation." But others "relied primarily on brutal layoffs, resistance to unionization, and a further shift of production overseas." All "without any regard for the employees whose lives might be upended or the communities that might be torn apart."[81]

These changes are so great that Obama hints that America might already be in a new historical era. Certainly, he says, America needs to respond to new problems in novel ways. He described politics under George W. Bush as a conflict in which "Republicans are fighting the last war, the war they waged and won in the eighties, while Democrats are forced to fight a rearguard action, defending the New Deal programs of the thirties."

But, he said, "Neither strategy will work anymore." He thus advocated at that time what he said was a new approach, including government "investments that can make America more competitive in the global economy" in such areas as "education, science and technology, and energy independence." And in terms of social policy he advocated raising the minimum wage, extending Ronald Reagan's Earned Income Tax Credit, wage insurance, union rights, safer pensions, and more affordable health care.[82]

The dogmas of the quiet past

Except that these ideas, fine as they may be, are really not so new. And Barack Obama seems to know it. In asking rhetorically what "a new economic consensus" might "look like," he says that "I won't pretend to have all the answers." And that apparent uncertainty is evident in the fact that, even while looking forward for something unprecedented, he nevertheless looks backward for precursors. He introduces these ideas as "a few examples of where we can break free of our current political stalemate; places where, in the tradition of Hamilton and Lincoln, we can invest in our infrastructure and our people" and "ways that we can begin to modernize and rebuild the social contract that FDR first stitched together in the middle of the last century." In "asking ourselves what mix of policies will lead to a dynamic free market and widespread economic security, entrepreneurial innovation and upward mobility" he says similarly that "we can be guided throughout by Lincoln's simple maxim: that we will do collectively, through our government, only those things that we cannot do as well or at all individually and privately." And when he says that there's an "alternative approach" to labor policy, he describes it as "one that recasts FDR's social compact to meet the needs of a new century."[83]

Barack Obama says as well that when looking for something new "we should be guided by what works." That is to say, we should be guided by something we've already seen. Indeed in looking for "what works" he argues that "our history should give us confidence that we don't have to choose between an oppressive, government-run economy and a chaotic and unforgiving capitalism." For Obama that seems to mean looking at what has been but not at what might have been. And also looking at the best of what has been rather than the worse of what has been. Admittedly, the "what works" approach appears to be both principled and practical, in the fine tradition of philosophical pragmatism. And yet reliance on experience can of course displace critical thinking and replace experimentation. It may thus be that in this area of economy and society Obama is trapped in the constraints of his own historical narrative.[84]

Ironically, it was Barack Obama's hero Abraham Lincoln who once said that sometimes "the dogmas of the quiet past, are inadequate to the stormy present ... As our case is new, so we must think anew and act anew." Obama too perceives how sometimes the dogmas of the past can define our thinking in limiting ways. "The result of" America's "business culture," he writes, "has been a prosperity that's unmatched in human history." And it should therefore "come as no surprise ... that we have a tendency to take our free-market system as a given, to assume that it flows naturally from the laws of supply and demand and Adam Smith's invisible hand. And from this assumption," he adds, "it's not much of a leap to assume that any government intrusion into the magical workings of the market—whether through taxation, regulation, lawsuits, tariffs, labor protections, or spending on entitlements—necessarily undermines private enterprise and inhibits economic growth." In addition to that, the "bankruptcy of communism and socialism as alternative means of economic organization has only reinforced this assumption. In our standard economics textbooks and in our modern political debates, laissez-faire is the default rule; anyone who would challenge it swims against the prevailing tide."[85]

And Obama is capable of course of stepping outside of this narrative, of swimming against this prevailing tide. "It's useful to remind ourselves, then," he rightly says, "that our free-market system is the result neither of natural law nor of divine providence. Rather, it emerged through a painful process of trial and error, a series of difficult choices between efficiency and fairness, stability and change. And although the benefits of our free-market system have mostly derived from the individual efforts of generations of men and women pursuing their own vision of happiness," he adds, "in each and every period of great economic upheaval and transition we've depended on government action to open up opportunity, encourage competition, and make the market work better."[86]

Yet these comments themselves reveal the extent to which Obama doesn't step outside the narrative, how he too swims with the prevailing tide. He clearly condemns free-market fundamentalism, but equally condones a free-market ideology that accepts government as an economic and social enabler, regulator, and mediator in scrupulously limited ways. He writes, for example, of how "government investment has helped pave the way for an explosion of *private* economic activity." Of government making "needed investments that *private* enterprise can't or won't make on its own." Of "Hamilton's and Lincoln's basic insight—that the resources and power of the national government *can facilitate, rather than supplant, a vibrant free market.*" Of how "we can be guided throughout by Lincoln's simple maxim: that we will do collectively, through our government, *only* those things that we cannot do as well or at all individually and privately" (my emphases, but still his words). Obama may qualify the idea of the "free market" quite profoundly, then, but he still believes the market should be as "free" as it can be.[87]

Barack Obama therefore is no more a communist or a socialist than he is a native Kenyan or a Muslim. His identification of "communism *and* socialism as alternative means of economic organization" (my emphasis again) implicitly acknowledges the difference between totalitarian and democratic economic systems, yet he dismisses both as roads to "bankruptcy." And his rejection of any government activity beyond the unavoidable shows he's not even a European-style social democrat but is rather an American-style liberal democrat, an ameliorator rather than a reformer.[88]

Obama's words about Theodore Roosevelt tell us this too. On the face of it they seem reformist. "Roosevelt also knew," Obama said in Osawatomie, "that the free market has never been a free license to take whatever you can from whomever you can. He understood the free market only works when there are rules of the road that ensure competition is fair and open and honest. And so he busted up monopolies, forcing those companies to compete for consumers with better services and better prices. And today, they still must. He fought to make sure businesses couldn't profit by exploiting children or selling food or medicine that wasn't safe. And today, they still can't." And yet Obama prefaced all this by noting that Roosevelt "praised what the titans of industry had done to create jobs and grow the economy. He believed then what we know is true today, that the free market is the greatest force for economic progress in human history. It's led to a prosperity and a standard of living unmatched by the rest of the world."[89]

Barack Obama's reasons for rejecting radical reformism are therefore both practical and ideological. The "free market" has generated the wealth and with it the pursuits of happiness Americans enjoy. And there is in his view an inseparability of property and liberty: a market that's as free as it can be is a hallmark of political and social liberty. "All the Founding Fathers," as we saw Obama say, "recognized the connection between private property and liberty." Yet Obama doesn't seem to see this as an ideological position. We saw earlier the assertive and affirmative functions that the verb "recognize" serves in the Obamian lexicon. That and the word "understood" are predicates to what Obama sees as unquestionable facts. As opposed to "feared," the predicate of ideological fantasy. These facts—the wealth-generating and happiness-creating function of the "free market" and the normally unbreakable association of property and liberty—are the bases of Barack Obama's narrative of American economic and social history. They are the dogmas of his quiet past, and they define and direct a narrative from which he cannot deviate.[90]

Barack Obama is certainly right to say that the Founders had some kind of faith in an association of property and liberty, but the ideological rather than factual nature of that faith is manifest in the fact—a fact Obama knows well enough—that they saw that association in different ways. As we saw earlier, Thomas Jefferson saw widespread property ownership as essential to the liberty and the survival of the new republic, however idealized his agrarianism was. Alexander Hamilton on the other hand saw finance and manufacturing as essential to the security and survival of the new republic, however idealized his industrialism was. Obama acknowledges this, but dismisses what "Jefferson feared" and embraces what "Hamilton understood" and what "Hamilton recognized." And yet when Obama characterizes the best of the history of the "free market" he does so in Jeffersonian rather than Hamiltonian terms. Sometimes very precisely Jeffersonian terms, as when Obama says that "the benefits of our free-market system have mostly derived from the individual efforts of generations of men and women pursuing their own vision of happiness." Liberty and property are thus reconciled and the Hamiltonian republic is thereby redeemed in Jeffersonian rhetoric, however idealized Obama's economic history is.[91]

Although sometimes thus idealized, Barack Obama does take a critical approach to American economy, inasmuch as he acknowledges the negative effects that corporate excesses can have on others. But that's not the same thing as a critical-theoretical approach, one that explores the meanings of liberty and property as concepts, or examines the ways in which these concepts are connected. In sum, Obama often accepts economic concepts as facts rather than as constructs. As a consequence, he cannot deconstruct them, and as a consequence of that he cannot show, for example, how sometimes in fact property and liberty aren't connected, or how sometimes in fact they're in conflict with each other.

A critical theory of liberty and property and economy and society need not be communistic or even socialistic—although I won't pretend to have all the answers either. But far from being revolutionary or in any way un-American, such a critical theory might nonetheless be necessary for thinking of new ways of making a more perfect union. It might even be necessary for finding ways of preserving that union.

Economic rights that have to be dealt with

For example, in terms of making a more perfect union. In a speech in Selma, Alabama, on March 4, 2007, Barack Obama said that "we've got to recognize that we fought for civil rights, but we've still got a lot of economic rights that have to be dealt with." And he spoke about disparities in health care, education, housing, employment, incarceration, and in hope. One year and two weeks later in Philadelphia, Pennsylvania, he explained the historical origins of these inequalities. We need, he said,

> to remind ourselves that so many of the disparities that exist in the African-American community today can be directly traced to inequalities passed on from an earlier generation that suffered under the brutal legacy of slavery and Jim Crow.
>
> Segregated schools were, and are, inferior schools; we still haven't fixed them, fifty years after *Brown v. Board of Education*, and the inferior education they provided, then and now, helps explain the pervasive achievement gap between today's black and white students.
>
> Legalized discrimination—where blacks were prevented, often through violence, from owning property, or loans were not granted to African-American business owners, or black homeowners could not access FHA mortgages, or blacks were excluded from unions, or the police force, or fire departments—meant that black families could not amass any meaningful wealth to bequeath to future generations. That history helps explain the wealth and income gap between black and white, and the concentrated pockets of poverty that persist in so many of today's urban and rural communities.
>
> A lack of economic opportunity among black men, and the shame and frustration that came from not being able to provide for one's family, contributed to the erosion of black families—a problem that welfare policies for many years may have worsened. And the lack of basic services in so many urban black neighborhoods—parks for kids to play in, police walking the beat, regular garbage pick-up and building code enforcement—all helped create a cycle of violence, blight and neglect that continue to haunt us.[92]

As Obama also said, "the path to a more perfect union means acknowledging that what ails the African-American community does not just exist in the minds of black people; that the legacy of discrimination—and current incidents of discrimination, while less overt than in the past—are real and must be addressed."[93]

Barack Obama's critical approach to American history therefore allows us to see that the legacies of past inequalities must be addressed, but without a critical theory it is hard to see that path to a more perfect union. Yet a critical-theoretical approach might help us see or see more clearly that property and liberty aren't always connected, or at least not in the ways we like to think they are. Sometimes indeed they're in conflict with each other, as when British colonial planters enslaved Africans and their descendants in order to enjoy the privileges of liberty and property afforded by the New World. And as when their postindependence descendants defended their by then peculiar institution on the grounds of their property "rights" in the people they continued to enslave.

If we think of property and liberty as less connected than we tend to do, and as more separable as they tend in fact to be, then we perhaps can do more to rebalance the two and thereby deal with the issues we need to address, those economic rights that have to be dealt with. And it has been done before, as when the Emancipation Proclamation and the Thirteenth Amendment liberated a people from their legal status as other people's property. And people do it every day, in a way, when they pay their taxes—or when some of them do. But the dogmas of the free market didn't and won't right any wrongs or advance the cause of equality, liberty, and the pursuit of happiness. Corporations and their beneficiaries won't do these things unless there's profit in it—or unless "WE THE PEOPLE" make them do it.

That he may "ride the storm and direct the whirlwind"

And for a further example, this time in terms of preserving the union. In his famous speech in Philadelphia, Barack Obama also said that "a similar anger" to that of African Americans also "exists within segments of the white community. Most working- and middle-class white Americans don't feel that they have been particularly privileged by their race. Their experience is the immigrant experience," he continued, and "as far as they're concerned, no one's handed them anything, they've built it from scratch. They've worked hard all their lives, many times only to see their jobs shipped overseas or their pension dumped after a lifetime of labor." And he added that this anger too has "often proved counterproductive," distracting "attention from the real culprits of the middle class squeeze—a corporate culture rife with inside dealing, questionable accounting practices, and short-term greed; a Washington dominated by lobbyists and special interests; economic policies that favor the few over the many."[94]

These comments opened Obama to criticisms of drawing false equivalences between the historical struggles and current sufferings of black and white Americans. But what he was drawing attention to was the fact, and it is a fact, that poorer white people are also "anxious about their futures, and feel their dreams slipping away … in an era of stagnant wages and global competition." That's one issue. And another related one is that such anxieties can lead to misdirected resentments when stoked by dissembling and divisive forces.[95]

The dangers of demagoguery have long been known. This is what FDR warned of when he said: "People who are hungry, people who are out of a job are the stuff of which dictatorships are made." But perhaps these fears were never expressed as eloquently as they were by Barack Obama's hero Alexander Hamilton. In August 1792, the Treasury Secretary wrote a report to President Washington entitled "Objections and Answers respecting the Administration of the Government." He didn't aim to impugn the "intention of the generality" of his detractors, but some of them he said had encouraged the "subversion of the republican system of the Country … by flattering the prejudices of the people, and exciting their jealousies and apprehensions, to throw affairs into confusion, and bring on civil commotion." And he carried on as follows:

> When a man unprincipled in private life[,] desperate in his fortune, bold in his temper, possessed of considerable talents … despotic in his ordinary demeanour—known to have scoffed in private at the principles of liberty—when such a man is seen to mount the hobby horse of popularity—to join in the cry of danger to liberty—to take every opportunity of embarrassing the General Government & bringing it under suspicion—to flatter and fall in with all the non sense of the zealots of the day—It may justly be suspected that his object is to throw things into confusion that he may "ride the storm and direct the whirlwind."[96]

Again, Barack Obama's critical approach to the history of American economy and society allows him to see that demagogues can distract "attention from the real culprits" who cause inequality, insecurity, and poverty. But, again, the absence of a critical-theoretical approach makes it harder to see *how* it is that they can do these things—how it is that, from the rise of slavery in late seventeenth century to our second Gilded Age, one percenters have managed so often to divide and rule, to ride the storm and direct the whirlwind.[97]

A more critical-theoretical approach might also allow a more extensive exploration of the meanings of property and liberty in the history of relations with Native Americans and the rest of the world. These are the subjects of the chapter that follows. Once again, one people's ideas about their rights to property can lead to nothing less than the annihilation of life, liberty, and the pursuit of happiness for another.

CHAPTER 7
BEYOND OUR BORDERS: NATIVE AMERICANS AND OTHER FOREIGN AFFAIRS

A conquest that ... contradicted America's founding principles

"WE HOLD THESE truths to be self-evident, that all men are Created equal, that they are endowed by their Creator with certain unalienable Rights, that among these are Life, Liberty, and the pursuit of Happiness." Barack Obama describes these words from the Declaration of Independence as "our starting point as Americans," as "the substance of our common creed," and as "the foundation of our government." In some respects these claims are true. As part of the founding document of the United States they are indeed the "starting point" of United States nationhood. And they are moreover a powerful philosophical claim about the nature of that nationhood, denoting its fundamental principles with all the moral imperative of a "creed." For Obama, furthermore, these principles were "made real" in law and government by "We the People" through a Constitution that crafted "a more perfect union." Not a perfect one in 1787 and not a perfect one today, but the deliberative democracy the Founders formed created the means to make an ever "more perfect union" in the course of time.[1]

And indeed African Americans achieved liberty and eventually equality, at least legally if not yet in every respect. Poorer whites also became enfranchised and attained improved economic rights, if not yet completely equal opportunity and security compared to the well-born. Women escaped the confines of coverture and finally won the vote, if not yet equal opportunity and pay. Immigrants arrived and struggled and strived and some of them thrived, and one group after another found their place in the United States. LGBT people have more recently achieved advances too, most especially in relation to equal marriage. And disabled Americans have had their needs increasingly recognized so that they too are closer to enjoying equal opportunity. For Barack Obama, therefore, for all the trials and tribulations, for all the struggles and setbacks, there has been progress; for all that the arc of the moral universe is long, it has nevertheless bent toward justice. A "more perfect union" has in his view been achieved, ever more in accord with "creed" of equality and the unalienable rights to life, liberty, and the pursuit of happiness for all.

Except for Native Americans. There may have been recent improvements in relations between the United States and the continent's original nations, but, while other groups have struggled for greater equality and liberty, the Native American struggle has been one for survival. Indeed, as the benefits of equality, liberty, and the pursuit of happiness were extending to more and more Anglo Americans, African Americans, and all kinds of immigrant Americans from the late eighteenth century, though the nineteenth century, and deep into the twentieth century, they were diminishing proportionally for Native Americans. Proportionally because the geographical expansion of the United States entailed the territorial expropriation of the continent's original inhabitants. And, as Barack Obama says, the conquest of Native Americans "tended to be justified in explicitly racist terms," which was bad enough, but it was also "an exercise in raw power." For these reasons, Obama says, it "was a conquest that, like slavery, contradicted America's founding principles."[2]

Except that it did not contradict America's founding principles. In some ways in fact the conquest of Native Americans was as closely in accord with those principles as the rejection of British imperialism was. The last of the accusations against George III that the Declaration of Independence made, for example, was that "he has excited domestic insurrections amongst us, and has endeavoured to bring on the inhabitants of our frontiers, the merciless Indian Savages, whose known rule of warfare, is an undistinguished destruction of all ages, sexes and conditions." The first part of the passage refers to Governor Dunmore of Virginia inviting slaves of rebellious colonists to join him in suppressing the anti-British insurrection by their own oppressors, and the second refers to British attempts to recruit Native Americans to their cause. The Declaration's reduction of the variety and complexity of different native nations' war conduct is fairly typical of the kind of "othering" people do even more of in moments of crisis than in normal times. But the word "Savages" was normal at all times, a conceptual weapon that was relentlessly deployed against Native Americans from the beginnings of European settlement in the Americas to US Independence and beyond.[3]

Reverend Robert Gray, for example, used it in a 1609 sermon entitled *A Good Speed to Virginia*, given in support of the then two-year-old and beleaguered mission to build a colony in Jamestown. The preacher asked the pressing question "by what right or warrant we can enter into the land of these Savages, take away their rightful inheritance from them, and plant ourselves in their place, being unwronged or unprovoked by them?" His answer inhered in the word "Savages" itself, which did not always connote mercilessness or brutality but did always connote the notion that Native Americans were uncivilized. That is, that they lived in a State of Nature and had neither property nor government, two fundamental features of civilization as Europeans defined it. This notion of Native Americans as "Savages" thus lay at the heart of the "agriculturalist argument" of Europeans for taking away Native Americans' "rightful inheritance" and planting themselves "in their place." And it was based on precisely the same theories of property and government, and of equality and unalienable rights, that informed the Declaration of Independence.[4]

The "agriculturalist argument" related first and foremost to private property, but was also necessarily tied to the matter of political territory. Or, to put that in the Roman-imperial legal terms upon which European settlement in America proceeded: *dominium* referred to private property ownership and *imperium* to the territorial sovereignty of a state. Both were essential components of European concepts of civilization. Native Americans were styled "Savages" because they supposedly practiced neither.

Some Native American tribes were primarily nomadic or seminomadic hunter-gatherers, others practiced settled, communal agriculture or horticulture, and many mixed these practices, but that made little difference to the English who practiced agriculture on private, fenced-off farms and estates. And because Native Americans supposedly exercised no *dominium*, it followed that they also exercised no *imperium*. For English people, one of the principal purposes of government was the protection of private property, or of "life, liberty, and possessions," or "life, liberty, and estates," in the words of John Locke. The absence of private property necessarily therefore implied the partial and perhaps even total absence of government. Locke made this connection himself, arguing that because Indians "exercise very little Dominion" they "have but a very moderate sovereignty." Again, Native Americans lived in various forms of social and political organizations, in villages, tribes, nations, and empires, but not in European-style nation states. They were therefore thought to have few or no laws or government, to live in a State of Nature. Indeed when Locke attempted to describe what human life was like before there was property and government, he wrote, in his *Second Treatise of Government* (1690): "In the beginning all the World was America."[5]

As Native Americans were deemed to possess no property, so they were deemed to possess no property rights, and so America was considered a "wilderness," either empty (*vacuum domicilium*) or unused and therefore unowned by its occupants (*res nullius*) and thus free for others to claim, settle, and use. As we saw in Chapter 6, the Declaration of Independence alludes to "the circumstances of our emigration and settlement here." In his original draft of that declaration Thomas Jefferson had elaborated that colonial settlements "were effected at the expence of our own blood & treasure, unassisted by the wealth or the strength of Great Britain." He also argued in his *Summary View of the Rights of British America* (1774) that migrants had left British jurisdiction and that no British authorities had any claims to American property or territory, and nor did Native Americans. It was settlers only who mixed their labor with the land and other resources and thereby made them their own and theirs alone.[6]

In turn, settlers freely formed colonial governments and then allied themselves to the British crown—the better to protect their lives, liberties, and property, whether from the unruly in their own community or from European enemies or from "merciless Indian Savages." As Jefferson explained in his *Summary View*, "That settlements having been thus effected in the wilds of America, the emigrants thought proper to adopt that system of laws under which they had hitherto lived in the mother country, and to continue their union with her by submitting themselves to the same common Sovereign." These are precisely the principles upon which the Declaration of Independence is predicated. The Declaration says "Governments are instituted among Men, deriving their just powers from the consent of the governed." But "whenever any Form of Government becomes destructive of" equality and the rights to life, liberty, and the pursuit of happiness, "it is the Right of the People to alter or to abolish it." Which is precisely what the Declaration of Independence did. The people had the right and duty also "to institute new Government, laying its foundation on such principles and organizing its powers in such form, as to them shall seem most likely to effect their Safety and Happiness." Which is precisely what the Constitution did.[7]

Barack Obama's claim that the conquest of Native American people and lands "contradicted America's founding principles" thus ignores the ideological kinship of the legal concepts of *dominium* and *imperium* with the Declaration's pronouncements about liberty, property, and government. Obama is of course entirely entitled to a different interpretation of the meanings of the Founders' words from the one they had, and indeed we all are, especially as he argues that the Founders themselves expected later generations to develop different interpretations of the meanings of their words and deeds. But it is worth noting nonetheless that what we may think now about the relation of liberty and property to Native American dispossession is not the same as what the Founders thought then. And what they thought then had catastrophic consequences for Native Americans.[8]

America's "original sin"

Barack Obama has often referred to slavery as America's "original sin," as many others also have. That may be apt as and when it applies to the United States, founded as the nation was on doctrines of equality and liberty that were antithetical to enslavement, and indeed Obama has usually used the more specific term "this nation's original sin." But if we integrate the colonies into American history more fully than Obama tends to do, then perhaps the term would apply more aptly to what colonial settlers did to Native Americans.[9]

Robert Gray's recounting of what came to be called the agriculturalist argument for appropriating Native-Americans' land came two years after the founding of Jamestown, but was part of a long tradition of imperialist thinking dating back to ancient Rome. The reverend's reiteration of it also arrived on the eve of the first Anglo-Powhatan War. The Jamestown colonists had settled in the midst of the Powhatan Empire of about thirty tribes located in the Atlantic tidewater between the Potomac River and the Great Dismal Swamp. Wahunsonacock (also called Powhatan) had assumed his guests were temporary, but their refusal to give gifts, to negotiate for land, and to intermarry, and then their refusal to answer questions about their departure, provoked him into attacking crops, livestock, and settlers in an attempt to drive them out. The war began in 1610, nine years before the arrival of the first recorded African Americans. It ended after a 1613 English raid that resulted in the capture of Powhatan's daughter Pocahontas, born Matoaka and also called Amonute, who became Rebecca Rolfe as a result of a diplomatic marriage that helped secure peace. Her new husband was John Rolfe, the tobacco pioneer who also recorded the arrival of the first African Americans in English North America.

Pocahontas fell fatally ill at the end of a two-year trip to London and was buried in Gravesend in March 1617. Her father died the following year and was succeeded by his brother, Opechancanough. By that time too tobacco-planting colonists had spread over 100 miles into his lands, and on March 22, 1622, he launched an attack that killed 347 settlers, a third of the English population, and that might have destroyed the entire colony were it not for Christian converts who warned the English on the morning of the raid. John Rolfe died in 1622, perhaps in the attack, or possibly as a result of privations proceeding from it. The killings precipitated a Second Anglo-Powhatan War of 1622 to 1628 in which the English drove the Powhatan off the Jamestown peninsula, although sporadic fighting continued until 1632. A final attempt by Opechancanough to drive the English out in a third war of 1644–46 eventuated in his death and the collapse of the Powhatan confederacy. Native American resistance to settlement was revived during Bacon's Rebellion of 1676. By then, though, the colony was too deeply entrenched to be uprooted.

Such wars characterized colonization in every region, inherent as they were to the very process of English settlement on Native American lands. They came late to New England because before the Pilgrims and Puritans arrived the Patuxet Indians were already all but wiped out by European diseases to which they had no immunity. But fur trade rivalry and the spread of settlement provoked first the Pequot War of 1636–37 and then the much more destructive Metacom's War of 1675–76 (formerly called King Philip's War), although that one ended serious Indian resistance in the heart of the region. The Dutch had largely defeated local Native Americans by the time their settlements became the English colonies of New York, East and West and finally New Jersey, and Delaware. William Penn established a peace with the Susquehannock that lasted several generations, although the spread of settlement eventuated in violence in the 1750s and 1760s, culminating in Pontiac's War of 1763–66 in the Great Lakes Region. Settlement conflict further south culminated with North Carolina's Tuscarora War of 1714–15 and South Carolina's Yamasee War of 1715–17.

Native Americans also entered wars between rival European imperial powers, aligning with whoever best accommodated their own strategic interests: King William' War of 1688–97 (part of the Nine Years' War), Queen Ann's War of 1702–13 (War of the Spanish Succession), Dummer's War of 1722–25 between northern Massachusetts and New France, King George's War of 1744–48 (part of the War of the Austrian Succession of 1740–48), and finally the French and Indian War of 1754–60 (which precipitated the Seven Years' War of 1756–63).

At the end of the Seven Years' War, the Great Proclamation of 1763 secured most of the land east of the Appalachian Mountains to Euro-American settlers and safeguarded most of the land beyond to Native Americans. But independence ended that agreement and augured rapid American expansion in the region from the mountains to the Mississippi River. The Declaration did not directly denounce the 1763 Proclamation Line, but the seventh set of grievances against king George said, "He has endeavoured to prevent the population of these States; for that purpose obstructing the Laws for Naturalization of Foreigners; refusing to pass others to encourage their migrations hither, and raising the conditions of new Appropriations of Lands." Certainly, though, the abolition of the Proclamation Line by the Declaration and then by the Treaty of Paris that acknowledged American Independence internationally in 1783 was a catastrophe for Native Americans.[10]

That said, some native nations fought for the United States in the War of Independence, including the Oneida and the Tuscarora of the Iroquois Confederacy that had first sided with settlers against other Native Americans as far back as Metacom's War. But most fought for the British, including the Cayuga, Mohawk, Onondaga, and Seneca, causing the disintegration of the Six Nations confederation (or "the people of the longhouse," as they collectively called themselves). Other nations were divided too, including the Cherokee, who cleaved into neutral and pro-British factions, some of whom continued fighting settlers in the western regions for over a decade after the end of the War of Independence. The British ultimately signaled the insincerity of their commitment to their erstwhile Native American allies by ceding western territories to the United States unconditionally.

The impulse to expand

If Barack Obama says little about Euro-American expansion and the settler wars of the colonial and revolutionary eras, he nevertheless acknowledges their intrinsic role in the history of the United States. "[I]f suspicion of foreign entanglements is stamped into our DNA," he wrote, "then so is the impulse to expand—geographically, commercially, and ideologically. Thomas Jefferson expressed early on the inevitability of expansion beyond the boundaries of the original thirteen states." Furthermore, in invoking Jefferson—the principal author of the Declaration of Independence, Virginia governor from 1779 to 1781, US minister to France from 1785 to 1789, secretary of state from 1790 to 1793, vice president from 1797 to 1801, and president from 1801 to 1809—Obama indicates the importance of government in the settlement of the West. He thereby makes an implicit criticism of the myth of individualism, a myth indeed that derives much of its power from a very selective collective memory of westward migration and settlement.[11]

Much, but not all. In Chapter 6 we saw how American entrepreneurs, ranging from Alexander Hamilton's eastern manufacturers to Abraham Lincoln's western homesteaders, depended on various kinds of public assistance, and in saying so Barack Obama offers an implicit criticism of a "free market" fundamentalism that imagines entrepreneurs heroically forging forward as rugged individuals without the assistance of government. We also see in the Epilogue how Obama sees individuals in the context of various levels of community, and sees them as enhanced as a consequence of that. Similarly, Obama admires the endeavors of America's "pioneers," as we see later in this chapter. But he is also clear, if only implicitly so in this instance, that western settlers also depended on public assistance, including Lincoln's 1862 Homestead Act that parceled out farms to those settlers as aforementioned. Government assistance also included the conducting of wars, the forced removal of Native American people, the deliberate destruction of their resources such as buffalo, and the making of treaties, often extortionate ones—and all in order to clear space for westward-bound migrants to settle. All in all, the American west could not have been "won" by pioneers alone. The frontiersman was a product of government initiatives; his individualism is a figment of antigovernment imaginations.

Another form of government involvement in western settlement was in the organization of territories. One of the conditions that allowed the Articles of

Confederation to come into effect in 1781 was that the landed states ceded their western territories to the United States. And in turn the Constitution of 1787 confirms: "The Congress shall have power to dispose of and make all needful Rules and Regulations respecting the Territory or other Property belonging to the United States." As a Virginia delegate to the Confederation Congress from 1783 to 1784, Thomas Jefferson himself proposed ordnances to organize the western territories, and these in turn influenced the Northwest and Southwest Ordnances of 1787 (renewed in slightly altered form when the Constitution came into effect in 1789).[12]

The rapid settlement of the regions those ordnances organized led in turn to the Northwest Indian War of 1785–95 between the United States and an alliance of Shawnee, Miami, Lenape, and Ottawa people, but when the British failed to come to their aid they were forced to cede what is now Ohio and much of Indiana in the Treaty of Greenville. The remaining Indiana Territory was taken in Tecumseh's War of 1810–13, although the brief Black Hawk War of 1832 followed a Sauk attempt to resettle in Illinois after being moved across the Mississippi into the Iowa Indian Territory. Tecumseh's war and the Creek War (1813–14) in the southeast became part of the wider War of 1812 (1812–15) against Great Britain. That in turn tipped into the First Seminole War that General Andrew Jackson engineered into a war against Spain that ended with the United States gaining East and West Florida—the Gulf Coast as well as the peninsula—in the Adams-Onís Treaty of 1819.

The treaty gained its name from the then Secretary of State John Quincy Adams, "who warned against US adventurism abroad," as Barack Obama says, but "became a tireless advocate of continental expansion and served as the chief architect of the Monroe Doctrine—a warning to European powers to keep out of the Western Hemisphere," as Obama also says. Named after James Monroe, president from 1817 to 1825, the Monroe Doctrine is an instance of confluence between foreign policy and western policy. We see others in the following pages, most especially with the Mexican American War of 1846–48, the Oregon Treaty of 1846, and the shift from internal to external expansionism from the 1890s. We'll also see a little later how Native Americans' ambiguous relationships with the United States make them in some respects a subject of American foreign policy as well as of its domestic history, as indeed is the case in Barack Obama's own thinking.[13]

The aforementioned Andrew Jackson traded on his military career successfully enough that he was president of the United States at the start of the Second Seminole War of 1835–42, a war that arose from resistance to the federal policy of removing Native Americans to "Indian Lands" west of the Mississippi River. Jackson had supported the Indian Removal Act of 1830, and the forced removals began with the Choctaw from 1830, the Chickasaw, Creek, and Seminole from 1832, and the Cherokee from 1835. Most of the Seminole were finally killed or removed in war, and up to 18,000 Cherokee who engaged in passive resistance were finally forced to go to what is now Oklahoma. A quarter to a third of them died on what became known as the Trail of Tears.

The scene was already set, however, for these processes to repeat themselves in the trans-Mississippi West. As Barack Obama mentioned, expansion seemed to be a part of America's metaphorical DNA. As he further recounted, Thomas Jefferson's "timetable for such expansion was greatly accelerated with the Louisiana Purchase and the Lewis and Clark expedition." After France regained Louisiana from Spain in the Treaty of San Ildefonso of 1800, President Jefferson sent envoys to Paris with the aim of purchasing the crucial trading port of New Orleans. Napoleon Bonaparte, however, beleaguered by the "black Jacobins" of St. Domingue, unexpectedly offered to sell the entire Louisiana Territory to the United States. Though it was in Jefferson's words "an act beyond the Constitution," the president could hardly pass up the opportunity to buy over 800,000 square miles of land for just $15 million. The United States thus gained a title unrivalled by other Europeans or Euro-Americans to the Mississippi River and a vast swathe of land from the Gulf of Mexico in the south to the Canadian border in the north, and all as far west as the Rocky Mountains: one-third of what is now the continental United States. This was of course yet another government action that helps account for how the west was "won."[14]

As was President Jefferson's rapid deployment of Meriwether Lewis and William Clark to head an expedition to explore this region. The Corps of Discovery left St. Louis in the spring of 1804 and returned just under two years later with plant and animal specimens, and with vast amounts of information recorded in their journals, enough to illustrate the possibilities for American settlers. They had in fact explored beyond the Rockies, reaching the Pacific Ocean by the winter of 1805, encouraging the notion that the United States could be and should be a continental nation. A notion that would become known as "manifest destiny."

Manifest destiny

The term was coined by a newspaper editor named John O'Sullivan in an article entitled "Annexation" and published in the July–August 1845 issue of the *Democratic Review*. O'Sullivan wrote of "our manifest destiny to overspread the continent allotted by Providence for the free development of our yearly multiplying millions." Few paid much heed to the phrase at the time, but it gradually came to be a shorthand way of justifying and celebrating American expansion, whatever its costs. Barack Obama contextualizes the term for our times, however. "As American soldiers and settlers moved steadily west and southwest," he wrote:

> successive administrations described the annexation of territory in terms of "manifest destiny"—the conviction that such expansion was preordained, part of God's plan to extend what Andrew Jackson called "the area of freedom" across the continent.
>
> Of course, manifest destiny also meant bloody and violent conquest—of Native American tribes forcibly removed from their lands and of the Mexican army defending its territory. It was a conquest that, like slavery, contradicted America's founding principles and tended to be justified in explicitly racist terms, a conquest that American mythology has always had difficulty fully absorbing but that other countries recognized for what it was—an exercise in raw power.[15]

Although both O'Sullivan and Obama were writing in their different ways about the same specific events, the descriptions they supplied could equally apply to any moment in the almost three centuries between the settling of Jamestown and the closing of the "frontier" by 1890. And even beyond.

The specific events in this instance began with the Anglo-American settler revolt against Mexico that resulted in Texan independence in 1836. After the United States annexed Texas in 1845, a war with Mexico followed that resulted in American acquisition of what is now Texas, California, and much of New Mexico, Arizona, Nevada, and Utah, and parts of Colorado and Wyoming. In the same year, the Oregon Treaty ended a joint occupancy that had existed with Britain and gave the United States exclusive possession of what is now part of Wyoming and Montana, and the entirety of what are now the states of Idaho, Oregon, and Washington. The United States thereby became a continental nation.

This seemingly inexorable expansion resulted in countless violent confrontations in the second half of the nineteenth century. The bloodiest and most decisive perhaps were the Texas Indian Wars of 1836–77, primarily between the United States and the Comanche, the Navajo Wars of 1849–66, the Apache Wars of 1849–1924, and Ute Wars of 1850–1923, also in the southwest, and, further north, the Sioux Wars of 1854–91. The US-Indian wars continued until the end of the "Renegade Period" of the Apache Wars in 1924, but 1890 marks a mournful moment that brought about the end of the Sioux Wars—the killing by the United States Army of up to 300 Lakota Indians, mostly older men and women and some children, most of them unarmed, at the Wounded Knee Massacre on the Pine Ridge Reservation in South Dakota on December 29, 1890.

That year also the decennial Census declared: "Up to and including 1880 the country had a frontier of settlement," defined as an area with a population density of two people per square mile. By 1890, however, "the unsettled area has been so broken into by isolated bodies of settlement that there can hardly be said to be a frontier line." That same census recorded a Native American population of just under a quarter of a million. The four-century process of resettlement that eventuated in this moment had reduced the indigenous population from a pre-Columbian minimum of two million in the region that is now the United States, with most historians estimating around five million, and some extending that figure to ten million.[16]

Even the confining of native nations to reservations, which began after the Pequot War of 1636–37 and continued as part of the process of conquest, did not prevent Indians from losing a lot of the little land they had left—even after the West was "won." The 1887 General Allotment Act, for instance, also called the Dawes Act after Henry L. Dawes of Massachusetts, chairman of the Senate Indian Affairs Committee, took communally owned Indian land and parceled it out again in (often adequate) family-sized allotments mainly to male heads of households—as part of a policy of "civilizing" Native American people. Reservation land was also parceled out to non-Indians, as indeed happened with the government-sponsored Oklahoma Land Rush of April 22, 1889, when some 50,000 white settlers thundered into Indian Territory and staked out a total of close to two million acres for themselves in just one day. Of the 138 million acres of land in Native

American possession in 1887, 86 million were handed over to white settlers before the Indian Reorganization Act of 1934 ended the reallocations begun under the Dawes Act.

Before the court of the conqueror

How did all this happen in a country whose "creed" claims that all men are created equal and are endowed with unalienable rights to life, liberty, and the pursuit of happiness? In a nation whose Constitution is supposed to respect that equality and protect those rights? The answers lie in the relation Native Americans were perceived to have to the principles and laws established by those founding documents.

We've already seen earlier in this chapter how Native Americans were excluded from benefiting from "America's founding principles" because they were deemed to exercise no *dominium* or *imperium* over their lands. They had no property rights as they had no property, and they had no civil rights as they had no civil government. That imperialist ideology remained a basis of law and policy in the continuing conquests of Native Americans by the United States. In the Supreme Court case of *Cherokee Nation v. Georgia* (1831), for example, in which the Cherokee were attempting to protect their land rights from the state of Georgia, Justice William Johnson gave the opinion that "Indian tribes" were "nothing more than wandering hordes, held together only by ties of blood and habit, and having neither rules nor government beyond what is required in a savage state." The self-serving nature of this ideology was supported in this instance by factual inaccuracy. Most Cherokee people by the 1830s had in fact adopted European-style property-ownership and farming practices, even to the point of embracing the enslavement of African Americans. They were thus among the so-called Five Civilized Tribes, alongside the Chickasaw, Choctaw, Creek (or Muscoge), and Seminole. Even then, though, they were still "savage." As Barack Obama says, the conquest of Native American peoples "tended to be justified in explicitly racist terms."[17]

Cherokee Nation v. Georgia was one of three Supreme Court cases—known as "The Marshall Trilogy" after the Chief Justice who rendered the majority (or in some instances unanimous) opinions—that attempted to establish the constitutional relationship of the United States and native nations. The events that gave rise to *Cherokee Nation v. Georgia* prove Barack Obama's point that "the Constitution's exquisite machinery would secure the rights of citizens, those deemed members of America's political community. But it provided no protection to those outside the constitutional circle." Those "outside the constitutional circle" included "the black man Dred Scott, who would walk into the Supreme Court a free man and leave a slave," as we saw in Chapter 4. They also included "the Native American whose treaties proved worthless before the court of the conqueror."[18]

Article I, Section 8 of the Constitution states that "Congress shall have the power to regulate Commerce with foreign nations and among the several states, and with the Indian tribes." The first case in the Marshall Trilogy that decided the practical meaning of these words was *Johnson v. M'Intosh* (1823), in which the inheritors of land that a

Euro-American named Thomas Johnson had purchased from the Piankeshaw Indians in the Illinois Territory from 1773 challenged a land patent that William M'Intosh (pronounced Macintosh) obtained from Congress 1818. The unanimous opinion of the Court favored M'Intosh over Johnson's heirs on the grounds that individual Americans had no right to make land transactions with Indians, or vice versa. Chief Justice John Marshall reasoned that Indians possessed "full sovereignty" over territory and were "the absolute owners and proprietors of the soil." He even stated that Indian sovereignty was organic, a natural right, not something granted by others. However, he added, "all the Indian tribes ... held their respective lands and territories each in common ... and there being among them no separate property in the soil." Therefore "their sole method of selling, granting, and conveying their lands ... is for certain chiefs of the tribe selling, to represent the whole tribe in every part of the transaction."[19]

The implication of that of course was that Native Americans didn't exercise *dominium*, even if they had some rights of *imperium*. And so, Marshall also argued, the "doctrine of discovery" extended ultimate sovereignty to the United States. The claim of king James I of England to North American territory had devolved first to the Virginia Company and since then to various others until it finally descended on the US federal government via western land cessions by the states and via the Treaty of Paris of 1783. That government therefore had the "sole right" to treat with Native Americans, and that included "the exclusive right of the United States to extinguish their title, and to grant the soil." In other words, Native American dispossession depended on government not only by practical necessity, but also by law.[20]

And it depended on the federal government, not on the states, as the next two cases in the Marshall Trilogy directed. The plaintiffs in *Cherokee Nation v. Georgia* were attempting to defend themselves from the expansion of Euro-American settlement onto their lands and from their own possible removal from their lands on the grounds that they were a sovereign nation. John Marshall ruled, however, "that an Indian tribe or nation within the United States is not a foreign state in the sense of the constitution," and that "the relationship of the tribes to the United States resembles that of a 'ward to its guardian.'" The Cherokee could not therefore defend themselves from the state of Georgia or from the federal Indian Removal Act of 1830 on the grounds of national sovereignty, though the Court could hear "a proper case with proper parties."

That case came up in the form of *Worcester v. Georgia* (1832), in which Marshall ruled that while the previous "dependent nation" ruling preserved federal government authority over Native Americans, "tribal sovereignty" nonetheless protected native nations from state authority. "The Cherokee nation, then, is a distinct community occupying its own territory in which the laws of Georgia can have no force," Marshall wrote. "The whole intercourse between the United States and this Nation, is, by our constitution and laws, vested in the government of the United States."[21]

In upholding the "right of the United States to extinguish their title, and to grant the soil," and in upholding the "dependent nation" doctrine, the Supreme Court was acting as Barack Obama's "court of the conqueror." On the other hand, in asserting the idea that "the relationship of the tribes to the United States resembles that of a 'ward to its guardian,'" the Court was attempting to offer some protections to those "outside the constitutional circle," even implying in some undefined way that Indians were at least partially inside "the constitutional circle." In defending "tribal sovereignty," furthermore, the Court was attempting to ensure that previous treaties between Native Americans and the United States were something more than "worthless."[22]

But it all came to naught. It is notable that Obama used lower case letters when he wrote of "the court of the conqueror." It may therefore be that, rather than the Supreme Court or any other court of law, Obama had in mind instead the executive "court" of Andrew Jackson—or indeed "King Andrew I" as he was sometimes styled by contemporaries who objected to what they saw as his egregious extensions of presidential power beyond those contained in the Constitution. A supporter of Indian removal and a sponsor and satisfied signer of the Indian Removal Act of 1830, Jackson was supposed to have said in response to *Worcester v. Georgia* that "John Marshall has made his decision; now let him enforce it!" What he certainly said, in a letter to his fellow Tennessee planter and former fellow soldier and business partner John Coffee, was that "the decision of the Supreme Court has fell still born, and they find that they cannot coerce Georgia to yield to its mandate."[23]

Jackson refused to oppose Georgia state policy, and indeed instead assisted it by negotiating the 1835 Treaty of New Echota, under which the Cherokee were supposed to move to Oklahoma. When many refused, his onetime vice president and then successor Martin Van Buren had almost 18,000 of them marched the more than 500 miles of the Trail of Tears, up to a third of them to their deaths along the way. Jackson also committed troops to the Second Seminole War in which almost 1,500 US soldiers and perhaps as many Seminole Indians died. At the end of the conflict almost 4,000 were forcibly marched to "Indian Territory" beyond the Mississippi. As Barack Obama also says, the conquest of Native American peoples was "an exercise in raw power."[24]

Washington thought it knew what was best

The 1871 Indian Appropriations Act marked a conceptual shift in the attitude of the US government toward Native Americans. Yet not enough of one to resolve the preexisting tensions and contradictions between the imperatives of the doctrines of dependent nationhood on the one hand and that of tribal sovereignty on the other. The Act declared that "no Indian nation or tribe" would any longer be recognized "as an independent nation, tribe, or power with whom the United States may contract by treaty," but Indians would instead be subject to federal legislation. That did not, however, extend constitutional rights to Native Americans. We've already seen how the Dawes Act of 1887 not only deprived Native Americans of the right to hold property their own way, but often also deprived them of their right to hold it at all.[25]

Nor did the act grant citizenship, even to those who lived off the reservations and among those recognized as citizens, as John Elk discovered. A Winnebago man born in Indian Territory, Elk renounced his tribal allegiance and moved from Oklahoma to

Omaha, Nebraska. But when he tried to register to vote in April 1880 he was denied the right to do so by election official Charles Wilkins. In the consequent court cases Elk claimed his right to be an American according to the citizenship clause of the Fourteenth Amendment that says: "All persons born or naturalized in the United States, and subject to the jurisdiction thereof, are citizens of the United States and of the State wherein they reside." And in turn he claimed his right to vote according to the Fifteenth Amendment's provision: "The right of citizens of the United States to vote shall not be denied or abridged by the United States or by any state on account of race, color, or previous condition of servitude."[26]

In *Elk v. Wilkins* (1884), however, the Supreme Court decided that "the Indian tribes, being within the territorial limits of the United States, were not, strictly speaking, foreign states, but they were alien nations, distinct political communities, with whom the United States might and habitually did deal as they thought fit, either through treaties made by the President and Senate or through acts of Congress in the ordinary forms of legislation." Therefore "The members of those tribes owed immediate allegiance to their several tribes, and were not part of the people of the United States. They were in a dependent condition, a state of pupilage, resembling that of a ward to his guardian." The 1871 Indian Appropriations Act made no difference as it was "coupled with a provision that the obligation of any treaty already lawfully made is not to be thereby invalidated or impaired, and its utmost possible effect is to require the Indian tribes to be dealt with for the future through the legislative and not through the treaty-making power."[27]

The 1887 Dawes Act did extend an offer of citizenship, however—on condition of acceptance of the Euro-American manner of land ownership. By 1900, 53,000 Native Americans had accepted citizenship on these terms, but the vast majority of the quarter million chose not to be "civilized" in this fashion. The United States granted citizenship to the 100,000 residents of Indian Territory in what is now Oklahoma in 1901, though, and it was later extended to those who fought in World War I. The Indian Citizenship Act finally granted it to all in 1924.

Nevertheless, even then and even now the rights of Native American citizens were and are incomplete, conditioned still by the often conflicting imperatives of national dependence and tribal sovereignty. The Indian Appropriations Act, with its denial of full sovereignty and provision for federal legislation came with significant potential for reducing Native American self-government and cultural autonomy. After that Act's passing in 1871 the Interior Department's Bureau of Indian Affairs sponsored the creation of boarding schools where Indian children would learn the English language, wear English clothes, and generally assimilate to English ways while also being drilled in Christianity. The Dawes Act was also driven by the seemingly undying notion that European traditions of land ownership were an essential element of "civilization." It was thus in the late nineteenth century that the United States entered a phase in its relations with Native Americans that Barack Obama once described as an era when "Washington thought it knew what was best for you."[28]

This new paternalism was in some respects a renewed paternalism. Early imperialists and colonizers expended great energy on converting Native Americans to Christianity and European civilization. The sixteenth-century English imperialist ideologue Richard Hakluyt (the younger), for instance, argued that "the people of America crye unto us their nexte neighboures to come and helpe them, and bringe unto them the gladd tidinges of the gospel," and indeed the legend "Come over and Help Us" appeared on the seal of the Massachusetts Bay Company in 1629, along with a picture of a praying Indian.[29]

Even the Virginia Company charters required settlers to convert Indians to the Christian faith, and the *True and Sincere Declaration of the Purpose and Ends of the Plantation begun in Virginia* (1610) claimed that the "principal and main ends" of the Company "were first to preach and baptize into Christian Religion, and by propagation of that Gospel to recover out of the arms of the Devil, a number of poor and miserable souls, wrapped up unto death, in almost invincible ignorance." Which was neither true nor sincere, but it was nevertheless important to make the pretense.[30]

Not surprisingly perhaps, the Puritans made the most effort in this endeavor. The minister John Eliot translated the Bible into Natick Algonquian language and his missions inspired the Massachusetts General Court to establish "praying towns" where Indians would learn the English language, wear English clothes, and generally adopt English ways before being drilled in the Calvinist version of Protestant Christianity. After the Jamestown attack and Metacom's War, the latter partly caused by Wampanoag resentment of English paternalism, there was greater emphasis on warfare and removal than on assimilation. It was only as the process of continental settlement approached completion in the final quarter of the nineteenth century that a renewed emphasis on assimilation appeared.

The Indian Reorganization Act of 1934 not only abolished the allotment system of the 1887 Dawes Act, but also ended some of the paternalism engendered by the 1871 Indian Appropriations Act. This "Indian New Deal," initiated by Commissioner of Indian Affairs John Collier, who knew more about and had more respect for Indian history and culture than any of his predecessors at the Bureau of Indian Affairs, allowed for more autonomous educational and other institutions, including the extension of the legal jurisdiction of tribal councils. The New Deal wasn't all new, though, as the Grand Coulee Dam on the Columbia River in Washington State, built between 1933 and 1942, flooded thousands of acres of Indian hunting and fishing grounds. Most Native American land is still held in trust by the United States, and so the matter of territorial sovereignty remains unresolved to this day.

As does the matter of Indian self-government. Presidents Dwight David Eisenhower and Harry S. Truman intended on "termination"—the abolition of reservations and the extension to Native Americans of all America's constitutional rights and protections. But that of course would also have eliminated tribal sovereignty and all aspects of Amerindian autonomy. Over 100 tribes were "terminated," and others were subjected to extensions of US federal and even state authority. Congress's Public Law 280 of 1953, for example, extended the criminal and legal authority of Alaska, California, Minnesota, Nebraska, Oregon, and Wisconsin over Indians on Indian lands. Tribal councils meanwhile had and still have no authority over crimes committed by non-Indians on Indian lands, and native nations must still go through the Bureau of Indian Affairs when filing suit against an American state.

The 1960s saw a revival of Native American campaigns for both civil rights and self-determination. The Indian Civil Rights Act of 1968 extended many of the provisions of the US Bill of Rights to Native Americans, which many welcomed, but which others saw as another erosion of Indian autonomy. Federal policy shifted decisively in favor of self-determination, however, with Richard Nixon's "Recommendations for Indian Policy" of July 1970. "It is long past time," the president wrote to Congress, "that the Indian policies of the Federal government began to recognize and build upon the capacities and insights of the Indian people. Both as a matter of Justice and as a matter of enlightened social policy, we must begin to act on the basis of what the Indians themselves have long been telling us. The time has come to break decisively with the past and to create the conditions for a new era in which the Indian future is determined by Indian acts and Indian decisions." It remains an assumption that Native Americans govern themselves except in areas already covered in US treaties and legislation. But the federal government retains legislative prerogative in Indian affairs.[31]

What makes us American

Given the complications of constitutional relations between the United States and Native Americans, how do the continent's original inhabitants fit into Barack Obama's history of "a more perfect union"? Obama's instinctive inclusiveness impels him to portray the history that Native Americans and other Americans share. But his respect for diversity encourages him to acknowledge distinctions, and his recognition of the often hard truths of history leads him to see where the facts don't conform to his normal American historical narrative. Ultimately, though, Barack Obama's American Indian history gets lost in precisely the same place as American Indian policy, in that indefinable space between dependent nationhood and tribal sovereignty.

In some ways Native Americans certainly seem outside the scope of Barack Obama's American history. As he said in his Second Inaugural Address, "What makes us exceptional—what makes us American—is our allegiance to an idea articulated in a declaration made more than two centuries ago: 'We hold these truths to be self-evident, that all men are created equal; that they are endowed by their Creator with certain unalienable rights; that among these are life, liberty, and the pursuit of happiness.'" And in *The Audacity of Hope* he referred to this passage from the Declaration as "our starting point as Americans," as "the substance of our common creed," and as "the foundation of our government." And in his speech on "A More Perfect Union" he said that the Founders "finally made real their declaration of independence at a Philadelphia convention" in a Constitution created by "We the people." And indeed in all these words and many others Barack Obama has implicitly defined his American history as a people's history.[32]

As a people's history, the scope of Barack Obama's American past is admirably inclusive. We saw right at the start of this book that Obama's historical interests extend beyond great men to include "all the faceless, nameless men and women, slaves and soldiers and tailors and butchers, constructing lives for themselves and their children and grandchildren, brick by brick, rail by rail, calloused hand by calloused hand, to fill in the landscape of our collective dreams." We've seen throughout this book how Obama includes these people at every juncture, and not for reasons of "political correctness" but for reasons of historical correctness. As he said himself in his Farewell Address, the rights to life, liberty, and the pursuit of happiness, "while self-evident, have never been self-executing," and so ultimately only "We, the People, through the instrument of our democracy, can form a more perfect union."[33]

Barack Obama's Americans are also not a people defined by religion or race or any kind of lineage, but rather by values that anyone can possess if they so wish, allegiances that anyone can adhere to if they choose to. If they so wish and if they choose to. That same process of choosing of course means that what makes some people American also makes other people Non-American. If the Declaration of Independence was "our starting point as Americans" it was other people's starting point as Non-Americans. Barack Obama's "We the people" may include all the people who subscribe to the rights and responsibilities written into the founding documents, but that kind of people's history excludes those who do not subscribe.

We saw in Chapter 2 how revolutionary Loyalists are silently excluded from Barack Obama's American history precisely because they refused "allegiance to an idea articulated in a declaration made more than two centuries ago." Many of those Loyalists were Native Americans, of course, and indeed many Native Americans were Loyalists because they felt their sovereign interests would be better served by retaining allegiance to the British Empire than they would be at the mercy of an independent and expanding United States. Many other Loyalists were European American or African American, and many of them had other options than remaining in an unwelcoming United States of America. Taking the option of migrating was not necessarily easy for any of them, even for relatively privileged European Americans, much less so for the hitherto enslaved. But few Native Americans naturally enough had any wish to abandon their ancestral homelands. They could not and did not disappear, and they therefore in some senses if not in all remained a part of American history, including Barack Obama's American history, in ways that we've seen already through this chapter so far.[34]

Yet the fact that they did so because of the facts of geography as well as because of acts of allegiance or non-allegiance means that Native Americans remained in a sense a part of the history of American foreign policy rather than becoming part of the history of America itself. At least as far as the logic of Barack Obama's people's history goes. Obama acknowledges, for example, that Native Americans as well as African Americans have often been "outside the constitutional circle," but the different ways in which Obama deals with that in each instance is instructive. It is therefore worth returning to that quote more fully to analyze the issue a little further. "The Constitution's exquisite machinery would secure the rights of citizens, those deemed members of America's political community," as Obama observes. "But it provided no protection to those outside the constitutional circle—the Native American whose treaties proved worthless before the court of the conqueror, or the black man Dred Scott, who would walk into the Supreme Court a free man and leave a slave."[35]

And yet, as we saw in Chapters 4 and 5, Obama contends with the matter of African Americans' relationship with citizenship by defining African Americans as being always of "the people" of the United States if not always a part of the polity of the United States. Obama began "A More Perfect Union" in Philadelphia in 2008, for example, by quoting the opening of the Constitution in the following way: "WE THE PEOPLE, in order to form a more perfect union." Missing out the words "of the United States" with no elliptical indication of the elision possibly acknowledges that enslaved African Americans were not deemed to be entitled to constitutional rights—that they were among "THE PEOPLE" but were not yet citizens of the United States. In "For We Were Born of Change" in Selma in 2015, however, Obama cites the Constitution subtly differently: "We the People … in order to form a more perfect union." Replacing the words "of the United States" with an elliptical indication of the elision possibly acknowledges that newly free African Americans were entitled to constitutional rights thanks to the Thirteenth, Fourteenth, and Fifteenth Amendments, but were nonetheless deprived of those rights by Jim Crow laws that were the subject of the march at Selma in 1965—that they were among "the people" but were not yet full citizens of the United States.[36]

But it's not always the case in Obama's writing that he thinks of Native Americans as similarly of "the people." When he writes, for example, about the "the Native American at the court of the *conqueror*," he implies the foreignness of Native Americans. As he does when he writes of "a *conquest* that, like slavery, contradicted America's founding principles," and that "manifest destiny also meant bloody and violent *conquest*." Similarly, Obama sums up the history of expansion as "a *conquest* that American mythology had always had difficulty fully absorbing but that others countries recognized for what it was— an exercise in raw power." A "conquest" is of course by definition committed over *another* nation, or an *other* people. Indeed when Obama writes of "a bloody and violent conquest— of Native American tribes forcibly removed from their lands and of the Mexican army defending its territory" he implies perhaps a Native American foreignness that's analogous to the unquestionable foreignness of the Mexican army. All of this is reinforced by Obama writing of "*American* soldiers and settlers" who "moved steadily west and southwest."[37]

The history that we share

On the other hand, when Barack Obama writes that historical treatment of Native Americans has "contradicted America's founding principles," and even when he writes that Native Americans have been "outside the constitutional circle," he implies that Native Americans were and are also entitled to liberty and equality under those principles and under that Constitution, or at least that they were more entitled than other kinds of foreigners.[38]

That impression of inclusion is reinforced by Obama's comments when condensing the long history of US mistreatment of Native Americans. Obama, for instance, summarized that past when he said at the first of the Tribal Nations Conferences that he initiated as president: "We know the history that we share. It's a history marked by violence and disease and deprivation. Treaties were violated. Promises were broken. You were told your lands, your religion, your cultures, your languages were not yours to keep. And that's a history that we've got to acknowledge if we are to move forward."[39]

Obama also referred in the same speech and in many others at these annual conferences to Native Americans as "First Americans." And the main message of this speech and subsequent ones was that Native Americans could and should be participants in "the American Dream." For Obama there was no contradiction here, and the next year he reached into the past in order to explain why. In doing so he showed how he sees Native Americans as included in the circle of American values—but without assimilation. "The truth is," he said, in reference to termination and other forms of paternalism,

for a long time, Native Americans were implicitly told that they had a choice to make. By virtue of the longstanding failure to tackle wrenching problems in Indian Country, it seemed as though you had to either abandon your heritage or accept a lesser lot in life; that there was no way to be a successful part of America and a proud Native American.

But we know this is a false choice. To accept it is to believe that we can't and won't do better ... We know that, ultimately, this is not just a matter of legislation, not just a matter of policy. It's a matter of whether we're going to live up to our basic values. It's a matter of upholding an ideal that has always defined who we are as Americans. E pluribus unum. Out of many, one.[40]

As well as these general summaries of the interweaving narratives of Native American and United States history, Barack Obama has also alluded to various particular moments of the "history that we share." One of those moments was the formation of the Iroquois Confederacy and its alliances with others, and he alluded at the same time to the alleged influence of the Iroquois Constitution on the US Constitution. At the Tribal Nations Conference of 2009 Obama spoke of a "new covenant" between the United States and the Indian Nations. "And I think we could learn from the Iroquois Confederacy," he said, "just as our Founding Fathers did when they laid the groundwork for our democracy. The Iroquois called their network of alliances with other tribes and European nations a 'covenant chain.' Each link represented a bond of peace and friendship," he continued, "But that covenant chain didn't sustain itself. It needed constant care, so that it would stay strong. And that's what we're called to do, to keep the covenant between us for this generation and for future generations."[41]

The "covenant chain" is a name for trade agreements and alliances first established between the Iroquois or Haudenosaunee and the Dutch in New Netherland, but renewed with the English during Metacom's War. It did indeed need care, and the Mohawk declared its collapse in 1753 due to everextending British incursions on their land, a factor in the outbreak of and Britain's early defeats in the French and Indian War of 1754–60. Obama's reference to what the Founders learned from "when they laid the groundwork for our democracy" hints at "The Great Law of Peace," a pre-Columbian agreement binding together the (originally) Five Nations of the Iroquois League, which became a more formal Confederacy in response to the threat of European settlement, and which became the Six Nations after the Tuscarora joined it in 1722. Originally an oral agreement, it was later written as symbols on Wampum belts and later still translated into English, and as well as being a historical narrative it contained 117 articles comprising a constitution.

Some historians have claimed that the decentralized structure of the Iroquois Confederacy influenced United States federalism, and that the representative and deliberative nature of the Confederacy's Grand Council influenced the US system of democracy and of constitutional checks and balances. As the leading constitutional scholar Jack Rakove has pointed out, however, there are significant institutional and procedural differences between the two constitutions, and there is no evidence of Iroquois influence in the voluminous documentation appertaining to the drafting and ratifying of the US Constitution, while there is an abundance of evidence that the Founders were influenced by a mixture of European theory and American experience. And indeed on the other occasions that Obama has written or spoken about the US Constitution he has placed it in these European American contexts. Even on this occasion his reference to Iroquois influence is only ambiguously hinting, perhaps nothing more than a diplomatic acknowledgment of the existence of the idea.[42]

Barack Obama hasn't confined his comments on Native American history to the Tribal conferences and *The Audacity of Hope*. Indeed in his speech marking the semicentennial of the 1965 Voting Rights March in Selma, Alabama, Obama included Native Americans. In a key passage of "For We Were Born of Change," Obama reflected on what he sees as the fundamental unity of American identity. He started the passage by asking his audience to "Look at our history." "We are Lewis and Clark and Sacajawea," he said next, "pioneers who braved the unfamiliar, followed by a stampede of farmers and miners, and entrepreneurs and hucksters. That's our spirit. That's who we are." A few lines later he said, "We're the ranch hands and cowboys who opened up the West, and countless laborers who laid rail, and raised skyscrapers, and organized for workers' rights." And shortly after that: "We're the fresh-faced GIs who fought to liberate a continent. And we're the Tuskegee Airmen, and the Navajo code-talkers, and the Japanese Americans who fought for this country even as their own liberty had been denied."[43]

Sacajawea was a Lemhi Shoshone Indian born in May 1788 who at age twelve was kidnapped by Hidatsa Indians. The next year she became the second wife of a Quebecois trapper named Toussaint Charbonneau, by whom she was pregnant when Meriwether Lewis and William Clark arrived and stayed over in the Hidatsa country in the winter of 1804–05. In February 1805 she gave birth to a son, Jean-Baptiste Charbonneau, and then in April she joined the Corps of Discovery as a guide and interpreter for the rest of its westward journey, saving the expedition's leaders' journals as they crossed what they gratefully named the Sacagawea River. After the expedition she returned to live among the Hidatsa for three years before accepting William Clark's invitation to live in St. Louis, where she died of an unknown illness in 1812. As well as being memorialized by the Shoshone and Hidatsa people and in various northwestern US place names, Sacajawea also became an official icon of the National Woman Suffrage Association in the early twentieth century. Another recognition of her status as a powerful woman came in 1977 with her induction into the National Cowgirl Hall of Fame in Fort Worth, Texas. And in 2001 President Bill Clinton made her an Honorary Sergeant of the United States Army.[44]

For Barack Obama, Sacajawea was one of America's "pioneers," as of course were Lewis and Clark, as were the "farmers and miners, and entrepreneurs and hucksters" who followed them. As of course were "the ranch hands and cowboys who opened up the West" and the "countless laborers" who laid the rails that crisscrossed the continent by the end of the century that began with Sacajawea's endeavors. In other words, Obama integrates her into the history of the United States, despite the phenomena he cites being so destructive of Native American civilization. Through it all and despite it all, Obama includes Native Americans as among the American people, among the "we" who are "born of change."[45]

Obama does the same of course with the "Navajo code-talkers," whose language proved impenetrable to the Axis Powers in World War II. They were thus listed along with "the fresh-faced GIs who fought to liberate a continent" and "the Tuskegee Airmen," the African American pilots and crews of the 332nd Fighter Group and 477th Bombardment Group of the United States Air Force who also served in World War II. And with the "Japanese-Americans who fought for this country even as their own liberty had been denied" by the un-Constitutional abomination of internment during that conflict.[46]

Some 25,000 Native Americans served in World War II, as many others have in other conflicts. Obama honored them specifically at the Tribal Nations Conference of November 2013, falling as it did that year in the week of Veterans' Day. "We draw strength," the president said, "from the Navajo Code Talkers whose skill helped win the Second World War. We draw strength from Woodrow Wilson Keeble, who many years after his death was finally awarded the Medal of Honor for his heroism in the Korean War. We draw strength from ... Lori Piestewa, who during the Iraq war was the first known Native American woman to give her life in combat for the United States. And we draw strength from all our men and women in uniform today." And he included "two pilots I rely on when I step onto Marine One—Major Paul Bisulca, from the Penobscot Nation, and Major Eli Jones, of the Shoshone Bannock" who "are carrying me around, keeping me safe."[47]

Barack Obama thus integrates Native Americans into his American history. Yet this inclusively perhaps inevitably sits slightly awkwardly alongside his respect for diversity, considering how ambiguous and ambivalent Native Americans' relations are with the United States. At those Tribal Nations Conferences Obama also accepted the legal, political, cultural, and historical facts of Native-American nationhood, however vaguely defined and ever-changing that nationhood has been. Hence he spoke in varying years of a "relationship between our nations," of "our unique nation-to-nation relationship," and of "a true nation-to-nation relationship with all of you."[48]

And when Obama writes of Native American history in *The Audacity of Hope*, he does so in chapter eight, entitled "The World Beyond Our Borders," the one about foreign policy.

A beacon of freedom and opportunity

Barack Obama readily acknowledges the contradictions in America's relations with other nations when he says that its "foreign policy has always been a jumble of warring impulses." As with policy toward Native Americans, there has been universalism in its approach and there has been relativism. Sometimes also there has been isolationism, other times excessive interventionism. Sometimes idealism, other times realism, still other times even cynicism. Sometimes it's been driven by enlightened self-interest, other times by economic self-interest. Sometimes right, other times might. And sometimes it's been good, other times bad. Obama's unsurprisingly ambivalent final verdict, then, is that "our record is mixed."[49]

Barack Obama's history of American foreign policy begins with the point that in the early American republic "a policy of isolationism often prevailed." Obama ascribes that isolationism to "a wariness of foreign intrigues that befitted a nation just emerging from a war of independence." And to that effect in *The Audacity of Hope* he quotes George Washington's Farewell Address: "Why," the first president asked, "by interweaving our destiny with that of any part of Europe, entangle our peace and prosperity in the toils of European ambition, rivalship, interest, humor or caprice?" And Obama quotes Washington's words again with regard to "America's 'detached and distant situation,' a geographic separation that would permit the new nation to 'defy material injury from external annoyance.'"[50]

Obama is ambivalent about this early isolationism. While "America's revolutionary origins and republican form of government might" have made Americans "sympathetic toward those seeking freedom elsewhere," he wrote, "America's early leaders cautioned against idealistic attempts to export our way of life." And Obama further quoted a later president, John Quincy Adams (1825–29), to the same effect: "America should not go 'abroad in search of monsters to destroy' nor 'become the dictatress of the world.'" And he characterized the attitude of Americans before the 1890s as a belief that America "protected by an ocean and with the bounty of a continent" and so "Providence had charged America with the task of making a new world, not reforming the old."[51]

Yet the United States did experience unhappy encounters with other nations long before it became a world power, as the nation never was entirely disconnected from the rest of the world, either geographically or politically. To begin with, the newly independent United States could not remove British troops from its northwest territories, or assert its fishing rights off British Canada, or its trading rights in the British Caribbean, or pay off its prerevolutionary debts to overseas merchants or nations, or maintain international confidence in its economy. All these factors played a large part in inspiring Americans to replace the Articles of Confederation with the Constitution and thereby make a stronger nation that could deal effectively with external exigencies as well as create a more perfect union within its own borders.

America's revolutionary origins and republican form of government, furthermore, made many sympathize with the French Revolution, and this sympathy was a defining characteristic of the Democratic-Republican Party. The Federalist Party's equally defining antipathy to it on the other hand inspired George Washington to announce the nation's neutrality, which actually amounted to annulling the French alliance that had helped America win its independence, and was therefore in fact an act of hostility. John Adams indeed became embroiled in an undeclared "Quasi-War" with France between 1798 and 1800.

And the United States was always a commercial nation, born as it was from an empire of trade, and so encounters on the seas were almost inevitable. One set of encounters comprised the Barbary Wars of 1801 to 1805 and of 1815, America's first hostilities with what we now call the "Muslim World." British impressment of American sailors into the Royal Navy and its other assaults on American sovereignty, plus the French Revolutionary and Napoleonic wars, eventually embroiled the United States in a series of trade boycotts from 1808 and finally the War of 1812, which, notwithstanding its name, officially ended with the Treaty of Ghent in 1814 but actually ended with Andrew Jackson's victory at the Battle of New Orleans in January 1815. After that, though, international affairs did allow greater scope for isolationism, and Barack Obama seems more sympathetic to it, at least in this early-middling era. He even sees a certain idealism in American isolationism. The country could, as Obama describes the attitude of the time, "best serve the cause of freedom by concentrating on its own development, becoming a beacon of hope for other nations and people around the globe."[52]

Barack Obama sees America as a beacon still, and he sees its exemplary aspects as one of its most important and influential international powers. As he said when introducing himself to America at the Democratic National Convention in Boston in 2004, and as he has told the same story in a similar way on many other occasions, "Through hard work and perseverance my father got a scholarship to study in a magical place, America, that shone as a beacon of freedom and opportunity to so many who had come before."[53]

And not only has America been a land of freedom and opportunity for immigrants, temporary and permanent, but also in Obama's view an inspiration for movements for liberty and opportunity elsewhere. In "For We Were Born of Change," for example, Obama argued that the willingness and ability of Americans to transform things for the better is "what makes us unique. That's what cements our reputation as a beacon of opportunity." And he gave examples:

Young people behind the Iron Curtain would see Selma and eventually tear down that wall. Young people in Soweto would hear Bobby Kennedy talk about ripples of hope and eventually banish the scourge of apartheid. Young people in Burma went to prison rather than submit to military rule. They saw what John Lewis had done. From the streets of Tunis to the Maidan in Ukraine, this generation of young people can draw strength from this place, where the powerless could change the world's greatest power and push their leaders to expand the boundaries of freedom.

They saw that idea made real right here in Selma, Alabama. They saw that idea manifest itself here in America.[54]

And yet, returning more specifically to the early republic's foreign affairs, as Obama hints in his aforementioned comments on the Louisiana Purchase and Thomas Jefferson's belief in "the inevitability of expansion beyond the boundaries of the original thirteen states," and on the Monroe Doctrine's "warning to European powers to keep out of the Western Hemisphere," America was sooner or later bound to encounter other powers besides native nations. The aforementioned war against Mexico was one instance, and, although the contemporaneous Oregon Treaty finally fixed the northern border of the Louisiana Purchase Territory, an encounter with Britain over the Canadian border might well instead have been another.[55]

But if US expansion on an international continent and its trade with nations overseas means it was never as geographically or as politically isolated as some imagined it to be, "the end of the Civil War and the consolidation of what's now the continental United States," as Obama says, nevertheless changed things. As did the massive industrialization we saw in the last chapter. "Intent on expanding markets for its goods, securing raw materials for its industry, and keeping sea lanes open for its commerce," Obama explains, "the nation turned its attention overseas."[56]

The world's dominant power

Barack Obama has severe doubts about America's first phase of international interventionism from the 1890s, and with the isolationism that prevailed in the 1920s and 1930s, and with various aspect of American foreign policy from Vietnam to Iraq. But he does see a brief moment of hope after World War I and a kind of Golden Age after World War II when America might have led and finally did lead in the making of a more stable international order, a more perfect global union.

After the completion of the continental conquest, and with greater need than ever to orient the world to its economic interests, the United States embarked on unprecedented overseas intervention. Obama mentions the annexation of Hawaii, the Spanish American War that gave the United States control of Puerto Rico, Guam, and the Philippines, all from 1898, and refers to the US presence in the latter from 1899 to 1902 as "an occupation that would involve thousands of US troops crushing a Philippine independence movement." Quite the opposite, then, of the spirit of nation born of an independence movement. Obama observes that "America would never pursue the systematic colonization practiced by European nations, but it shed all inhibitions about meddling in the affairs of countries it deemed strategically important," citing Theodore Roosevelt's "corollary to the Monroe Doctrine" that the United States "would intervene in any Latin American or Caribbean country whose government it deemed not to

America's liking." From the 1890s to 1917, then, American foreign policy was "barely distinguishable from those of the other great powers, driven" as it was "by realpolitik and commercial interests."[57]

Barack Obama is no isolationist, however, at least not as regards the twentieth century and since. In *The Audacity of Hope* he quotes Theodore Roosevelt's words, apparently approvingly this time, that " 'The United States of America has not the option as to whether it will or it will not play a great part in the world. It must play a great part. All that it can decide is whether it will play that part well or badly.' " And Obama is clear on the different ways in which the United States has played its part both well and badly.[58]

Despite America's new interests and interventions from the 1890s, a residual isolationism remained influential, and Woodrow Wilson initially avoided involvement in World War I, at least "until the repeated sinking of American vessels by German U-boats and the imminent collapse of the European continent made neutrality untenable." The United States emerged from that war, furthermore, "as the world's dominant power," although Wilson "now understood" that America's interests depended as never before on "peace and prosperity in faraway lands," rather than on assertions of American military might. Wilson thus attempted "to reinterpret the idea of America's manifest destiny" (in Obama's words) by making "the world safe for democracy" (in Wilson's words). Hence the president's attempts "to encourage the self determination of all peoples and provide the world a legal framework that could help avoid future conflicts" through a League of Nations and a new set of international laws and courts. As Obama said, citing Wilson's idea of a spirit of democracy, "It is surely the manifest destiny of the United States to lead in the attempt to make this spirit prevail."[59]

However, some at home felt that such laws represented "an encroachment on American sovereignty" and a "foolish constraint on America's ability to impose its will around the world." And so "traditional isolationists in both parties" and "Wilson's stubborn unwillingness to compromise" meant that the United States ultimately refused to join the League of Nations and the World Court, and then it reduced its own armed forces, just in time for when it would need them more than ever before. Obama asserts a Churchillian disdain for isolationism at this point, describing the United States in the 1930s as "standing idly by as Italy, Japan, and Nazi Germany built up their military machines." The Senate in particular was guilty of failing to aid "countries invaded by the Axis powers" and of "repeatedly ignoring" President Franklin Roosevelt's "appeals as Hitler's armies marched across Europe." Obama indeed quotes FDR's point that there is "no such thing as security for any nation—or any individual—in a world ruled by the principles of gangsterism." And the attack on Pearl Harbor proved for Obama that isolationists made a "terrible mistake."[60]

"In the aftermath of World War II," though, as Barack Obama writes, "the United States would have a chance to apply these lessons to its foreign policy." And for quite a while it did, despite certain difficulties. Obama describes three choices the United States faced at that juncture. From the right came advocates of a "unilateral foreign policy" proposing "an immediate invasion of the Soviet Union" to "disable the emerging communist threat." From the left, even with isolationism "thoroughly discredited," came a view that "downplayed Soviet aggression" and that in light of "Soviet losses and the country's critical role in the Allied victory, Stalin should be accommodated."[61]

As Obama says, though, "America took neither path," but followed a third and middle way instead, one in which "President Truman, Dean Acheson, George Marshall, and George Kennan" married "Wilson's idealism to hard-headed realism," that entailed "an acceptance of America's power" and "a humility regarding America's ability to control events around the world." This was also wise, in Obama's view, "because the battle against communism was also a battle of ideas, a test of what system might best serve the hopes and dreams of billions of people around the world." America therefore needed "allies that shared the ideals of freedom, democracy, and the rule of law, and that saw themselves as having a stake in a market-based economic system." Alliances of that kind, Obama pointedly adds, "entered into freely and maintained by mutual consent, would be more lasting—and stir less resentment—than any collection of vassal states American imperialism might secure." Additionally, US commitment to "international institutions and ... norms" would signal America's "willingness to show restraint in the exercise of its power;" giving the country credit to spare for whenever it did need to use force.[62]

Obama then cites US "containment with respect to communist expansion," alliances with NATO and Japan, and commitment to the United Nations as the bases of its postwar diplomatic policy. A wider security policy as well as US economic interest were further well-served by the Marshall Plan that reconstructed Europe's "war-shattered economies," while the Bretton Woods agreement, the General Agreement on Tariffs and Trade, the International Monetary Fund, and the World Bank served as guardians of global economic stability. Obama describes this world order in almost triumphalist terms. Its results were, he said, "a successful outcome to the Cold War, an avoidance of nuclear catastrophe, the effective end of conflict between the world's great military powers, and an era of unprecedented economic growth at home and abroad." All this was "perhaps the Greatest Generation's greatest gift to us after the victory over fascism."[63]

Yet Obama spends longer writing about the political principles than he does about the historical details of the era, perhaps because his account of foreign policy is more politically and didactically driven than the rest of his historical analyses. What it all leads up to is the point where it all went wrong, how the system "could fall victim to" what he calls "the distortions of politics, the sins of hubris, the corrupting effects of fear."[64]

The distortions of politics, the sins of hubris, the corrupting effects of fear

The Soviet threat and the expansion of communism in China and North Korea led American policy makers, Barack Obama observes, to see all international developments "through the lens of the Cold War." And so "For decades" America tolerated and even aided "thieves like [Congolese dictator] Mobutu [Sese Seko], thugs like [Panamanian dictator Manuel] Noriega, so long as they opposed communism." And on occasion "US covert operations would engineer the removal of democratically elected leaders in countries like Iran—with seismic repercussions that haunt us to this day." The enormity of American firepower also allowed "the 'iron triangle' of the Pentagon, defense contractors, and congressmen with large defense expenditures in their districts" to amass "great power in shaping US foreign policy," leading them too to see "the world through a military lens rather than a diplomatic one."[65]

Also, and in Obama's view "Most important," was the breakdown of "a degree of domestic consensus surrounding foreign policy" where party politics "usually ended at the water's edge" and foreign policy officials "were expected to make decisions based on facts and sound judgment, not ideology or electioneering." Obama cites the most obvious example of this phenomenon when he says that "McCarthyism destroyed careers and crushed dissent," but he doesn't exonerate Democrats. "Kennedy would blame Republicans for a 'missile gap' that didn't exist on his way to beating Nixon," Obama observes, although not without noting that Nixon "himself had made a career of Red-baiting his opponents." Indeed "Presidents Eisenhower, Kennedy, and Johnson would all find their judgment clouded by fear that they would be tagged as 'soft on communism.'" And, furthermore, "Cold War techniques of secrecy, snooping, and misinformation ... became tools of domestic politics, a means to harass critics, build support for questionable policies, or cover up blunders." Obama's assessment of all this is as measured yet as hard-hitting as it ought to be: "The very ideals that we had promised to export overseas," he writes, "were being betrayed at home."[66]

And all this, Obama writes, "came to a head in Vietnam." Barack Obama notes the negative effects of that war on "those who fought," on the nation's armed forces, and on American "credibility and prestige abroad." But, he says, "perhaps the biggest casualty of that war was the bond of trust between the American people and their government—and between Americans themselves." Terrible images of horrific realities in Vietnam undermined public confidence in the competence and truthfulness of politicians. An increasingly cynical left, Obama wrote, complained of "American arrogance, jingoism, racism, capitalism, and imperialism." An increasingly cynical right blamed the loss of the war and American prestige on "the protesters, the hippies, Jane Fonda, the Ivy League intellectuals and liberal media who denigrated patriotism, embraced a relativistic worldview, and undermined American resolve to confront godless communism." Many Americans, Obama rightly points out, "remained somewhere in the middle," but "the caricatures were what shaped public impressions during election time." And so it was in this "era of division rather than an era of consensus—that most Americans alive today formed whatever views they may have on foreign policy."[67]

Barack Obama refers at this point to the "tactically brilliant" Richard Nixon and Henry Kissinger, but also calls their policies at home and in Cambodia "morally rudderless" (even without at this point mentioning the CIA-assisted overthrow of the democratically elected government of Salvador Allende in favor of military dictator Augusto Pinochet in Chile in 1973). The great promise of Jimmy Carter, "who—with his emphasis on human rights—seemed prepared to once again align moral concerns with a strong defense," was alas lost to oil shortages, the Iranian hostage crisis, and the Soviet invasion of Afghanistan.[68]

Ronald Reagan emerged victorious from all this chaos, and Obama's judgement of him is ambivalent, perhaps best described as ultimately grudgingly respectful. Obama writes of Reagan's "clarity about communism" being "matched by his blindness regarding other sources of misery in the world." He also recalls his own younger days of bemoaning "Reagan's policies toward the Third World: his administration's support for the apartheid regime of South Africa, the funding of El Salvador's death squads, the invasion of tiny, hapless Grenada," and of finding Star Wars "ill conceived." And "the chasm between Reagan's soaring rhetoric and the tawdry Iran-Contra deal," Obama recalls, "left me speechless." On the other hand, Obama agreed with "aspects of Reagan's worldview," including his insistence on condemning "oppression behind the Iron Curtain." And, he says, "when the Berlin Wall came tumbling down, I had to give the old man his due, even if I never gave him my vote."[69]

On the other hand, in a speech in Tiergarten during his first presidential campaign, Obama folded Reagan's famous imprecation to Mikael Gorbachev into the actions of Berliners and credited them with all that followed. "When you, the German people, tore down that wall," he said, "walls came tumbling down all around the world. From Kiev to Cape Town, prison camps were closed, and the doors of democracy were opened." And in his 2015 speech commemorating the great march against disfranchisement in Alabama, Obama credited Reagan's words and the actions of Germans and other peoples to the inspiration of the American Civil Rights Movement. "Young people behind the Iron Curtain," he said, "would see Selma and eventually tear down that wall."[70]

As Obama says, the fall of Soviet and eastern European communism, added to Nixon's earlier rapprochement with China, rendered Reaganism obsolete, and Obama is generous in asserting that "George H. W. Bush's return to a more traditional, 'realist' foreign policy would result in a steady management of the Soviet Union's dissolution and an able handling of the first Gulf War," before Bush I's presidency was undone by an unsteady economy. Bill Clinton gets due recognition for helping to "end long-festering conflicts in the Balkans and Northern Ireland and advance democratization in Eastern Europe, Latin America, Africa, and the former Soviet Union." Clinton also "understood"— that specially selected verb of validation in the Obamian lexicon—"that globalization involved not only new economic challenges but also new security challenges." Many Americans, however, did not understand this, and to them "foreign policy in the nineties lacked any overarching theme or grand imperatives." Until September 11, 2001, when "Americans felt their world turned upside down."[71]

Their world turned upside down

Americans had hitherto felt safe at home, at least from foreign enemies if not always from each other, but the 9/11 attacks meant that "chaos had come to our doorstep." After this, Barack Obama wrote, the United States "would have to act differently, understand the world differently." The administration of the day, alas, still saw the world in Cold War terms, through a military lens rather than a diplomatic one.[72]

Certainly, the Bush II administration began its response in a context of internal support and international sympathy. Obama mentions that senators voted 98–0 and congressmen and congresswomen 420–1 to allow the president to "use all necessary and appropriate force against those nations, organizations or persons" responsible for the attacks, and that citizens applied to join the armed forces and the CIA in record numbers. He mentions too the memorable *Le Monde* headline, "Nous sommes tous Américains," and the less well-remembered but equally notable prayers for the terrorists' victims in Middle-Eastern mosques. Also, Obama observes, NATO invoked its charter's Article 5, for the first time in its forty-two-year history, to the effect that "an attack on one of its members 'shall be considered an attack against them all.'" And he even concedes that the administration made a "good start" in Afghanistan, quickly expelling the Taliban from Kabul and killing or capturing numerous Al Qaeda operatives, although he notes that we learned later that the administration may have missed an opportunity to trap Osama bin Laden at Tora Bora. Otherwise, the response was "steady, measured, and accomplished with minimal casualties."[73]

However, a necessary new foreign policy that would "adapt our military planning, intelligence operations, and homeland defenses to the threat of terrorist networks" and also "build a new international consensus around the challenges of transnational threats" never materialized. Instead, as Obama puts it, all the Bush administration came up with was "an assortment of outdated policies from eras gone by, dusted off, slapped together, and with new labels affixed. Reagan's 'Evil Empire' was now 'the Axis of Evil.' Theodore Roosevelt's version of the Monroe Doctrine—the notion that we could pre-emptively remove governments not to our liking—was now the Bush Doctrine, only extended beyond the Western Hemisphere to span the globe." Indeed, "manifest destiny was back in fashion; all that was needed, according to Bush, was American firepower, American resolve, and a 'coalition of the willing.'" And as well as the "distortion of politics" and the "sins of hubris," the Cold War's "corrupting effects of fear" made an unwelcome return as well, as "those who questioned the Administration's rationale for" the 2003 invasion of Iraq "were accused of being 'soft on terrorism' or 'un-American.'"[74]

Yet for a while it all appeared to work. The Iraq invasion initially seemed successful, and the president received sufficient popular and political support to be reelected easily in 2004. In the longer term, however, the exposure of the lies told in support of the war, the long-term commitment required to suppress anarchy in Iraq, and the unleashing of other and horrific forces elsewhere in the Middle East once again undermined the trust of Americans in their government and the trust of the world in America.

Barack Obama opposed the Iraq war at the time, presciently predicting that even a successful invasion "will require a US occupation of undetermined length, at undetermined cost, with undetermined consequences." The precise predictions he did make were that an invasion "without a clear rationale and without strong international support will only fan the flames of the Middle East ... and strengthen the recruitment arm of al Qaeda." Saddam Hussein, however "brutal" and "ruthless" he was, Obama said, "poses no imminent and direct threat to the United States or his neighbors"—comments serving as a critique of the Bush Doctrine of Pre-emptive War in favor of a doctrine of restraint and self-defense. "Let's fight" instead, Obama said, "to make sure our so-called allies in the Middle East, the Saudis and the Egyptians, stop oppressing their own people, and suppressing dissent, and tolerating corruption and inequality, and mismanaging their economies so that their youth grow up without education, without prospects, without hope, the ready recruits of terror cells."[75]

A part of America's story

In the first year of his own presidency, Barack Obama addressed American-Middle East relations at the University of Cairo. In a speech entitled and promising "A New Beginning," he broached "the issue of Iraq" directly, once again saying that action in Afghanistan was justifiable self-defense, but the "war of choice" in Iraq and events since had "reminded America of the need to use diplomacy and build international consensus to resolve our problems whenever possible." Reminded because, he added, "we can recall the words of Thomas Jefferson, who said: 'I hope that our wisdom will grow with our power, and teach us that the less we use our power the greater it will be.'" Obama also placed recent conflict in longer context. "The relationship between Islam and the West includes centuries of co-existence and cooperation," he said, "but also conflict and religious wars. More recently, tension has been fed by colonialism that denied rights and opportunities to many Muslims, and a Cold War in which Muslim-majority countries were too often treated as proxies without regard to their own aspirations."[76]

Obama also addressed the issue of force more generally, and in doing so he simultaneously reiterated his universalist values and the practical limits of their applicability, a foreign affairs analogue perhaps to the "philosophical pragmatism" discerned in Obama by historian and political scientist James T. Kloppenberg. "I know there has been controversy about the promotion of democracy in recent years," Obama said, "So let me be clear: no system of government can or should be imposed upon one nation by any other." However, he continued, "That does not lessen my commitment ... to governments that reflect the will of the people. Each nation gives life to this principle in its own way, grounded in the traditions of its own people. America does not presume to know what is best for everyone ... But," he added, "I do have an unyielding belief that all people yearn for certain things: the ability to speak your mind and have a say in how you are governed; confidence in the rule of law and the equal administration of justice; government that is transparent and doesn't steal from the people; the freedom to live as you choose." And "Those," he argued, "are not just American ideas, they are human rights, and that is why we will support them everywhere."[77]

And so Obama grounded this new beginning, as he tried to ground US relations with Native Americans, on shared values and in a shared history that for him represent the best of the past. "Islam has always been a part of America's story," he said. "The first nation to recognize my country was Morocco," and "In signing the Treaty of Tripoli in 1796, our second President John Adams wrote, 'The United States has in itself no character of enmity against the laws, religion or tranquility of Muslims.' " Obama added also that "since our founding, American Muslims have enriched the United States. They have fought in our wars, served in government, stood for civil rights, started businesses, taught at our Universities, excelled in our sports arenas, won Nobel Prizes, built our tallest building, and," in a reference to Muhammad Ali, "lit the Olympic Torch." And, in a reference to Keith Ellison's 2008 election to the House of Representatives, Obama added that "when the first Muslim-American was recently elected to Congress, he took the oath to defend our Constitution using the same Holy Koran that one of our Founding Fathers—Thomas Jefferson—kept in his personal library."[78]

"So let there be no doubt," Obama said, "Islam is a part of America. And I believe that America holds within her the truth that regardless of race, religion, or station in life, all of us share common aspirations—to live in peace and security; to get an education and to work with dignity; to love our families, our communities, and our God. These things we share. This is the hope of all humanity."[79]

And so, just as some Americans and other westerners need to let go of stereotypes of Muslims, so some Muslims, Obama said, must let go of an image of America as "a self-interested empire." Rather, he argued, "The United States has been one of the greatest sources of progress that the world has ever known. We were born out of revolution against an empire." And, returning to his most repeated themes, "We were founded upon the ideal that all are created equal, and we have shed blood and struggled for centuries to give meaning to those words—within our borders, and around the world. We are shaped by every culture, drawn from every end of the Earth, and dedicated to a simple concept: *E pluribus unum*: 'Out of many, one.' " Obama thus once again walked those very fine lines between idealism and pragmatism, and between universalism and particularism, that also characterize his thoughts and words about Native Americans.[80]

A few months after Cairo, Barack Obama went to Oslo to accept what he admitted was the slightly surprising award of his Nobel Peace Prize. In his speech on that occasion—"A Just and Lasting Peace"—Obama reiterated his belief in the right to self-defense but also in restraint under the rule of law. He described a time when international relations were similar to a State of Nature. "War, in one form or another," he said, "appeared with the first man. At the dawn of history, its morality was not questioned; it was simply a fact, like drought or disease—the manner in which tribes and then civilizations sought power and settled their differences." In time, though, "the concept of a 'just war' emerged, suggesting that war is justified only when certain conditions were met: if it is waged as a last resort or in self-defense; if the force used is proportional; and if, whenever possible, civilians are spared from violence."[81]

And it is through the implementation and gradual improvement of these laws that, for Obama, a more perfect world has slowly emerged. A "quarter century after the United States Senate rejected the League of Nations—an idea for which Woodrow

Wilson received this prize—" as Obama noted, "America led the world in constructing an architecture to keep the peace: a Marshall Plan and a United Nations, mechanisms to govern the waging of war, treaties to protect human rights, prevent genocide, restrict the most dangerous weapons." And "Yes," he conceded, "terrible wars have been fought, and atrocities committed. But there has been no Third World War. The Cold War ended with jubilant crowds dismantling a wall. Commerce has stitched much of the world together. Billions have been lifted from poverty. The ideals of liberty and self-determination, equality and the rule of law have haltingly advanced."[82]

A useful metaphor

Barack Obama began his chapter on "The World Beyond Our Borders" in *The Audacity of Hope* with personal, political, and historical reflections on a nation he has long known well: Indonesia. At the end of just under ten pages, Obama says, with the methodological scrupulousness of any academic, "it's dangerous to extrapolate from the experiences of a single country. In its history, geography, culture, and conflicts, each nation is unique." And yet Indonesia is for him a useful way to introduce his thoughts on the wider world because of its typicality. So as Obama also says, this time with the generalizing compulsiveness of any academic, "And yet in many ways Indonesia serves as a useful metaphor for the world beyond our borders—a world in which globalization and sectarianism, poverty and plenty, modernity and antiquity constantly collide."[83]

Indonesia thus "provides a handy record of US foreign policy over the past fifty years. In broad outline at least," Obama notes,

> it's all there: our role in liberating former colonies and creating international institutions to help manage the post–World War II order; our tendency to view nations and conflicts through the prism of the Cold War; our tireless promotion of American-style capitalism and multinational corporations; the tolerance and occasional encouragement of tyranny, corruption, and environmental degradation when it served our interests; our optimism once the Cold War ended that Big Macs and the Internet would lead to the end of historical conflicts; the growing economic power of Asia and the growing resentment of the United States as the world's sole superpower; the realization that in the short term, at least, democratization might lay bare, rather than alleviate, ethnic hatreds and religious divisions—and that the wonders of globalization might also facilitate economic volatility, the spread of pandemics, and terrorism.[84]

Barack Obama actually commences his essay on Indonesia in the manner of a travel-writer, beginning with a brief account of the geography, demography, and economy of Indonesia today. But he soon becomes a storyteller, noting next that after being ruled "by succession of sultanates and often-splintering kingdoms for most of its history, the archipelago became a Dutch colony ... in the 1600s, a status that would last for more than three centuries." After Japanese occupation during World War II, the Dutch returned, but, after a four-year war, Indonesia achieved its independence. The United States, playing *its role in liberating former colonies*, helped by threatening the Netherlands with an end to its Marshall Plan funding. At that point, Barack Obama the historical analyst takes over, saying of postindependence Indonesians that "for the past sixty years the fate of their nation has been directly tied to US foreign policy."[85]

The United States, *concerned with the spread of communism under the banner of anticolonialism*, soon found itself disappointed with first independent President Sukarno's equidistance from Washington and Moscow, and then with his upping "the anti-Western rhetoric, nationalizing key industries, rejecting US aid, and strengthening ties with the Soviets and China." Viewing *nations and conflicts through the prism of the Cold War*, the CIA began covertly supporting Indonesian insurrectionaries, including General Suharto, whose purges from 1965 and coup of 1967 resulted in the deaths of between 500,000 and a million people, with another 750,000 others imprisoned or exiled. Violent repression continued "throughout the seventies and eighties," and did so "with the knowledge, if not outright approval, of US administrations."[86]

America's *tolerance and occasional encouragement of tyranny, corruption, and environmental degradation* continued as "The US military conducted joint exercises with the Indonesian military and training programs for its officers." And America's *tireless promotion of American-style capitalism and multinational corporations* continued as "President Suharto turned to a cadre of American economists to design Indonesia's development plan, based on free-market principles and foreign investment." That meant collusion by American public servants and private individuals in funneling money from the US Agency for International Development and the World Bank into a country rife corruption from top to bottom. Even so, "As far as the United States was concerned, Indonesia had become a model of stability, a reliable supplier of raw materials and importer of Western goods, a stalwart ally and bulwark against communism." That resulted in Indonesia becoming an economic "Asian Tiger," complete with "Nike," "Gap," "surfers and rock stars," "five-star hotels, Internet connections," and "Kentucky Fried Chicken." But also "slums, smog, and nightmare traffic."[87]

And in turn American *optimism once the Cold War ended that Big Macs and the internet would lead to the end of historical conflicts* led to pressure on "Indonesia to curb its human rights abuses, especially with the ending of military aid after the 1992 massacres in East Timor and the rise of a democratic movement in the country. A catastrophic financial crash in 1997 and subsequent austerity measures mandated by "the Western-dominated International Monetary Fund" resulted in protests that finally forced Suharto's resignation and the nation's first free elections the following year.[88]

All that, however, has resulted in a growing *resentment of the United States as the world's sole superpower* and the aggravation rather than the alleviation of *ethnic hatreds and religious divisions*. The end of the twentieth century and beginning of the present one has seen an unprecedented spread of "Anti-American sentiment" in Indonesia and "the growth of militant, fundamentalist Islam in the country," in place of "a tolerant, almost syncretic brand of the faith, infused with the Buddhist, Hindu, and animist traditions of earlier periods" that had previously prevailed.[89]

We might live as Indonesians lived

Barack Obama, furthermore, interweaves some of his own story into this history of Indonesia, America, and the world. For Obama, international relations may in the main be defined by powerful politicians and global corporations, but they're also about the lesser-told stories of interactions between diplomatic officials, businessmen and women, working people, and students like his Kenyan father and his Javanese stepfather in America, and his mother in Indonesia.

Barack Obama moved with his mother, Stanley Ann Dunham, to Indonesia in 1967, "two years after the purge began, the same year that Suharto assumed the presidency." She had married Lolo Soetoro, whom she met during their time as students at the University of Hawaii, and she worked at first as an English teacher in the American Embassy while he did his service in the Indonesian army. Like almost all Americans, she knew nothing of the purges at the time, and her husband recommended that "some things were best forgotten." Obama described Jakarta as "a sleepy backwater in those days" where forgetting was easy, at least for the foreign-born, and a place "where the city center and wealthier sections of town—with their colonial elegance and lush, well-tended lawns" quickly gave way "to clots of small villages with unpaved roads and open sewers, dusty markets, and shanties of mud and brick and plywood and corrugated iron that tumbled down gentle banks to murky rivers where families bathed and washed laundry like pilgrims in the Ganges."[90]

His mother and stepfather were "not well off in those early years" and, unable to afford the international school, they sent young Barack to "local Indonesian schools." And so he "ran the streets with the children of farmers, servants, tailors, and clerks" and enjoyed "a joyous time, full of adventure and mystery—days of chasing down chickens and running from water buffalo, nights of shadow puppets and ghost stories and street vendors bringing delectable sweets to our door." Not all Americans interacted with local people so eagerly, though, some expressing "condescension toward Indonesians" and showing an "unwillingness to learn anything about the country that was hosting them."[91]

Yet, for all their comparative integration, Barack Obama's family was inevitably distinct. "I knew that relative to our neighbors we were doing fine," he wrote, and "unlike many, we always had enough to eat." Ann Dunham was happy to be paid in reliable dollars rather than in rupiahs. And after the army, Lolo Soetoro worked for an American oil company for much more money. "We might live as Indonesians lived," Obama wrote, "but every so often my mother would take me to the American Club, where I could jump in the pool and watch cartoons and sip Coca-Cola to my heart's content." And his family's status "was determined not only by our wealth but by our ties to the West." He was thus able to show his friends "books of photographs, of Disneyland or the Empire

State Building," and "sometimes we would thumb through the Sears Roebuck catalog and marvel at the treasures on display," all of which, "I knew, was part of my heritage and set me apart." And furthermore, "my mother and I were citizens of the United States, beneficiaries of its power, safe and secure under the blanket of its protection."[92]

After four years of this life, Obama's mother sent him home to Hawaii to live with his grandparents and continue his education. Her "ties to Indonesia," however, "would never diminish," and for the remainder of her life she would repeatedly return to conduct postgraduate research in anthropology and to work for international agencies promoting women's economic prospects. Barack Obama himself would return from time to time, and in any case remained always "haunted by memories—the feel of packed mud under bare feet as I wander through paddy fields; the sight of day breaking behind volcanic peaks; the muezzin's call at night and the smell of wood smoke; the dickering at the fruit stands alongside the road; the frenzied sound of a gamelan orchestra, the musicians' faces lit by fire." He also wrote in 2006 that "I would like to take Michelle and the girls to share that piece of my life, to climb the thousand-year-old Hindu ruins of Prambanan or swim in a river high in Balinese hills." And, in 2017, he did.[93]

Barack Obama thus tells the story of his own sojourn in Indonesia, of his interactions with the country and its people, of the relationship of his mother and his stepfather, of their relationships with Indonesia and its people, and those of other Americans abroad as well. And of Indonesia itself, and of its relationship with the United States, and of Indonesia as a metaphor for the history of American relations with the world during a long, complex, and changing era lasting sixty years. This little essay is thus a masterclass in how to synthesize history—a history of the self, of individual relationships, of communities, of two nations, of American foreign relations, and of the world, all in one, all in less than ten erudite pages. Barack Obama is a great historian in many ways, but if he has one signature skill then it is this facility for synthesis.

But Obama's final verdict on America's foreign policy in the distant and recent past is that "our record is mixed—not just in Indonesia but across the globe. At times, American foreign policy has been farsighted, simultaneously serving our national interests, our ideals, and the interests of other nations. At other times American policies have been misguided, based on false assumptions that ignore the legitimate aspirations of other peoples, undermine our own credibility, and make for a more dangerous world."[94]

And that's the case not just in Indonesia and not just across the globe but also in America as well. For these words might also apply to Obama's own reckoning of US relations with Native Americans. As we saw earlier in this chapter, at least some recent American policy toward native nations and people *has been farsighted, simultaneously serving our national interests, our ideals, and the interests of other nations*. But for much of its history, American policies toward Indians have indeed been *based on false assumptions that ignore the legitimate aspirations of native peoples*. In fact, thinking back to the ideology of *dominium* and *imperium* that was deployed to justify European colonization and US westward expansion, there would have been no American history as we know it without those *false assumptions that ignore the legitimate aspirations of native peoples*.

He lived to see

And just as Barack Obama says that "our record is mixed" through the story of a single country, so he expresses his gift for synthesis in the story of a single individual. And the story has a very similar message, one that doesn't shy from injustice and oppression but which is nevertheless ultimately optimistic.

Hartford "Sonny" Black Eagle was an Apsaalooke Indian who was born on the Crow Reservation in Montana in December 1933 and who became a traditional healer and spokesman for the Crow tribe first and later for other nations too. He was also known by the Crow name *Alaxalusshixiassaah*, meaning "Thundering Hoof." He summed up his philosophy with the words, "There is but one race: Humanity." In 2008, when Barack Obama made the first ever visit by a presidential candidate to an Indian reservation, Black Eagle made him his adoptive son, a member of the Apsaalooke people, and gave him the Crow name *Awe Kooda Bilaxpak Kuxshish*, meaning "One Who Helps People Throughout the Land." Obama proudly mentioned these honors at every Tribal Nations Conference between 2009 and 2011, and promised to try to live according to the meaning of his Native American name.[95]

Hartford "Sonny" Black Eagle passed away in November 2012 at the age of seventy-eight, shortly before the fourth Tribal Nations Conference. Barack Obama paid tribute to him on that occasion. He described his adoptive father first as "a revered elder" to the Crow Nation and a "respected elder" to many others. And, after mentioning again that "Sonny Black Eagle adopted me into the Crow Nation during my 2008 campaign," Obama said that "we can celebrate his remarkable life and all that happened along the way, because Sonny's story is not just one man's journey to keep his culture alive, but one country's journey to keep perfecting itself."[96]

And Obama proceeded to tell Sonny Black Eagle's life and America's history in the following way, including what was misguided and what was farsighted, including the suffering and the striving but also including the mutual making a more perfect union. "So Sonny Black Eagle was born in 1933 just outside of Lodge Grass, Montana," Obama said.

That's where his grandparents raised him after his mother died of tuberculosis; where he tended to cattle as a child; and where as an adult, he raised a family of his own. And Sonny was brought up in the traditional Crow ways, with the same values that many of you share—a reverence for the Earth, to cherish the Earth and to cherish each other; to honor ancestors and preserve traditions.

Staying true to those values wasn't always easy. As a child, if Sonny spoke Crow in school, his teachers would strike his hand with a ruler. As a teenager, when he went to eat at local restaurants he was sometimes met with a sign on the door that said, "No Indians or dogs allowed." In the 1950s, as Sonny and his wife Mary began a new life together, the government put in place a new policy of forced assimilation—a move that harkened back to the days when Native religions and languages were banned. The policy was called "termination" for a reason—it was meant to end tribal governments in America once and for all.

So Sonny, like many of you, knew intolerance and knew injustice. He knew what it was like to be persecuted for who you are and what you believe. But as time went by, year by year, decade by decade, as Native Americans rallied together and marched together, as students descended on Alcatraz and activists held their ground at Frank's Landing, as respect and appreciation for your unique heritage grew and a seminal struggle played itself out, Sonny lived to see something else. He saw a new beginning.

He lived to see a government that turned the page on a troubled past and adopted a new policy towards Native Americans—a policy centered on self-determination and the right for tribal governments to do whatever you think is best to strengthen your communities.

Over the past 40 years, that policy has had a major impact. It has empowered you to build up stronger institutions. It has enabled you to establish more effective law and order. It has laid the foundation for a true and lasting government-to-government relationship with the United States.

And over those decades, as Sonny went from being a father to a great-great-grandfather; and as he taught his family the Crow language and his community the Crow customs; as he became a living symbol of the perseverance of the entire Crow nation, Sonny stayed true to those fundamental values—to those fundamental values—to cherish the Earth and each other, to honor ancestors and preserve traditions.

And these are not just Sonny's values. In fact, they're not just values cherished by Native Americans. These should be and are American values. And they lie at the heart of some of our country's greatest challenges—to rebuild the middle class; to build ladders of opportunity for everybody who's working hard; to protect our planet; to leave our children something better than we inherited; to make sure Americans remain optimistic about the future and that this country of ours remains the place where no matter who you are or what you look like or where you come from or what your last name is, you can make it here if you try.[97]

This story of Hartford "Sonny" Black Eagle was not the only time Obama expressed his vision of American history through the life of a single individual. Nor was it the first time he did so in such a masterful and moving manner, as we will see as we conclude our journey in Barack Obama's American history.

EPILOGUE
OUT OF MANY, ONE: AMERICAN HISTORY'S BARACK OBAMA

She lived to see

On November 2, 2004, Barack Obama was elected US senator for the state of Illinois. In his victory speech that evening, in the Ballroom of the Hyatt Regency hotel in Chicago, he recalled:

> I told some of you about a story a couple of days ago where, during a rally that the clergy had organized on the South Side of Chicago, I was asked to meet with a woman who had attended a reception beforehand. And she was a woman who had voted absentee for me already and wanted to shake my hand and take a picture with me. And she came to the reception and she was very gracious and said how proud she was to have voted for me and how proud she was of the campaign that we had run. We shook hands, we hugged, we took a picture and all of this would be unexceptional except for the fact that she was born in 1899. Her name was Margaret Lewis. She may be watching television tonight. She's one hundred four. She will be one hundred five on November twenty-fourth.[1]

The senator-elect had done some reflecting on Margaret Lewis's life. "Trying to imagine," he said, "what it would be like for this woman, an African American woman born in 1899, born in the shadow of slavery. Born in the midst of Jim Crow. Born before there were automobiles or roads to carry those automobiles. Born before there were airplanes in the sky, before telephones and televisions and cameras. Born before there were cell phones and the Internet. Imagining her life spanning three centuries." And he continued his imaginings in his eminently eloquent fashion:

> she lived to see World War I; she lived to see the Great Depression; she lived to see World War II; and she lived to see her brothers and uncles and nephews and cousins coming home and still sitting in the back of a bus.
>
> She lived to see women get the right to vote. She lived to see FDR drag this nation out of its own fear and establish the GI bill and social security and all the programs that we now take for granted. She saw unions rising up and she saw immigrant families coming from every direction making a better life for themselves in this nation.

And yet she still was held back by her status until finally she saw hope breaking through the horizon and the Civil Rights Movement. And women who were willing to walk instead of riding the bus after a long day's work doing somebody else's laundry and looking after somebody else's children. And she saw young people of every race and every creed take a bus down to Mississippi and Alabama to register voters and some of them never coming back. And she saw four little girls die in a Sunday school and catalyze a nation. And then she saw the Civil Rights Act of 1964 passed and the Voting Rights Act of 1965 passed.

And she saw people lining up to vote for the first time and she was among those voters and she never forgot it. And she kept on voting each and every election, each and every election she kept voting thinking that there was a better future ahead, despite her trials, despite her tribulations, continually believing in this nation and its possibilities. Margaret Lewis believed. And she still believes at the age of one hundred four that her voice matters, that her life counts, that her story is sacred, just like the story of every person in this room and the stories of their parents and grandparents, the legacy that we've established. The history of so many people building, calloused hand by calloused hand, brick by brick, a better future for our children.[2]

This is of course a deeply moving story of a very senior citizen, but it's also a fascinating interpretation of the history of a nation. Let's examine it as a historical essay.

The period of time covered by these words connects three centuries, as Obama says, and includes the whole of the twentieth one. But Obama doesn't settle for a periodization based only on calendrical happenstance. Rather, he frames the era of Margaret Lewis's life as beginning in "the shadow of slavery" and reaching to the day she could vote for only the fifth African American in 115 years to win a seat in the US Senate.

This framing establishes the era as one of transformation, beginning in oppression but encompassing progress and ending in an instance of liberation. Through her life in his words, then, we bear witness to the evidence of all these phenomena. Of segregation: from the racism it was founded on, represented by the painted minstrel "Jim Crow," to the quotidian tribulations of separate and unequal worlds, to the material inequality and poverty all that imposed, to the violence these iniquities were founded on, as represented by the protesters who never came home and by the children killed in the bombing of the 16th Street Baptist Church in Birmingham, Alabama, in September 1963. But we also see the struggle against segregation and disfranchisement, and we see victory in the form of federal legislation outlawing discrimination and enforcing the most fundamental of democratic freedoms. And we see Margaret Lewis finally employ that freedom to help elect a fellow African American to the highest legislature in the land.

But Barack Obama's essay is not just a narrative of events. It is in fact replete with interpretive themes. Narrative itself is interpretative of course, and the aforementioned framing shows us trial, tribulation, and finally triumph. In addition, Obama doesn't shy from highlighting injustice, oppression, and murder in the events he portrays and the language he uses. He shows too how the struggle to right these wrongs is long. And that liberation is not a gift given by the privileged but a prize won by the citizens fighting for it, "building, calloused hand by calloused hand, brick by brick, a better future for our children"—a phrase Obama has used at other times, as we saw at the beginning of this book.[3]

And yet, for all the divisiveness caused by iniquity, the struggle for equality is all about unity. Young people of "every race and every creed" campaign for justice, "a nation is catalyzed" by a terrorist outrage, and citizens of all backgrounds come together to win wars overseas in 1917–18 and in 1941–45, despite what divides them at home. The story of African American hardship and liberation is also for Obama indivisible from the stories of similar trials and triumphs of women, of immigrants, of workers, of the poor, of all races.

And out of unity comes progress, Barack Obama's ultimate historical theme. Equal rights and votes for African Americans and for women are obviously victories, but Obama reinforces the idea that they represent progress with his far from accidental allusions to technological transformations, in the same way we saw at the start of Chapter 6. There were no automobiles, roads, or airplanes "in the shadow of slavery," no telephones, televisions, or cameras. And "Jim Crow" never gave us cell phones or the internet. These things come with votes for women, with the New Deal for the poor, with Civil Rights for black Americans. Political and material modernity arrive together, hand-in-hand, equality and liberty related inextricably to metaphorical pursuits of happiness.

Yet, all the while, for all the essay's range in time and all its sweeping themes, Margaret Lewis remains at the center of this American history, the focus of its narrative and interpretation. *She* was "born in the shadow of slavery" and the "midst of Jim Crow." There were no automobiles or roads, airplanes, telephones, televisions, cameras, cell phones, or internet when *she* was born. Mrs. Lewis may be just one individual, but Barack Obama affirms her agency and her worth with his own rhetorical power: "her voice matters … her life counts … her story is sacred."

By placing her in the context of all that she has lived to see, he portrays her life in epic style. And yet, for Barack Obama there is even more to Margaret Lewis than her epic individuality. First and perhaps most obviously, her story is exemplary—it is "just like the story of every person in this room and the stories of their parents and grandparents, the legacy that we've established." Yet she is also something more than exemplary in Obama's telling of her life, something that tells us much about how he thinks about the nature of the American experience. Her individuality is important and her experience is epic in its own right, but also because of all that she connects with and all that she has lived to see. That refrain, "She lived to see," positions Mrs. Lewis as both an active agent in her own story and an interested observer of those of others, a participant in and a witness to all the great events of the twentieth century. She is thus both an individual and more, a member of a larger community, an engaged citizen of a democratic nation.

The great historian Benedict Anderson described a nation as an "imagined community," one in which an individual feels affinity with millions of other people, people he or she has never met. Margaret Lewis certainly imagines her nation this way, but she also acts and sees, participates and bears witness, and she helps make transformations happen. She is Obama's American syncretism personified—one out of many among the "We the people" who make a more perfect union. For Barack Obama, Margaret Lewis *is* the American national community, and the American national community *is* Margaret Lewis.[4]

The Joshua generation

Which brings us to the matter of how Barack Obama tells the story of himself. How he has, in the words of E. J. Dionne and Joy-Ann Reid, "regularly historicized himself." His story is again in his own telling a history of an individual in the context of a community. Or rather three connected communities and their interrelated histories: in the African American community; in an American progressive political community; and in an American national community too. And these communities not only have connected presents, but connected pasts as well. Let's look at his relationship with each of them in turn.[5]

Barack Obama has of course written an autobiography, *Dreams from my Father: A Story of Race and Inheritance*, first published in 1995 and updated and republished in 2004, the year he gave the keynote address at the Democratic National Convention and that he ran for and won that seat in the US Senate. There will no doubt be either an updated version or more likely a new one soon. There have been numerous biographies too, and there will no doubt be many more to come. But autobiographies and biographies are necessarily about someone's becoming. This book however has focused on what Barack Obama became, or at least on the American historian he became once his views on this subject were more or less settled. Similarly, the following account of his accounts of himself within the stream of American history is largely limited to what he has said since he became who he is.[6]

Nevertheless, it's worth noting first that in writing his life Obama employed the idioms of over two centuries of African American autobiography, including idioms of becoming, beginning with *A Narrative of the Uncommon Sufferings and Surprising Deliverance of Briton Hammon, a Negro Man* (1760), and continuing with Ukawsaw Gronniosaw and Olaudah Equiano in the eighteenth century, Frederick Douglass, Solomon Northup, and Harriet Jacobs in the nineteenth century, and Booker T. Washington, W. E. B. Du Bois, Langston Hughes, Richard Wright, Zora Neale Hurston, James Baldwin, Malcolm X, and Maya Angelou in the twentieth century. And many, many others besides. The literary theorist Robert Stepto calls this kind of storytelling a "narrative of ascent," beginning in "Sufferings" but ending in "Deliverance," and it's also a kind of individualized analogue of the radical Whiggish narrative of hard-won national progress. Obama has obviously never suffered all the pains his predecessors did, as he readily admits. But his telling of the history of himself follows a similar narrative of early difficulty, self-discovery, then of a journey to freedom—freedom of the mind if not of the body, as it was in the days of slavery—and finally of entry into a community of fellows.[7]

Another great scholar of the African American experience, perhaps the greatest, Henry Louis Gates Jr., has written that former slaves wrote autobiographies in part to "demonstrate" their "membership in the human community" after enslavement had defined them as property. Barack Obama never had to prove his humanity as he was born long enough after the end of enslavement. But his story was still about finding membership in communities that had difficulty accommodating his hybridity. Like Frederick Douglass and many others, though, he finally found it in an American nation that has slowly become more accepting of people like him. But, again like Douglass, Obama found it in the African American community first.[8]

On March 4, 2007, Barack Obama gave a speech at Brown Chapel in Selma, Alabama, at a commemoration of the 1965 Voting Rights March, although it was also an early event in the Democratic primaries preceding the presidential election of the following year. The speech was actually perhaps closer to a sermon, probably the closest Obama has ever come to fully fledged homiletics. Among the many things he spoke about that day were the fears and doubts some had about him running for president, fears for his life first and foremost but doubts about his life experience as well. He mentioned however a letter he'd received from Reverend Otis Moss Jr. in which the renowned preacher from Cleveland, Ohio, said that "if there's some folks out there who are questioning whether or not you should run, just tell them to look at the story of Joshua because you're part of the Joshua generation." And so in Selma Obama duly proceeded to talk "about Moses and Aaron and Joshua."[9]

Obama gave due thanks first of course to the Moses generation of which Otis Moss Jr. was a member, to those who struggled for civil rights in the first place. We are, Obama said, "in the presence today of a lot of Moseses. It's because they marched that we elected councilmen, congressmen. It is because they marched that we have Artur Davis and Keith Ellison. It is because they marched that I got the kind of education I got, a law degree, a seat in the Illinois senate and ultimately in the United States senate … It is because they marched that I stand before you here today. I'm here because somebody marched. I'm here because you all sacrificed for me. I stand on the shoulders of giants." And Obama duly named many giants. "There were people like Anna Cooper and Marie Foster," he said, "and Jimmy Lee Jackson and Maurice Olette, C. T. Vivian, Reverend Lowery, John Lewis, who said we can imagine something different and we know there is something out there for us, too."[10]

But Obama also employed the kind of scriptural and allegorical language that many generations of African Americans had used before, beginning with the enslaved, who drew hope and inspiration from Moses leading his people out of slavery and from Joshua leading them into freedom in the Promised Land. "Like Moses," Obama said of the Civil Rights leaders he was among, "they challenged Pharaoh, the princes, powers who said that some are atop and others are at the bottom, and that's how it's always going to be … Thank God," he continued,

He's made us in His image and we reject the notion that we will for the rest of our lives be confined to a station of inferiority, that we can't aspire to the highest of heights, that our talents can't be expressed to their fullest. And so because of what they endured, because of what they marched; they led a people out of bondage.

They took them across the sea that folks thought could not be parted. They wandered through a desert but always knowing that God was with them and that, if they maintained that trust in God, that they would be all right. And it's because they marched that the next generation hasn't been bloodied so much.[11]

Obama then spoke of his own generation's mission, but in making this rhetorical transition he implicitly but unmissably reminded us of the last public words of an American Moses, Reverend Martin Luther King Jr. "I thank the Moses generation," Obama said, "but we've got to remember, now, that Joshua still had a job to do. As great as Moses was, despite all that he did, leading a people out of bondage, he didn't cross over the river to see the Promised Land. God told him your job is done. You'll see it. You'll be at the mountain top and you can see what I've promised. What I've promised to Abraham and Isaac and Jacob. You will see that I've fulfilled that promise but you won't go there."[12]

At Bishop Charles Mason Temple in Memphis, Tennessee, on April 3, 1968, the evening before he died, Martin Luther King famously meditated on his own mortality. His speech, "I've been to the Mountaintop," is worth quoting at some length because King drew those parallels and continuities from Biblical time to American time that slaves had drawn on before and that Barack Obama has drawn on since. But it's also worth quoting at length just because. "And you know," King said,

if I were standing at the beginning of time, with the possibility of taking a kind of general and panoramic view of the whole of human history up to now, and the Almighty said to me, "Martin Luther King, which age would you like to live in?" I would take my mental flight by Egypt and I would watch God's children in their magnificent trek from the dark dungeons of Egypt through, or rather across the Red Sea, through the wilderness on toward the Promised Land. And in spite of its magnificence, I wouldn't stop there.

I would move on by Greece and take my mind to Mount Olympus. And I would see Plato, Aristotle, Socrates, Euripides and Aristophanes assembled around the Parthenon. And I would watch them around the Parthenon as they discussed the great and eternal issues of reality. But I wouldn't stop there.

I would go on, even to the great heyday of the Roman Empire. And I would see developments around there, through various emperors and leaders. But I wouldn't stop there.

I would even come up to the day of the Renaissance, and get a quick picture of all that the Renaissance did for the cultural and aesthetic life of man. But I wouldn't stop there.

I would even go by the way that the man for whom I am named had his habitat. And I would watch Martin Luther as he tacked his ninety-five theses on the door at the church of Wittenberg. But I wouldn't stop there.

I would come on up even to 1863, and watch a vacillating President by the name of Abraham Lincoln finally come to the conclusion that he had to sign the Emancipation Proclamation. But I wouldn't stop there.

I would even come up to the early thirties, and see a man grappling with the problems of the bankruptcy of his nation. And come with an eloquent cry that we have nothing to fear but "fear itself." But I wouldn't stop there.

Strangely enough, I would turn to the Almighty, and say, "If you allow me to live just a few years in the second half of the 20th century, I will be happy."[13]

But alas of course he didn't live a few years more. After reflecting on the "difficult days ahead" and rehearsing his ideas for building a better future for all, he said "But it really doesn't matter with me now, because I've been to the mountaintop." And he continued:

Like anybody, I would like to live a long life. Longevity has its place. But I'm not concerned about that now. I just want to do God's will. And He's allowed me to go up to the mountain. And I've looked over. And I've seen the Promised Land. I may not get there with you. But I want you to know tonight, that we, as a people, will get to the Promised Land![14]

And so Barack Obama promised his own Moses that he would lead the Joshua generation into that Promised Land.

The stories—became our story, my story

While no decent person doubted Barack Obama's African and American heritage, there were those at least back then who more reasonably questioned his "African American" heritage. As Obama said in that same speech in Selma, "a lot of people been asking, well, you know, your father was from Africa, your mother, she's a white woman from Kansas. I'm not sure that you have the same experience." And he duly noted that he was not himself descended from slaves and indeed that his mother's "great great-great-great-grandfather had owned slaves."[15]

But he had his answers to these questions all the same. In the Selma sermon he recounted his own family memory of British imperialism in Kenya to establish parallels with the black experience in America. "You see," he said, "my Grandfather was a cook to the British in Kenya. Grew up in a small village and all his life, that's all he was—a cook and a house boy. And that's what they called him, even when he was 60 years old. They called him a house boy. They wouldn't call him by his last name. Sound familiar?" And he added that his grandfather "had to carry a passbook around because Africans in their own land, in their own country, at that time, because it was a British colony, could not move about freely." He thus implicitly but clearly compared his African grandfather's circumstances with those of American slaves who had to carry a pass if they were off their masters' lands. "They could only go where they were told to go," he said, "They could only work where they were told to work." And "So," Obama insisted, "don't tell me I don't have a claim on Selma, Alabama. Don't tell me I'm not coming home to Selma, Alabama."[16]

As David Remnick and others have noted, and as Barack Obama himself indicates in his own autobiography, Onyango Obama's personal experience of British imperial rule was not unremittingly bleak—as oppressive and as murderous as that rule was for so many others. But in any case, besides race and inheritance, Obama also had his own personal sense of belonging in the African American community and in the course of that community's history, one he expressed with arresting eloquence in *Dreams from My Father*. Recalling the first time he heard Reverend Jeremiah Wright preach about "the audacity to hope" at Trinity United Church of Christ in Chicago, he wrote:

And in that single note—hope!—I heard something else; at the foot of that cross, inside the thousands of churches across the city, I imagined the stories of ordinary black people merging with the stories of David and Goliath, Moses and Pharaoh, the Christians in the lion's den, Ezekiel's field of dry bones. The stories—of survival, and freedom, and hope—became our story, my story; the blood that had spilled was our blood; the tears our tears.[17]

Most African Americans one way or another and sooner or later came to accept Obama's answers to their questions, and to acknowledge this son of Kansas and Kenya as one of their own. And many also came to embrace a certain sense of his place in American history. In the final weeks of the 2008 presidential election, after it was broadcast on National Public Radio on October 28 and attributed to a St. Louis job trainer named Ed Welch, a poem became popular:

Rosa sat so Martin could walk,

Martin walked so Obama could run

Obama is running so our children can fly![18]

A tall, gangly, self-made Springfield lawyer

In previous chapters as well as above we've seen how Barack Obama has been inspired by previous black leaders such as Martin Luther King and before him Frederick Douglass and many others too. And that reminds us that Barack Obama's American communities are connected with each other. These men were not only African American leaders, but American leaders also, members of both the black community and also a broader American progressive community. Thus it is that while Obama reached out to the African American community in his speech in Selma in March 2007 he also reached out beyond. We are "in the presence today of a lot of Moses. We're in the presence today of giants whose shoulders we stand on, people who battled," he said, "not just on behalf of African Americans but on behalf of all of America." And right after mentioning their battles "on behalf of all of America," he described their sacrifices in the terms that Abraham Lincoln used in his Gettysburg Address of 1863. Obama spoke of those that "battled for America's soul, that shed blood, that endured taunts and ... torment and in some cases gave the full measure of their devotion."[19]

Just a few moments before that, Obama had mentioned Lincoln by name, and a place where Lincoln had been, and also holy words that Lincoln had read, and another phrase that Lincoln had used. "You know," he reminded his audience, "several weeks ago, after I had announced that I was running for the Presidency of the United States, I stood in front of the Old State Capitol in Springfield, Illinois; where Abraham Lincoln delivered his speech declaring, drawing on scripture, that a house divided against itself could not stand."[20]

Part of the reason for Barack Obama's frequent mentions of Abraham Lincoln is a wish to align himself with America's progressive historical traditions—traditions that allied, at least eventually, with African Americans' causes. We've seen already how Obama identifies closely with America's earlier Founding Fathers, but it's notable that he only does so on an intellectual and political level, that he doesn't seem to identify with these mostly slaveholding men on an intimate and personal level. The instructive exception is Benjamin Franklin. Obama recalled once thinking about the parallel between his own and Franklin's commitment to public service, quoting this Founding Father saying to his mother: " 'I would rather have it said, He lived usefully, than, He died rich.' " But public service was not necessarily the particular distinction that made Obama identify especially with Franklin. As we saw in Chapter 1, Franklin held slaves early in his life, but he changed. His last public act, in the wake of an American Revolution that he did so much to shape, was to call for an end to enslavement.[21]

But even the connection Barack Obama made with Benjamin Franklin was fleeting, in contrast to the one he has made repeatedly with Abraham Lincoln. Obama has long identified with the sixteenth president. Part of the affinity is based on geography, as Hawaiian-born Obama is an adoptive son of Illinois as Kentucky-born Lincoln was. Hence Obama began his keynote encomium for John Kerry's presidential election campaign in 2004 with the following salutation: "On behalf of the great state of Illinois, crossroads of a nation, Land of Lincoln, let me express my deepest gratitude for the privilege of addressing this convention." Abraham Lincoln was thus the first person most of us ever heard Barack Obama speak of.[22]

Furthermore, when Obama announced his own run for the presidency in February 2007, he didn't do so in his own home town of Chicago, but did so in Lincoln's city of Springfield, in "the shadow of the Old State Capitol, where," indeed, "Lincoln once called on a divided house to stand together." Obama had of course served in the Capitol and in the capital as an Illinois state senator, so it made sense in that respect that he should make his announcement there. But Obama's attention to Lincoln was not just a situational happenstance and not just a passing gesture.[23]

The reference to the "divided house" was not the only Lincolnian rhetorical moment of Obama's announcement address, nor was it necessarily the most telling. Obama alluded to this proverbial other times too, combining references to Lincoln's 1858 speech with borrowings from his inaugural address of 1861: "As Lincoln said to a nation far more divided than ours," Obama said, "we are not enemies but friends. Though passion may have strained, it must not break our bonds of affection." And Obama also quoted the paraphrasing of the Biblical Ezekiel in Lincoln's "House Divided" speech: ' "Of strange, discordant, and even hostile elements, we gathered from the four winds, and formed and fought to battle through.' " And for the final words of his announcement Obama lifted a line from Lincoln's 1863 Gettysburg Address: "let us finish the work that needs to be done, and usher in a new birth of freedom on this Earth."[24]

And these quotations were more than just oratorical affectations. Obama truly believes that Lincoln has lessons to teach us today, and he even rhetorically positioned Lincoln as talking directly to us. "He tells us that there is power in words," Obama said, "He tells us that there is power in conviction. That beneath all the differences of race and region, faith and station, we are one people. He tells us that there is power in hope." And it was "through his will and his words," Obama further noted, that "he moved a nation and helped free a people. It is because of the millions who rallied to his cause that we are no longer divided, North and South, slave and free."[25]

And location, quotation, and historical instruction weren't the only means Barack Obama used that day to forge a link with Lincoln. He also invited a physical and therefore personal as well as a professional and political comparison of himself and the man he aimed to follow from the State House to the White House. Obama merged Lincoln's biographical narrative with his own aspirations when he spoke as he did of "the life of a tall, gangly, self-made Springfield lawyer" who "tell us that a different future is possible."[26]

It can of course be dangerous for a politician to identify so intimately with a historical figure as legendary as Lincoln. In *The Audacity of Hope*, Obama recalled the occasion in 2005 when the editors at *Time* asked him to contribute to a special issue of the magazine on the meaning of the sixteenth president today. Not having time to write something new, Obama gave them the text of a speech he'd given a few months before in Springfield at the dedication of a new Lincoln Presidential Library. The editors permitted this, but asked Obama to "personalize it a bit more—say something about Lincoln's impact on my life." He thus altered a passage in the speech to say that "in Lincoln's rise from poverty, his ultimate mastery of language and law, his capacity to overcome personal loss and remain determined in the face of repeated defeat—in all this, he reminded me not just of my own struggles."[27]

As Obama rather ruefully recounts, former Ronald Reagan speechwriter Peggy Noonan subsequently pounced. In an article entitled "Conceit of Government" in the *Wall Street Journal*, she wrote of the "previously careful Sen. Barack Obama, flapping his wings in *Time Magazine* and explaining that he's a lot like Abraham Lincoln, only sort of better." She then qualified this claim, but with burns. "There is nothing wrong with Barack Obama's resume," she continued, "but it is a log-cabin-free zone. So far it is also a greatness-free zone. If he keeps talking about himself like this it always will be." Obama responded with his customary equanimity and humor, simply writing "Ouch!"[28]

We know now of course that Barack Obama's résumé has not remained a "greatness-free zone." And nor did his attachment to his presidential predecessor diminish once he occupied the White House himself. In *The Atlantic* magazine in 2012 Obama revealed that he sometimes went to the Lincoln Bedroom to "reread the handwritten Gettysburg Address encased in glass," that at other times he reflected "on the Emancipation Proclamation, which hangs in the Oval Office," and that he occasionally pulled "a volume of" Lincoln's "writings from the library in search of lessons to draw." Lincoln's words, Obama wrote, remind us "that though we may have our differences, we are one people, and we are one nation, united by a common creed." And that "he calls on us through the ages to commit ourselves to the unfinished work he so nobly advanced—the work of perfecting our Union."[29]

My story is part of the larger American story

Barack Obama has often said similar words to those quoted immediately above: "though we may have our differences, we are one people, and we are one nation, united by a common creed." It's not surprising then that, as well as relating personally to the African American community and to Abraham Lincoln and through him to an American progressive continuity, he should also relate his own story to the larger American story.

As we saw at the start of this book, when Barack Obama introduced himself to the nation on the night of July 27, 2004, he portrayed himself as a product of America's past and a part therefore of its present and future. He began with his immigrant heritage and the enduring story of American opportunity, saying that "my presence on this stage is pretty unlikely. My father was a foreign student, born and raised in a small village in Kenya. He grew up herding goats, went to school in a tin-roof shack. His father—my grandfather—was a cook, a domestic servant to the British." The story of opportunity and upward mobility was driven home by his adding that "my grandfather had larger dreams for his son. Through hard work and perseverance my father got a scholarship to study in a magical place, America, that shone as a beacon of freedom and opportunity to so many who had come before him."[30]

Obama didn't neglect his other grandparents and parent either, associating them also with well-known American historical phenomena. His grandfather, he noted, "worked on oil rigs and farms through most of the Depression." Then, "The day after Pearl Harbor," he "signed up for duty; joined Patton's army, marched across Europe." At the same time, "Back home, my grandmother raised their baby and went to work on a bomber assembly line. After the war, they studied on the GI Bill, bought a house through FHA, and later moved west all the way to Hawaii in search of opportunity."[31]

Yet, while embedding his family story in American history and tradition, Obama also noted something about his origins that was new and yet also in his view not new. His American grandparents "had big dreams for their daughter. A common dream," he said, but one that was "born of two continents." Because "While studying here," Obama explained, "my father met my mother. She was born in a town on the other side of the world, in Kansas." He of course was born in Kenya. But Obama used this newness, his own racial and not just national hybridity, to emphasize something he sees as an American tradition—the idea that "America can change," that it has long been multicultural, that it can therefore embrace new kinds of newness, as it has in the past embraced what once was new but now is not. "My parents shared not only an improbable love," he said, but "they shared an abiding faith in the possibilities of this nation. They would give me an African name, Barack, or 'blessed,' believing that in a tolerant America your name is no barrier to success." And indeed "They imagined me going to the best schools in the land, even though they weren't rich, because in a generous America you don't have to be rich to achieve your potential." And so "I stand here today," he concluded, "grateful for the diversity of my heritage, aware that my parents' dreams live on in my two precious daughters. I stand here knowing that my story is part of the larger American story, that I owe a debt to all of those who came before me, and that, in no other country on earth, is my story even possible."[32]

Barack Obama told his story in a similar way when he was compelled to reintroduce himself in the midst of a political storm started in part by his pastor Reverend Jeremiah Wright and in part by the sensationalist habits of the media. Obama explained that his belief in a better future "comes from my unyielding faith in the decency and generosity of the American people. But it also comes from my own American story." And he then rendered his story this way:

> I am the son of a black man from Kenya and a white woman from Kansas. I was raised with the help of a white grandfather who survived a Depression to serve in Patton's Army during World War II and a white grandmother who worked on a bomber assembly line at Fort Leavenworth while he was overseas. I've gone to some of the best schools in America and lived in one of the world's poorest nations. I am married to a black American who carries within her the blood of slaves and slaveowners—an inheritance we pass on to our two precious daughters. I have brothers, sisters, nieces, nephews, uncles and cousins, of every race and every hue, scattered across three continents, and for as long as I live, I will never forget that in no other country on Earth is my story even possible.[33]

E pluribus unum. Out of many, one

These themes—of individuality and community, of inclusiveness and unity, of the interconnectedness of everyone—accord with the themes of some of Obama's most well-known words. At his national-name-making keynote address in Boston in 2004 he said that "there is not a liberal America and a conservative America—there is the United States of America. There is not a Black America and a White America and Latino America and Asian America—there's the United States of America."[34]

Obama noted in *The Audacity of Hope* that when people met him they sometimes cited this particular "line in my speech at the 2004 Democratic National Convention" and that it therefore "seemed to strike a chord." He reflected that for those people "it seems to capture a vision of America finally freed from the past of Jim Crow and slavery, Japanese internment camps and Mexican braceros, workplace tensions and cultural conflict—an America that fulfills Dr. King's promise that we be judged not by the color of our skin but by the content of our character." And then he explained exactly what that vision means to him, and his reflections on it express not only a sense of belonging, but even perhaps a sense of being. "I have no choice," he wrote,

> but to believe in this vision of America. As the child of a black man and a white woman, someone who was born in the racial melting pot of Hawaii, with a sister who's half Indonesian but who's usually mistaken for Mexican or Puerto Rican, and a brother-in-law and niece of Chinese descent, with some blood relatives who resemble Margaret Thatcher and others who could pass for Bernie Mac, so that family get-togethers over Christmas take on the appearance of a UN General Assembly meeting, I've never had the option of restricting my loyalties on the basis of race, or measuring my worth on the basis of tribe.[35]

These personal feelings manifested themselves in political terms in some other famous words from the speech in Boston. "If there is a child on the south side of Chicago who can't read," he said,

> that matters to me, even if it's not my child.
> If there's a senior citizen somewhere who can't pay for their prescription drugs, and has to choose between medicine and the rent, that makes my life poorer, even if it's not my grandparent.
> If there's an Arab American family being rounded up without benefit of an attorney or due process, that threatens my civil liberties.
> It is that fundamental belief ... I am my brother's keeper, I am my sister's keeper that makes this country work. It's what allows us to pursue our individual dreams and yet still come together as one American family.
> *E pluribus unum.* Out of many, one.[36]

These ideas seem to some to contradict America's traditional values and historical habits of individualism and self-reliance, but for Barack Obama there is no contradiction. "For alongside our famous individualism," he said, "there's another ingredient in the American saga. A belief that we're all connected as one people." We saw in Chapter 6 how Obama calmly demolished the myth of economic self-reliance by pointing out how "government has been called upon throughout our history to build the infrastructure, train the workforce, and otherwise lay the foundations necessary for economic growth." We saw in Chapter 7 how he similarly calmly demolished the myth of the individualistic frontiersman by pointing out how government purchased and organized the western territories and fought and conquered their native inhabitants.[37]

But above all, for Obama, communities ideally do not inhibit individualism but allow it, do not suppress self-reliance but enable it. As we saw in Chapter 1, Obama's analysis of some of the best-remembered communities in American history—the Puritan towns of Massachusetts—show he has no fondness for those that inhibit individuality by oppression or exclusion. For him, communities should be and at their historical best have been inclusive and affirmative for every individual member. In some respects Obama's model is therefore that of the slave community. The community in which, as we saw in Chapter 4, slaves sat around a fire "singing freedom songs," the community that welcomed those sold away from their homes and gave them new ones, that hid and fed fugitives, and that generally sustained individuals and a people long besieged by enslavement and racism. Churches and schools were the community institutions that supported individuals and a people through the time of Jim Crow, and that provided the places where many came together to mount and maintain the Civil Rights Movement. And when people marched in that Movement, they marched as one.[38]

Yet, as specifically constituted as some of these communities may be, for Obama they are ultimately all American. For all of this for Barack Obama began with the Declaration of Independence, a document that's often more associated with individual liberty than with concepts of community. Obama has often said for sure that the Declaration espouses the individual liberties that were later "made real" as Constitutional rights. But for him the principles of the Declaration are also collective. All three characterizations of the Declaration that Obama gives in *The Audacity of Hope*, as explored earlier in and throughout this book, contain the same plural possessive determiner. The Declaration is "*our* starting point as Americans," contains "the substance of *our* common creed," and forms "the foundation of *our* government." For Obama, as for John Locke and his theories of society and government, and as for America's Founders and their Declaration and Constitution, individual rights and individualism are shared ideas and ideals, and they are created, protected, preserved, and advanced by collective endeavor and common institutions.[39]

WE THE PEOPLE

As we've also seen, Obama is fond of quoting the opening words of the US Constitution, or at least some of them: "WE THE PEOPLE, in order to form a more perfect union," as he put it, in part in capitals, in the transcription of his speech on "A More Perfect Union." The inherently collective concept of "We the People" is the foundation of Barack Obama's American syncretism, a concept he expressed so eloquently in his speech in Selma in 2015, marking the semi-centenary of Bloody Sunday, "For We Were Born of Change":

We are Lewis and Clark and Sacajawea ... farmers and miners, and entrepreneurs and hucksters. That's our spirit.

We are Sojourner Truth and Fannie Lou Hamer . . . and we're Susan B. Anthony . . . That's our character.

We're the immigrants . . . Holocaust survivors, Soviet defectors, the Lost Boys of Sudan. We're the hopeful strivers who cross the Rio Grande . . . That's how we came to be.

We're the slaves who built the White House and the economy of the South. We're the ranch hands and cowboys who opened up the West, and countless laborers who laid rail, and raised skyscrapers, and organized for workers' rights.

We're the fresh-faced GIs who fought to liberate a continent. And we're the Tuskegee Airmen, and the Navajo code-talkers, and the Japanese Americans who fought for this country even as their own liberty had been denied. We're the firefighters who rushed into those buildings on 9/11, the volunteers who signed up to fight in Afghanistan and Iraq.

We are the gay Americans whose blood ran in the streets of San Francisco and New York, just as blood ran down this bridge.

We are storytellers, writers, poets, artists who abhor unfairness, and despise hypocrisy, and give voice to the voiceless, and tell truths that need to be told.

We are the inventors of gospel and jazz and blues, bluegrass and country, and hip-hop and rock and roll . . .

We are Jackie Robinson . . .

We are the people Langston Hughes wrote of . . . We are the people Emerson wrote of.[40]

Barack Obama's ideas about individuality and community, and about citizenship and nationality, thus infuse all of his American history. And he summarized them again in his farewell address in January 2017, this time less poetically, more scholastically, yet just as eloquently as in Selma. He gave the farewell address in Chicago, where it all began and where he "learned that change only happens when ordinary people get involved and they get engaged, and they come together to demand it." He spoke of this phenomenon as "the beating heart of our American idea—our bold experiment in self-government"—encapsulating both individuality and collectivity in this particular usage of the term "self-government." He spoke of the "common creed"—"that we are all created equal, endowed by our Creator with certain unalienable rights, among them life, liberty, and the pursuit of happiness," but noted "that these rights, while self-evident, have never been self-executing; that We, the People, through the instrument of our democracy, can form a more perfect union." And he similarly said, a little later in the speech, repeatedly using his favorite subject pronoun, we: "Our Constitution is a remarkable, beautiful gift. But it's really just a piece of parchment. It has no power on its own. We, the people, give it power. We, the people, give it meaning. With our participation, and with the choices that we make, and the alliances that we forge. Whether or not we stand up for our freedoms. Whether or not we respect and enforce the rule of law."[41]

Once again then we see individuality and community not in competition but in cooperation and in confluence, each enhancing the power of the other. Obama proceeded to speak in Chicago of "The freedom to chase our individual dreams through our sweat and toil and imagination, and the imperative to strive together, as well, to achieve a common good, a greater good." And "For 240 years, our nation's call to citizenship has given work and purpose to each new generation." And in each example that followed that general statement we again see individuals endeavoring in common to create something for the betterment of all. "It's what led patriots to choose republic over tyranny, pioneers to trek west, slaves to brave that makeshift railroad to freedom," he said. "It's what pulled immigrants and refugees across oceans and the Rio Grande. It's what pushed women to reach for the ballot. It's what powered workers to organize. It's why GIs gave their lives at Omaha Beach and Iwo Jima, Iraq and Afghanistan. And why men and women from Selma to Stonewall were prepared to give theirs, as well."[42]

Yes, we can

Barack Obama even insinuated his own election slogan—which contained again that same subject pronoun—into the course of American history, drawing a direct line from the "We the People" of 1787 to the "Yes, we can" of 2008, and through all points in between. He had used "Yes, we can" in the 2004 Illinois Senate campaign, but revived it in January 2008 after unexpectedly winning the Iowa Caucus and then unexpectedly losing the New Hampshire Primary. And he tied it to moments in American history by associating it with the concept of hope that, as we saw in the Introduction, he had so successfully articulated in his Keynote Speech at the Democratic National Convention four years before. "We've been warned against offering the people of this nation false hope," he told his crowd in Nashua on that January night in 2008. "But in the unlikely story that is America," he continued, "there has never been anything false about hope."

> For when we have faced down impossible odds, when we've been told we're not ready or that we shouldn't try or that we can't, generations of Americans have responded with a simple creed that sums up the spirit of a people.
> Yes, we can.
> It was a creed written into the founding documents that declared the destiny of a nation.
> Yes, we can.
> It was whispered by slaves and abolitionists as they blazed a trail towards freedom through the darkest of nights.
> Yes, we can.
> It was sung by immigrants as they struck out from distant shores and pioneers who pushed westward against an unforgiving wilderness.
> Yes, we can.
> It was the call of workers who organized, women who reached for the ballot, a president who chose the moon as out new frontier, and a King who took us to the mountaintop and pointed the way to the Promised Land.

Yes, we can, to justice and equality. Yes, we can, to opportunity and prosperity. Yes we can heal this nation. Yes we can repair this world. Yes we can.[43]

In his victory speech on the evening of presidential election day some months later in November he said: "This is our moment. This is our time, to put our people back to work and open doors of opportunity for our kids; to restore prosperity and promote the cause of peace; to reclaim the American dream and reaffirm that fundamental truth, that, out of many, we are one; that while we breathe, we hope. And where we are met with cynicism and doubts and those who tell us that we can't, we will respond with that timeless creed that sums up the spirit of a people: Yes, we can."[44]

And at the end of it all, in his presidential farewell address, he said it again. Except it wasn't the end of it all. Continuities come from the past but don't end in the present, and so Obama projected this one into the future. "I am asking you," he urged his audience in January 2017, "to hold fast to that faith written into our founding documents; that idea whispered by slaves and abolitionists; that spirit sung by immigrants and homesteaders and those who marched for justice; that creed reaffirmed by those who planted flags from foreign battlefields to the surface of the moon; a creed at the core of every American whose story is not yet written: Yes, we can. Yes, we did. Yes, we can."[45]

Calling "Yes, we can" a "timeless creed" may well be anachronistic. And associating it with the idea that "all men are created equal" and endowed with unalienable rights to life, liberty, and the pursuit of happiness—ideas he and others have called a "creed"—may well overburden this humble election slogan. But he used it time and time again anyway, and maybe it's a measure of Obama's sense of his own belonging to a nation and its past—his sense of being, his oneness with his homeland and its history—that he felt that yes, he could.[46]

Barack Obama's American syncretism is closely related to what is perhaps his greatest gift as a historian: his facility for synthesis. His ability to perceive the stories of the individual and the nation simultaneously. His ability to tell the story of each in the form of the other—to make us see the image of an individual person in a nation and the image of a nation in an individual person. That's how he has written and spoken of himself, and that's how he spoke of Margaret Lewis. His story was part of hers, hers was part of his, and both of theirs was part of the larger American story—a story of two people, but also of one people.

And his homage to her was not the only time he told the story this way.

A more perfect union

On November 4, 2008, Barack Obama was elected president of the United States. In his victory speech that evening, in Grant Park in Chicago, he recalled:

This election had many firsts and many stories that will be told for generations. But one that's on my mind tonight's about a woman who cast her ballot in Atlanta.

She's a lot like the millions of others who stood in line to make their voice heard in this election except for one thing—Ann Nixon Cooper is 106 years old.[47]

The president-elect had done some reflecting on Ann Nixon Cooper's life. "She was," he said, "born just a generation past slavery; a time when there were no cars on the road or planes in the sky; when someone like her couldn't vote for two reasons—because she was a woman and because of the color of her skin. And tonight," he continued, "I think about all that she's seen throughout her century in America—the heartache and the hope; the struggle and the progress; the times we were told that we can't, and the people who pressed on with that American creed: Yes we can." And he continued his imaginings in his eminently eloquent fashion.

At a time when women's voices were silenced and their hopes dismissed, she lived to see them stand up and speak out and reach for the ballot. Yes we can.

When there was despair in the dust bowl and depression across the land, she saw a nation conquer fear itself with a New Deal, new jobs, a new sense of common purpose. Yes we can.

When the bombs fell on our harbor and tyranny threatened the world, she was there to witness a generation rise to greatness, and a democracy was saved. Yes we can.

She was there for the buses in Montgomery, the hoses in Birmingham, a bridge in Selma and a preacher from Atlanta who told a people that We Shall Overcome. Yes we can.

A man touched down on the moon, a wall came down in Berlin, a world was connected by our own science and imagination. And this year, in this election, she touched her finger to a screen and cast her vote, because after 106 years in America, through the best of times and the darkest of hours, she knows how America can change.[48]

Much of course has come to pass since that November night in 2008. As Barack Obama said in his goodbye as president to the American people in January 2017: "Yes, our progress has been uneven. The work of democracy has always been hard. It's always been contentious. Sometimes it's been bloody. For every two steps forward, it often feels we take one step back. But," he said, "the long sweep of America has been defined by forward motion, a constant widening of our founding creed to embrace all and not just some."[49]

"The arc of the moral universe is long, but it bends towards justice," as Barack Obama likes to say. Is this overly idealistic? Maybe. But the nineteenth-century abolitionist preacher who coined the phrase during the struggle against slavery might have felt somewhat vindicated by the eventual elevation of an African American to the highest office in the land. And the twentieth-century Civil Rights preacher who borrowed the phrase might have felt that night that he'd reached his Promised Land. But Barack Obama often adds his own coda to the phrase coined by Theodore Parker and borrowed by Martin Luther King—"as long as we help it bend that way." Margaret Lewis helped it bend that way. Ann Nixon Cooper helped it bend that way. Millions of others have helped it bend that way.[50]

It took more than a century to get from "just a generation past slavery" to the time when Ann Nixon Cooper "touched her finger to a screen" to help elect the first black president in American history. And America has seen the "darkest of hours" as well as the "best of times" in its odyssey from the days of Ulysses Grant to a night in Grant Park. And yet, as Barack Obama spoke that evening of Ann Nixon Cooper and all that she had lived to see, we too knew how America can change, as we too lived to see a moment in the making of a more perfect union.

NOTES

INTRODUCTION

1. "The Audacity of Hope: Keynote Address at the 2004 Democratic National Convention, *Boston, MA, July 27, 2004*," in E. J. Dionne Jr. and Joy-Ann Reid, eds., *We Are the Change We Seek: The Speeches of Barack Obama* (London, New York : Bloomsbury, 2017), 6.

2. Ibid., 7, 12.

3. "Iowa Caucus Night: *January 3, 2008, De Moines, Iowa*," *Change We Can Believe In: Barack Obama's Plan to Renew America's Promise* (New York: Three Rivers Press, 2008), 207.

4. "Declaration of Candidacy: *February 10, 2007, Springfield, Illinois*," ibid., 195, 196, 201, 202, 195–96, 193.

5. Ibid., 195–96.

6. Ibid., 193.

7. "A More Perfect Union: *March 18, 2008, Philadelphia, Pennsylvania*," ibid., 215.

8. Ibid., 216, 217.

9. "Remarks by the President in a Farewell Address, McCormick Place, Chicago, Illinois," The White House, Office of the Press Secretary, January 10, 2017. Available online: https://obamawhitehouse.archives.gov/the-press-office/2017/01/10/remarks-president-farewell-address. I have always tried to cite speeches from sources as close to Barack Obama as possible. Using these "official" transcriptions allows me to analyze grammar unedited by others, the usefulness of which I hope will soon be apparent. Official material from his years as President is now "frozen in time" online at https://obamawhitehouse.archives.gov/. For 2008 campaign material I have used *Change We Can Believe In*, cited above. For material not available from these sources I have whenever possible used the most authoritative published versions available, such as Dionne and Reid, eds., *We Are the Change We Seek*, cited above, and Mary Frances Berry and Josh Gottheimer, *Power In Words: The Stories Behind Barack Obama's Speeches, from the State House to the White House* (Boston: Beacon Press, 2010).

10. "Remarks by the President in a Farewell Address, McCormick Place, Chicago, Illinois."

11. Barack Obama, *The Audacity of Hope: Thoughts on Reclaiming the American Dream* (New York: Crown, 2006), 361–62.

12. "The Audacity of Hope," Dionne and Reid, eds., *We Are the Change We Seek*, 12; "Declaration of Candidacy," *Change We Can Believe In*, 193; "A More Perfect Union," *Change We Can Believe In*, 216.

13. Obama quotes Faulker in "A More Perfect Union," *Change We Can Believe In*, 222, and in *Dreams from My Father: A Story of Race and Inheritance* (New York: Crown, 1995, 2004), x. The other quotes here, as above, are from *The Audacity of Hope*, 362.

14. Indeed E. J. Dionne and Joy-Ann Reid noted that "few other Presidents (Lincoln was one) have been more insistent than Obama on offering a running class in American history and its meaning." See *We Are the Change We Seek*, xix.

15. These quotes and those below will reappear in fuller form and be duly noted later in the book.

16. "New Hampshire Primary Night: *January 8, 2008, Nashua, New Hampshire*," *Change We Can Believe In*, 212; "Remarks by the President at the 50th Anniversary of the Selma to Montgomery Marches, Edmund Pettus Bridge, Selma, Alabama," The White House, Office of the Press Secretary, March 7, 2015. Available online: https://obamawhitehouse.archives.gov/the-press-office/2015/03/07/remarks-president-50th-anniversary-selma-montgomery-marches.

17. In any case, academic historians sometimes use these techniques too. And we all make mistakes as well; I certainly have. No, I'm not going to tell you what or where they are.

18. *The Audacity of Hope*, 362. As a Briton living in France and working at a French university, I'm aware that Barack Obama's "our" and "we" don't actually apply to me. I can't be bothered, however, and I don't want to bother you, with either the extensive quote-editing or extended explanations required to be clear about that fact on every occasion it arises. So let's just acknowledge it here and move on without any further ado.

PROLOGUE

1. The media missed or understated many aspects of the contexts of these sermons, such as the fact that Reverend Wright was quoting former US Ambassador Edward Peck, who was himself quoting Malcolm X using the poultry-based proverb in relation to the assassination of President John F. Kennedy. The media also paid little attention to Wright's long and distinguished career in public service. Or at least they didn't allow context to diminish the impact of the more sellable content. For fuller accounts see "A More Perfect Union: *March 18, 2008, National Constitution Center, Philadelphia, Pennsylvania*," in Mary Frances Berry and Josh Gottheimer, eds., *Power In Words: The Stories Behind Barack Obama's Speeches, from the State House to the White House* (Boston: Beacon Press, 2010), 175–81, 195–96, and David Remnick, *The Bridge: The Life and Rise of Barack Obama* (New York: Picador, 2010), 468–72, 495, 517–22.

2. Berry and Gottheimer, eds., *Power in Words*, 175.

3. Michael Powell, "Following Months of Criticism, Obama Quits His Church," *New York Times*, June 1, 2008, available online: http://www.nytimes.com/2008/06/01/us/politics/01obama.html.

4. T. Denean Sharpley-Whiting, ed., *The Speech: Race and Barack Obama's "A More Perfect Union"* (London, New York: Bloomsbury, 2009). The quotations throughout are taken from "A More Perfect Union: *March 18, 2008, Philadelphia, Pennsylvania*," in *Change We Can Believe In: Barack Obama's Plan to Renew America's Promise* (New York: Three Rivers Press, 2008), 215–32. For the delivery and reception of the speech, see "A More Perfect Union," Berry and Gottheimer, eds., 179–81, and Remnick, *The Bridge*, 522–33.

5. "A More Perfect Union," *Change We Can Believe In*, 222, 224.

6. Ibid., 227.

7. Barack Obama, *Dreams from My Father: A Story of Race and Inheritance* (New York: Crown, 1995, 2004) and *The Audacity of Hope: Thoughts on Reclaiming the American Dream* (New York: Crown, 2006). "A More Perfect Union," *Change We Can Believe In*, 227.

8. Ibid., 215.

9. *The Audacity of Hope*, 53. The capitals here are copied from Obama's own published words. The possible reasons for this typography are explored later in this prologue and further still in other parts of the book.

10. "A More Perfect Union," *Change We Can Believe In*, 227.

11. *The Audacity of Hope*, 53, 92.

12. "A More Perfect Union," *Change We Can Believe In*, 216.

13. See Robert Greene II, "Barack Obama Radically Expanded Our Appreciation of African-American History," *The Nation*, February 2, 2017. Available online: https://www.thenation.com/article/barack-obama-radically-expanded-our-appreciation-of-african-american-history/.

14. Mark S. Ferrara, *Barack Obama and the Rhetoric of Hope* (London: Macfarlane, 2013), 14, 23.

15. Ibid., 15.

16. *The Audacity of Hope*, 53. "Remarks by the President at the 50th Anniversary of the Selma to Montgomery Marches, Edmund Pettus Bridge, Selma, Alabama," The White House, Office of the Press Secretary, March 7, 2015. Available online: https://obamawhitehouse.archives.gov/the-press-office/2015/03/07/remarks-president-50th-anniversary-selma-montgomery-marches.

17. "A More Perfect Union," *Change We Can Believe In*, 215.

18. Ibid., 230. E. J. Dionne, Jr. and Joy-Ann Reid have already noted something we see here and will see throughout this book—how Obama uses often "perfect" as a verb rather than an adjective: *We Are the Change We Seek: The Speeches of Barack Obama* (London, New York: Bloomsbury, 2017), xx.

19. *The Audacity of Hope*, 97.

20. *The Audacity of Hope*, 89; James T. Kloppenberg, *Reading Obama: Dreams, Hope, and the American Political Tradition* (Princeton: Princeton University Press, 2011), especially xi–xiii, 17–18, 62–64, 83, 110–11, 169–72, 193.

21. Thomas J. Sugrue has also referred to Barack Obama's "whig history" of the American Civil Rights Movement in his *Not Even Past: Barack Obama and the Burden of Race* (Princeton: Princeton University Press, 2010), 4, 52. For the nature of this historiography, Herbert Butterfield, *The Whig Interpretation of History* (London: G. Bell, 1931) remains remarkably useful.

22. The term "Founding Fathers," referring either to signers of the Declaration of Independence or the Constitution, or sometimes to American revolutionaries more generally, was first used by Warren G. Harding in a speech to the Republican National Convention in 1916 and then in his presidential inaugural address in 1921, though it's credited to his "literary clerk" Judson T. Welliver (Berry and Gottheimer, *Power in Words*, xxvi). Obama alternates between this term and just the word "Founders," which was common usage in the nineteenth century.

23. See Edward Vallance, *The Glorious Revolution: 1688—Britain's Fight for Liberty* (London: Little, Brown, 2006); Tim Harris, *Revolution: The Great Crisis of the British Monarchy, 1685–1720* (London: Allen Lane, 2006); Steve Pincus, *1688: The First Modern Revolution* (New Haven: Yale University Press, 2011).

24. John Locke, *Two Treatises of Government*, Peter Laslett, ed., *Cambridge Texts in the History of Political Thought* (Cambridge: Cambridge University Press, 1988); Ronald Hamowy, ed. [John Trenchard and Thomas Gordon], *Cato's Letters: Or, Essays on Liberty, Civil and Religious, and Other Important Subjects*, two volumes (Indianapolis: Liberty Fund, 1995); Caroline Robbins, *The Eighteenth Century Commonwealthman: Studies in the Transmission, Development, and Circumstance of English Liberal Thought from the Restoration of Charles II until the War with the Thirteen Colonies* (Cambridge, MA: Harvard University Press, 1959); Bernard Bailyn, *The Ideological Origins of the American Revolution* (Cambridge, MA: Harvard University Press, 1966).

25. *The Audacity of Hope*, 53; Gunnar Myrdal, *An American Dilemma: The Negro Problem and Modern Democracy* (New York: Harper, 1944); Pauline Maier, *American Scripture: How America Declared its Independence from Britain* (New York: Alfred A. Knopf, 1997). Robert

N. Bellah first wrote about the issue in "Civil Religion in America," *Dædalus: Journal of the American Academy of Arts and Sciences*, vol. 96, no. 1 (Winter 1967), 1–21.

26. Sam Leith, *You Talkin' to Me: Rhetoric from Aristotle to Obama* (London: Profile Books, 2011), 221–22, 224–28; Ferrara, *Rhetoric of Hope*, 18, 113–15; Wolfgang Mieder, *"Yes We Can": Barack Obama's Proverbial Rhetoric* (New York: Peter Lang, 2009), 71–72; Camille Tardy, "Transcendentalism and the Way to Freedom," MA thesis (Université Jean Moulin—Lyon 3, 2016), 96–106. "Remarks at the 50th Anniversary of the Selma to Montgomery Marches."

27. *The Audacity of Hope*, 90.

28. "Inaugural Address by President Barack Obama, United States Capitol," The White House, Office of the Press Secretary, January 21, 2013. Available online: https://obamawhitehouse. archives.gov/the-press-office/2013/01/21/inaugural-address-president-barack-obama.

29. The best among such critics are perhaps Mark Lawrence McPhail in his debate with David A. Frank in their unusual and excellent dialectical essay, "Barack Obama's Address to the 2004 Democratic National Convention: Trauma, Compromise, Consilience, and the (Im) possibility of Racial Reconciliation," *Rhetoric and Public Affairs*, vol. 8, no. 4 (2005), 571–94. And, with regards more to "A More Perfect Union," Ebony Utley and Amy L. Heyse in "Barack Obama's (Im)perfect Union: An Analysis of the Strategic Failures and Successes of His Speech on Race," *Western Journal of Black Studies*, vol. 33, no. 3(Fall 2009), 153–63.

30. "Remarks by the President in a Farewell Address, McCormick Place, Chicago, Illinois," The White House, Office of the Press Secretary, January 10, 2017. Available online: https://obamawhitehouse. archives.gov/the-press-office/2017/01/10/remarks-president-farewell-address.

31. Ibid.

32. *The Audacity of Hope*, 248. Martin Luther King used the phrase often: see Wolfgang Mieder, *"Making a Way Out of No Way": Martin Luther King's Sermonic Proverbial Rhetoric* (New York: Peter Lang, 2010). Theodore Parker's use of it can be found in *Ten Sermons of Religion by Theodore Parker, Of Justice and the Conscience* (Boston: Crosby, Nichols, 1853), 84–85.

33. "How Far We've Come: Remarks at John Lewis's Sixty-fifth Birthday Gala, *Atlanta, Georgia: February 21, 2005*," Dionne and Reid, eds., *We Are the Change We Seek*, 20; "John Lewis's Sixty-Fifth Birthday Gala: *February 21, 2005, Georgia Tech Hotel and Conference Center, Atlanta, Georgia*," in Berry and Gottheimer, eds., *Power in Words*, 51; "United States Senate Victory Speech: *November 2, 2004, Hyatt Ballroom, Chicago, Illinois*," ibid., *Power in Words*, 39.

34. *The Audacity of Hope*, 362.

35. "A More Perfect Union," *Change We Can Believe In*, 230–32. David Remnick relates the story of Ashley Baia and notes that Obama had told her tale in speeches before, the first time indeed a week before the South Carolina Primary, on Martin Luther King's birthday of January 20, 2008, and where the great Civil Rights leader grew up at Ebenezer Baptist Church in Atlanta, Georgia. Remnick, *The Bridge*, 499–500, 505, 522.

CHAPTER 1: OUR STARTING POINT AS AMERICANS

1. Barack Obama, *The Audacity of Hope: Thoughts on Reclaiming the American Dream* (New York: Crown, 2006), 53.

2. Probably the easiest way to access the Declaration of Independence (and the Constitution and Bill of Rights) is via the US National Archives' "Founding Documents" collection where one can see digitized originals and transcriptions. Available online: https://www.archives.gov/founding-docs.

3. One of the best introductions to the Atlantic approach remains David Armitage and Michael J. Braddick, eds., *The British Atlantic World, 1500–1800* (New York: Palgrave Macmillan, 2002; second edition, 2010), while I had a go at synthesizing the subject in *British America, 1500–1800: Creating Colonies, Imagining an Empire* (London: Bloomsbury, 2010). This approach encourages the use of terms such as "English America" and (after the 1707 Act of Union) "British America" to indicate indeed the Englishness or Britishness of early America. However, I've deliberately subtitled this chapter "The American Colonies" to indicate Barack Obama's emphasis on American-ness in early America. A notable and honorable exception among historians is Alan Taylor in *American Colonies: The Settling of North America* (London: Penguin, 2001).

4. "Weekly Address: Celebrating Independence Day," The White House, Office of the Press Secretary, July 4, 2013. "Remarks by the President at Fourth of July Celebration, South Lawn," The White House, Office of the Press Secretary, July 4, 2013. Available online: https://obamawhitehouse.archives.gov/the-press-office/2013/07/04/weekly-address-celebrating-independence-day and https://obamawhitehouse.archives.gov/the-press-office/2013/07/04/remarks-president-fourth-july-celebration.

5. The University of Massachusetts at Boston Commencement Address, June 2, 2006, is available online: http://obamaspeeches.com/074-University-of-Massachusetts-at-Boston-Commencement-Address-Obama-Speech.htm.

6. "The Audacity of Hope: Keynote Address at the 2004 Democratic National Convention, Boston, MA, July 27, 2004," E. J. Dionne Jr. and Joy-Ann Reid, eds., *We Are the Change We Seek: The Speeches of Barack Obama* (London, New York: Bloomsbury, 2017), 6.

7. Barack Obama's "Remarks at the Selma Voting Rights March Commemoration in Selma, Alabama, March 4, 2007" is available via John Woolley and Gerhard Peters, University of California, Santa Barbara, "The American Presidency Project." Available online: http://www.presidency.ucsb.edu/ws/?pid=77042. David Remnick, *The Bridge: The Life and Rise of Barack Obama* (New York: Alfred A. Knopf, 2010), 29–41, 49–55, 62–68.

8. "A More Perfect Union: *March 18, 2008, Philadelphia, Pennsylvania*," in *Change We Can Believe In: Barack Obama's Plan to Renew America's Promise* (New York: Three Rivers Press, 2008), 215.

9. For the stories behind the writing of the speech, see "A More Perfect Union: *March 18, 2008, National Constitution Center, Philadelphia, Pennsylvania*," in Mary Frances Berry and Josh Gottheimer, eds., *Power in Words: The Stories Behind Barack Obama's Speeches, from the State House to the White House* (Boston: Beacon Press, 2010), 175–81, and Remnick, *The Bridge*, 517–22.

10. "President Barack Obama's Inaugural Address," The White House, Office of the Press Secretary, Blog, January 21, 2009. Available online: https://obamawhitehouse.archives.gov/blog/2009/01/21/president-barack-obamas-inaugural-address.

11. "A More Perfect Union," *Change We Can Believe In*, 215.

12. John Dickinson, *Letters from a Farmer in Pennsylvania, to the Inhabitants of the British Colonies in America* (Philadelphia: David Hall and William Sellers, 1768), 3.

13. "A More Perfect Union," *Change We Can Believe In*, 215.

14. *The Audacity of Hope*, 199; University of Massachusetts at Boston Commencement Address.

15. Mary Frances Berry and Josh Gottheimer replace the semicolon with a comma in their edition of the speech in *Power in Words*, 182, but E. J. Dionne and Joy-Ann Reid keep the semicolon in theirs in *We Are the Change We Seek*, 52. Dionne and Reid also reproduce the version without commas around the clause "who traveled across an ocean to escape tyranny and persecution," in keeping with the original text given to the press on March 18, 2008. I have followed the version in *Change We Can Believe In*, with both semicolon and commas, produced by the "Obama for America" campaign immediately after the election of 2008.

16. See for example Fernand Braudel, *The Mediterranean and the Mediterranean World in the Age of Philip II*, 2 vols., trans. Sian Reynolds (New York: Harper and Row, 1972).

17. *The Audacity of Hope*, 199.

18. University of Massachusetts at Boston Commencement Address, June 2, 2006.

19. John Winthrop, "A Modell of Christian Charity" (1630), Collections of the Massachusetts Historical Society (Boston, 1838), 3rd series 7: 31-48, available online: https://history. hanover.edu/texts/winthmod.html.

20. Ibid.

21. Ibid.

22. University of Massachusetts at Boston Commencement Address, June 2, 2006.

23. *The Audacity of Hope*, 61.

24. See especially Robert Middlekauff, *The Mathers: Three Generations of Puritan Intellectuals, 1596–1728* (Los Angeles: University of California Press, 1999) and Richard Francis, *Judge Sewall's Apology: The Salem Witch Trials and the Formation of an American Conscience* (New York: Harper Collins, 2005).

25. *The Audacity of Hope*, 198, 199, 214, 195–96.

26. Ibid., 335.

27. Ibid., 8. That's a point Obama repeated word-for-word in "We Cannot Abandon the Field of Religious Discourse: Keynote Address at the Call to Renewal Conference, *Washington, DC, June 28, 2006*," Dionne and Reid, eds. *We Are the Change We Seek*, 32. See also "Call to Renewal Keynote Address: *June 28, 2006, National City Church, Washington, DC*," in Berry and Gottheimer, eds., *Power in Words*, 81.

28. The text of the Mayflower Compact can be found at Yale University Law School's Avalon Project. Available online: http://avalon.law.yale.edu/17th_century/mayflower.asp.

29. James T. Kloppenberg, *Reading Obama: Dreams, Hope, and the American Political Tradition* (Princeton: Princeton University Press, 2011), 31–35, 172–74, 196–97.

30. "The Audacity of Hope," Dionne and Reid, eds., *We Are the Change We Seek*, 11.

31. *The Audacity of Hope*, 55, 87, 101.

32. There's a huge body of work on New England towns, but the latest book to look out for is Mark S. Peterson, *The City-State of Boston: A Tragedy in Three Acts, 1630–1865* (New Haven: Yale University Press, forthcoming).

33. *The Audacity of Hope*, 54. Isaiah Berlin, *Two Concepts of Liberty* (Oxford: Oxford University Press, 1958).

34. The quote can be found in many sources, but one is Edmund S. Morgan, ed., *Not Your Usual Founding Father: Selected Readings from Benjamin Franklin* (New Haven: Yale University Press, 2006), 141; *The Audacity of Hope*, 361; "Weekly Address: Celebrating Independence Day," The White House, Office of the Press Secretary, July 4, 2014. Available online: https://obamawhitehouse. archives.gov/the-press-office/2014/07/04/weekly-address- celebrating-independence-day.

35. Nian-Heng Shuang, *Benjamin Franklin in American Thought and Culture, 1790–1990* (Philadelphia: American Philosophical Society, 1994), 52.

36. Available online as Benjamin Franklin, "Observations Concerning the Increase of Mankind, 1751," *Founders Online*, National Archives: http://founders.archives.gov/documents/Franklin/01-04-02-0080, sourced from Leonard W. Labaree, ed., *The Papers of Benjamin Franklin*, vol. 4, July 1, 1750, through June 30, 1753 (New Haven: Yale University Press, 1961), 225–34.

37. The document is digitized and available online: https://digitalhistory.hsp.org/pafrm/doc/memorial-pennsylvania-society-promoting-abolition-slavery-senate-and-representatives (Historical Society of Pennsylvania) and https://www.archives.gov/legislative/features/franklin (US National Archives).

38. According to Jared Sparks's *The Life of Benjamin Franklin* (Boston: Tappan and Dennet, 1844), the words "a long and useful life" were spoken by Dr. John Jones, who attended Franklin on his deathbed. See also H. W. Brands, *The First American: The Life and Times of Benjamin Franklin* (New York: Anchor Books, 2010).

39. University of Massachusetts at Boston Commencement Address, June 2, 2006.

40. A transcription of Rolfe's letter to Sandys is available online via the Library of Congress: http://www.loc.gov/teachers/classroommaterials/presentationsandactivities/presentations/timeline/colonial/virginia/rolf.html.

41. Jack P. Greene, *Pursuits of Happiness: The Social Development of Early Modern British Colonies and the Formation of American Culture* (Chapel Hill: University of North Carolina Press, 1988); James Horn, *A Land As God Made It: Jamestown and the Birth of America* (New York: Basic Books, 2005). On the origins and development of slavery and race, see especially Winthrop Jordan, *White over Black: American Attitudes toward the Negro, 1550–1812* (Chapel Hill: University of North Carolina Press, 1968); Edmund S. Morgan, *American Slavery, American Freedom: The Ordeal of Colonial Virginia* (New York: W. W. Norton, 1975); Ibram X. Kendi, *Stamped from the Beginning: The Definitive History of Racist Ideas in America* (New York: Nation Books, 2016). Major studies of slavery throughout American history include Ira Berlin, *Many Thousands Gone: The First Two Centuries of Slavery in North America* (Cambridge, MA: Harvard University Press, 1998) and David Brion Davis, *Inhuman Bondage: The Rise and Fall of Slavery in the New World* (Oxford: Oxford University Press, 2006).

42. James Horn and Philip D. Morgan, "Settlers and Slaves: European and African Migration to Early Modern British America," in Carole Shammas and Elizabeth Mancke, eds., *The Creation of the Atlantic World* (Baltimore: Johns Hopkins University Press, 2005), 24.

43. See for example *The Audacity of Hope*, 96, and "A More Perfect Union," *Change We Can Believe In*, 215.

44. "A More Perfect Union," *Change We Can Believe In*, 215.

45. Manisha Sinha, *The Slave's Cause: A History of Abolition* (New Haven: Yale University Press, 2016).

46. "A More Perfect Union," *Change We Can Believe In*, 215.

47. Ibid., 215, 215–16.

CHAPTER 2: THE SUBSTANCE OF OUR COMMON CREED

1. Barack Obama, *The Audacity of Hope: Thoughts on Reclaiming the American Dream* (New York: Crown, 2006), 53.

Notes

2. In "A More Perfect Union: *March 18, 2008, Philadelphia, Pennsylvania*," *Change We Can Believe In: Barack Obama's Plan to Renew America's Promise* (New York: Three Rivers Press, 2008), 215. Obama described how the founders "made real" their Declaration of Independence in the Constitutional Convention of 1787.

3. Available online: http://www.oed.com/.

4. Ibid.

5. "The Audacity of Hope: Keynote Address at the 2004 Democratic National Convention, *Boston, MA, July 27, 2004*," E. J. Dionne Jr. and Joy-Ann Reid, eds., *We Are the Change We Seek: The Speeches of Barack Obama* (London, New York: Bloomsbury, 2017), 7. All the other speeches quoted here are available online: https://obamawhitehouse.archives.gov/ briefing-room/speeches-and-remarks. "Inaugural Address by President Barack Obama, United States Capitol," The White House, Office of the Press Secretary, January 21, 2013. Available online: https://obamawhitehouse.archives.gov/the-press-office/2013/01/21/ inaugural-address-president-barack-obama; "Inaugural Address by President Barack Obama, United States Capitol," The White House, Office of the Press Secretary, January 21, 2013. Available online: https://obamawhitehouse.archives.gov/the-press-office/2013/01/21/ inaugural-address-president-barack-obama; "Remarks by the President in a Farewell Address, McCormick Place, Chicago, Illinois," The White House, Office of the Press Secretary, January 10, 2017. Available online: https://obamawhitehouse.archives.gov/ the-press-office/2017/01/10/remarks-president-farewell-address.

6. *The Audacity of Hope*, 53.

7. Pauline Maier, *American Scripture: How America Declared its Independence from Britain* (New York: Alfred A. Knopf, 1997), 168, 154.

8. Thomas Jefferson's letter to John Quincy Adams, July 18, 1824, is quoted in Maier, *American Scripture*, 186, and eulogists Caleb Cushing and John Sergeant are also in Maier, 189, 191.

9. Ibid., 202.

10. Ibid., xiv, xix.

11. Ibid., 215.

12. Ibid., 208.

13. "Declaration of Candidacy: *February 10, 2007, Springfield, Illinois*," *Change We Can Believe In*, 195–96.

14. The University of Massachusetts at Boston Commencement Address, June 2, 2006, is available online: http://obamaspeeches.com/074-University-of-Massachusetts-at-Boston-Commencement-Address-Obama-Speech.htm. "Knox College Commencement Address: June 4, 2005, Galesburg, Illinois," in Mary Frances Berry and Josh Gottheimer, eds., *Power in Words: The Stories Behind Barack Obama's Speeches, from the State House to the White House* (Boston: Beacon Press, 2010), 58.

15. "Weekly Address: Celebrating Independence Day," The White House, Office of the Press Secretary, July 4, 2013. "Remarks by the President at Fourth of July Celebration, South Lawn," The White House, Office of the Press Secretary, July 4, 2013. Available online: https:// obamawhitehouse.archives.gov/the-press-office/2013/07/04/weekly-address-celebrating-independence-day and https://obamawhitehouse.archives.gov/the-press-office/2013/07/04/ remarks-president-fourth-july-celebration.

16. There was also a Quebec Act that created a highly unaccountable kind of colonial government in the formerly French Canadian colony and redrew its borders southward to include territory that the traditionally English colonies considered theirs under their original charters. This

the colonists' counted as a fifth "Intolerable Act," though it was not intended by MPs to be one of the four Coercive Acts.

17. "President Barack Obama's Inaugural Address," The White House, Office of the Press Secretary, Blog, January 21, 2009. This part of Obama's Inaugural Address has sometimes been said to reference events at Valley Forge. But in fact Washington is thought to have had these words (by Thomas Paine—see below) read to his soldiers as they were about to cross the Delaware River in December 1776. This was indeed, as Obama says, "the year of America's birth," whereas Washington and his army camped at Valley Forge in the winter of 1777–78.

18. Thomas Paine, "The Crisis, Number 1, 1776," in Bruce Kuklick, ed., *Thomas Paine: Political Writings* (Cambridge: University of Cambridge Press, 2000), 54, 49.

19. Adams on Paine's *Common Sense* is cited in Maier, *American Scripture*, 173.

20. Eric Foner, *Tom Paine and Revolutionary America* (Oxford: Oxford University Press, 1976); John Keane, *Tom Paine: A Political Life* (London: Bloomsbury, 1995).

21. Maier, *American Scripture*, 41.

22. Ibid., 41–44.

23. "Weekly Address," July 4, 2013; John to Abigail Adams, July 2, 1776, Maier, *American Scripture*, 162.

24. All versions of the Declaration of Independence (and the Constitution and Bill of Rights) are digitized and available at the US National Archives' "Founding Documents" collection. Available online: https://www.archives.gov/founding-docs.

25. *The Audacity of Hope*, 87; Thomas Jefferson to Henry Lee, May 8, 1825, is partly cited in Maier, *American Scripture*, 124, and wholly in Merrill D. Peterson, ed., *Jefferson: Writings* (New York: Library of America, 1984), 1500-01. Jefferson always used an apostrophe in the possessive "its."

26. Jefferson to James Madison, August 30, 1823, and John Adams to Timothy Pickering, August 6, 1822, are quoted in Maier, *American Scripture*, 124.

27. Danielle Allen, *Our Declaration: A Reading of the Declaration of Independence in Defense of Equality* (New York: Liveright, 2015), especially pages 45–125; Richard D. Brown, *Knowledge Is Power: The Diffusion of Information in Early America, 1700-1865* (Oxford: Oxford University Press, 1989).

28. Peter Laslett, ed., John Locke, *Two Treatises of Government* (Cambridge: Cambridge University Press, 1988), Chapter 2, 6.

29. *The Audacity of Hope*, 87.

30. Richard Tuck, ed., Thomas Hobbes, *Leviathan* (Cambridge: Cambridge University Press, 1996), 223.

31. *The Audacity of Hope*, 53; James T. Kloppenberg, *Reading Obama: Dreams, Hope, and the American Political Tradition* (Princeton: Princeton University Press, 2011), 42–44, 53, 93–94, 101–02, 273–74.

32. J. G. A. Pocock, *The Machiavellian Moment: Florentine Political Thought and the Atlantic Republican Tradition* (Princeton: Princeton University Press, 1975).

33. David Remnick, *The Bridge: The Life and Rise of Barack Obama* (New York: Alfred A. Knopf, 2010), 98–122, 182–200, 205–18. Kloppenberg, *Reading Obama*, 16–19, 42–44, 93–94, 158–60. Bernard Bailyn, *The Ideological Origins of the American Revolution* (Cambridge, MA: Harvard University Press, 1966); Gordon S. Wood, *The Creation of the American Republic, 1776-1787* (Chapel Hill: The University of North Carolina Press, 1969).

34. Ronald Hamowy ed., [John Trenchard and Thomas Gordon], *Cato's Letters: Or, Essays on Liberty, Civil and Religious, And other Important Subjects, Two Volumes* (Indianapolis: Liberty Fund, 1995).

35. Bailyn, *The Ideological Origins of the American Revolution*; Wood, *The Creation of the American Republic*; Jack P. Greene, *The Intellectual Construction of America: Exceptionalism and Identity from 1492 to 1800* (Chapel Hill: The University of North Carolina Press, 1997).

36. "Inaugural Address by President Barack Obama, United States Capitol," The White House, Office of the Press Secretary, January 21, 2013.

37. See the U.S. National Archives' "Founding Documents" collection. Available online: https://www.archives.gov/founding-docs.

38. The linking hyphens are not in Jefferson's draft or the Committee of Five's submission or the Continental Congress's first versions of the Declaration. They first appear in the "Dunlap Broadside," a single-page version produced on the evening of July 4 to publicize independence and its justifications. More such dashes were afterwards added by Timothy Matlack, the secretary of the Continental Congress, for the parchment version to be distributed to the new states. It is worth noting then that the dashes were added to help others follow the arguments being made. See Allen, *Our Declaration*, 152.

39. "Remarks by the President at Independence Day Celebration," The White House, Office of the Press Secretary, July 6, 2010. Available online: https://obamawhitehouse.archives.gov/the-press-office/remarks-president-independence-day-celebration.

40. "Weekly Address," July 4, 2013.

41. My emphases.

42. "A More Perfect Union," *Change We Can Believe In*, 215.

43. Obama created exactly the same effect, in speaking about the contemporary United States, when he said "It was here, in Springfield, where I saw that all that is America converge—farmers and teachers, businessmen and laborers, all of them with a story to tell, all of them seeking a seat at the table, all of them clamoring to be heard": "Declaration of Candidacy: *February 10, 2007, Springfield, Illinois,*" *Change We Can Believe In*, 194.

44. John Dickinson, *Letters from a Farmer in Pennsylvania, to the Inhabitants of the British Colonies in America* (Philadelphia: David Hall and William Sellers, 1768), 3.

45. "A More Perfect Union," *Change We Can Believe In*, 215.

46. Carl Lotus Becker, *The History of Political Parties in the Province of New York, 1760–1776* (Madison: University of Wisconsin, 1909), 22.

47. *The Audacity of Hope*, 95. Here Obama is citing Joseph J. Ellis's *Founding Brothers: The Revolutionary Generation* (New York: Vintage Books, 2002), 89. In the section referred to, Ellis was remarking that although Thomas Jefferson's attack on the slave trade and slavery in his draft of the Declaration was edited out of the final version, "it nevertheless captured the nearly rhapsodic sense that the American Revolution was both a triumphant and transformative moment in world history, when all laws and human relationships dependent on coercion would be swept away forever." We'll return to Jefferson's attack on slavery shortly.

48. Thomas Jefferson to Henry Lee, May 8, 1825, Peterson, ed., *Jefferson: Writings*, 1501.

49. Thomas Jefferson, Letter to Edward Coles, August 25, 1814, in Joyce Appleby and Terrence Ball, eds., *Thomas Jefferson: Political Writings* (Cambridge: Cambridge University Press, 1999), 493.

50. See the U.S. National Archives' "Founding Documents" collection. Available online: https://www.archives.gov/founding-docs.

51. Ibid.

52. Thomas Jefferson, *Notes on the State of Virginia*, Query XVIII, "Manners," in Peterson, ed., *Jefferson: Writings*, 289.

53. Jefferson, *Notes on the State of Virginia*, Query XIV, "Laws," in Peterson, ed., *Jefferson: Writings*, 264.

54. Ibid., 264–65.

55. Ibid.

56. Ibid., 265–66.

57. Ibid., 266.

58. Ibid., 265.

59. Ibid., 266–67.

60. Ibid., 264, 270.

61. Ibid., 270.

62. She was born Sarah but known as Sally. Annette Gordon-Reed, the principal historian of Sally Hemings and Thomas Jefferson, styles her Sally and so I follow her lead. See *The Hemingses of Monticello: An American Family* (New York: W. W. Norton, 2008)—a masterpiece of forensic research and beautiful writing.

63. Fawn Brodie, *Thomas Jefferson: An Intimate History* (New York: W. W. Norton, 1974); Annette Gordon-Reed, *Thomas Jefferson and Sally Hemings: An American Controversy* (Charlottesville: University of Virginia Press, 1997) and *The Hemingses of Monticello*. See also Gordon-Reed and Peter S. Onuf, *"Most Blessed of the Patriarchs": Thomas Jefferson and the Empire of the Imagination* (New York: Liveright, 2016) and Onuf, *The Mind of Thomas Jefferson* (Charlottesville: University of Virginia Press, 2007). I say "black" children, but Betty was the daughter of an African woman named Susanna and an English sea captain named John Hemings and was therefore half white. As Sally was the daughter of Betty and John Wayles, she was three-fourths white. As her children were fathered by Thomas Jefferson, they were seven-eights white. They were nevertheless legally black according to America's "one-drop rule," and they were enslaved because slavery was a matrilineal inheritance. When the Hemingses moved to Ohio, however, they "passed" as white.

64. Paul Leicester Ford, ed., *The Autobiography of Thomas Jefferson, 1743–1790*, (Philadelphia: University of Pennsylvania Press, 2005), 76–77. These words are also found in Peterson, ed., *Jefferson: Writings*, 44.

65. See especially Sylvia Frey, *Water from the Rock: Black Resistance in a Revolutionary Age* (Princeton: Princeton University Press, 1991).

66. The full text of the petition can be found in Christopher Cameron, *The Abolitionist Movement: Documents Decoded* (Santa Barbara, CA: ABC-Clio, 2014), 20–22.

67. The full text of the petition can be found in Philip B. Kurland and Raplph Lerner, eds., *The Founders' Constitution* (Chicago: University of Chicago Press, 1987), Vol. 1, Chapter 14, Document 9.

68. The full text of this petition can be found in Cameron, *The Abolitionist Movement*, 25–27.

69. James Otis, *The Rights of the British Colonies Asserted and Proved* (Boston: Edes and Gill, 1764), 29.

70. "A More Perfect Union: *March 18, 2008, Philadelphia, Pennsylvania*," *Change We Can Believe In*, 230–32.

71. Further details and all the primary sources connected to this case are available online via the Massachusetts Historical Society: https://www.masshist.org/endofslavery/index.php.

72. Ibid.

73. Arthur Zilversmit, *The First Emancipation: The Abolition of Slavery in the North* (Chicago: University of Chicago Press, 1967); David Brion Davis, *The Problem of Slavery in the Age of Revolution, 1770–1823* (Ithaca: Cornell University Press, 1975; Oxford: Oxford University Press, 1999).

74. *The Audacity of Hope*, 53.

75. *The Audacity of Hope*, 53, 86, 53; "A More Perfect Union," 215.

CHAPTER 3: THE FOUNDATION OF OUR GOVERNMENT

1. Barack Obama, *The Audacity of Hope: Thoughts on Reclaiming the American Dream* (New York: Crown, 2006), 53.

2. The Virginia Declaration of Rights is available online: http://edu.lva.virginia.gov/docs/hires/ VirginiaDeclarationofRights.pdf (Library of Virginia). John Hancock to "Certain States," Philadelphia, July 6, 1776, cited in Pauline Maier, *American Scripture: How America Declared its Independence from Britain* (New York: Alfred A. Knopf, 1997), 126.

3. Arthur Zilversmit, *The First Emancipation: The Abolition of Slavery in the North* (Chicago: University of Chicago Press, 1967). Documents related to the end of slavery in Massachusetts are available online via the Massachusetts Historical Society: https://www. masshist.org/endofslavery/index.php.

4. It is true that the Virginia Declaration of Rights was incorporated into that state's constitution, but the slaveholders of the Old Dominion could of course trust themselves not to overinterpret its applicability in a way that they couldn't trust all their other countrymen.

5. "A More Perfect Union: *March 18, 2008, Philadelphia, Pennsylvania*," in *Change We Can Believe In: Barack Obama's Plan to Renew America's Promise* (New York: Three Rivers Press, 2008), 215.

6. Ibid., 215. The capitalization of "WE THE PEOPLE" as well as the elision of "of the United States" is in this book, which, produced by "Obama for America" after the 2008 campaign, I take to be the authoritative version.

7. I've listed above the Constitutional clauses that are (almost) explicitly about slavery. But, as David Waldstreicher's *Slavery's Constitution: From Revolution to Ratification* (New York: Hill and Wang, 2009) points out, six of the Constitution's eighty-four clauses directly affected slavery and another five did so indirectly. The Constitution and Bill of Rights as well as the Declaration of Independence are digitized and probably most easily available at the US National Archives' "Founding Documents" collection. Available online: https://www. archives.gov/founding-docs.

8. "A More Perfect Union," *Change We Can Believe In*, 215.

9. Ibid.

10. Danielle Allen, *Our Declaration: A Reading of the Declaration of Independence in Defense of Equality* (New York: Liveright, 2015), especially pages 45–125.

11. The Articles of Confederation are also available on the website of the US National Archives: https://www.archives.gov/historical-docs/articles-of-confederation.

12. "Proceedings of Commissioners to Remedy Defects of the Federal Government," 1786, is available online via the Yale University Law Department's Avalon Project: http://avalon.law. yale.edu/18th_century/annapoli.asp.

13. Charles A. Beard, *An Economic Interpretation of the Constitution of the United States* (New York: Macmillan, 1913). An excellent short explication of the Constitution is Jack N. Rakove, *The Annotated U.S. Constitution and Declaration of Independence* (Cambridge, MA: Harvard University Press, 2009). See also Rakove, *The Beginnings of National Politics: An Interpretive History of the Continental Congress* (New York: Alfred A. Knopf, 1979).

14. "A More Perfect Union," *Change We Can Believe In*, 215, 216. Accounts of Obama's education and evaluations of its influence can be found in David Remnick, *The Bridge: The Life and Rise of Barack Obama* (New York: Alfred A. Knopf, 2010), 98–122, 182–200, 205–18, and James T. Kloppenberg, *Reading Obama: Dreams, Hope, and the American Political Tradition* (Princeton: Princeton University Press, 2011), 1–84. On Obama's teaching of Constitutional law at the University of Chicago, see Remnick, 261–67.

15. For both the Declaration of Independence and the Constitution see the U.S. National Archives' "Founding Documents" collection. Available online: https://www.archives.gov/founding-docs.

16. James Madison, "Vices of the Political System of the United States." Also available from the US National Archives: https://founders.archives.gov/documents/Madison/01-09-02-0187.

17. *The Audacity of Hope*, 87.

18. "A More Perfect Union," *Change We Can Believe In*, 215, 216. Abraham Lincoln's Gettysburg Address of November 19, 1863, is available via the US National Archives: https://www.loc.gov/rr/program/bib/ourdocs/Gettysburg.html.

19. *The Audacity of Hope*, 86–87.

20. Ibid., 87–88.

21. Ibid., 92.

22. Ibid., 93.

23. Ibid., 87.

24. Ibid., 88.

25. James Madison, Federalist No. 10, 1788, Isaac Kramnick, ed., *The Federalist Papers* (London: Penguin, 1987), 124.

26. Ibid., 126.

27. Ibid., 126–27.

28. Ibid., 127.

29. Ibid., 127, 128.

30. *The Audacity of Hope*, 91.

31. Douglass Adair, *Fame and the Founding Fathers*, Trevor Colbourn, ed. (New York: W. W. Norton, 1974).

32. *The Audacity of Hope*, 93.

33. There were originally supposed to be twelve amendments in the Bill of Rights. One of those not adopted at the time enumerated the proportion of congressmen to the population, but has since been superseded by legislation. The other one had also been superseded and was also pretty much forgotten, until a Texan legislative aid named Gregory Watson launched a campaign that finally saw it adopted in 1992. The Twenty-Seventh Amendment directs that "No law, varying the compensation for the services of the Senators and Representatives, shall take effect, until an election of Representatives shall have intervened." See also Pauline Maier, *Ratification: The People Debate the Constitution* (New York: Simon and Schuster, 2010).

34. *The Audacity of Hope*, 91.

35. The text of the *Marbury v. Madison* ruling is available online via the Supreme Court Center: https://supreme.justia.com/cases/federal/us/5/137/case.html.

36. "Thomas Jefferson to William Charles Jarvis, September 28, 1820," in Joyce Appleby and Terrence Ball, eds., *Thomas Jefferson: Political Writings: Cambridge Texts in the History of Political Thought* (Cambridge: Cambridge University Press, 1999), 381.

37. *The Audacity of Hope*, 79, 89.

38. Ibid., 92, 89.

39. Ibid., 89–90.

40. Ibid., 91.

41. Ibid., 91–92.

42. "Inaugural Address by President Barack Obama, United States Capitol," The White House, Office of the Press Secretary, January 21, 2013. Available online: https://obamawhitehouse. archives.gov/the-press-office/2013/01/21/inaugural-address-president-barack-obama.

43. Ibid.

44. *The Audacity of Hope*, 85.

45. Ibid., 92.

46. Garry Wills, "Two Speeches on Race," *The New York Review of Books*, May 1, 2008. Available online: http://www.nybooks.com/articles/2008/05/01/two-speeches-on-race/. As a Law student at Harvard, Barack Obama assisted Professor Laurence H. Tribe with an article entitled "The Curvature of Constitutional Space: What Lawyers Can Learn from Modern Physics," for the *Harvard Law Review* (November 1989). The article argued, in opposition to the conservative concept of judicial neutrality and restraint, that the power and authority of the state affects all aspects of culture, including the law, just as a star curves light and gravity around it. Furthermore, in *On Reading the Constitution* (Cambridge, MA: Harvard University Press, 1991), Tribe and Michael C. Dorf credited Obama and fellow student Robert Fisher with the likening of the history of constitutional interpretation to a "conversation" (the theme Obama returned to in *The Audacity of Hope*). The authors said that the two students had "influenced our thinking on virtually every subject discussed in these pages." For more on this, see Kloppenberg, *Reading Obama*, 56–62.

47. *The Audacity of Hope*, 92, 89, 90.

48. Ibid., 90, 93.

49. Ibid., 92–93.

50. Ibid., 94, 94–95, 93–94.

51. For Kloppenberg on Obama's "philosophical pragmatism," see *Reading Obama*, most especially xi–xiii, 3–4, 17–18, 62–64, 83, 110–11, 169–72, and 193. For the influence of other thinkers besides James and Dewey, especially Reinhold Niebuhr, John Rawls, Richard Rorty, and Richard J. Bernstein, see the whole of chapter 2. And for Obama's legal education and thought, especially the influence of Laurence Tribe, see 37–62, 69–71, 109, 153–72, 174–77, and 184–85. Actually, just read the whole book—it's great. Not that I agree with everything Prof Kloppenberg says. He tends, for example, to emphasize Obama's "historicism" and "particularism," while my stress on Obama's belief in "evolutionary intent" tends (as seen in this chapter) to place more emphasis on Obama's "universalism," albeit a historicized kind of universalism. This difference may be merely a matter of emphasis, or may be a result of Kloppenberg approaching Obama as a social, legal, and political thinker and me approaching Obama more as a historian, or it may be a bit of both. That said, chapter 3 of *Reading Obama* is called "Obama's American History," although again the Kloppenberg approach is more from the perspective of political theory than mine, which comes more from the angle of historiography. By a remarkable coincidence,

by the way, John Dewey's granddaughter, Professor Alice Dewey, supervised Stanley Ann Dunham's PhD thesis on "Peasant Blacksmithing in Indonesia: Surviving and Thriving Against All Odds" (University of Hawaii, 1992), and the two became personal friends. Stanley Ann Dunham (November 29, 1942–November 7, 1995) was, of course, Barack Obama's mother. Kloppenberg, 255, 268, and Remnick, *The Bridge*, esp. 83–87.

52. *The Audacity of Hope*, 92; Joseph M. Bessette, "Deliberative Democracy: The Majority Principle in Republican Government," in Robert A. Goldwin and William A. Schambra, eds., *How Democratic Is the Constitution?* (Washington: American Enterprise Institute, 1980), 102–16; and Bessette, *The Mild Voice of Reason: Deliberative Democracy and American National Government* (Chicago: University of Chicago Press, 1994).

53. *The Audacity of Hope*, 95. President Obama's successor has also commented on the tried and tested checks and balances of the Constitution, and he appears to have significantly less reverence for America's fundamental laws and system of government than Obama does. "It's a very rough system. It's an archaic system. It's really a bad thing for the country," he said. Matthew Rozsa, "Donald Trump doesn't like the 'archaic' Constitution: 'It's really a bad thing for the country,'" *Salon*, May 1, 2017.

54. "A More Perfect Union," *Change We Can Believe In*, 215; *The Audacity of Hope*, 199, 61; University of Massachusetts at Boston Commencement Address, June 2, 2006, available online: http://obamaspeeches.com/074-University-of-Massachusetts-at-Boston-Commencement-Address-Obama-Speech.htm.

55. *The Audacity of Hope*, 217.

56. Ibid., 93.

57. Pictures of the tombstone are available online and free to see via the Thomas Jefferson Foundation at Monticello: https://www.monticello.org/site/research-and-collections/jeffersons-gravestone.

58. The Virginia Statute for Religious Freedom is available online at the US National Archives: https://founders.archives.gov/documents/Jefferson/01-02-02-0132-0004-0082.

59. Ibid.

60. Ibid.

61. See the U.S. National Archives' "Founding Documents" collection. Available online: https://www.archives.gov/founding-docs.

62. To John Adams, April 11, 1823. Available online at the US National Archives: https://founders.archives.gov/documents/Jefferson/98-01-02-3446.

63. *The Audacity of Hope*, 217.

64. Ibid., 217–18.

65. Ibid., 218.

66. Ibid.

67. Ibid., 218. John Leland is also famous for the Cheshire Mammoth Cheese. Yes, really! On January 1, 1802, on behalf of the people of Cheshire, Massachusetts, Leland presented President Jefferson with a four-foot wide, thirteen-foot round, 1,235 pound block of cheese made from the milk of "Republican" cows and bearing the legend "Rebellion to tyrants is obedience to God" in its red crust. Leland also gave the Sunday sermon two days later in the House of Representatives, and Jefferson made a rare trip to Capitol Hill for the special occasion.

68. "We Cannot Abandon the Field of Religious Discourse: Keynote Address at the Call to Renewal Conference, *Washington, DC, June 28, 2006*," E. J. Dionne Jr. and Joy-Ann Reid, eds., *We Are the Change We Seek: The Speeches of Barack Obama* (London: Bloomsbury, 2017), 27.

69. *The Audacity of Hope*, 214. Of course I have no idea whether Barack Obama thought about John Lennon when he wrote these words. But it is worth noting that during the Chicago anti-Iraq-war rally of October 2, 2002, at which Obama gave his now-famous anti-Iraq-war speech, Lennon's "Give Peace a Chance" was playing on the PA. Obama leaned over to his friend and fellow Project Vote activist and civil rights campaigner Bettylu Saltzman and said "Can't they play something else?" See Remnick, *The Bridge*, 345.

70. *The Audacity of Hope*, 218.

71. Ibid., 221, 219. Obama repeated many of these same words in his address to the Call to Renewal Conference in June 2006: "We Cannot Abandon the Field of Religious Discourse," Dionne and Reid, eds., *We Are the Change We Seek*, 21–37, and "Call to Renewal Keynote Address: *June 28, 2006, National City Church, Washington, DC*," Mary Frances Berry and Josh Gottheimer, eds., *Power in Words: The Stories Behind Barack Obama's Speeches, from the State House to the White House* (Boston: Beacon Press, 2010), 66–85.

72. "The Audacity of Hope: Keynote Address at the 2004 Democratic National Convention, *Boston, MA, July 27, 2004*," Dionne and Reid, eds., *We Are the Change We Seek*, 11.

73. *The Audacity of Hope*, 91, 95.

74. Ibid., 93.

75. Ibid.

76. Ibid., 91.

77. Ibid., 21–22. Of course Obama published these words in 2006, long before the election of the forty-fifth president, who is also not fond of foreigners or of freedom of the press.

78. *The Audacity of Hope*, 93. That Jefferson's agrarian republic was largely a figment of his imagination is one of the subjects of my previous book, *The Tobacco-Plantation South in the Early American Atlantic World* (New York: Palgrave Macmillan, 2013).

79. *The Audacity of Hope*, 93.

80. Thomas Jefferson's First Inaugural Address is available online at the Library of Congress website: https://www.loc.gov/rr/program/bib/inaugurations/jefferson/index.html.

81. Ibid.

82. *The Audacity of Hope*, 85–86.

83. Ibid., 86, 88.

84. Jefferson's First Inaugural Address: https://www.loc.gov/rr/program/bib/inaugurations/jefferson/index.html.

85. *The Audacity of Hope*, 95.

86. Jefferson, *Notes on the State of Virginia*, Query XVIII, "Manners," in Merrill D. Peterson, ed., *Jefferson: Writings* (New York: Library of America, 1984), 289; "A More Perfect Union," *Change We Can Believe In*, 215.

CHAPTER 4: A NEW BIRTH OF FREEDOM

1. "A More Perfect Union: *March 18, 2008, Philadelphia, Pennsylvania*," in *Change We Can Believe In: Barack Obama's Plan to Renew America's Promise* (New York: Three Rivers Press, 2008), 215.

2. Barack Obama, *The Audacity of Hope: Thoughts on Reclaiming the American Dream* (New York: Crown, 2006), 96.

3. The Constitution and Bill of Rights as well as the Declaration of Independence are digitized and probably most easily available at the US National Archives' "Founding Documents" collection. Available online: https://www.archives.gov/founding-docs.

4. As David Waldstreicher's *Slavery's Constitution: From Revolution to Ratification* (New York: Hill and Wang, 2009) shows, there were in fact six clauses that directly affected slavery and another five that did so indirectly, some of them following the implications of the three-fifths clause. I've focused on the ones that are (almost) explicitly about slavery. Moreover, as Waldstreicher says, enslavement was so deeply embedded in American life that "slavery was as important in the making of the Constitution as the Constitution was to the survival of slavery" (page 17).

5. "Remarks by the First Lady at the Democratic National Convention," The White House, Office of the First Lady, July 25, 2016. Available online: https://obamawhitehouse.archives.gov/the-press-office/2016/07/25/remarks-first-lady-democratic-national-convention.

6. "Q&A: Did Slaves Build the White House," The White House Historical Association. Available online https://www.whitehousehistory.org/questions/did-slaves-build-the-white-house.

7. Ibid.

8. James Madison's "Original Notes on the Debates in the Federal Convention" are available online from the US National Archives: https://www.loc.gov/item/mjm023093/convention; https://www.loc.gov/item/mjm023109.

9. Details and documents about the end of slavery in Massachusetts are available online via the Massachusetts Historical Society: https://www.masshist.org/endofslavery/index.php.

10. Ibid.

11. "A More Perfect Union," *Change We Can Believe In*, 215-16; *The Audacity of Hope*, 95.

12. *The Audacity of Hope*, 92; "A More Perfect Union," *Change We Can Believe in*, 216.

13. "The Audacity of Hope: Keynote Address at the 2004 Democratic National Convention, *Boston, MA, July 27, 2004*," E. J. Dionne Jr. and Joy-Ann Reid, eds., *We Are the Change We Seek: The Speeches of Barack Obama* (London, New York: Bloomsbury, 2017), 12.

14. I give this example as it featured in the movie *Twelve Years a Slave* (dir. Steve McQueen, 2013), based on the narrative of Solomon Northup. For more on slave religion, see especially Eugene D. Genovese, *Roll, Jordan, Roll: The World the Slaves Made* (New York: Vintage Books, 1976) and Albert J. Raboteau, *Slave Religion: The "Invisible Institution" in the Antebellum South* (Oxford: Oxford University Press, 1978; updated edition, 2004). For its origins and early development, see Sylvia R. Frey and Betty Wood, *Come Shouting to Zion: African American Protestantism in the American South and British Caribbean to 1830* (Chapel Hill: University of North Carolina Press, 1998).

15. Barack Obama, *Dreams from My Father: A Story of Race and Inheritance* (New York: Crown, 1995, 2004), 294. Obama repeated the passage when he spoke about Reverend Jeremiah Wright in Philadelphia in March 2008: "A More Perfect Union," *Change We Can Believe In*, 220.

16. "Remarks by the First Lady at the Democratic National Convention," "President Barack Obama's Inaugural Address," The White House, Office of the Press Secretary, Blog, January 21, 2009. Available online: https://obamawhitehouse.archives.gov/blog/2009/01/21/president-barack-obamas-inaugural-address; "Inaugural Address by President Barack Obama, United States Capitol," The White House, Office of the Press Secretary, January 21, 2013. Available online: https://obamawhitehouse.archives.gov/the-press-office/2013/01/21/inaugural-address-president-barack-obama.

17. "The Audacity of Hope," Dionne and Reid, eds., *We Are the Change We Seek*, 15.

18. "President Barack Obama's Inaugural Address."

19. "Inaugural Address by President Barack Obama."

20. During the 2008 campaign Barack Obama was opportunistically alleged to be all these things, but managed to avert the development of a consensus on any of them. The "birther" movement nevertheless gained momentum after Obama's election as president, as American birth is a qualification for that office. It was of course nothing but a barely disguised racist campaign to delegitimize his presidency, fake news promulgated by very dishonest people.

21. "Remarks by the President at the Groundbreaking Ceremony of the National Museum of African American History and Culture, The National Mall," The White House, Office of the Press Secretary, February 22, 2012, available online: https://obamawhitehouse.archives. gov/the-press-office/2012/02/22/remarks-president-groundbreaking-ceremony-national-museum-african-americ; "Weekly Address: Celebrating the National Museum of African American History and Culture," The White House, Office of the Press Secretary, September 24, 2016, available online: https://obamawhitehouse.archives.gov/the-press-office/2016/09/24/weekly-address-celebrating-national-museum-african-american-history-and.

22. "Remarks by the President at the Groundbreaking Ceremony of the National Museum of African American History and Culture."

23. "Remarks by the President at Commemoration of the 150th Anniversary of the 13th Amendment, U.S. Capitol, Washington, D.C.," The White House, Office of the Press Secretary, December 9, 2015. Available online: https://obamawhitehouse.archives.gov/the-press-office/2015/12/09/remarks-president-commemoration-150th-anniversary-13th-amendment.

24. "Remarks by the President at the Groundbreaking Ceremony of the National Museum of African American History and Culture"; "Remarks by the First Lady at the Democratic National Convention"; Remarks by the President at Reception in Honor of the National Museum of African American History and Culture, Grand Foyer," The White House, Office of the Press Secretary, September 23, 2016. Available online: https://obama whitehouse.archives.gov/the-press-office/2016/09/23/remarks-president-reception-honor-national-museum-african-american.

25. "Remarks by the President at the 50th Anniversary of the Selma to Montgomery Marches, Edmund Pettus Bridge, Selma, Alabama," The White House, Office of the Press Secretary, March 7, 2015. Available online: https://obamawhitehouse.archives.gov/the-press-office/2015/03/07/remarks-president-50th-anniversary-selma-montgomery-marches.

26. Ibid.

27. "A More Perfect Union," *Change We Can Believe In*, 217.

28. "Remarks by the President at the Groundbreaking Ceremony of the National Museum of African American History and Culture."

29. "Remarks by the President at Commemoration of the 150th Anniversary of the 13th Amendment"; "A More Perfect Union," *Change We Can Believe In*, 215; *The Audacity of Hope*, 92.

30. "A More Perfect Union," *Change We Can Believe In*, 215.

31. Thomas Jefferson, "Letter to John Holmes, August 22, 1820," Joyce Appleby and Terrence Ball, eds., *Thomas Jefferson: Political Writings* (Cambridge: Cambridge University Press, 1999), 496.

32. The full text of the Exposition and Protest is available online thanks to the South Carolina State Library: https://dc.statelibrary.sc.gov/handle/10827/21911.

33. "Election Night: *November 4, 2008, Chicago, Illinois*," in *Change We Can Believe In*, 275.

34. Various versions of the Gettysburg Address are available via the US National Archives: https://www.loc.gov/rr/program/bib/ourdocs/Gettysburg.html.

35. Daniel Webster's "Second Reply to Hayne" is available online from the Library of Congress: https://www.loc.gov/item/2005687410/.

36. Ibid.

37. Cited in Sean Wilentz, *The Rise of American Democracy: Jefferson to Lincoln* (New York: Norton, 2005), 322.

38. William W. Freehling, *Prelude to Civil War: The Nullification Controversy in Southern Carolina, 1816–1836* (New York: Harper and Row, 1965). Lincoln probably borrowed the particular phraseology from the abolitionist and Unitarian Minister Theodore Parker, who said, borrowing from Webster, that "Democracy is direct self-government, over all the people, by all the people, for all the people" in an address entitled "The effect of slavery on the American people: A sermon preached at the Music hall, Boston, on Sunday, July 4, 1858." Lincoln owned copies of Parker's sermons. It may have derived originally from John Wycliffe who in 1384 said that "The Bible is for the Government of the People, by the People, and for the People," according to the 1951 edition of *Familiar Quotations* by John Bartlett.

39. *The Audacity of Hope*, 96.

40. Available at the U.S. National Archives' "Founding Documents" collection. Available online: https://www.archives.gov/founding-docs.

41. "Remarks by the President at Commemoration of the 150th Anniversary of the 13th Amendment." A published, printed version of Charles Sumner's popular "The Crime Against Kansas" speech is available to view online from the website of the United States Senate: https://www.senate.gov/artandhistory/history/resources/pdf/CrimeAgainstKSSpeech.pdf

42. For more on this moment, see Joanne Freeman, *The Field of Blood: Congressional Violence and the Road to Civil War*, forthcoming from Farrar, Straus, and Giroux. Professor Freeman has also shown elsewhere how common and ritualized violence actually was. See also her earlier book, *Affairs of Honor: National Politics in the New Republic* (New Haven: Yale University Press, 2002).

43. As Barack Obama called Lincoln in his "Declaration of Candidacy: *February 10, 2007, Springfield, Illinois,*" *Change We Can Believe In*, 201.

44. *The Audacity of Hope*, 95.

45. Material relevant to the Dred Scott case is available online via the Library of Congress: https://www.loc.gov/rr/program/bib/ourdocs/DredScott.html. The full text of the Scott v Sandford decision is available online from the Supreme Court website: https://supreme.justia.com/cases/federal/us/60/393/case.html.

46. Ibid.

47. There are of course many sources for Lincoln's speeches. A full transcription of the "House Divided" speech is available online at the site of National Parks Service Lincoln Home National Historic Site, sourced from Mark E. Neely, Jr., *The Abraham Lincoln Encyclopedia* (New York: Da Capo Press, 1982): https://www.nps.gov/liho/learn/historyculture/housedivided.htm.

48. Ibid.

49. Robert W. Johannsen, ed., *The Lincoln-Douglas Debates of 1858* (Oxford: Oxford University Press, 1965).

50. *The Audacity of Hope*, 96.

51. Ibid.

52. Ibid., 96-97.

53. "Remarks by the President at Commemoration of the 150th Anniversary of the 13th Amendment."

54. *The Audacity of Hope*, 97.

55. Peter P. Hinks, ed., *David Walker's Appeal to the Coloured Citizens of the World* (University Park: Penn State University Press, 2000).

56. All issues of *The Liberator* are available online: http://fair-use.org/the-liberator/.

57. Henry Mayer, *All on Fire: William Lloyd Garrison and the Abolition of Slavery* (New York: St. Martin's Press, 1998). For Garrison and other abolitionist figures mentioned by Obama, and for how (as with Obama) black and white abolitionists worked together, see Manisha Sinha's new, epic, and brilliant *The Slave's Cause: A History of Abolition* (New Haven: Yale University Press, 2016).

58. Douglas R. Egerton, *He Shall Go Out Free: The Lives of Denmark Vesey* (Lanham: Rowman and Littlefield, second edition, 2004).

59. Frederick Douglass, "The Meaning of the Fourth of July for the Negro," in Philip S. Foner, ed., *Frederick Douglass: Selected Speeches and Writings, Abridged and Adapted by Yuval Taylor* (Chicago: Lawrence Hill, 1999), 196-97 (the whole speech runs from page 188 to 205).

60. Ibid., 191.

61. Ibid., 204.

62. Ibid., 204, 205.

63. William S. McFeely, *Frederick Douglass* (New York: W. W. Norton, 1991). "The Meaning of the Fourth of July," 191. "President Barack Obama's Inaugural Address"; "A More Perfect Union," *Change We Can Believe In*, 215; *The Audacity of Hope*, 97. Barack Obama has quoted Frederick Douglass directly on this point: "And, as Frederick Douglass once stated: 'Power concedes nothing without a demand. It never did, and it never will,'" in "An Honest Government, A Hopeful Future: *August 28, 2006, University of Nairobi, Nairobi, Kenya*," Mary Frances Berry and Josh Gottheimer, eds., *Power in Words: The Stories Behind Barack Obama's Speeches, from the State House to the White House* (Boston: Beacon Press, 2010), 94. Douglass spoke these famous words in his "West India Emancipation" speech of August 3, 1857: "West India Emancipation, speech delivered in Canandaigua, New York, August 3, 1857," Foner, ed., *Frederick Douglass*, 367. For a course on "Current Issues in Racism and the Law" at the University of Chicago, Professor Obama set as readings Douglass's "The Right to Criticize the American Institutions" (a speech before the American Anti-Slavery Society. May 11, 1847) and "Is It Right and Wise to Kill a Kidnapper" (article in *The North Star*, July 28, 1848). See David Remnick, *The Bridge: The Life and Rise of Barack Obama* (New York: Alfred A. Knopf, 2010), 263. Remnick also tells us that the great scholar Henry Louis Gates Jr. told him that he sees Obama as a "post-modern Frederick Douglass": "they both launched their careers with speeches and their first books were autobiographies. They spoke and wrote themselves into being: tall, elegant, eloquent figures of mediation, conciliation, and compromise" (*The Bridge*, 525). Wolfgang Mieder has also noted similarities in the rhetoric of Douglass and Obama: *"Yes We Can": Barack Obama's Proverbial Rhetoric* (New York: Peter Lang, 2009), 14, 69–70. President Obama's successor also apparently admires Douglass, saying at the beginning of Black History Month in 2017 that "Frederick Douglass is an example of somebody who's done an amazing job and is being recognized more and more, I noticed." See David A. Graham, "Donald Trump's Narrative of the Life of Frederick Douglass," *The Atlantic*, February 1, 2017. Available online: https://www.theatlantic.com/politics/archive/2017/02/frederick-douglass-trump/515292/.

64. Sarah Hopkins Bradford, *Harriet, the Moses of Her People* (New York: Geo. R. Lockwood & Son, 1886; Chapel Hill: University of North Carolina Press, 2012), 72-73.

65. Interview with Henry Stewart, Canada, 1863, in John W. Blassingame, ed., *Slave Testimony: Two Centuries of Letters, Speeches, Interviews, and Autobiographies* (Baton Rouge: Louisiana State University Press, 1977), 415.

66. Bradford, *Harriet, The Moses of Her People*, 22.

67. Catherine Clinton, *Harriet Tubman: The Road to Freedom* (New York: Little, Brown, 2005).

68. Kate Clifford Larson, *Bound for the Promised Land: Harriet Tubman: Portrait of an American Hero* (New York: Ballantine Books, 2004), 177.

69. *The Audacity of Hope*, 97. Robert E. McGlone, *John Brown's War against Slavery* (Cambridge: Cambridge University Press, 2009).

70. *The Audacity of Hope*, 97.

71. Ibid., 97–98.

72. Ibid., 98.

73. "Declaration of Candidacy," *Change We Can Believe In*, 201.

74. Ibid.

75. Available online: https://www.nps.gov/liho/learn/historyculture/firstinaugural.htm.

76. Ibid.

77. Ibid.

78. Ibid.

79. Doris Kearns Goodwin, *Team of Rivals: The Political Genius of Abraham Lincoln* (New York: Simon and Schuster, 2005) and Eric Foner, *The Fiery Trial: Abraham Lincoln and the War against Slavery* (New York: W. W. Norton, 2011). President Obama's successor has also commented on the causes of the Civil War, saying "I mean had Andrew Jackson been a little later you wouldn't have had the Civil War. He was a very tough person, but he had a big heart. He was really angry that he saw what was happening with regard to the Civil War, he said 'There's no reason for this.' People don't realize, you know, the Civil War, if you think about it, why? People don't ask that question, but why was there the Civil War? Why could that one not have been worked out?" People have in fact been asking that question often and for a long time. The best place to find the answer is of course in the secession declarations where southern state leaders expressed their determination to defend slavery. The forty-fifth president is either unaware of these declarations or simply doesn't believe that slavery was an important enough issue to fight about. Jonah Engel Bromwich, "Trump on the Civil War: 'Why Could That One Not Have Been Worked Out?'" *The New York Times*, May 1, 2017. Available online: https://www.nytimes.com/2017/05/01/us/politics/trump-andrew-jackson-fact-check.html.

80. "Declaration of Candidacy," *Change We Can Believe In*, 195. The *New York York Tribune* letter is available to see online at site of the Library of Congress Abraham Lincoln Papers: https://memory.loc.gov/cgi-bin/ampage?collId=mal&fileName=mal2/423/4233400/malpage.db&recNum=0.

81. "Remarks by the President at Commemoration of the 150th Anniversary of the 13th Amendment."

82. *The Audacity of Hope*, 98.

83. "Declaration of Candidacy," *Change We Can Believe In*, 195; "What I Am Opposed to Is a Dumb War: Speech against the Iraq War, *Chicago, IL, October 2, 2002*," Dionne and Reid, eds., *We Are the Change We Seek*, 1–2.

84. "Remarks by the President at Commemoration of the 150th Anniversary of the 13th Amendment."

CHAPTER 5: WE SHALL OVERCOME

1. Barack Obama, "A More Perfect Union: *March 18, 2008, Philadelphia, Pennsylvania*," in *Change We Can Believe In: Barack Obama's Plan to Renew America's Promise* (New York: Three Rivers Press, 2008), 215.

2. The Constitution and Bill of Rights as well as the Declaration of Independence are digitized and probably most easily available at the US National Archives' "Founding Documents" collection. Available online: https://www.archives.gov/founding-docs.

3. "A More Perfect Union," *Change We Can Believe In*, 216; "Remarks by the President at Commemoration of the 150th Anniversary of the 13th Amendment, US Capitol, Washington, DC," The White House, Office of the Press Secretary, December 9, 2015. Available online: https://obamawhitehouse.archives.gov/the-press-office/2015/12/09/remarks-president-commemoration-150th-anniversary-13th-amendment. W. E. B. Du Bois, *Black Reconstruction in America* (New York: The Free Press, 1935), 30.

4. "Remarks by the President at the 50th Anniversary of the Selma to Montgomery Marches, Edmund Pettus Bridge, Selma, Alabama," The White House, Office of the Press Secretary, March 7, 2015. Available online: https://obamawhitehouse.archives.gov/the-press-office/2015/03/07/remarks-president-50th-anniversary-selma-montgomery-marches.

5. The text of the American Antiquities Act is available online at the site of the National Parks Service: https://www.nps.gov/history/local-law/anti1906.htm.

6. Gregory Downs and Kate Masur were interviewed by Kritika Agarwal, "Monumental Effort: Historians and the Creation of the Nation Monument to Reconstruction," *AHA Today*, January 24, 2017. Available online: http://blog.historians.org/2017/01/national-monument-reconstruction/. Eric Foner, *Reconstruction: America's Unfinished Revolution, 1863-1877* (New York: Harper Collins, 1988); Willie Lee Rose, *Rehearsal for Reconstruction: The Port Royal Experiment* (Oxford: Oxford University Press, 1976).

7. The President's "Proclamation for the Establishment of the Reconstruction Era National Monument," The White House, Office of the Press Secretary, January 12, 2017, is available online: https://obamawhitehouse.archives.gov/the-press-office/2017/01/12/presidential-pro clamations-establishment-reconstruction-era-national. The quotations below come from the Proclamation, except where specified and footnoted.

8. Ibid.

9. Ibid.

10. Barack Obama, *The Audacity of Hope: Thoughts on Reclaiming the American Dream* (New York: Crown, 2006), 97.

11. Ibid., 97–98.

12. " 'The President and his Speeches': *Douglass' Monthly*, September, 1862," in Philip S. Foner, ed., *Frederick Douglass: Selected Speeches and Writings, Abridged and Adapted by Yuval Taylor* (Chicago: Lawrence Hill, 1999), 511. Lincoln cited in Mark E. Steiner, "Lincoln and Citizenship," in Charles M. Hubbard, ed., *Lincoln, the Law, and Presidential Leadership* (Carbondale: Southern Illinois University Press, 2015), 47–48.

13. "Proclamation for the Establishment of the Reconstruction Era National Monument."

14. W. E. B. Du Bois, *The Negro* (original 1915; New York: Cosimo Classics, 2010), 125.

15. "Proclamation for the Establishment of the Reconstruction Era National Monument."

16. "Remarks by the President at Commemoration of the 150th Anniversary of the 13th Amendment."

17. The text of this Civil Rights Act is available online at the Library of Congress website: https://memory.loc.gov/cgi-bin/ampage?collId=llsl&fileName=014/llsl014.db&recNum=58.

18. "Proclamation for the Establishment of the Reconstruction Era National Monument."

19. Ibid.; Foner, *Reconstruction: America's Unfinished Revolution*, especially 354-55.

20. Ibid.

21. Du Bois, *Black Reconstruction in America*, 30. It is worth remembering that by far the most common form of election fraud in the United States was and still is racially motivated voter suppression.

22. "Proclamation for the Establishment of the Reconstruction Era National Monument."

23. Ibid.

24. Ibid.

25. Ibid.

26. Ibid.

27. Ibid.

28. Ibid.

29. "Remarks by the President at Howard University Commencement Ceremony," Howard University, The White House, Office of the Press Secretary, Washington, DC, May 7, 2016. Available online: https://obamawhitehouse.archives.gov/the-press-office/2016/05/07/remarks-president-howard-university-commencement-ceremony.

30. "Proclamation for the Establishment of the Reconstruction Era National Monument."

31. Ibid.

32. Ibid.

33. As noted above, one of Professor Foner's books refers to Reconstruction as *America's Unfinished Revolution*, and another is called *Nothing but Freedom: Emancipation and Its Legacy* (Baton Rouge: Louisiana State University Press, 2007).

34. The Equal Justice Initiative's report on lynching is available online: https://eji.org/reports/lynching-in-america.

35. "Remarks by the President at Commemoration of the 150th Anniversary of the 13th Amendment."

36. "Remarks by the President at the 50th Anniversary of the Selma to Montgomery Marches."

37. For the 1875 Civil Rights Act, see Jerome A. Barron, C. Thomas Dienes, Wayne McCormack, Martin H. Redish, *Constitutional Law: Principles and Policy, Cases and Materials*, 8th Edition (New York: LexisNexis, 2012), 106. The text of the 1883 Civil Rights Cases ruling is available online via the Supreme Court website: https://supreme.justia.com/cases/federal/us/109/3/case.html.

38. *Plessy v. Ferguson* is available at: https://supreme.justia.com/cases/federal/us/163/537/case.html.

39. *Williams v. Mississippi* at available at: https://supreme.justia.com/cases/federal/us/170/213/case.html.

40. *Giles v. Harris* is available at: https://supreme.justia.com/cases/federal/us/189/475/case.html.

41. "How Far We've Come: Remarks at John Lewis's Sixty-fifth Birthday Gala, *Atlanta, Georgia: February 21, 2005*," E. J. Dionne Jr. and Joy-Ann Reid, eds., *We Are the Change We Seek: The Speeches of Barack Obama* (London, New York: Bloomsbury, 2017), 15.

42. "Remarks by the President at the 50th Anniversary of the Selma to Montgomery Marches"; "Proclamation for the Establishment of the Reconstruction Era National Monument." As a law professor at the University of Chicago, for a course called "Current Issues in Racism and the Law," Barack Obama set such primary sources as the Emancipation Proclamation, the Reconstruction Amendments, the South Carolina Black Codes, the *Plessy v. Ferguson* ruling, and excerpts from works by Frederick Douglass, Booker T. Washington, W. E. B. Du Bois, Marcus Garvey, Martin Luther King, and Malcolm X. He also set work by contemporary conservative jurists opposed to affirmative action, including Robert Bork, Charles Cooper, and Lino Graglia. His secondary readings included George M. Fredrickson, *The Arrogance of Race: Historical Perspectives on Slavery, Racism, and Social Inequality* (Middletown, CT: Wesleyan University Press, 1988) and Kwame Anthony Appiah's "The Uncompleted Argument: Du Bois and the Illusion of Race," *Critical Inquiry*, vol. 12, no. 1, " 'Race,' Writing, and Difference," (Autumn 1985), 21–37. See David Remnick, *The Bridge: The Life and Rise of Barack Obama* (New York: Alfred A. Knopf, 2010), 263.

43. "Remarks by the President at the 50th Anniversary of the Selma to Montgomery Marches."

44. In August 1917 A. Philip Randolph and Chandler Owen founded *The Messenger* as the "only radical Negro magazine in America". For the explanation of the term "New Negro," see their article, "The New Negro—What Is He?" from the August 1920 issue of the magazine, available online: http://nationalhumanitiescenter.org/ows/seminars/aahistory/NewNegro.pdf. And see J. Hector St. John de Crèvecouer, "What Is an American?" in Albert E. Stone, ed., *Letters from an American Farmer and Sketches of Eighteenth-Century America* (Harmondsworth: Penguin, 1986), 66-105.

45. "Remarks by the President at Reception in Honor of the National Museum of African American History and Culture, Grand Foyer," The White House, Office of the Press Secretary, September 23, 2016. Available online: https://obamawhitehouse.archives.gov/the-press-office/2016/09/23/remarks-president-reception-honor-national-museum-african-american.

46. "To Secure These Rights" is available online via the Harry S. Truman Presidential Library and Museum at the University of Missouri: https://www.trumanlibrary.org/civilrights/srights1.htm.

47. The *Brown v. Board of Education* verdict is available online at the Supreme Court website: https://supreme.justia.com/cases/federal/us/347/483/case.html.

48. Ibid. It is interesting that Obama or his speechwriters or the transcriber who posted the speech on the White House website used the term "students who walked passed angry crowds," rather than the more obvious-sounding "students who walked past angry crowds." Using thus the verb rather than the adverb underlines the active agency of the young people and in turn, therefore, their courage. (That said, the article in place of the preposition for the eighth word in "The students who walked passed angry crowds the integrate our schools" is certainly just a typo.)

49. For the *Browder v. Gayle* decision see: https://law.justia.com/cases/federal/district-courts/FSupp/142/707/2263463/.

50. *The Audacity of Hope*, 361.

51. "How Far We've Come," Dionne and Reid, eds., *We Are the Change We Seek*, 16.

52. "Remarks by the President at the 50th Anniversary of the Selma to Montgomery Marches."

53. "A More Perfect Union," *Change We Can Believe In*, 216.

54. "Remarks by the President at the 50th Anniversary of the Selma to Montgomery Marches."

55. "How Far We've Come," Dionne and Reid, eds., *We Are the Change We Seek*, 17; "Remarks by the President at the 50th Anniversary of the Selma to Montgomery Marches."

56. Obama's thoughts on these issues are instructive enough that as long ago as 2010 Thomas J. Sugrue, one of America's most influential historians of race and civil rights, called Obama "the nation's most influential historian of race and civil rights." See *Not Even Past: Barack Obama and the Burden of Race* (Princeton: Princeton University Press, 2010), 3. Of course Obama, as the above examples show, has said much more still since then.

57. "Remarks by the President at the 50th Anniversary of the Selma to Montgomery Marches." "How Far We've Come," Dionne and Reid, eds., *We Are the Change We Seek*, 17.

58. "Remarks by the President at Howard University Commencement Ceremony, Howard University."

59. Ibid.

60. Ibid.

61. Ibid.

62. Ibid.

63. Barack Obama, *Dreams from My Father: A Story of Race and Inheritance* (New York: Crown, 1995, 2004); *The Audacity of Hope*, 97.

64. Quoted in Sugrue, *Not Even Past*, 50. For more on this, and on the influence of the different strands of the Civil Rights Movement on Obama's own personal and intellectual evolution, see chapter 1, " 'This Is My Story': Obama, Civil Rights, and Memory," 11–55.

65. Sugrue, *Not Even Past*, 24–25, 41.

66. "Remarks by the President at the 50th Anniversary of the Selma to Montgomery Marches."

67. "How Far We've Come," Dionne and Reid, eds., *We Are the Change We Seek*, 16; "Remarks by the President at the 50th Anniversary of the Selma to Montgomery Marches."

68. Sugrue also makes point that Obama sees the Civil Rights Movement as a popular one that pressured politicians; see especially page 136. "Remarks by the President at Reception in Honor of the National Museum of African American History and Culture."

69. *The Audacity of Hope*, 228.

70. *The Audacity of Hope*, 228; "Remarks by the President at the 50th Anniversary of the Selma to Montgomery Marches."

71. Ibid.; "Remarks by the President at Reception in Honor of the National Museum of African American History and Culture."

72. "Remarks by the President at the 50th Anniversary of the Selma to Montgomery Marches."

73. *The Audacity of Hope*, 362.

74. "Remarks by the President at the 50th Anniversary of the Selma to Montgomery Marches."

75. "How Far We've Come," Dionne and Reid, eds., *We Are the Change We Seek*, 17; "Remarks by the President at the 50th Anniversary of the Selma to Montgomery Marches."

76. "Remarks by the President at the 50th Anniversary of the Selma to Montgomery Marches." President Obama's successor in office also supports the right to protest, sometimes, describing some of those defending Confederate statues at Charlottesville, for example, as "very good people." Sometimes, however, he's less supportive, advocating, for example, that if a sportsman protests violence against African Americans then his employee should "fire that son of a bitch." Adam Serwer, "Trump's War of Words with Black Athletes," *The Atlantic*, 23 September, 2017. Available online: https://www.theatlantic.com/politics/archive/2017/09/trump-urges-nfl-owners-to-fire-players-who-protest/540897/.

77. "Remarks by the President at the Groundbreaking Ceremony of the National Museum of African American History and Culture, The National Mall," The White House, Office

of the Press Secretary, February 22, 2012. Available online: https://obamawhitehouse. archives.gov/the-press-office/2012/02/22/remarks-president-groundbreaking-ceremony- national-museum-african-americ.

78. "Remarks by the President at Reception in Honor of the National Museum of African American History and Culture."

79. "Remarks by the President at the Groundbreaking Ceremony of the National Museum of African American History and Culture."

80. "Remarks by the President at Reception in Honor of the National Museum of African American History and Culture"; "Weekly Address: Celebrating the National Museum of African American History and Culture," The White House, Office of the Press Secretary, September 24, 2016. Available onlone: https://obamawhitehouse.archives.gov/the-press-office/2016/09/24/ weekly-address-celebrating-national-museum-african-american-history-and.

81. "Weekly Address: Celebrating the National Museum of African American History and Culture." For a detailed telling of the Civil Rights Movement and the era it defined it's hard to beat the "Taylor Branch Trilogy": *Parting the Waters: America in the King Years, 1954-63*; *Pillar of Fire: America in the King Years, 1963-65*; and *At Canaan's Edge: America in the King Years, 1965-1968* (New York: Simon and Schuster, 1988, 1998, 2006).

82. "Remarks by the President at the 50th Anniversary of the Selma to Montgomery Marches."

83. "Remarks by the President at the 50th Anniversary of the Selma to Montgomery Marches"; "Remarks by the President at Commemoration of the 150th Anniversary of the 13th Amendment."

84. Remnick, *The Bridge*, 494.

85. "Remarks by the President at the 50th Anniversary of the Selma to Montgomery Marches." E. J. Dionne and Joy-Ann Reid also rate this speech as among Obama's "most beautiful," describing it as "an American elegy": *We Are the Change We Seek*, 253. It is also worth noting that Obama's inclusiveness in this oration is especially impressive, given Susan B. Anthony's refusal to support black men's right to vote as long as women were denied the same right. Some saw and some still see that move by Anthony as motivated merely by a wish to maintain the powerful coalition of black and white men and women, and by fear of it being weakened if a quarter of its constituency were enfranchised alone. Others saw and see it as motivated or at least informed by racism. Whatever the case, Obama applies the same standards to Anthony as he does to Thomas Jefferson, crediting her and him alike for helping make a more perfect union the ways they did, whatever other imperfections they may have had.

86. Remnick, *The Bridge*, 585, and "The Promise," *The New Yorker*, February 15, 2010. Available online: https://www.newyorker.com/magazine/2010/02/15/the-promise-2.

87. "Remarks by the President at the 50th Anniversary of the Selma to Montgomery Marches."

88. "Remarks by the President at Howard University Commencement Ceremony."

89. Ibid.

90. "Remarks by the President at the 50th Anniversary of the Selma to Montgomery Marches."

91. Ibid.

92. Ibid.

93. Ibid.

94. "A More Perfect Union," *Change We Can Believe In*, 222.

CHAPTER 6: THE CHIEF BUSINESS OF THE AMERICAN PEOPLE

1. "Election Night: *November 4, 2008*, Chicago, Illinois," in *Change We Can Believe In: Barack Obama's Plan to Renew America's Promise* (New York: Three Rivers Press, 2008), 278-79.

2. Ibid.

3. "Remarks by the President in a Farewell Address, McCormick Place, Chicago, Illinois," The White House, Office of the Press Secretary, January 10, 2017. Available online: https://obamawhitehouse.archives.gov/the-press-office/2017/01/10/remarks-president-farewell-address.

4. Barack Obama, *The Audacity of Hope: Thoughts on Reclaiming the American Dream* (New York: Crown, 2006), 149.

5. Ibid., 151, 153, 154.

6. Ibid., 155-56.

7. Ibid., 53.

8. Ibid., 149.

9. "Remarks by the President at Fourth of July Celebration, South Lawn," The White House, Office of the Press Secretary, July 4, 2013. Available online: https://obamawhitehouse. archives.gov/the-press-office/2013/07/04/remarks-president-fourth-july-celebrationJuly04; The University of Massachusetts at Boston commencement address, June 2, 2006, is also available online: http://obamaspeeches.com/074-University-of-Massachusetts-at-Boston-Commencement-Address-Obama-Speech.htm.

10. John M. Murrin, *Beneficiaries of Catastrophe: The English Colonies in America* (Washington, DC: American Historical Association, 1991, revised edition, 1997).

11. Gabriel Thomas, *An Historical and Geographical Account of the Province and Country of Pensilvania and of West-New-Jersey in America* (London: A. Baldwin, 1698), 28-30.

12. Ibid., 30-31.

13. Ibid., 31-32.

14. Ibid., 32-33.

15. Ibid., 33-35.

16. Ibid., 35-36, 44.

17. Ibid., 43-44.

18. "A More Perfect Union: *March 18, 2008, Philadelphia, Pennsylvania*," in *Change We Can Believe In*, 215.

19. University of Massachusetts at Boston Commencement Address.

20. James Horn and Philip D. Morgan, "Settlers and Slaves: European and African Migration to Early Modern British America", in ed. Carole Shammas and Elizabeth Mancke, *The Creation of the Atlantic World* (Baltimore: The Johns Hopkins University Press, 2005), 24.

21. Ibid.

22. Ibid.

23. Ibid.

24. Ibid. For an overview see David Brion Davis, *Inhuman Bondage: The Rise and Fall of Slavery in the New World* (Oxford: Oxford University Press, 2006).

25. Thomas, *An Historical and Geographical Account of the Province and Country of Pensilvania and of West-New-Jersey*, 35.

26. "A More Perfect Union: *March 18, 2008, Philadelphia, Pennsylvania*," in *Change We Can Believe In*, 215; *The Audacity of Hope*, 54.

27. "A More Perfect Union," 215.

28. *The Audacity of Hope*, 53; "A More Perfect Union," *Change We Can Believe In*, 215.

29. Various versions of the Declaration of Independence, including Jefferson's original draft, are digitized and available at the U.S. National Archives' "Founding Documents" collection. Available online: https://www.archives

30. The Constitution is also available at the US National Archives' "Founding Documents" collection: https://www.archives.gov/founding-docs.

31. See Sven Beckert's magnificent *Empire of Cotton: A Global History* (New York: Vintage, 2014).

32. "Remarks by the President at the Groundbreaking Ceremony of the National Museum of African American History and Culture, The National Mall," The White House, Office of the Press Secretary, February 22, 2012. Available online: https://obamawhitehouse.archives.gov/the-press-office/2012/02/22/remarks-president-groundbreaking-ceremony-national-museum-african-americ.

33. "Remarks by the President at Commemoration of the 150th Anniversary of the 13th Amendment, US Capitol, Washington, DC," The White House, Office of the Press Secretary, December 9, 2015. Available online: https://obamawhitehouse.archives.gov/the-press-office/2015/12/09/remarks-president-commemoration-150th-anniversary-13th-amendment.

34. "Remarks by the President at the 50th Anniversary of the Selma to Montgomery Marches, Edmund Pettus Bridge, Selma, Alabama," The White House, Office of the Press Secretary, March 7, 2015. Available online: https://obamawhitehouse.archives.gov/the-press-office/2015/03/07/remarks-president-50th-anniversary-selma-montgomery-marches.

35. A number of mighty tomes have recently explored the links between the British Empire, the US, capitalism, and slavery. As well as Professor Beckert's *Empire of Cotton*, see especially Simon P. Newman, *A New World of Labor: The Development of Plantation Slavery in the British Atlantic* (Philadelphia: University of Pennsylvania Press: Philadelphia, 2013); Edward E. Baptist, *The Half Has Never Been Told: Slavery and the Making of American Capitalism* (New York: Basic Books, 2014); Trevor Burnard, *Planters, Merchants, and Slaves: Plantation Societies in British America, 1650–1820* (Chicago: University of Chicago Press, 2015); and most recently Sven Beckert and Seth Rockman, eds., *Slavery's Capitalism: A New History of American Economic Development* (Philadelphia: University of Pennsylvania Press, 2017).

36. *The Audacity of Hope*, 151.

37. *The Audacity of Hope*, 151. For the Declaration of Independence, see the US National Archives' "Founding Documents" collection. Available online: https://www.archives.gov/founding-docs. Thomas Jefferson, *A Summary View of the Rights of British America*, in Merrill D. Peterson, ed., *Jefferson: Writings* (New York: Library of America, 1984), especially 107-08 and 118-20.

38. *The Audacity of Hope*, 87.

39. Ibid., 149.

40. Ibid., 151.

41. Ibid.

42. Ibid., 151.

43. Ibid.

44. *Notes on the State of Virginia* (1787), Query XIX, The Present State of Manufactures, Commerce, Interior and Exterior Trade? in Peterson, ed., *Jefferson: Writings*, 290-91.

45. Ibid., 290.

46. Steven Sarson, *The Tobacco Plantation South in the Early American Atlantic World* (New York: Palgrave Macmillan, 2013), and for the later era see Keri Leigh Merritt, *Masterless Men: Poor Whites in the Antebellum South* (Cambridge: Cambridge University Press, 2017).

47. *The Audacity of Hope*, 151. Some records have Hamilton born in 1755. Obama indeed concedes that "Jefferson was not entirely wrong to fear Hamilton's vision for the country, for we have always been in a constant balacing act between self-interest and community, markets and democracy, the concentration of wealth and power and the opening up of opportunity." *The Audacity of Hope*, 193.

48. Alexander Hamilton's "Report on the Subject of Manufactures" are available online at the website of the US National Archives: https://founders.archives.gov/documents/ Hamilton/01-10-02-0001-0007. The quote here is on pages 157–58. William Blake's "Jerusalem" is in W. H. Stephenson, ed., *Blake: The Complete Poems* (Abingdon: Routledge, Third Edition, 1987), 29A, "Preface to Milton."

49. Thomas Jefferson's First Inaugural Address is available online at the Library of Congress website: https://www.loc.gov/rr/program/bib/inaugurations/jefferson/index.html.

50. Cathy Matson, ed., *The Economy of Early America: Historical Perspectives and New Directions* (University Park: Penn State University Press, 2011) provides a very thorough account of early American economic thought and development.

51. John Quincy Adams's inaugural address is available online via the website of the Library of Congress: https://www.loc.gov/rr/program/bib/inaugurations/jqadams/index.html.

52. *The Audacity of Hope*, 153. For Jackson to Biddle see Thomas P. Govan, "Fundamental Issues of the Bank War," *The Pennsylvania Magazine of History and Biography*, Vol. 82 (No. 3, Jul., 1958), 311.

53. Sean Wilentz, *Andrew Jackson* (New York: Henry Holt, 2005).

54. *The Audacity of Hope*, 152.

55. Ibid.

56. Ibid., 152-3.

57. "Remarks by the President in a Farewell Address, McCormick Place, Chicago, Illinois."

58. *The Audacity of Hope*, 154.

59. Ibid.

60. The text of the decision in *Pembina Consolidated Silver Mining Co. v. Pennsylvania* is available online via the Supreme Court website: https://supreme.justia.com/cases/federal/us/125/181/ case.html.

61. *The Audacity of Hope*, 154.

62. "Remarks by the President on the Economy in Osawatomie, Kansas: Osawatomie High School, Osawatomie, Kansas," The White House, Office of the Press Secretary, December 06, 2011. Available online: https://obamawhitehouse.archives.gov/the-press-office/2011/12/06/ remarks-president-economy-osawatomie-kansas. Rebecca Edwards, *New Spirits: Americans in the Gilded Age, 1865–1905* (Oxford: Oxford University Press, 2005); Richard White, *The Republic for Which It Stands: The United States during Reconstruction and the Gilded Age, 1865–1896* (Oxford: Oxford University Press, 2017). For a terrific coverage of this whole era

of American economic history, see H. W. Brands, *The Money Men: Capitalism, Democracy, and the Hundred Years' War over the American Dollar* (New York: W. W. Norton, 2006).

63. "Remarks by the President on the Economy in Osawatomie, Kansas"; *The Audacity of Hope*, 153.

64. "Remarks by the President on the Economy in Osawatomie, Kansas." Maureen A. Flanagan, *America Reformed: Progressives and Progressivisms, 1890s–1920s* (Oxford: Oxford University Press, 2007).

65. David M. Kennedy, *Over Here: The First World War and American Society* (New York, Oxford: Oxford University Press, 2004), 65.

66. *The Audacity of Hope*, 149, 153.

67. Gary Dean Best, *The Dollar Decade: Mammon and the Machine in 1920s America* (Westport, CT: Praeger, 2003).

68. *The Audacity of Hope*, 153.

69. Ibid., 154.

70. Ibid.

71. Ibid., 154, 177.

72. Ibid., 154-55.

73. Ibid., 154.

74. Ibid., 177.

75. Ibid., 155, 176-77.

76. Ibid., 155; David M Kennedy, *Freedom from Fear: The American People in Depression and War, 1929–1945* (Oxford: Oxford University Press, 1999); Elliot A. Rosen, *Roosevelt, the Great Depression, and the Economics of Recovery* (Charlottesville: University of Virginia Press, 2005).

77. *The Audacity of Hope*, 156, 157.

78. Ibid., 157, 158.

79. Ibid., 158, 178.

80. Ibid., 180, 178-79, 180.

81. Ibid., 155, 156.

82. Ibid., 158, 159. Obama also explained one aspect of the appeal of this ideology in a speech in 2005: "And it is especially tempting because each of us believes that we will always be the winner in life's lottery, that we will be Donald Trump, or at least that we won't be the chump that he tells 'You're fired!'" "Knox College Commencement Address: *June 4, 2005, Galesburg, Illinois*," in Mary Frances Berry and Josh Gottheimer, eds., *Power in Words: The Stories Behind Barack Obama's Speeches, from the State House to the White House* (Boston: Beacon Press, 2010), 61. Doug Rossinow, *The Reagan Era: A History of the 1980s* (New York: Columbia University Press, 2015).

83. *The Audacity of Hope*, 159, 180.

84. Ibid., 159, 158.

85. The term "dogmas of the quiet past" comes from Abraham Lincoln's Annual Message to Congress of December 1, 1862, available online: https://www.archives.gov/legislative/features/sotu/lincoln.html. Barack Obama used the term in his own Annual Message to Congress in 2016: "America has been through big changes before—wars and depression, the influx of new immigrants, workers fighting for a fair deal, movements to expand civil rights. Each time, there

have been those who told us to fear the future; who claimed we could slam the brakes on change; who promised to restore past glory if we just got some group or idea that was threatening America under control. And each time, we overcame those fears. We did not, in the words of Lincoln, adhere to the 'dogmas of the quiet past.' Instead we thought anew, and acted anew." "Remarks of President Barack Obama – State of the Union Address As Delivered," The White House, Office of the Press Secretary, January 13, 2016, available online: https://obamawhitehouse.archives.gov/the-press-office/2016/01/12/remarks-president-barack-obama-%E2%80%93-prepared-delivery-state-union-address. Although, as I argue here, the newness is not really so new. The Obama quotes in this paragraph are from *The Audacity of Hope*, 149-50, 150.

86. *The Audacity of Hope*, 150.

87. Ibid., 152, 159.

88. Ibid., 150.

89. "Remarks by the President on the Economy in Osawatomie, Kansas."

90. *The Audacity of Hope*, 151.

91. Ibid., 151, 150.

92. Barack Obama's "Remarks at the Selma Voting Rights March Commemoration in Selma, Alabama, March 4, 2007" is available via John Woolley and Gerhard Peters, University of California, Santa Barbara, "The American Presidency Project." Online: http://www.presidency.ucsb.edu/ws/?pid=77042. "A More Perfect Union: *March 18, 2008, Philadelphia, Pennsylvania*," in *Change We Can Believe In*, 222–23. On the history of the reparations issue, see Ana Lucia Araujo, *Reparations for Slavery and the Slave Trade: A Transnational and Comparative History* (London, New York: Bloomsbury, 2017).

93. "A More Perfect Union," in *Change We Can Believe In*, 227-28.

94. Ibid., 225. On this matter, see William Julius Wilson, "Why Obama's Race Speech is a Model for the Political Framing of Race and Poverty," in T. Denean Sharpley-Whiting, ed., *The Speech: Race and Barack Obama's "A More Perfect Union"* (London, New York: Bloomsbury, 2009), 132-41, although some of the other essays in the same collection are more critical of Obama's approach.

95. "A More Perfect Union," *Change We Can Believe In*, 225.

96. Barack Obama quotes these words by Franklin Roosevelt in *The Audacity of Hope*, 155. Alexander Hamilton's "Objections and Answers respecting the Administration of the Government" is available at the US National Archives "Founders Online" site: https://founders.archives.gov/documents/Hamilton/01-12-02-0184-0002. It somehow seems fitting that this quote came to my attention not only through the scholarly work of world-leading Hamilton scholar Joanne Freeman, but also through her tweeting it. The line in quotation marks is Hamilton's adaptation of a stanza from Joseph Addison's *The Campaign*, his 1705 poem honouring the victory of John Churchill, Duke of Marlborough, at the Battle of Blenheim during the War of the Spanish Succession. Hamilton, however, may have had in mind the line's reappearance in Alexander Pope's epic mock-satirical poem *The Dunciad* (1728–43). Pope was referring specifically to a theater manager he styled "The Angel of Dulness."

97. "A More Perfect Union," *Change We Can Believe In*, 226.

CHAPTER 7: BEYOND OUR BORDERS

1. Barack Obama, *The Audacity of Hope: Thoughts on Reclaiming the American Dream* (New York: Crown, 2006), 53.

2. Ibid., 281.

3. All relevant versions of the Declaration of Independence, the Constitution, and the Bill of Rights are digitized and available at the US National Archives' "Founding Documents" collection. Available online: https://www.archives.gov/founding-docs.

4. Robert Gray, *A Good Speed to Virginia* (London: William Welbie, 1609), 23.

5. Peter Laslett, ed., John Locke, *Two Treatises of Government* (Cambridge: Cambridge University Press, 1988), 319.

6. See US National Archives' "Founding Documents" collection. Available online: https://www.archives.gov/founding-docs.

7. Ibid. Thomas Jefferson, "A Summary View of the Rights of British America," in Merrill D. Peterson, ed., *Jefferson: Writings* (New York: Library of America, 1984), 107.

8. I'm feeling especially cautious about commenting on Barack Obama's comments on Native Americans because of a mauling I once received about my own. For comments on my inadvertent Euro-centrisms, see James H. Merrell, "Second Thoughts on Colonial Historians and American Indians," *The William and Mary Quarterly*, vol. 69, no. 3 (2012), 451–512. For my original errors, see *British America, 1500–1800: Creating Colonies, Imagining an Empire* (London, New York: Bloomsbury, 2010). After reading Professor Merrell's article, I wrote to him to confess that he had busted me and to say that I'd try to do better in the future. He kindly wrote back to say that we're all on a life-long learning curve. Merrell's *The Indians' New World: Catawbas and their Neighbors from European Contact through the Era of Removal* (Chapel Hill: University of North Carolina Press, 1989) is one of the greatest books on this subject. As is Daniel K. Richter, *Facing East from Indian Country: A Native History of Early America* (Cambridge, MA: Harvard University Press, 1981) and Richard White, *The Middle Ground: Indians, Empires, and Republics in the Great Lakes Region, 1650–1815* (Cambridge: Cambridge University Press, 1991).

9. See for example *The Audacity of Hope*, 96, 231, and "A More Perfect Union: *March 18, 2008, Philadelphia, Pennsylvania*," in *Change We Can Believe In: Barack Obama's Plan to Renew America's Promise* (New York: Three Rivers Press, 2008), 215.

10. US National Archives' "Founding Documents": https://www.archives.gov/founding-docs.

11. *The Audacity of Hope*, 281.

12. U.S. National Archives' "Founding Documents": https://www.archives.gov/founding-docs.

13. *The Audacity of Hope*, 281.

14. Ibid.

15. O'Sullivan is quoted and the concept of Manifest Destiny is explored in Thomas R. Hietala, *Manifest Design: American Exceptionalism and Empire* (Ithaca: Cornell University Press, 1985), 255. *The Audacity of Hope*, 281.

16. Alan Taylor, *American Colonies: The Settling of North America* (London: Penguin, 2001), 40; Russell Thornton, *American Indian Holocaust and Survival: A Population History since 1492* (Norman: University of Oklahoma Press, 1987).

17. *The Audacity of Hope*, 281. The records of the case of *Cherokee Nation v. Georgia* are available online via the website of the US Supreme Court: https://supreme.justia.com/cases/federal/us/30/1/case.html.

18. *The Audacity of Hope*, 95.

19. The records of the case of *Johnson v. M'Intosh* are available at: https://supreme.justia.com/cases/federal/us/21/543/case.html.

20. Ibid.

21. *Worcester v. Georgia* is available at: https://supreme.justia.com/cases/federal/us/31/515/case. html.

22. These three court cases and the treaties, laws, and concepts mentioned throughout the rest of this section of this chapter are available in the three volumes of Donald L. Fixico, ed., *Treaties with American Indians: An Encyclopedia of Rights, Conflicts, and Sovereignty* (Santa Barbara, CA: ABC-CLIO, 2008).

23. Ronald N. Satz, *American Indian Policy in the Jacksonian Era* (Norman: University of Oklahoma Press, 1974), 49. See also R. Douglas Hurt, *The Indian Frontier, 1763–1846* (Albuquerque: University of New Mexico Press, 2003); Theda Perdue, *The Cherokee Nation and the Trail of Tears* (New York: Viking, 2007); Steve Inskeep, *Jacksonland: President Andrew Jackson, Cherokee Chief John Ross, and a Great American Land Grab* (London: Penguin, 2015). Barack Obama set readings on these court cases and also excerpts from Emer de Vattel, *The Law of Nations, Or, Principles of the Law of Nature, Applied to the Conduct and Affairs of Nations and Sovereigns, with Three Early Essays on the Origin and Nature of Natural Law and on Luxury*, first published in French 1758 and in English in 1760, in a course on Current Issues in Racism and the Law during his time as a teacher at the University of Chicago. See David Remnick, *The Bridge: The Life and Rise of Barack Obama* (New York: Alfred A. Knopf, 2010), 263.

24. *The Audacity of Hope*, 281.

25. Quoted in the Supreme Court's account of "Indian Treaties": https://law.justia.com/ constitution/us/article-2/19-indian-treaties.html.

26. US National Archives' "Founding Documents" collection where one can see digitized originals and transcriptions. Available online: https://www.archives.gov/founding-docs.

27. The *Elk v. Wilkins* decision is available via the Supreme Court website: https://supreme.justia. com/cases/federal/us/112/94/case.html.

28. "Remarks by the President During the Opening of the Tribal Nations Conference & Interactive Discussion with Tribal Leaders," The White House, Office of the Press Secretary, November 5, 2009. Available online: https://obamawhitehouse.archives.gov/the-press-office/ remarks-president-during-opening-tribal-nations-conference-interactive-discussion-w.

29. Richard Hakluyt, "A Discourse Concerning Western Planting," E. R. G. Taylor, ed., *The Original Writings and Correspondence of the Two Richard Hakluyts* (Abingdon: Ashgate, The Hakluyt Society, 2016), Vol II, 216.

30. Laurence French, *Legislating Indian Country: Significant Milestones in Transforming Tribalism* (New York: Peter Lang, 2007), 126; Lawrence C. Kelly, *True and Sincere Declaration of the Purpose and Ends of the Plantation Begun in Virginia* (London: George Eld, 1610), 2.

31. Lawrence C. Kelly, *The Assault on Assimilation: John Collier and the Origins of Indian Policy Reform* (Albuquerque: University of New Mexico Press, 1983).

32. "Inaugural Address by President Barack Obama, United States Capitol," The White House, Office of the Press Secretary, January 21, 2013. Available online: https://obamawhitehouse. archives.gov/the-press-office/2013/01/21/inaugural-address-president-barack-obama; *The Audacity of Hope*, 53; "A More Perfect Union," *Change We Can Believe In*, 215.

33. *The Audacity of Hope*, 361–62; "Remarks by the President in a Farewell Address, McCormick Place, Chicago, Illinois," The White House, Office of the Press Secretary, January 10, 2017. Available online: https://obamawhitehouse.archives.gov/the-press-office/2017/01/10/remarks-president-farewell-address.

34. "Inaugural Address by President Barack Obama, United States Capitol."

35. *The Audacity of Hope*, 95.

36. "A More Perfect Union," *Change We Can Believe In*, 216; "Remarks by the President at the 50th Anniversary of the Selma to Montgomery Marches, Edmund Pettus Bridge, Selma, Alabama," The White House, Office of the Press Secretary, March 7, 2015. Available online: https://obamawhitehouse.archives.gov/the-press-office/2015/03/07/remarks-president-50th-anniversary-selma-montgomery-marches.

37. *The Audacity of Hope*, 281.

38. Ibid., 281, 95.

39. "Remarks by the President During the Opening of the Tribal Nations Conference & Interactive Discussion with Tribal Leaders."

40. "Remarks by the President at the White House Tribal Nations Conference," The White House, Office of the Press Secretary, December 16, 2010. Available online: https://obamawhitehouse.archives.gov/the-press-office/2010/12/16/remarks-president-white-house-tribal-nations-conference.

41. "Remarks by the President at Tribal Nations Conference, US Department of the Interior, Washington, DC," The White House, Office of the Press Secretary, November 13, 2013. Available online: https://obamawhitehouse.archives.gov/the-press-office/2013/11/13/remarks-president-tribal-nations-conference.

42. Jack N. Rakove, *Original Meanings: Politics and Ideas in the Making of the Constitution* (New York: Vintage, 1997).

43. "Remarks by the President at the 50th Anniversary of the Selma to Montgomery Marches."

44. The United States Bureau of American Ethnology gives an official spelling of Sacagawea, the one most commonly used in the journals of Lewis and Clark. The Hidatsa called her Sakakawea, meaning "bird woman" in their language. It is interesting though that Barack Obama uses Sacajawea, closest to her Shoshone birth name and meaning "boat-puller" or "boat launcher" in their language. Frederick E. Hoxie, *Lewis & Clark and the Indian Country: The Native American Perspective* (Urbana: University of Illinois Press, 2007).

45. "Remarks by the President at the 50th Anniversary of the Selma to Montgomery Marches."

46. Ibid.

47. "Remarks by the President at Tribal Nations Conference," November 13, 2013.

48. "Remarks by the President at the White House Tribal Nations Conference," December 16, 2010; "Remarks by the President During the Opening of the Tribal Nations Conference & Interactive Discussion with Tribal Leaders, November 05, 2009," "Remarks by the President at Tribal Nations Conference, Reagan Building, Washington, DC," The White House, Office of the Press Secretary, November 5, 2015. Available online: https://obamawhitehouse.archives.gov/the-press-office/2015/11/05/remarks-president-tribal-nations-conference.

49. *The Audacity of Hope*, 280.

50. Ibid., 281. George Washington's "Farewell Address" is available online from the US National Archives: https://founders.archives.gov/documents/Washington/99-01-02-00963.

51. *The Audacity of Hope*, 280. John Quincy Adams's "Speech on Independence Day" of July 4, 1821, to the US House of Representatives is available via the website of the Miller Center for Public Affairs at the University of Virginia: https://millercenter.org/the-presidency/presidential-speeches/july-4-1821-speech-us-house-representatives-foreign-policy.

52. *The Audacity of Hope*, 280, 281. My student Sarah Loustalet-Turon is doing a fascinating PhD dissertation that shows that early US domestic and international history was more deeply affected by North Africa, the Middle East, and the Barbary Wars than hitherto thought.

53. "The Audacity of Hope: Keynote Address at the 2004 Democratic National Convention, *Boston, MA, July 27, 2004*," E. J. Dionne Jr. and Joy-Ann Reid, eds., *We Are The Change We Seek: The Speeches of Barack Obama* (London, New York: Bloomsbury, 2017), 6.

54. "Remarks by the President at the 50th Anniversary of the Selma to Montgomery Marches, Edmund Pettus Bridge."

55. *The Audacity of Hope*, 281.

56. Ibid.

57. *The Audacity of Hope*, 281–82.

58. Ibid., 282.

59. Ibid., 282–83.

60. Ibid., 283. The Theodore Roosevelt quote comes from his article "Nationalism and International Relations," in *Outlook*, April 1, 1911, and the one from Franklin Roosevelt from his fireside chat of December 9, 1941, two days after the attack on Pearl Harbor: https://millercenter.org/the-presidency/presidential-speeches/december-9-1941-fireside-chat-19-war-japan.

61. *The Audacity of Hope*, 284.

62. Ibid., 284–85.

63. Ibid., 285.

64. Ibid., 285–86.

65. Ibid., 286.

66. Ibid., 286–87.

67. Ibid., 287–88.

68. Ibid., 288.

69. Ibid., 288–89.

70. "A World That Stands as One: *July 24, 2008, Berlin, Germany*," *Change We Can Believe In*, 264; "Remarks by the President at the 50th Anniversary of the Selma to Montgomery Marches, Edmund Pettus Bridge."

71. *The Audacity of Hope*, 290. Richard Crockatt, *The Fifty Years War: The United States and the Soviet Union in World Politics, 1941–1991* (Abingdon: Routledge, 1995).

72. *The Audacity of Hope*, 292.

73. Ibid., 292. British Prime Minister Tony Blair's ill-fated vow to stand "shoulder-to-shoulder" with the United States goes mercifully unmentioned.

74. *The Audacity of Hope*, 292–93.

75. "What I Am Opposed to Is a Dumb War: Speech against the Iraq War, *Chicago, IL, October 2, 2002*," in Dionne and Reid, eds., *We Are the Change We Seek*, 3, 4.

76. "Remarks by the President at Cairo University, 6-04-09," The White House, Office of the Press Secretary (Cairo, Egypt), June 4, 2009. Available online: https://obamawhitehouse.archives.gov/the-press-office/remarks-president-cairo-university-6-04-09 and https://obamawhitehouse.archives.gov/issues/foreign-policy/presidents-speech-cairo-a-new-beginning.

77. Ibid. James T. Kloppenberg, *Reading Obama: Dreams, Hope, and the American Political Tradition* (Princeton: Princeton University Press, 2011), especially xi–xiii, 3–4, 17–18, 62–64, 83, 110–11, 169–72, 193.

78. "Remarks by the President at Cairo University."

79. Ibid.

80. Ibid.

81. "Remarks by the President at the Acceptance of the Nobel Peace Prize, Oslo City Hall, Oslo, Norway," The White House, Office of the Press Secretary, December 10, 2009. Available online: https://obamawhitehouse.archives.gov/the-press-office/remarks-president-acceptance-nobel-peace-prize.

82. Ibid.

83. *The Audacity of Hope*, 279.

84. Ibid., 279–80.

85. Ibid. 271–72.

86. Ibid., 272–73, 276. The passages in italics in this and the next few paragraphs are from Obama's generalizations about American foreign policy from pages 279–80 of *The Audacity of Hope*, as block-quoted on page 271 of this book.

87. Ibid., 275, 276.

88. Ibid., 276–77, 277.

89. Ibid., 278.

90. Ibid., 273.

91. Ibid., 274.

92. Ibid., 274, 274–75.

93. Ibid., 275–76, 278–79.

94. Ibid., 280.

95. Adrian Jawort, "President Obama's Adoptive Crow Father, 'Sonny' Black Eagle, Walks On," *Indian Country Today*, November 29, 2012. Available online: https://indiancountrymedia network.com/news/native-news/president-obamas-adoptive-crow-father-sonny-black-eagle-walks-on/.

96. "Remarks by the President at the Tribal Nations Conference, US Department of the Interior, Washington, D.C.," The White House, Office of the Press Secretary, December 05, 2012. Available online: https://obamawhitehouse.archives.gov/the-press-office/2012/12/05/remarks-president-tribal-nations-conference.

97. Ibid.

EPILOGUE

1. "United States Senate Victory Speech: *November 2, 2004, Hyatt Ballroom, Chicago, Illinois*," Mary Frances Berry and Josh Gottheimer, eds., *Power In Words: The Stories Behind Barack Obama's Speeches, from the State House to the White House* (Boston: Beacon Press, 2010), 37.

2. Ibid., 37-38.

3. Ibid., 38; see also *The Audacity of Hope*, 362.

4. Benedict Anderson, *Imagined Communities: Reflections on the Origin and Spread of Nationalism* (New York: Verso, 1983; revised and extended ed., 2006).

5. E. J. Dionne Jr. and Joy-Ann Reid, eds., *We Are the Change We Seek: The Speeches of Barack Obama* (London, New York: Bloomsbury, 2017), xxi.

6. Barack Obama, *Dreams from My Father: A Story of Race and Inheritance* (New York: Crown, 1995, 2004). For biographies, see David Mendell, *Obama: From Promise to Power* (New York: Harper Collins, 2007), and David Remnick, *The Bridge: The Life and Rise of Barack Obama* (New York: Alfred A. Knopf, 2010).

7. Chapter six of David Remnick's *The Bridge* is about Barack Obama's autobiography and is aptly entitled "A Narrative of Ascent," (pages 219–55). Remnick cites Robert Stepto on page 231.

8. David Remnick cites Henry Louis Gates, Jr. on pages 254–55 of *The Bridge*. Remnick also recounts the young Obama's dilemmas about race and personal identity (pages 71–82, 89-97, 98-255). As of course does Obama's own *Dreams from My Father*. See also James T. Kloppenberg, *Reading Obama: Dreams, Hope, and the American Political Tradition* (Princeton: Princeton University Press, 2011), 249–65.

9. Barack Obama's "Remarks at the Selma Voting Rights March Commemoration in Selma, Alabama, March 4, 2007" is available via John Woolley and Gerhard Peters, University of California, Santa Barbara, "The American Presidency Project." Online: http://www. presidency.ucsb.edu/ws/?pid=77042. David Remnick opens his epic biography of Barack Obama with a Prologue entitled "The Joshua Generation," which tells the story of Selma and how the then presidential candidate spoke at Brown Chapel in 2007: *The Bridge*, 3–25. And of course the title of Remnick's book evokes not only the bridge at Selma but also Obama's own spanning of communities and place in time. Indeed it brings to mind what John Lewis himself told David Remnick the day before the first black president's inauguration: "Barack Obama is what comes at the end of that bridge in Selma" (p. 575).

10. "Remarks at the Selma Voting Rights March Commemoration in Selma, Alabama, March 4, 2007."

11. Ibid.

12. Ibid.

13. The original typed speech is available to view online at the website of The Martin Luther King, Jr. Center for Nonviolent Social Change ("The King Center"): http://www.thekingcenter.org/archive/document/ive-been-mountaintop.

14. Ibid.

15. "Remarks at the Selma Voting Rights March Commemoration in Selma, Alabama, March 4, 2007."

16. Ibid.

17. *Dreams from My Father*, 294. Obama repeated the passage when he spoke about Reverend Jeremiah Wright in Philadelphia in March 2008: "A More Perfect Union: *March 18, 2008, Philadelphia, Pennsylvania*," in *Change We Can Believe In: Barack Obama's Plan to Renew America's Promise* (New York: Three Rivers Press, 2008), 220. Remnick, *The Bridge*, 29–41, 49–55, 62–68.

18. Thomas J. Sugrue, *Not Even Past: Barack Obama and the Burden of Race* (Princeton: Princeton University Press, 2010), 11, 141. David Remnick tells us of a moment early in Barack Obama's Harvard law school days when, on a visit to Chicago, a friend saw him reading Taylor Branch's *Parting the Waters: America in the King Years, 1954–63* (New York: Simon and Schuster, 1988), number one in the "Taylor Branch Trilogy." Obama nodded at the book and told his friend, "Yes, it's *my* story." Remnick, *The Bridge*, 13.

19. "Remarks at the Selma Voting Rights March Commemoration in Selma, Alabama, March 4, 2007."

20. Ibid.

21. Barack Obama, *The Audacity of Hope: Thoughts on Reclaiming the American Dream* (New York: Crown, 2006), 361.

22. "The Audacity of Hope: Keynote Address at the 2004 Democratic National Convention, *Boston, MA, July 27, 2004*," Dionne and Reid, eds., *We Are the Change We Seek*, 6.

23. "Declaration of Candidacy: *February 10, 2007, Springfield, Illinois*," in *Change We Can Believe In*, 195.

24. "Election Night: *November 4, 2008, Chicago, Illinois*," *Change We Can Believe In*, 277; "Declaration of Candidacy," *Change We Can Believe In*, 201, 202.

25. "Declaration of Candidacy," *Change We Can Believe In*, 201, 196.

26. "Declaration of Candidacy: *February 10, 2007, Springfield, Illinois*," in *Change We Can Believe In*, 201. See also Kloppenberg, *Reading Obama*, 244–47, and Meider, *"Yes We Can,"* 15, 68–69, 138. It's worth noting too that on his way to his inauguration, Barack Obama did a whistle-stop train tour along the same route Lincoln took in 1861, and then took his oath of office on the Lincoln Bible.

27. *The Audacity of Hope*, 122–23.

28. Ibid., 123. "What I see in Lincoln's Eyes," *Time Magazine*, June 27, 2005, 74. Peggy Noonan, "Conceit of Government: Why are our politicians so full of themselves," *Wall Street Journal*, updated June 29, 2005. Available online: https://www.wsj.com/articles/ SB122487035712667167.

29. Barack Obama, "Perfecting Our Union: The President of the United States reflects on what Abraham Lincoln means to him, and to America," *The Atlantic*, February, 2012. Available online: https://www.theatlantic.com/magazine/archive/2012/02/perfecting-our-union/308832/. Though already well familiar with the life and thought of Abraham Lincoln, Obama first read Doris Kearns Goodwin's Pulitzer Prize winning book *Team of Rivals: The Political Genius of Abraham Lincoln* (New York: Simon and Schuster, 2005) shortly after announcing his bid for the presidency in 2007. He called the writer soon after and she remained a kind of unofficial historical advisor to the president during his time in office. See Remnick, *The Bridge*, 475–76. Garry Wills long ago noted the resemblances between Barack Obama and Abraham Lincoln, comparing the former's "A More Perfect Union" of 2008 with the latter's Cooper Union Speech in New York in 1860: "Two Speeches on Race," *The New York Review of Books*, May 1, 2008. Available online: http://www.nybooks.com/ articles/2008/05/01/two-speeches-on-race/.

30. "The Audacity of Hope," Dionne and Reid, eds., *We Are the Change We Seek*, 6.

31. Ibid.

32. Ibid., 6–7. Obama largely wrote this speech himself because, as David Axelrod later related, Obama said to him that "I want to talk about my story as part of the larger American story." Berry and Gottheimer, eds., *Power in Words*, 12.

33. "A More Perfect Union," *Change We Can Believe In*, 216–17.

34. "The Audacity of Hope," Dionne and Reid, eds., *We Are the Change We Seek*, 11.

35. *The Audacity of Hope*, 231.

36. "The Audacity of Hope," Dionne and Reid, eds., *We Are the Change We Seek*, 11.

37. Ibid. *The Audacity of Hope*, 151.

38. "The Audacity of Hope," Dionne and Reid, eds., *We Are the Change We Seek*, 12.

39. "A More Perfect Union," *Change We Can Believe In*, 53; *The Audacity of Hope*, 215. Steve Pincus gives an intriguingly contrarian collectivist reading of the Declaration of Independence in *The Heart of the Declaration: The Founders' Case for an Activist Government* (New Haven: Yale University Press, 2016).

40. "A More Perfect Union," *Change We Can Believe In*, 216. "Remarks by the President at the 50th Anniversary of the Selma to Montgomery Marches, Edmund Pettus Bridge, Selma, Alabama," The White House, Office of the Press Secretary, March 7, 2015. Available online: https://obamawhitehouse.archives.gov/the-press-office/2015/03/07/remarks-president-50th-anniversary-selma-montgomery-marches.

41. "Remarks by the President in a Farewell Address, McCormick Place, Chicago, Illinois," The White House, Office of the Press Secretary, January 10, 2017. Available online: https://obamawhitehouse.archives.gov/the-press-office/2017/01/10/remarks-president-farewell-address.

42. Ibid.

43. "New Hampshire Primary Night: *January 8, 2008, Nashua, New Hampshire*," *Change We Can Believe In*, 212. As Mary Frances Berry and Josh Gottheimer explain, the refrain may have originated with United Farm Workers' campaign of 1972 led Cesar Chavez and Dolores Huerta—"*Sí, se puede.*" *Power in Words*, xi, 27–33, 146, and Remnick, *The Bridge*, 371. Wolfgang Mieder also notes that the Pointer Sisters' 1973 hit—"Yes We Can Can"—not only has that title but also has lyrics which very much match Barack Obama's message: to "try to live as brothers," to "respect the women of the world," to "make this land a better land," and "If we want it, yes we can, can." "*Yes We Can,*" 104–05, 131.

44. "Election Night," *Change We Can Believe In*, 279.

45. "Remarks by the President in a Farewell Address."

46. *The Audacity of Hope*, 53.

47. "Election Night," *Change We Can Believe In*, 278.

48. Ibid, 278–79. Mrs. Cooper was known to the Obama campaign as she was also the grandmother of sociologist of racial attitudes and race relations Lawrence Bobo, the W. E. B. Du Bois Professor of the Social Sciences at Harvard University, where he teaches in both the Department of Sociology and the Department of African and African American Studies. As David Remnick rightly notes, in Obama's telling, "Ann Nixon Cooper was an emblem not only of her race, but of her nation": *The Bridge*, 559, 560.

49. "Remarks by the President in a Farewell Address."

50. *The Audacity of Hope*, 248; "How Far We've Come: Remarks at John Lewis's Sixty-fifth Birthday Gala, *Atlanta, Georgia: February 21, 2005*," Dionne and Reid, eds., *We Are the Change We Seek*, 20; "United States Senate Victory Speech," Berry and Gottheimer, eds., *Power in Words*, 39. Wolfgang Mieder, *"Making a Way Out of No Way": Martin Luther King's Sermonic Proverbial Rhetoric* (New York: Peter Lang, 2010). *Ten Sermons of Religion by Theodore Parker, Of Justice and the Conscience* (Boston: Crosby, Nichols, 1853), 84–85.

INDEX

Index

Index

Carpetbaggers 175
Carr, Peter 88
Carter, Jimmy 233, 266
Castle William (Boston, MA) 65
Catholicism 21, 41, 45, 57, 62, 71–2, 121
Cato's Letters (John Trenchard and Thomas Gordon 1720–3) 73
Cayuga Indians 246
Cedar Creek, Battle of 158
Central Intelligence Agency 266, 268, 272
Chaffee, Calvin C., 148
Chaney, James 190
Charbonneau, Jean-Baptiste 259
Charbonneau, Toussaint 259
Charles I, king of England 41
Charles II, king of England 72
Charleston, SC 90, 143, 151, 153, 164, 174, 177, 192, 223
Charlottesville, VA 87, 321 n.76
Chattanooga, TN 196
Chavez, Cesar 335 n.43
Cheese, Cheshire Mammoth 311 n.67
Cheesecake 210
Cherokee Indians 246, 247, 250, 252
Cherokee Nation v. Georgia (1831) 250–2
Chesapeake Bay 52, 53–4, 93, 212
Chicago, Illinois 116, 136, 202, 205, 206, 227, 228, 277, 284, 285, 289, 291, 292, 293
Chickasaw Indians 247, 250
Chickens, coming home to roost 14, 34
Chile 266
China 30, 64, 208, 265, 267, 272
Choctaw Indians 247, 250
choice, freedom of 19, 44, 127
Christ, Jesus 42, 119, 135, 150, 178
Chronicle of His Time in Virginia, A (John Leland 1845) 121
Church of England (*see* Anglicanism)
Church of Scotland (*see* Presbyterianism)
Churchill, John, duke of Marlborough 327n.96
Churchill, Winston 264
Cicero 70
Citizens of New Orleans 182
City upon a Hill 9, 37, 39, 41–3, 44, 46, 110, 212
Civil Militia 36, 49, 65, 80, 90, 101, 105, 112, 125, 220–1, 227
Civil Rights Act (1866) 173, 174
Civil Rights Act (1875) 174, 181
Civil Rights Act (1957) 190
Civil Rights Act (1964) 190, 193, 278
Civil Rights Cases (1883) 181, 182
Civil Rights Movement 1, 7, 24, 25–6, 122, 138, 139, 164, 168, 169, 178–9, 183, 205, 233, 238, 267, 278, 279, 281–2, 290, 293, 294
  early campaign (1865–1945) 184–5

  later campaign (1945–65) 186–92
  limits of and extent of 202–4
  and non-violence 192–5
  as part of mainstream American history 198–202
  as a popular movement 195–8
Civil War (English/British) 31, 41, 71, 73, 125
Civil War (US) 2, 3, 7, 16, 17, 56, 131, 134, 143–4, 150, 155, 168, 178, 191, 225, 263
  causes of 94, 113, 130, 145, 151–2, 163–5, 170, 317 n.79
  historiography of 151–2, 161, 165, 170, 171, 317 n.79
  military conduct of 151, 158, 165–6, 170–1, 179
  Reconstruction and 169–72, 173, 179
Civil Works Administration 231
Civilian Conservation Corps 231
Clark, William 139, 201, 248, 259–60, 290
Clay, Henry 142, 143, 146, 223–4
Clayton Act (1914) 229
Cleveland, OH 281
Clinton, Bill 169, 233–4, 260, 267
Clinton, Hillary 131–2
  wins popular vote by near 3,000,000 in 2016 election 105
Coercive Acts (*see* Intolerable Acts)
Coffee, John 252
Colbert, Burwell 87
Cold War 264–7, 268, 269, 271, 272
Collier, John 254
Collins, Addie Mae 141, 190, 191, 278
Colonial British America (*see* American colonies)
colonizationism 86, 88
Colorado 249
Columbia River 254
Columbia University 73
Columbian Orator 154
Colvin, Claudette 189
Comanche Indians 249
Combahee River, SC 158
Commission on Civil Rights 186
Commission on Industrial Relations 229
Committee of Five 50, 69, 97–8, 306 n.38
Committees of Correspondence 99
Committees of Inspection 80
Committees of Safety 80
Common Sense (Thomas Paine, 1776) 67–8, 103
communism 24, 236, 265, 266, 267, 272
Compromise of 1833, 143, 223–4
Compromise of 1850, 146
  see also Fugitive Slave Act 1850
Compromise of 1877, 175–6
  see also "Redemption"
Concord, MA 49, 65, 137, 198

Index

Index

Index

Index

Index

Index

Index